RESOLVING LAND DISPUTES IN EAST ASIA

Economic development and mass urbanisation have unleashed unprecedented levels of land disputes in the region. In China and Vietnam especially, courts and other legal institutions struggle to find lasting solutions. It is against this background of legal failure that this book brings together leading scholars to understand how state agencies, land users and land developers engage imaginatively with each other to resolve disputes. Drawing on empirically rich case studies, contributors explore the limits of law and legal institutions in resolving land disputes and reveal insights into how key actors in East Asia understand land disputes. Their studies reveal promising dispute resolution practices and point to the likely ways that states will deal with land disputes in the future.

HUALING FU is a Professor of Law in the Faculty of Law of the University of Hong Kong, where his research interests include public law, human rights and legal institutions in China.

JOHN GILLESPIE is a Professor of Law and Director of the Asia Pacific Business Regulation Group at Monash University, Melbourne, Australia. He specialises in law and development, regulatory theory and socialist-transforming Asia.

RESOLVING LAND DISPUTES IN EAST ASIA

Exploring the Limits of Law

Edited by

HUALING FU

and

JOHN GILLESPIE

CAMBRIDGE
UNIVERSITY PRESS

CAMBRIDGE
UNIVERSITY PRESS

University Printing House, Cambridge CB2 8BS, United Kingdom

Cambridge University Press is part of the University of Cambridge.

It furthers the University's mission by disseminating knowledge in the pursuit of education, learning and research at the highest international levels of excellence.

www.cambridge.org
Information on this title: www.cambridge.org/9781107066823

First published 2014

Printed in the United Kingdom by Clays, St Ives plc

A catalogue record for this publication is available from the British Library

Library of Congress Cataloging in Publication data
Resolving land disputes in East Asia : exploring the limits of law / edited by Hualing Fu, John Gillespie.
pages cm
ISBN 978-1-107-06682-3 (Hardback)
1. Land tenure – Law and legislation – East Asia. 2. Land use – Law and legislation – East Asia. 3. Land reform – Law and legislation – East Asia. 4. Eminent domain – East Asia. I. Fu, Hualing, editor of compilation. II. Gillespie, John, editor of compilation.
KNC201.R47 2014
346.504′32–dc23
2014002365

ISBN 978-1-107-06682-3 Hardback

CONTENTS

FIGURES

TABLES

LIST OF CONTRIBUTORS

LEI CHEN is an Associate Professor at the School of Law, City University of Hong Kong. His research focuses on comparative law and Chinese private law, particularly contract and property law from historical, comparative and empirical perspectives. He is a fellow of the Hong Kong Institute of Arbitrators and on the roster of arbitrators of HKIAC and Beijing Arbitration Commission.

JIE CHENG is an Associate Professor of law at Tsinghua University Law School. She teaches constitutional law, comparative constitutional law, and Hong Kong and Macau Basic Law. Her research fields include constitutionalism in transitional society, Hong Kong and Macau Basic Law, freedom of information, and administrative reconsideration in China. She was a visiting scholar at Yale Law School (2003–2004, Fulbright Senior Visiting Scholar), Oslo University Human Rights Center (2001) and Sciences Po Paris (2008), and Nathaniel Fensterstock Visiting Associate Professor of Law at Columbia University Law School (2013).

HUALING FU is a Professor of Law in the Faculty of Law of the University of Hong Kong. He graduated from the Southwestern University of Politics and Law in Chongqing, and received postgraduate degrees in Canada. His research interests include public law, legal institutions and dispute resolution in China, and he has published widely in those areas. He has recently published *Liu Xiaobo, Charter 08 and the Limits of China's Political Reform* (2012) (co-edited with Jean Philippe Beja and Eva Pils).

JOHN GILLESPIE is a Professor and Director of the Asian Regulatory Group in the Department of Business Law, Monash University. His research and teaching interests include East Asian comparative law, law and development theory, regulatory theory, and land disputes. He has published widely on these topics and has consulted to international donors such as the World Bank, UNDP, IFC, Danida, the Asia

Foundation, and AusAid on legal development projects in East Asia. He is currently a Hauser Global Visiting Professor at the Law School, New York University.

SAY H. GOO is Professor and Director of the Asian Institute of International Financial Law (AIIFL), and Deputy Director of the Ronald Coase Centre for Property Rights Research (RCCPRR), Hong Kong University, and serves on the Editorial Board of *Property Law Review*. He is currently Honorary Visiting Professor at the University of Exeter Law School.

XIN HE is Professor of Law at City University of Hong Kong. He studies China's legal systems from a perspective of law and society. His recent articles include 'Black Hole of Responsibility: The Role of Adjudication Committee in A Chinese Court', and 'Pragmatic Discourse and Gender Inequality in China' (with Kwai Hang Ng), both in the *Law & Society Review*.

CHRISTOPHER HEURLIN is an Assistant Professor of Government and Asian Studies at Bowdoin College. He received his PhD in Political Science from the University of Washington in 2011. His research focuses on contentious politics, NGO–state relations, and law and society. His articles have appeared in *Voluntas* and *German Politics*.

TOAN LE works at the Department of Business Law and Taxation, Faculty of Business and Economics, Monash University. He is a graduate of the University of Melbourne and Deakin University, and his research interests and publications are in the field of commercial law reform and the development of legal capacities in Vietnam. Toan is currently a PhD candidate examining land tenure rights reforms in Vietnam at Monash University.

ALICE LEE is an Associate Professor at the University of Hong Kong, and specialises in property law (real property and intellectual property) and legal education. As Associate Dean of the Faculty of Law, she has contributed to the development of effective teaching practices. In recognition of her excellence in teaching, she has received two teaching awards from the University of Hong Kong.

DUAN LIN was a Professor at the Department of Sociology, National Taiwan University, and earned his PhD from the University of Heidelberg. His specialities included not only the sociology of religion, law and culture, but also Max Weber, social theory and Confucianism.

He published two books in Chinese: *Confucian Ethics and Legal Culture* (1992, 2002) and *Max Weber on Traditional Chinese Law* (2003).

EVA PILS is Associate Professor of Law at the Chinese University of Hong Kong (CUHK). She studied law, philosophy and Sinology in Heidelberg, London and Beijing, and holds a PhD in law from the University of London. Her scholarship focuses on human rights and China, with publications addressing the role and situation of Chinese human rights defenders, property law and land rights in China, the status of migrant workers, the Chinese petitioning system, and conceptions of justice in China. Eva was the founding (co-)director and is a member of CUHK's Centre for Rights and Justice.

NGUYEN HUNG QUANG is the Managing Partner of NHQUANG & Associates, a law firm engaged in legal practice and development consulting in Hanoi and Ho Chi Minh City, Vietnam. He has published extensively and applied his research findings in legal development projects focusing on the rule of law, land disputes and access to justice in Vietnam.

HUA SHAO is an Associate Professor at the Central South University School of Law in Hunan, China. She received her PhD from Wuhan University, and specialises in the legal profession and dispute resolution. She has published widely on mediation, arbitration and the development of the Chinese legal profession.

PO-FANG TSAI is currently an Assistant Professor at the Department of Sociology, National Taiwan University, and works in the field of sociology of law. His PhD dissertation concerns the social theory of rights discourse in citizenship studies, and his research interests include citizenship studies, sociology of law, cultural sociology, human rights, modernity and social theory.

FRANK K. UPHAM is the Wilf Family Professor of Property Law and Co-Director of the US–Asia Law Institute at the New York University School of Law, as well as the Faculty Director of NYU Law's semester study abroad programme in Shanghai. His research interests include the role of law in Japanese and Chinese societies, with a special interest in property rights issues. He has spent considerable time at various Asian institutions, especially universities in Japan and China. His book *Law and Social Change in Postwar Japan* received the Thomas J. Wilson Prize in 1987, and he has published numerous articles on topics related to law and society in Asia.

SUSAN H. WHITING is Associate Professor of Political Science and Adjunct Associate Professor of Law and International Studies at the University of Washington, Seattle. She specialises in Chinese and comparative politics, with particular emphasis on the political economy of development. She has published on property rights, fiscal reform, governance, contract enforcement and dispute resolution to numerous publications. She has also conducted extensive research in China and has contributed to studies of governance, fiscal reform and non-governmental organisations under the auspices of the World Bank, the Asian Development Bank and the Ford Foundation, respectively.

CHANGDONG ZHANG is an Assistant Professor of Political Science at Peking University. He received his PhD from the University of Washington in 2011. His research interests include taxation politics, state–business relationships, and state and society with a focus on China.

PREFACE

The idea to publish a book dealing with land disputes in East Asia evolved during conversations between John Gillespie and Hualing Fu, when John worked in the Faculty of Law, Hong Kong University as a visiting professor in 2011. At this time, new land disputes were erupting in China and Vietnam on a daily basis, and the insurrection in Wukan village in the Pearl River Delta, less than 60 km from Hong Kong, was making international headlines. In November 2011, a group of scholars from around the world gathered at Hong Kong University to discuss how land disputes are resolved in East Asia. To understand this complex phenomenon, participants in the workshop examined land disputes from a wide interdisciplinary perspective. This discussion not only centered on China and Vietnam, but also drew comparative insights from land disputes in the economically developed East Asian regions, especially Taiwan and Hong Kong. After numerous follow-up discussions and the commissioning of new chapters, this book emerged from the workshop.

We wish to thank Professor Albert Chen for supporting the Hong Kong workshop, the University of Hong Kong for supplying the convivial facilities, and the Asia Business Regulation Group, Monash University, for providing funding. Particular thanks to Flora Leung for logistical and organizational support.

We also wish to thank our editor, Sarah Russell, for her attention to detail and keeping the project on track. Finally, we have enjoyed working with Cambridge University Press. Our sincere thanks go to all involved.

John Gillespie and Hualing Fu

PART I

Theorizing land disputes in socialist Asia

1

Resolving land disputes in East Asia

Exploring the limits of the law

JOHN GILLESPIE AND HUALING FU

Introduction

Land disputes are increasing in East Asia as economic and demographic growth intensifies the demand for farmland and urban spaces. Nowhere is this more evident than in China and Vietnam. Reforms that brought socialist Asia into the globalized economy and returned private property have also sparked intense competition between farmers and residents with outsiders, such as private developers and government agencies. In China and Vietnam, industrial parks, transport infrastructure, and new residential developments are encroaching on farmland, sparking increasingly violent clashes with farmers. China alone experienced more than 500 daily land disputes and protests in 2011,[1] with the Wukan village insurrection, discussed in Chapter 6 in this book, making newspaper headlines around the world.

From a legal perspective, the proliferation of land disputes is puzzling, because it is occurring at the same time as governments in China and Vietnam are clarifying property rights and improving formal dispute resolution institutions, such as the courts. Rather than promoting uniformity, order, and predictability, the authors in this book reveal that law reforms have produced mixed results. Land claims and property rights often conflict, producing unpredictable and multi-layered dispute resolution processes. Highly ambiguous and contested patterns of land access persist in these countries. Consequently, courts and administrative agencies, such as grand mediation, struggle to use property rights to

[1] See Max Fisher, "How China Stays Stable Despite 500 Protests Every Day," *The Atlantic*, January 5, 2012, available at: www.theatlantic.com/international/archive/2012/01/how-china-stays-stable-despite-500-protests-every-day/250940.

find lasting solutions to land disputes. Far from state legal processes dominating, no single actor or set of regulatory traditions can gain the upper hand in many land cases.

Taiwan and Hong Kong have been added to this study because they furnish valuable comparative insights into how closely related, but significantly wealthier, societies have enlisted the law to resolve land disputes. These regions are connected to China and Vietnam through shared neo-Confucian values and, perhaps more significantly, a common pre-colonial system of land regulation (discussed in Chapters 3, 10, 12, and 14). This system, which was perfected during the Tang Dynasty in China, linked central imperial governance with village control over land. As Chapters 8 and 11 reveal, echoes of this system are found in the customary land systems found in rural China and Vietnam, and, more surprisingly, in highly developed urban spaces in Taipei and Hong Kong (Chapters 13 and 15). These findings connect with other socio-legal studies about advanced industrial countries that show how state land systems are interwoven with informal land systems.[2]

Authors apply different disciplinary approaches to understand how state agencies and communities imaginatively interact to conceptualize and resolve land disputes. They explore if legislative, judicial, and administrative reforms are capable of resolving land disputes, or if more fundamental reforms are required? This approach contrasts with studies that focus exclusively on either the role of property rights and state institutions or on local communities. Authors search for solutions to land disputes in the dynamic interaction between the relevant actors.

Mapping the causes of land disputes in East Asia

Land disputes and the political economy

Much has been written from a political economy perspective about the origins and nature of land disputes in socialist Asia.[3] Although this

[2] For a discussion about regulatory land communities, see Robert C. Ellickson, "Unpacking the Household: Informal Property Rights around the Hearth," *Yale Law Journal*, 116 (2006), 226 at 271–276; Amnon Lehavi, "How Property Can Create, Maintain or Destroy Community," *Theoretical Inquiries into Law*, 10(1) (2008), 43 at 52–65.

[3] See, generally, Y. T. Hsing, *The Great Urban Transformation: Politics of Land and Property in China* (Oxford University Press, 2010); George C. S. Lin, *Developing China: Land, Politics and Social Conditions* (London: Routledge, 2009); Peter Ho, *Institutions in Transition: Land Ownership, Property Rights and Social Conflict in China* (Oxford University Press, 2005).

literature differs in detail, there is a broad consensus about the demographic and economic forces underlying land conflicts in this region. Population[4] and industrial growth have produced historically unprecedented levels of urbanization, necessitating the continuous conversion of rural land for urban development.

At the time of its founding six decades ago, urbanization in the People's Republic of China (PRC) was little more than 10 percent. By 2011, for the first time in Chinese history, more people lived in urban than rural areas.[5] In the thirty years since economic reforms began, urbanization has grown from 15 percent to 50 percent, adding an additional 500 million urban dwellers.[6]

The scale of urbanization in China is unprecedented. For example, at the height of US urban renewal projects during the New Deal period in the 1930s, Pittsburgh's Golden Triangle and Lower Hill redevelopments displaced 28,000 residents. The number of displaced people due to construction projects in the PRC is estimated to have reached a staggering 50 million, including 17 million due to the construction of dams.[7] In 2003 alone, 180,000 Beijing residents were resettled. "This is human upheaval on a scale seen previously only in time of war or extreme natural catastrophe."[8] Government policies in China are set to shift a further 250 million farmers to cities by 2025.[9]

Vietnam exhibits a similar, although proportionally, smaller urbanization trajectory. In the last twenty years, the urban population has risen from 15 percent to 30 percent, and it is expected to reach 45 percent in the next twenty years.[10] Reflecting higher levels of wealth and economic

[4] At 0.47 percent per annum, the population growth in China is considerably slower than the 1.04 percent in Vietnam. See United Nations Sources, available at: www.tradingeconomics.com/vietnam/population-growth-annual-percent-wb-data.html.

[5] See Bloomberg News, "China's Urban Population Exceeds Countryside for First Time," January 17, 2012, available at: www.bloomberg.com/news/2012-01-17/china-urban-population-exceeds-rural.html.

[6] See United Nations, "World Urbanisation Prospects, the 2012 Revision," Population Database, available at: http://esa.un.org/unup, last accessed February 28, 2013.

[7] Huang Dongdong, *Development, Resettlement and Governance* (Beijing: Law Press, forthcoming).

[8] Thomas Campanella, *The Concrete Dragon: China's Urban Revolution and What it Means for the World* (New York: Princeton Architectural Press, 2008), p. 166.

[9] See Ian Johnson, "China's Great Uprooting: Moving 250 Million into Cities," *New York Times*, June 15, 2013, available at: www.nytimes.com/2013/06/16/world/asia/chinas-great-uprooting-moving-250-million-into-cities.html?pagewanted=all&_r=0.

[10] See United Nations, "World Urbanisation Prospects, the 2012 Revision."

development, the urbanization rate in Taiwan is 75 percent.[11] As a city-state, Hong Kong has for more than a century maintained high urbanization levels.[12]

The patterns of land disputes between China and Vietnam share similarities and significant differences. In both countries, farmers fight with each other for scarce farmland. Despite the process of urbanization in both countries, land disputes in rural areas among farmers remain a serious issue, although the patterns of dispute may fluctuate according to the employment of the migrants in the cities. China and Vietnam are also experiencing large-scale conversion of rural land to urban and industrial use – leading to clashes between farmers and developers. To gauge the scale of land acquisition, between 1995 and 2005, Chinese cities increased in land area by 59 percent.[13] In Vietnam, the area of farmland taken over in the last decade reached 1 million hectares, greater than the 810,000 hectares redistributed during the socialist land reforms in the 1950s.[14]

And there are significant differences between China and Vietnam. As Xin He discusses in Chapter 7 in this book, urban renewal projects have become a major source of land disputes in China. Vietnam has not yet accumulated the wealth needed to replace poor quality housing stock on a significant scale. But, in both countries, increasing numbers of land-taking disputes in peri-urban and rural areas are being experienced. Faced with high urban densities, housing and industrial developers have little option but to expand into farmland.

In what Annette Kim[15] termed fiscal socialism, local governments in China and Vietnam used their urban planning controls to compel private developers to provide public services and amenities that could not be financed from government budgets. Local governments

[11] See National Statistics of the Republic of Taiwan, June 2013, available at: www.stat.gov.tw/mp.asp?mp=4.

[12] In the 1950s, Hong Kong was 85 percent urban reach, and close to 100 percent urban by 1990. See United Nations, "World Urbanisation Prospects, the 2012 Revision."

[13] See Lin, *Developing China*, p. 180.

[14] See Vu Tuan Anh, "Land Issues in the Process of Implementing the 1992 Constitution," *Vietnam Economic Review*, 216 (2012), 16–27.

[15] Annette Kim, "A Market Without the 'Right' Property Rights: Ho Chi Minh City, Vietnam's Newly-Emerged Private Real Estate Market," *Economics of Transition*, 12(2) (2004), 275–305; Jieming Zhu, "Local Developmental State and Order in China's Urban Development During Transition," *International Journal of Urban and Regional Research* (2004), 424–447.

used their extensive powers over land allocation to recruit private developers to realize state planning schemes. The large increases in land value generated by fiscal socialism were sufficient to pay for roads, pavements, utilities, and even schools. Fiscal socialism, however, could function only if farmers were paid low rates of compensation for their land.

As the authors have observed, it is the unequal sharing of rapid economic growth and, in particular, the increasing economic divide between rural and urban populations that have animated many land disputes in socialist Asia. Many of the land-takings have taken place in the peri-urban and urban fringe areas where the interface between wealthy urban and poorer rural communities is most evident. Tensions are further exacerbated when rural communities see their land taken for private developments, such as golf courses and luxury apartments, rather than for public purposes that might benefit the public and the nation.

As Jie Cheng observes in Chapter 4, tax raised by local governments from land sales increased exponentially after 1994 when a tax-sharing system began, further propelling demand for farmland. She cites a report prepared by the Chinese Academy of Social Science in 2010, showing that the percentage of tax revenue from land sales increased from 3 percent in 1998 to 11 percent by 2008. This amount further increased by an astonishing 63 percent in 2009. The report concluded that pressure to increase tax income is a potent force driving land-takings in China. With tax revenues in decline and expenditure on the rise, local governments face the hard choice of making more land sales or falling into deep debt.

Land disputes and social cleavages

Land disputes are not only attributable to economic and demographic factors, but they are also anchored in historical contests that reflect long-standing beliefs and practices. As the authors in this book observe, many conflicts occur at the intersection of major social cleavages, such as claims by a resurgent Catholic Church for the return of land seized by the revolutionary government in Vietnam, and claims by farmers for their spiritual connection to village altars and cemeteries. Land disputes are also influenced by less visible, but nonetheless potent, everyday acts of resistance to state power. As Mark Seldon and Elizabeth Perry observed in relation to China:

> These take such forms as private acts of evasion, flight and foot dragging, which, in the absence of manifestos or marches, may nevertheless effectively enlarge the terrain of social rights.[16]

Authors in this book add the additional insights that legal challenges through administrative petitions and court litigation pressure state officials to justify their actions, and, in the process, open new ways of conceptualizing and asserting private and community property claims. Authors also describe how social media not only mobilizes public opinion, but is also a key source of inspiration and instruction for land claimants, and is reshaping the interaction between land users and state regulators.

Growing numbers of land disputes

Statistics concerning land disputes in China and Vietnam are fragmented, making the precise identification of trends problematic. There is, nevertheless, a broad consensus that the number and complexity of land disputes in China and Vietnam is growing. Details are provided in the chapters introducing China (Chapter 3) and Vietnam (Chapter 10). To set the scene, a longitudinal survey conducted by Landesa in China shows that the number of land-taking cases has increased every year since 2001 when the study began.[17] The survey also found that, in 2011, farmers were, on average, offered compensation rates of US$17,850 per acre, about 10 percent of the US$740,000 per acre that state authorities received for the land. It is unsurprising that the dissatisfaction rates among farmers eclipsed the satisfaction rates by a margin of two to one.[18] This discontent has translated into numerous, sometimes violent, land disputes in China.[19]

According to statistics prepared by the Government Inspectorate in Vietnam, there were 700,000 land complaints from 2009 to 2012, and more than 70 percent concerned compulsory land acquisition.[20]

[16] Mark Seldon and Elizabeth Perry, "Introduction: Reform, Conflict and Resistance in Contemporary China," in Elizabeth Perry and Mark Seldon (eds.), *Chinese Society: Change, Conflict and Resistance* (London: Routledge, 2010), p. 3.

[17] See Landesa, "Summary of 2011, 17-Province Survey Findings: Insecure Land Rights the Single Greatest Challenge Facing China's Sustainable Development," April 26, 2012, Research Report Landesa, p. 2.

[18] *Ibid.* [19] See Fisher, "How China Stays Stable Despite 500 Protests Every Day."

[20] See VNS, "Red Tape Leads to Property Disputes," *Viet Nam News*, September 19, 2012, available at: http://vietnamnews.vn/politics-laws/230281/red-tape-leads-to-property-disputes.html.

Conceptualizing land disputes

This book explores the idea that land disputes are socially constructed. The way in which land disputes are conceptualized profoundly influences not only what is considered to be a dispute, but also the appropriateness of dispute resolution forums and outcomes. In their seminal article "The Emergence and Transformation of Disputes: Naming, Blaming and Claiming," William Felstiner, Richard Able, and Austin Sarat observed that, in attributing blame, actors shape the trajectory of disputes.[21] For example, if actors believe they are only partially to blame, then they are unlikely to escalate grievances into claims or disputes. Felstiner *et al.* concluded that disputes are rarely ordered by uncontested sets of norms and practices; but rather they are socially constructed from different conceptual frameworks.

Taking this idea further, scholars in a wide range of fields, such as socio-legal studies,[22] sociology,[23] and economics,[24] argue that the tacit assumptions and norms in which people are embedded, shape the conceptual frameworks they find compelling. According to Felstiner *et al.*, it is to these frameworks that actors turn when attributing blame in disputes. A core question considered in this book is whether land disputes are more easily resolved when the main actors, both state and non-state, share conceptually compatible frameworks and generally agree about the cause of the dispute and the appropriate outcomes. Conversely, do negotiations break down and disputes become intractable when actors lack compatible frameworks for determining blame and redress?

Particularly in rapidly transforming societies,[25] such as socialist-transforming Asia, diverse educational, economic, and social experiences generate differences in the distribution of knowledge. This fragmentation of knowledge produces a diversity of conceptual frameworks. As the case

[21] See William Felstiner, Richard Able, and Austin Sarat, "The Emergence and Transformation of Disputes: Naming, Blaming and Claiming," *Law & Society Review*, 15(3/4) (1980), 631–654.

[22] See, generally, Susan Silbey, "After Legal Consciousness," *Annual Review of Law and Social Science*, 1 (2005), 323–368; Lawrence Lessig, "The Regulation of Social Meaning," *University of Chicago Law Review*, 62(3) (1995), 958-961.

[23] See Peter Berger and Thomas Luckmann, *The Social Construction of Reality* (New York: Anchor Books, 1966), p. 65.

[24] See Avner Greif, *Institutions and the Path to the Modern Economy* (New York: Cambridge University Press, 2006).

[25] See Jerrold Long, "Private Lands, Conflict and Institutional Evolution in the Post-Public Lands," *Pace West Environmental Law Review*, 28(3) (2011), 670–789.

studies in this book demonstrate, the most intractable land disputes seem to occur at knowledge boundaries found, for example, at the peri-urban interface between globally connected cities and farming communities.

Drawing on the authors' studies, it is possible to identify three main frameworks used to conceptualize land disputes in socialist Asia. In practice, the actors involved in disputes rarely rely on just one framework and often interweave ideas from one framework into another. Before discussing the ramifications of this blurring and hybridization, we discuss the three main conceptual frameworks below.

Seeing like a state

James Scott argues that the process of simplification, codification, and standardization – much of what land laws, cadastral plans, and land titles do – is an essential aspect of governing modern states.[26] Because societies more often than not comprise "a reality so complex and variegated as to defy easy short-hand description," states must first transform societies into "neat constructs of science" before they can govern.[27] This regulatory technology enables states to govern without fine-grained knowledge about everyday practices – to govern at a distance on a large scale. To recreate the modernist ideal of orderly planned cities and industrial agriculture, governments throughout East Asia imported European planning schemes and land titling systems.[28]

A central aspect of modernist land management is governance through codification and abstraction. This transformation assumes a shift from particularism to universalism, and from substantive to procedural justice. Authors in this book query if this transformation uniformly applies to China and Vietnam (see Chapters 8, 9, and 11).[29] Although

[26] See James Scott, *Seeing Like a State: How Certain Schemes to Improve the Human Condition Have Failed* (New Haven, CT: Yale University Press, 1998), pp. 11–22.

[27] See Scott, *Seeing Like a State*, pp. 11–22.

[28] See, generally, Anan Ganjanapan, "The Northern Thai Land Tenure System: Local Customs versus National Laws (Ching Mai Province)," *Law & Society Review*, 28(3) (1994), 609–622; Franz von Benda-Beckmann and Keebet von Benda-Beckmann, "Property, Politics, and Conflict: Ambon and Minangkabau Compared," *Law & Society Review*, 28(3) (1994), 589–607.

[29] See also William Hurst, Mingxing Liu, Yongdong Liu, and Ran Tao, "Reassessing Collective Petitioning in Rural China: Civic Engagement, Extra-State Violence, and Regional Variation," (2010) APSA 2009 Toronto Meeting Paper, 2009, revised 2013, available at: http://papers.ssrn.com/sol3/papers.cfm?abstract_id=1448983.

they point to increased codification, the case studies also show the ongoing importance of interpersonal relationships, the treatment of each land dispute as *sui generis*, and, as a consequence, the lack of general principles that apply predictably and systematically to every case. In Chapter 4, Jie Cheng makes the additional point that litigants are most likely to win land cases by challenging the exercise of official powers rather than questioning procedural defects. All of this suggests that "seeing like a state" takes on a different form in socialist East Asia than in western Europe.

Scott also notes that officials are not content with merely promoting state governance; in "seeing like a state," they displaced rival modes of regulation. For example, officials used laws to define boundaries of control and discredit or omit practices that were considered inconvenient or resistant to control. Nowhere was this approach more obvious than in the Soviet land planning introduced into China and Vietnam during the 1960s.[30] Revolutionary governments in Europe and Asia sought to sweep away backward traditional cultures that had become associated with class oppression and feudalism. Marx followed a well-established European intellectual tradition that depicted Asian societies in undifferentiated ways as "semi-barbarians," portrayals that generated socialist antipathy, or at least indifference, to neo-Confucian and "feudal" culture.[31] To varying degrees, governments in China and Vietnam believed that a universal "proletarian culture" would link the working classes in different countries, and "Asiatic" and "feudal" modes of production would dissolve in the face of this unifying force.[32]

Soviet planning drew directly from the same intellectual traditions as the "city beautiful" movement that shaped land governance in Europe and North America.[33] Soviet land planners enjoyed close links with French *urbanisme*, which emphasized large-scale urban redevelopment and long-lasting streetscapes. What the Soviets found attractive about

[30] See Yehua Dennis Wei, "Planning Chinese Cities: The Limits of Transitional Institutions," *Urban Geography*, 26(3) (2005), 201–221.

[31] Karl Marx, "Otechestvenniye Zapiski" (1887), reproduced in Shlomo Avineri, "Introduction," in Shlomo Avineri (ed.), *Karl Marx on Colonialism and Modernization* (New York: Doubleday, 1969), p. 6.

[32] See, for example, Truong Chinh, "Marxism and Vietnamese Culture," report delivered to the Second National Cultural Conference, July 1948, reproduced in *Truong Chinh Selected Writings* (Hanoi: Gioi Publishers, 1994), pp. 251–252.

[33] See Scott, *Seeing Like a State*, ch. 4; William Logan, "The Russians on the Red River: The Soviet Impact on Hanoi's Town Scape 1955–1990," *Europe–Asia Studies*, 47(3) (1995), 443–468.

Baron Haussmann was his penchant for re-engineering the physical landscape to change social behavior. When integrated into Soviet central planning, this utopian planning became even more rigid than in Europe. Soviet planners insisted that economic and social planning could be understood only in Marxist–Leninist terms, which defined out-of-existence private markets and other modes of self-regulation. Following Soviet practices, land planning in China and Vietnam took place at stratospheric levels of abstraction that dismissed customary land regulation as unbounded, inefficient, and potentially subversive.[34]

In both China and Vietnam, the technology of land governance declined after the revolution. As Phung Minh, a French-trained land surveyor, recalled in his memoirs, skills and technical competencies eroded during the high socialist period (1954–1986) when professional cadastral mapping effectively ceased in Hanoi. He depicted housing and land management during this period as arbitrary and haphazard.[35] And he thought that the culture of revolutionary resistance did not generate respect for rule-based land management, because revolutionaries sought to subvert state power structures. Reinforcing this antipathy toward the technology of regulation, many senior cadres who migrated to Hanoi from rural areas after 1954 were unfamiliar with, even contemptuous of, the title by registration system operating in former colonial centers.

Following economic reforms in the 1970s and 1980s, governments in China and Vietnam once again turned their attention to the technology of land governance (see Chapters 3 and 10). They upgraded cadastral planning and land-titling technologies to render landholdings intelligible and secure. Although the governments in these countries now tolerate private markets and other modes of self-regulation, they continue to insist on state land management. Reforms have ensured that state officials will continue to manage the property rights regime and private property markets.

There is another distinctly modernizing feature of land law and planning. As Michael Lief[36] observed in relation to peri-urban China and Vietnam:

[34] See Wei, "Planning Chinese Cities."

[35] See Phung Minh, "40 Nam Quan Ly Nha Cua O Ha Noi" ("40 Years of Housing Management in Hanoi"), unpublished paper, Hanoi, October 16–17, 1998.

[36] See Michael Lief, "Peri-Urban Asia: A Commentary on Becoming Urban," *Pacific Affairs*, 84(3) (2011), 531.

> the expansion of urban administrative structures into formerly rural settings is understood to be an effort not only to regulate urbanization, to bring villagers' spontaneous activities in line with the laws of the state, but to rein in their frontier lawlessness more broadly, to "civilize" the countryside.

In short, state regulation aims to displace the "local personalism of traditional village practices," which must be wiped away before villagers can join modern society.

This "seeing like a state" mindset has influenced the way policy-makers and land officials conceptualize land disputes. Authors (see Chapter 4) in this book show that officials blame land disputes on unclear laws and incomplete procedures. If formal legal structures are not at fault, then officials attribute failings to administrative shortcomings or outright corruption. Officials also blame the public for lacking "legal consciousness" and circumventing land laws and procedures. Underlying this diagnosis is the assumption that states are the optimal regulators, and that state laws and regulatory technologies should displace informal land practices.

The case studies about Taiwan and Hong Kong provide a glimpse into what can happen when societies judicialize and democratize. In both countries, governments "see like states" in planning land and housing developments, but their instrumental powers are checked by courts and, more recently, by democratic processes. In Hong Kong, courts from the early days of the colony played a prominent role in resolving land disputes by balancing competing property rights (see Chapter 14). More recently, democratic reforms in both countries have encouraged public participation in every stage of the land-planning process and enabled civil protests to pressure officials into recognizing customary land entitlements and preventing developers from compromising land rights.

Economic development and property rights

Recycling property rights

Belief in the capacity of property rights to promote economic development and social stability in East Asia is not new. In 1880, the French Colonial Inspector of Native Affairs in Vietnam opined that:

> The establishment of property ownership will be the prosperity of the country: the rights to sell, to buy, to mortgage – to execute all the

> conveyances of property will augment the country's wealth in circulating the capital which is now frozen by many cultivators.[37]

Similar arguments were made to support the introduction of property rights in the PRC and by the British in Hong Kong.

Far from unlocking the wealth of indigenous cultivators, property rights during the period of colonial domination secured wealth for foreign investors and local elites.[38] The accumulation of estates made possible by land titling dispossessed large numbers of farmers, resulting in subsistence incomes as tenants and wage laborers.[39] The inequities generated by the private enclosure of land excited social unrest throughout the colonial period, and is considered by many historians as the single most important catalyst for socialist revolution in China and Vietnam.[40]

Revolutionary land policies in these countries could hardly have differed more from colonial property rights. A core objective of Marxist–Leninism was to replace private property rights with state and collective ownership. The Chinese Constitution of 1954 followed this line by providing for the people's ownership of land (see Chapter 3). In order to appease the capitalist South, both the 1946 and 1960 Constitutions in the Democratic Republic of Vietnam retained private landownership. Following victory over the South in 1975, the post-reunification 1980 Constitution of the Socialist Republic of Vietnam adopted the Soviet formulation of people's ownership and state management of land.[41]

Karl Marx and Friedrich Engels dismissed legally protected property rights in the West as bourgeois instruments "for the mutual guarantee of their property and interests."[42] To displace "bourgeois" property rights, Soviet theorists conceptualized land as a "special commodity" or public

[37] Jean Louis Bassford, *Land Development Policy in Cochin China under the French (1865–1925)* (Ann Arbor, MI: University Microfilms International, 1984), pp. 129–130.

[38] See Chapter 12 in this book; Martin Murray, *The Development of Capitalism in Colonial Indochina (1870–1940)* (Berkeley, CA: University of California Press, 1980), pp. 132–140.

[39] See David Biggs, "Property and Poverty in Southern Vietnam," in Hue-Tam Ho Tai and Mark Sidel (eds.), *State, Society and the Market in Contemporary Vietnam* (London: Routledge, 2013), pp. 15–32.

[40] See Edwin E. Moise, "Land Reform and Land Reform Errors in North Vietnam," *Pacific Affairs*, 49 (1976), 70–92 at 72.

[41] 1980 Constitution of the Socialist Republic of Vietnam, Art. 20.

[42] Karl Marx and Friedrich Engels, *The German Ideology*, ed. R. Pascal (New York: International Publishers, [1846] 1960), p. 59.

good. In contrast to "bourgeois" property, land in Soviet theory was not a tradable commodity and could not be used for private exchange and personal advantage.[43] Party elites in both China and Vietnam followed this Marxist–Leninist trope until market reforms in the 1970s and 1980s unleashed housing and land markets (see Chapters 3 and 10).

Early post-Mao reforms in China (1978–1982) and *doi moi* (renovation) reforms in Vietnam (1979–1986) focused on agricultural de-collectivization and market opening. In both countries, individual household contracts gave farmers control over the management, output, and marketing of agricultural production in exchange for payments in the form of crops and labor to the village, and taxes to the state. This household responsibility system effectively ended decades of state collectivization in favor of private agricultural production.

Responding to pressure from below, in 1993, the Chinese state extended the term of household contracts from fifteen to thirty years, and in 1998 for an additional period of thirty years. Throughout this period, land-use rights in agricultural land remained with the village authorities, giving them significant management powers over land use and disposal. The Rural Land Contracting Law 2002 continued this policy by conferring land-use rights on households, rather than on individuals. The law's primary purpose is to prevent large-scale arbitrary reallocations of land and to allow transfers of land between households. Generally, farmers have two land-use rights over rural land. The first is the right to contract out the land for agricultural production, and the second is the right to use land to construct a residential homestead. Attempts to individualize rights over agricultural land in the Land Law 2007 were blocked, ensuring the retention of strong state management powers over rural land rights. A recent survey conducted by Landesa found that only 36.7 percent of farmers surveyed held the land contracts and land-use rights stipulated by the law.[44]

Land reforms in Vietnam took a different trajectory.[45] Vietnamese farmers are now allotted individualized land titles, but as the case studies discussed in this book show, this reform has not appreciably

[43] The writings of Soviet legal academics were influential during this period in China and Vietnam. See, for example, Pa-Ven Sko-Mo-Ro-Kho- Nop, "Phap Luat Xo Viet Bao Ve Quyen Loi Dan Su" ("Soviet Law Protecting Civil Rights"), (2) (1961), 42–44.

[44] See Landesa, "Summary of 2011, 17-Province Survey Findings," p. 2.

[45] See, generally, Benedict Kerkvliet, "Agricultural Land in Vietnam: Markets Tempered by Family, Community and Socialist Practices," *Journal of Agrarian Change*, 6(3) (2006), 285–305.

improved their bargaining position compared with that of Chinese farmers. Rather than retaining the household responsibility system and land contracts, the Land Law 1988 established individual land-use rights for agricultural land in Vietnam. Responding to bottom-up pressure, the state has incrementally increased the rights attached to land. For example, the Land Law 1993 gave farmers rights to transfer and mortgage agricultural land-use rights, but limited land tenure to twenty years. Amendments in 2013 to the Land Law 2003 increased the tenure rights to fifty years. Even so, in practice farmers have few opportunities to mobilize their land-use rights against the state in land-taking cases – effectively nullifying their legal advantage over Chinese farmers.

Neo-liberal property rights

International pressure from foreign governments, international donor agencies, and foreign investors has also shaped internal debates about land reform in China and Vietnam. Reprising colonial enthusiasm for property rights, international donors such as the World Bank have been especially vocal in advocating transparent and robust private property rights. Donors were influenced by Harold Demsetz's assertion that private property is the solution for resource tragedies.[46] According to Demsetz, the privatization of property off-sets negative social costs, such as exclusion from natural resources, because the individual pursuit of self-interest increases overall social welfare. This classical economic notion that societies are better off when people can reap what they sow dates back to the classical economics of Adam Smith. The World Bank has added the neo-liberal economic objective of minimizing government oversight and maximizing Coasian bargaining between private property-holders.[47]

More recently, New Institutional Economic (NIE) theorists added weight to Demsetz's claim by arguing that legally protected property rights are essential for economic development.[48] Douglass North famously claimed:

[46] See Harold Demsetz, "Toward a Theory of Property Rights," *American Economic Review*, 57(2) (1967), 347–359.

[47] See Ronald Coarse, "The Problem of Social Cost," *Journal Law and Economics*, 3 (1960), 1–44.

[48] See, generally, Oliver Williamson, *The Economic Institutions of Capitalism* (New York: Free Press, 1985).

> the inability of societies to develop effective, low-cost enforcement of contracts is the most important source of both historical stagnation and contemporary underdevelopment in the Third World.[49]

By the early 1990s, international donors seized on NIE theory to stress the importance of institutions - especially stable property rights - in promoting an orderly transition from socialism in China and Vietnam.

Hernando de Soto, a leading exponent of this view, invoked the metaphor of a bell jar to explain the difference between registered and unregistered property rights.[50] Those within the bell jar enjoy state protection of their registered property rights, while he opined that those outside the bell jar must fend for themselves. The assumption underlying this metaphor is that state regulators and courts protect property rights more effectively than community-based, self-regulatory systems. Supporters of de Soto urged developing countries to upgrade their land regulation systems by replacing customary informality with land management technology.[51]

Other theorists are less certain than de Soto that "with each new year, the link between economic prosperity and property rights protection becomes increasingly clearer."[52] They criticize de Soto for drawing too sharp a distinction between state-backed property rights and self-regulation.[53] In their estimation, it is questionable whether systems based on inalienable property rights provide the most effective mechanism where there is ambiguity about access to land and the resolution of disputes.[54] Property rights, they maintain, do little to change the disparities in wealth and power that animate many land contests.

[49] See Douglass C. North, *Institutions, Institutional Change and Economic Performance* (Cambridge University Press, 1990), p. 54.

[50] Hernando de Soto, *The Mystery of Capitalism: Why Capitalism Triumphs in the West and Fails Everywhere Else* (London: Black Swan, 2000), pp. 47–62.

[51] See Asian Development Bank, "The Impact of Land Markets on the Poor: Implementing de Soto," Making Markets Work Better for the Poor Discussion Paper 3, Hanoi, 2004.

[52] See Property Rights Alliance, "2012 Report International Property Rights Index," p. 3, available at: http://www.internationalpropertyrightsindex.org.

[53] See Alan Gilbert, "On the Mystery of Capitalism and the Myths of Hernando de Soto: What Difference Does Legal Title Make," *International Planning Review*, 24 (2002), 1–19; Jonathan Manders, "Sequencing Property Rights in the Context of Development: A Critique of the Writings of Hernando de Soto," *Cornell International Law Journal*, 37(1) (2004), 177–198.

[54] See also Leah M. Trzcinski and Frank K. Upham, "The Integration of Conflicting Donor Approaches: Land Law Reform in Cambodia," *Journal of International Cooperation Studies*, 20(1) (2012), 129–146.

Adding to the mounting criticism, still other scholars argue that donors underestimated the regulatory role of informal institutions, such as family and business networks, in maintaining and stabilizing domestic regulatory systems.[55] They point to the high growth periods in northeast Asia, especially in China and Vietnam, where formal property rights played a marginal role in economic development.[56] Donald Clarke argues that "it is impossible to make the case that formal legal institutions have contributed in an important way to China's remarkable economic success."[57] If anything, economic success has fostered the development of law, rather than the reverse. Rapid economic development continues to thrive today despite ongoing shortcomings in the statutory protection of private property.[58]

Fuzzy property rights

China and Vietnam listened to advice from international donors and then proceeded to develop their own unique land rights systems. For specifics, refer to Chapters 3 and 11 in this book. Party leaders in both China and Vietnam refused to countenance a return to private landownership, and instead created land-use rights that, in some circumstances, convey tenure rights, such as unlimited duration, transfer, and mortgage rights that resemble full ownership. A movement away from the socialist notion that land is a "special commodity" toward individual land rights has advanced incrementally in both countries. This transition reflects intense internal debates about the continued role of the state in managing the economy and land. As Frank Upham argues forcefully in Chapter 2, in the long term, economic growth depends on the possibility

55 See Donald C. Clarke, "Economic Development and the Rights Hypothesis: The China Problem," *American Journal of Comparative Law*, 51 (2003), 89–111; Manders, "Sequencing Property Rights in the Context of Development"; Frank K. Upham, "From Demsetz to Deng: Speculations on the Source," *New York University Journal of International Law and Politics*, 41(3) (2009), 522–602.

56 See Katharina Pistor, "The Standardization of Law and its Effect on Developing Economies," *American Journal of Comparative Law*, 50 (2002), 101; John Ohnesorge, "Law and Development Orthodoxies and the Northeast Asian Experience," in Gerald McAlinn and Caslav Pejovic (eds.), *Law and Development in Asia* (London: Routledge, 2012), pp. 7, 16–30.

57 See Clarke, "Economic Development and the Rights Hypothesis."

58 See Ronald Gilson and Curtis Milhaupt, "Economically Benevolent Dictators: Lessons for Developing Democracies," *American Journal of Comparative Law*, 59(1) (2011), 227–288.

of shifting property rights to those who have the ability to put resources to more effective use.

Despite more than two decades of legislative reforms, the terms ambiguity and "fuzziness" are often used to describe property rights in China and Vietnam, or for that matter, any legal right. Katherine Verdery coined the term "fuzzy" to describe the forms of property rights found in post-socialist Europe.[59] The transition out of socialism, Verdery observed, did not entirely transform the institutional structures and epistemic settings that supported socialism. On the contrary, the transformation changed some structures, but left others relatively intact. In consequence, the property rights that emerged contained a complex mixture of private rights and collective obligations that differed from one context to another, leading Verdery to describe them as "fuzzy property rights."

Verdery's observations are not limited to Europe, or in fact to a transformation out of socialism. The authors in this book narrate many examples where the transformation of socialism in China and Vietnam has generated fragmented institutional and epistemic structures that have generated fuzzy property rights. As we will see in the next section – about China – fuzzy property rights are not only found where village land practices suppressed under socialism percolate up to the surface following de-collectivization. The state itself creates fuzzy property rights by treating state-owned or state-controlled enterprises differently from other sectors.

Authors in this book have also observed state officials using fuzzy property rights in land-taking and compensation cases. Especially in China, the vague land-use rights issued to farmers following de-collectivization have aggravated land grabs by officials.[60] Fuzzy property rights provide political and legal justification for predatory land-grabbing, and serve as effective tools to silence farmers who have lost their land. Fuzzy property rights also give courts considerable discretionary powers in deciding private land claims against citizens and the state. As John Gillespie observed in relation to housing disputes in Hanoi:

[59] See Katherine Verdery, "Fuzzy Property Rights, Power and Identity," in Michael Burawoy and Katherine Verdery (eds.), *Uncertain Transition: Ethnographies of Change in the Postsocialist World* (Lanham, MD: Rowman & Littlefield, 1999), pp. 53–81.

[60] See Robin Dean and Tobias Damm-Luhr, "A Current Review of Chinese Land Use and Policy: A 'Breakthrough' in Rural Reform?" *Pacific Rim Law and Policy Journal*, 19(1) (2010), 121–159.

> Judges quickly exhaust the possibilities of statutory land rights and legal doctrines and either push cases back to state officials or use "reason and sentiment in applying the law" . . . a type of situational justice, to resolve cases.[61]

Authors also reveal a close connection between politically sensitive cases and party intervention (see Chapters 4, 5, 9, and 11). Although the details differ from case to case, in general it falls to party organizations at provincial and central levels to resolve highly sensitive land-taking cases. Under the direction of the party, courts creatively interpret or entirely disregard property rights to secure predetermined outcomes.[62] In these cases, every aspect of property rights is fuzzy.

In other circumstances, fuzzy property rights are the source of considerable creativity, where judges, officials, and mediators use conceptual ambiguity to find flexible solutions to land disputes that are not otherwise available in law. For example, in Chapters 6, 8, and 9, the use of grand mediation in China is discussed, which brings the party, state officials, and disputants together to explore extra-legal methods of dispute resolution. Chapter 11 shows how provincial party leaders in Vietnam take advantage of fuzzy property rights to circumvent ineffective legal procedures and negotiate directly with land claimants.

The chapters on Taiwan and Hong Kong provide a useful counter-narrative to socialist Asia. Colonial powers brought property rights and a judicial system capable of enforcing them to these countries. For example, Japanese colonizers introduced a land-titling system to Taiwan, which, subject to various modifications, provides the basis for a rights-based land system today (see Chapter 12). In Hong Kong, the British imported English land laws, courts, and judges. And as Chapters 15 and 16 show, more than a decade after de-colonization, litigation provides a viable means of resolving most types of property dispute.

What these countries clearly demonstrate is that capitalism and democracy, or at least, liberal political values, play a major role in protecting property rights in society. Yet, even in highly developed legal systems, property rights become fuzzy when they collide with customary land claims.

[61] John Gillespie, "Exploring the Limits of Judicial Review in Urban Land Disputes in Vietnam," *Law & Society Review*, 45(2) (2011), 241–275 at 243.

[62] For a discussion of this practise in Vietnam, see Mark Sidel, "Property State Corruption and the Judiciary: The Don Son Land Case and its Implications," in Hue-Tam Ho Tai and Mark Sidel (eds.), *State, Society and the Market in Contemporary Vietnam* (London: Routledge, 2013), pp. 103–122.

Community conceptualizations of land disputes

So far we have focused on state-based conceptualizations of land disputes. What makes this book distinctive is its multi-actor focus; it not only considers state regulation, but also decenters the analysis by considering what other actors think about land disputes.[63] Decentered analysis provides a valuable corrective to state mythologizing that only central authorities possess regulatory solutions to land disputes. It also sheds light on the remarkable resilience of community land regulation, which continues to flourish despite unprecedented economic development and globalization in East Asia. The importance of community governance to ethnic minorities is well known;[64] what is less well documented and understood is the vital role it plays in urban, peri-urban, and rural centers in East Asia, and elsewhere.[65]

Far from being a fringe phenomenon, studies show that in some developing countries more than 80 percent of the population live under community land systems.[66] For example, an International Finance Corporation survey puts the level of land transactions taking place outside the state land tenure system in Hanoi at over 75 percent.[67] Similarly high levels of unofficial land use are reported in rural and urban areas in China.[68] Chapters 13, 15, and 16 show customary land systems flourishing in highly developed Asian cities, such as Hong Kong and Taipei. In fact, community land systems play a significant role in regulating land and housing disputes in most cases discussed in this book.

[63] For a discussion about decentering regulatory analysis, see Julia Black, "Regulatory Conversations," *Journal of Law and Society*, 29(1) (2002), 163–196.

[64] See, generally, Kerstin Andersen, "Communal Tenure and the Governance of Common Property Resources in Asia", Land Tenure Working Paper 20, Food and Agriculture Organization of the United Nations, 2011, pp. 2–5; World Bank, *Village Justice in Indonesia: Case Studies on Access to Justice, Village Democracy and Governance* (Washington, DC: World Bank, 2004).

[65] Richard Ford, "Law's Territory: A History of Jurisdiction," *Michigan Law Review*, 97 (1999), 843–930; Mariana Valverde, "Seeing Like a City: The Dialectic of Modern and Premodern Ways of Seeing in Urban Governance," *Law & Society Review*, 45(2) (2011), 277–312.

[66] See Stephen Golub, "A House without Foundations," in T. Carothers (ed.), *Promoting the Rule of Law Abroad: In Search of Knowledge* (Washington, DC: Carnegie Endowment for International Peace, 2006), pp. 105–136.

[67] See Stoyan Tenev, Amanda Carlier, Omar Chaudry, and Quynh-Trang Nguyen, *Informality and the Playing Field in Vietnam's Business Sector* (Washington, DC: International Finance Corporation, 2003), p. 68.

[68] See Samuel Ho and George Lin, "Emerging Land Markets in Rural and Urban China: Policies and Practices," *China Quarterly*, 175 (2003), 681 at 696–698.

Some authors in this book partially attribute the resilience of community governance to personal choice – in some circumstances, people prefer community governance to state regulation. In other cases, it is explained by necessity; where there is limited penetration of, or poorly performing, state institutions, people turn to community systems to determine what they can and cannot do with their land. Other authors ascribe the resilience of community systems not only to preference or necessity, but also, more importantly, to the interdependence between state and community systems (see Chapters 11 and 13). They argue that differences between these regimes are often overstated, and that informality and formality describe regulatory styles or technologies, rather than binary cleavages between separate modes of governance. This argument connects with the previous discussion about fuzzy property rights occurring where different regulatory systems overlap.

Before proceeding further, it is necessary to define what is meant by the term "community governance." Recent scholarly analysis of communities has focused on geographically proximate groups that share some common connection other than physical proximity.[69] Community in this sense involves an element of belonging and intra-community empathy, mutual commitment to shared values and norms, and collaboration in the pursuit of common goals.[70] As Robertson observed, "being embedded in a background context of beliefs, practices, goals, etc. is what makes perception of anything possible, and is also what gives that perception its 'shape.'"[71] Community governance is intersubjective, in the sense that shared understandings about the optimal way to regulate land are generated largely within epistemologically compatible social or organizational groups.

Taking this concept further, others argue that community governance is possible in groups that lack any physical proximity.[72] Members of these virtual communities may knowingly, or even unknowingly, share common epistemological frameworks that orient them toward common understandings about access to land and dispute resolution. Virtual communities not only encompass actors who share common interests

[69] See Monica Colombo, Cristina Mosso, and Norma De Piccoli, "Sense of Community and Participation in Urban Contexts," *Journal of Community and Applied Social Psychology*, 11 (2001), 457 at 458–459.

[70] See Amitai Etzioni, "Creating Good Communities and Good Societies," *Contemporary Sociology*, 29 (2000), 188.

[71] See Michael Robertson, "Picking Positivism Apart: Stanley Fish on Epistemology and Law," *Southern California Interdisciplinary Law Journal*, 8 (1999), 401 at 417.

[72] See Black, "Regulatory Conversations," p. 174.

in land, but also might include members of the public who are united through the mass media and especially social media.

Rather than identifying communities by their degree of mutuality, theorists believe it makes more sense to mark out boundaries between communities.[73] Factors that differentiate communities include different validity claims, sets of epistemologies, and tacit understandings, as well as different levels of attachment and identification with the community. What this suggests is that land communities are distinguishable according to their cohesiveness and epistemic understandings of land regulation.

In sum, land communities differ in the way in which they embed property relationships in wider sets of social, political, and economic relationships. "Embeddedness" is used here as a metaphor to indicate the relative extent to which property relates to legal, social, and economic domains. Different degrees and kinds of embeddedness are illustrated in the four land communities discussed below.

One: traditional land communities

Traditional communities comprise close-knit groups that organize around consolidating ideologies, religions, or village traditions, and employ comprehensive internal norms to validate their community.[74] They are sometimes functionally or physically insulated from society, although some members of these communities might engage with the outside world.[75] The recent origin or hybrid nature of regulatory traditions does not diminish their potency. As Benedict Anderson reminds us, "invented traditions and 'imaged communities' are just as authentic to villagers as traditions with an 'objective' historical provenance."[76] Communal land tenure, where communities or villages have well-defined, exclusive rights to jointly own and/or manage land, is a feature of some, but certainly not all, traditional communities. In China and Vietnam, communal land tenure is most widely practiced in remote areas, especially in the mountainous zones

[73] See Brian Tamanaha, *Realistic Socio-Legal Theory* (Oxford University Press, 1998), pp. 170–172.

[74] See, generally, Andersen, "Communal Tenure and the Governance of Common Property Resources in Asia."

[75] See Ellickson, "Unpacking the Household," pp. 271–276.

[76] See Benedict Anderson, *Imagined Communities: Reflections on the Origin and Spread of Nationalism*, 2nd edn. (London: Verso, 2006), pp. 9–35.

settled by ethnic minorities.[77] Nevertheless, some authors (Chapters 8, 9, and 11) show that traditional communities also flourish in highly developed rural and even urban locales.

Franz and Keebet von Benda-Beckmann[78] observed that traditional communities typically "treat property relations as only one aspect or strand of more encompassing categorical relationships, in which kinship relations, property relations and relations of political authority are largely fused in a many-stranded or multiplex relationship." In other words, property relations remain embedded in relational and/or spiritual practices and have not yet re-embedded in legal relationships. Traditional communities remain a common form of social organization in rural China and Vietnam, and the community structure continues to shape the way in which land disputes are resolved and the degree to which state law may be involve in dispute resolution (see Chapters 7 and 11). Consider the Đông Dương villagers, discussed in Chapter 11, who invoked moral and spiritual claims to land that conflicted with the exclusive property rights recognized by the Vietnamese Land Law 2003.

Revolution and modernization have exposed many villagers to the outside world, resulting in spontaneous urbanizing with or without state support and guidance. Authors show how people create their own urban transformation by replacing agriculture with small businesses and rental accommodation, for example. Through this transformation, property relationships are changing to accommodate new conditions, but remain embedded in personalistic village connections.

Two: spontaneous land communities

Spontaneous land communities arise when residents who live in the same area, or citizens connected through the mass and/or personal media, come together to oppose land developments (see Chapters 5, 7, and 11).[79] Spontaneous communities differ from traditional communities

[77] Although China and Vietnam are signatories to the *United Nations Declaration of Indigenous Peoples' Rights* of 2007, they recognize ethnic minorities as disadvantaged groups, but do not recognize indigenous land rights. See Andersen, "Communal Tenure and the Governance of Common Property Resources in Asia," p. 6.

[78] Franz and Keebet von Benda-Beckmann, "Multiple Embeddedness and Systemic Implications: Struggles over Natural Resources in Minangkabau since the Reformasi," *Asian Journal of Social Science*, 38 (2010), 172–186 at 175.

[79] See, generally, Nguyen Quang Vinh and Michael Leaf, "City Life in the Village of Ghosts: A Case Study of Popular Housing in Ho Chi Minh City," *Habitat International*, 20(2) (1999), 175–190.

in that they lack strong organizational structures and coherent sets of regulatory traditions that are capable of galvanizing collective resistance. As the case studies in this book show, spontaneous land communities organize collective action around agents of change. These entities play a crucial role in coordinating collective action, filtering and constituting ideas, and keeping people connected.

Although most spontaneous land communities discussed by the authors (see Chapters 8, 9, and 11) were physically connected to a geographical location, the growing use of blogs, social media, and Weibo in particular, is creating virtual communities. Bloggers are often more prepared than the official media to test the boundaries of party-state narratives. The Osin blog in Vietnam, for example, linked the resolution of land disputes to party legitimacy, thus holding Vietnam's leaders accountable for socioeconomic problems. In China, Weibo has developed a virtual polity in which claims were made, judgments were made, and punishment was delivered, all by citizens independent of state power in the real world.

What is different about spontaneous land communities is the multiple embeddedness of property relations. Since members of these communities cannot invoke village customs or practices to legitimize their claims, they are less likely than traditional communities to embed property in relational or spiritual connections. Instead, they attempt to link property rights to a wide range of political, economic, and legal relationships. For example, spontaneous communities discussed in this book drew on socialist revolutionary arguments to legitimize their "rightful resistance" to land claims by capitalist investors (see Chapters 5, 7, and 11). They also embedded property in economic relationships based on employment and the commodity value of land. In China, spontaneous land communities used the courts as platforms to advance their claims (see Chapters 3, 4, and 8). In Taiwan (see Chapter 12) and Hong Kong (see Chapter 14), spontaneous land communities framed their complaints in the language of property rights and successfully prosecuted their claims through the courts and public protests.

Three: planned land communities

Planned land communities are created by land developers to resolve collective action problems that crop up for residents living in close proximity in high-rise apartments or gated communities. Under Chinese Property Law, homeowners in gated communities are required to create homeowners associations (HOA) to manage common property within the community on behalf all homeowners. HOAs have become one of the most active groups protesting about property and in challenging arbitrary corporate and government powers. They promote democratic decision-making within gated communities and social networking between HOAs.[80]

In contrast to the other land communities, residents living in planned communities are brought together by a formal set of legal conditions incorporated into governing documents.[81] As a consequence, their property claims are primarily, although not exclusively, embedded in legal relationships. As the discussion in Chapter 11 shows, members of planned communities also draw on political connections to advance their claims.

Four: state land communities

State agencies, judges, and associated land professionals, such as lawyers, are not generally considered members of a community; nevertheless, like other land communities, they embed property in particular sets of relationships. As previously discussed, in adopting modernist approaches to land management, states throughout East Asia have disembedded property from relational connections. They have passed laws that categorize property-holders, property objects, rights, duties, and rules for the appropriation and transfer of property rights. Legal property rights are meant to trump political, economic, and personalistic relationships. But, as the authors make clear, especially in China and Vietnam, law-based property rights and planning processes are interwoven with political and personalistic relationships, creating "fuzzy property rights." The intervention of party politics, as well as collusion and corruption, suggests that, in practice, as distinct from legal theory, property rights have yet to disembed from political and relational connections. This gap between the assertion of legal autonomy made by the state and practice on the ground undermines the legitimacy of state land communities in the eyes of farmers and other land users.

[80] Benjamin L. Read, "Democratizing the Neighborhood? New Private Housing and Home-Owner Self-Organization in Urban China," *China Quarterly*, 49 (2003), 31–59.

[81] See, generally, Choon Piew Pow, "Securing the 'Civilized' Enclaves: Gated Communities and the Moral Geographies of Exclusion in (Post-)Socialist Shanghai," *Urban Studies*, 44(8) (2007), 1539–1558.

A key difference between Taiwan and Hong Kong, on the one hand, and China and Vietnam, on the other hand, is the extent to which state land communities have detached property rights from political, economic, and personal relations. This relative autonomy translates into court protection of property rights and the civil space for land protests in Taiwan and Hong Kong.

Intersecting land communities

Land disputes are often characterized as clashes between modernity and tradition; however, the multi-embeddedness of property rights discussed above suggests shortcomings with this view. Most land communities discussed in this book drew from modernity and tradition to legitimize their property rights. Disputes revolved around differences in the emphasis communities placed on legal, political, social, and economic aspects of property relationships. Different emphases resulted in different understandings about what constituted socially just and fair dispute resolution processes and outcomes.

In most disputes in China and Vietnam, no single land community, including the state, was sufficiently powerful to displace rival understandings about land disputes. In this polycentric regulatory environment, lasting settlements are most likely to occur where land users and state agencies negotiate together in relatively unmediated dialogues to find common ground. In Taiwan and Hong Kong, the state land community has largely, but not entirely, displaced rival modes of property regulation. Courts, as a corollary, play a major role in resolving land disputes.

The social dimensions of land disputes

As Frank Upham points out in Chapter 2, rapid economic development in China, Vietnam, and elsewhere creates winners as well as losers. Since land is a scarce and highly valuable commodity, land expropriation and the resulting demolition and relocation create tangled webs of financial, social, and psychological harm. Losers in East Asia and elsewhere do not go quietly, and their grievances are a major source of conflict that involves individual and community stakeholders.

In China and Vietnam, where land must be converted and expropriated for economic development purposes, land-taking is highly contentious, not just because it affects the economic interest of individuals and communities. Upham notes that, "land not only has economic value; it also constitutes the basis for social relations through the creation of individual, group, and community identities." Land disputes are also contentious because they shape political, social, and legal institutions, and the political economy.

Land expropriation is a core component of the economic growth policy in China and Vietnam, and the party-state, authoritarian at its core, proves to be highly efficient in achieving its developmental agenda. In China, land appropriation takes place at great speed and through simple procedures. Unsurprisingly, this authoritarian efficiency generates disputes and conflict on a massive scale. The party-state, while aware of the complications, has been trying to submerge land disputes in mediation for ad hoc resolution to achieve short-term social harmony. Mediation may preempt social contention in the short term, but it does not resolve underlying conflicts, and in the long term, the process may generate more conflict than the original dispute. According to Upham, mediation may be damaging in two unique ways. First, mediation encourages "expressive violence" among the weaker parties, or "mob culture" of a sort, to counter the powerful developers and the government. Second, mediation creates a parallel system that is independent of, and competes with, formal judicial institutions and procedures. In the long term, it undermines the legitimacy of law and the political system. Land expropriation creates tremendous social trauma that may not be avoidable in economic transition, but a better-designed dispute resolution system that is transparent, participatory, and responsive may reduce the harm and produce long-term stability.

Country case studies

This book is divided into four sections that deal with case studies in China, Vietnam, Taiwan, and Hong Kong. Each country section begins with a chapter introducing the history of land regulation and its connection to contemporary land disputes. The introduction is then followed by chapters providing detailed cases studies about land disputes.

China narrative

In Chapter 3, Lei Chen traces the evolution of China's land tenure system in both rural and urban areas. His chapter sets a historical and institutional context in which the current land law and policy operate. After identifying the defining characteristics of China's land tenure system and pointing out the major problems that generate land disputes, the chapter offers a concise discussion of the recent overhaul of the legal and regulatory framework for land dispute resolution, with a special focus on contentious expropriation of land and the resulting issue of fair compensation. Chen concludes that Chinese law and legal institutions are offering enhanced protection of property rights and creating more meaningful substantive and procedural limits on state powers.

In Chapter 4, Jie Cheng puts the legal system to the test by offering a focused study of land-taking cases adjudicated in Chinese courts. Through a meticulous examination of 200 court cases that applied the Land Management Law, Cheng presents powerful evidence to illustrate the limited role of courts. Cases reveal that courts struggle to balance state interest in expropriation and individual entitlement to land, and to provide meaningful protection for the evictees' land entitlements. Although the courts are more neutral and offer better protection of land rights in civil disputes between two equal private parties, the courts defer to government authorities in adjudicating the authorities' disputes with private parties. Because of their constitutional and political status, courts can play only a limited role in contentious land disputes, tipping the scale decisively toward the interests of the collective and the state. Cheng concludes that, without achieving the necessary level of judicial independence and other institutional change, the capacity of the courts to offer effective land dispute resolution in China is highly constrained.

In Chapter 5, Eva Pils goes beyond the positive law and formal legal framework for land disputes. She explores the contrasting conceptions of land rights in the context of land expropriation. For Pils, the expropriators, including developers and the government standing behind them, and evictees, including their supporters and sympathizers, form two radically different perspectives on land rights. From a statist perspective, expropriation of land is essential for China's continuous economic growth, and given public ownership of land in the socialist system, is legally and morally justifiable. But, from the perspective of evictees and their representatives, expropriation, as it has been practiced in China, is predatory, corrupt, and in any event fundamentally unfair. The current property regime and the politics of expropriation have generated inevitable and often irreconcilable disputes that are bound to recur.

In Chapter 6, Hualing Fu uses the famous Wukan protest against predatory land-taking as a case study to illustrate the potential of successful political mobilization in protecting property rights. The Wukan protest highlights a commonly observed irony in China that the government encourages citizens to settle their disputes through law, but at the same time creates multiple barriers to block citizens' access to justice for meaningful legal remedies. In the end, frustrated citizens whose land is taken without proper compensation abandon the law and take the matter into their own hands. In the process, the citizens realize that, if they speak unequivocally and act collectively and firmly, their collective action increases the likelihood of the government taking its own law more seriously. Thus, there emerges the alternative of a mobilization-based trajectory in which people organize themselves and act forcefully on specific social and economic issues. Organized protest creates better opportunities for dialogue between protesters and the government, and for reaching a mutually beneficial result of channeling contentious land disputes back to legal institutions for effective resolution.

In Chapter 7, Xin He provides a more positive interpretation of the potential of courts to offer effective protection of property rights in housing demolition cases. Ordinarily, land disputes are characterized by power disparity between the parties. The disputes take place largely between private citizens as plaintiffs and powerful developers and the government behind them as defendants, and as such, courts are not able to act fairly and effectively to correct the regulatory capture. However, the balance tips toward the plaintiffs when they act collectively and forcefully in and outside the courts to generate enough political pressure so that judges are forced to rule according to law. Public protest within the framework of law, as He frames it, can enhance transparency, accountability, and judicial independence, and, as He concludes, the court can be used as an effective public forum for social and legal development.

The two subsequent chapters offer empirical evidence to illustrate the limits of state law in resolving land disputes in rural areas. In Chapter 8, Susan Whiting and Hau Shao explore the enhanced role of mediation in solving rural disputes, and the impact of the extensive use of mediation on the legal system in general and on the courts in particular. Through sample surveys and in-depth interviews, the authors examine the degree to which mediation undermines the ability of the courts to provide predictable and determinant legal norms to guide dispute resolution, and inadvertently emboldens villagers to use violence. Farmers prefer formal rules and courts to solve high-stakes disputes, but political constraints prevent the courts from developing the capacity to offer effective remedies. These authors conclude that the unchecked and unprincipled use of mediation undermines the function of the legal system and creates popular dissatisfaction.

In Chapter 9, Changdong Zhang and Christopher Heurlin explore the reasons why courts are timid in handling disputes through extensive field work on rural land disputes. The authors point out that local government officials prevent disputes reaching courts to hide corrupt practices from their superiors. For example, officials push land disputes through mediation and use their administrative authority to block access to courts. The paradox is that imposed mediation may block farmers' access to courts, but cannot close off access to justice. Frustrated with the process and end result, farmers contest mediation and take their cases to the streets. Mediation as it is practiced in rural China provokes farmers and generates the very problem it tries to resolve.

Vietnam narrative

In Chapter 10, Toan Le and Nguyen Hung Quang show how cycles of adoption and reception have shaped land laws in Vietnam. First, the Chinese, and then the French, left their laws. Revolutionary land management practices borrowed from Maoist China and the former Soviet Union replaced, but did not entirely displace, the previous land regimes. More recently, Vietnam embarked on another cycle of borrowing, this time attempting to create private land-use rights that commodified land. The authors argue that the rapid increase in land disputes in Vietnam has arisen not only from increased pressure on farmland, but also from a clash in the epistemic understandings between state officials and developers, on the one hand, and farmers, on the other hand, about who should have access to land and on what conditions.

In Chapter 11, John Gillespie draws on a series of case studies to examine why land disputes have proliferated in Vietnam at the same time as the state is perfecting property rights and formal dispute resolution agencies. He examines three disputes that reflect the previously discussed traditional, spontaneous, and planned land communities. In each case study, he shows that the state legal regime has not displaced pre-existing self-regulatory practices. For example, state land-use rights did not recognize or extinguish farmers' spiritual and moral claims to land circulating in the traditional Đông Dương village. The findings from the case studies point to a plurality of land regulation,[82] where the state is only one of many regulators seeking to control access to land.

[82] For a discussion about legal pluralism in East Asia, see Jane Collier *et al.*, "Editors' Introduction," *Law & Society Review*, 28 (1994), 417–428; Andrew J. Harding, "Comparative Law and Legal Transplantation in South East Asia: Making Sense of the 'Nomic Din,'" in D. Nelken and J. Feest (eds.), *Adapting Legal Cultures* (Oxford: Hart, 2001).

In each case study, the state lacked the power to unilaterally impose its solutions on the land users and needed to cooperate with the other land communities to find mutually acceptable outcomes. As in China, however, land users had few opportunities to press their case through either formal state forums or via public discourse. It was only by staging civil disobedience campaigns that they managed to leverage a position on the negotiating table.

Taiwan narrative

In Chapter 12, Po-Fang Tsai and Duan Lin show that the Taiwanese land regime is constructed from different legal systems – the new overlying and interweaving with the old. Imperial Qing dynasty land laws that aimed to pacify the local population were replaced by Japanese colonial laws during the late nineteenth century. Like the French colonial laws in Vietnam and the English colonial laws in Hong Kong, the Japanese laws were modeled on Western land title rules that abolished the link in Imperial Chinese law between group status and land rights. The colonial laws also centralized land control, a process that facilitated the creation of a new landlord class. Finally, the land laws separated administrative and judicial functions. For the first time, land disputants were given the option of taking their grievances to the courts for resolution. Unlike the Vietnamese, the Taiwanese did not abrogate their colonial legal system. After decades of gradual consolidation and reform, the court system is now sufficiently independent from the executive arm of government to effectively adjudicate land-taking cases.

In Chapter 13, Duan Lin and Po-Fang Tsai go on to show how formal state apparatus, such as administrative mechanisms and the courts, deal with disputes over land used for ancestor worship. When the Chinese Nationalist Government recovered Taiwan in 1945 and started to apply modern Chinese civil law to Taiwan, ancestor worship land lost its legal status and was treated as common property. This change in legal status disrupted the personal relationships underlying this traditional practice and generated numerous land disputes. In an attempt to rectify this problem, the government introduced the Ancestral Worship Property Ordinance 2007, which once again recognized the legal status of ancestral worship property. But, as Lin and Tsai narrate, the Ordinance has not resolved disputes because it does not adequately reflect the fluid and contextual relationships that govern this type of property. What the authors demonstrate is that, although formal state institutions can regulate most land disputes, they lack the flexibility to deal with nuanced relational property interests, such as ancestral worship property, which do not fit neatly within the narrow parameters of property law.

Hong Kong narrative

In Chapter 14, Say H. Goo explores how the English land law system took root and flourished in Hong Kong. He describes an entire system transfer. The English colonists not only brought land laws, but also the entire institutional trappings, including judges, lawyers, educational system, and even the judicial architecture of the English legal system. Over time, the law spread beyond the colonial elites and came to govern most land transactions. But the English law did not entirely displace pre-existing regulatory practices. It did not apply to the villages and farmland of the New Territories and coexisted in an uneasy relationship with a thriving unofficial housing market.

In Chapter 15, Say H. Goo takes up this story about the plural land systems in Hong Kong. To avoid disputes with land users in the New Territories, the colonial administration allowed the construction of new houses for male children during the nineteenth century. This initiative, which was formalized as the small house policy in 1972, recognized customary land practices that predated colonization. But, with the large population growth in the New Territory coupled with rapidly increasing land values, the policy currently threatens the integrity of land-planning schemes. What the study shows is that land law provides no effective solutions to complex resource disputes arising from land scarcity. Ultimately, the residents of the New Territories relied on the powerful Heung Yee Kuk association to voice their concerns through public discourse and political processes.

Contrasting with the uncertainty surrounding the small house policy, courts routinely deal with disputes over Tso and Tong ancestral worship land. Here, the common law courts have shown their capacity to work customary practices into the formal legal rules governing the ownership and management of this kind of property.

In Chapter 16, the connection between land disputes and political discourse reappears as Alice Lee discusses the regulation of unauthorized buildings and structures in Hong Kong. For decades, authorities in Hong Kong turned a blind eye to unauthorized buildings constructed on rooftops and other available spaces in the city. Faced with a rapidly increasing population and prohibitively expensive housing prices, the authorities tacitly accepted unauthorized buildings as a means of housing the urban poor. This relaxed regulatory approach changed following revelations of building violations during the 2011 elections. Intense media scrutiny of the candidates, itself a product of increasing democratization, spilled over into an official rethink about the regulation of unauthorized buildings.

This link between democratization and land disputes is also evident in the discussion about the Mei Foo Sun Chuen estate. In this case, neighbors complained that a twenty-story housing development was being constructed on land set aside as a buffer zone between existing apartment towers. Members of protest organizations staged a "lie-down" protest to prevent construction and to mobilize media support to campaign against the project. Mass civil disobedience provided an effective mode of communication when protestors lacked legal forums for expressing their views.

It is instructive to contrast the Taiwanese and Hong Kong cases with the Chinese and Vietnamese cases. Taiwanese and Hong Kong courts routinely resolve land disputes that clearly fall within the parameters covered by the land law. But where disputes escalate beyond simple legal questions about the validity of ownership or control and involve issues such as the small house policy or complex planning issues about environmental amenity, then disputants need to organize and mobilize to influence public policy. Recent democratization in Taiwan and Hong Kong has relaxed controls over the formation of protest organizations and the use of civil protest, leveling the playing field against state-backed developers in ways that the legal protection of property rights cannot achieve.

Conclusions

In rapidly urbanizing and developing societies, such as China and Vietnam, land pressures and ongoing disputes are inevitable. Land-taking creates ongoing and contested relationships between state agencies, developers, and land users. Without clear legal authority, unequivocal juridical foundations or irrefutable land compensation strategies, agreements will break down and be reshaped through fresh conflicts until a new consensus is reached. Dispute resolution is therefore highly dynamic, and land disputes are rarely settled once and for all.

The case studies reveal the complexity of land disputes and the importance of decentering the analysis to consider what all the relevant actors think. We have also seen that conflicts are socially constructed.

Even when there is agreement about compensation, for example, disputes may continue if actors form different views about what constitutes fair and reasonable access to land. The findings further show how emotion transforms disputes and puts solutions based on pragmatic dialogue out of reach. The case studies show that governments in China and Vietnam take steps only infrequently to reduce the emotional intensity of disputes before outbreaks of civil disobedience and violence. For example, grand mediation in China, which is the main government response to proliferating land disputes, has proved to be relatively ineffective in reducing the scale and intensity of conflicts. When land-taking is perceived as a mere conspiracy between the power and money, there is little trust of local state institutions, legal or otherwise. Especially in an age when social media rapidly spreads information about land disputes, land users form clear views about the justice and appropriateness of land-taking and compensation and are difficult to manipulate through state-managed mediation and litigation.

Suppression may produce short-term results in land-grabbing, but it is likely to backload social tension and conflict to a future date. Behind China's authoritarian efficiency is a hidden social havoc that is surfacing slowly but resiliently. A more consultative and accommodative approach that is inclusive of the voices of all stakeholders in decision-making and goes through proper procedures reduces tension and violent conflict, and produces more peaceful expropriation and resettlement. Procedural justice matters for East Asians as much as it matters for Westerners.

Land disputes are often polycentric, involving multiple parties fighting for the same interest and multiple institutions jointly offering solutions. As such, they are ill-suited for traditional court-centered litigation, and judicial reasoning does not offer the best options for land dispute resolution. This is especially true in countries like China and Vietnam, where the courts are weak and cannot act effectively and independently on highly politicized issues such as land-taking. Dependence breeds corruption, and corruption undermines trust. In addition, legal rules and procedures in China and Vietnam are too "fuzzy" to provide sufficient guidance for dispute resolution. As is often the case in China and Vietnam, the courts eagerly push land-taking cases away for political resolution.

Lasting settlements are most likely to occur where land users and state agencies negotiate together in relatively unmediated exchanges. This dialogue may occur where informal connections link the social organizations representing land users with party and government agencies.

Without these linkages, social organizations often lack effective ways of making local party-state agencies accountable to land users. Low-level political participation in policy implementation is possible in the authoritarian systems of China and Vietnam, but institutional channels for resolving land disputes are rigidly restricted. Tight state management of formal dispute resolution has the unintended consequence of driving land users into non-institutional channels. Frustrated land users organize themselves to demonstrate their dissatisfaction and, with the support of the wider community as well as public and social media, they sometimes force the government to compromise.

There are signs of a more "responsible and responsive" state emerging in China and Vietnam. The Wukan reforms point to a renewed interest in grass-roots democracy as a means of opening dialogue that might resolve disputes that prove intractable to mediation and court actions. Settlement is most likely to occur where land users have the power to deliberate with state officials on a relatively equal footing. For this to happen, land users need to organize and mobilize their resources, which, together with domestic and international support, may force the state and developers to the negotiation table. Political mobilization at the grass-roots level may, over time, force the state to take its own laws and procedures seriously in handling land disputes.

Finally, it is unrealistic to rely entirely on dispute resolution to mitigate land disputes. Fiscal measures, such as removing the benefits of land sales and taxation, can reduce the incentives for local government to take land and pay low compensation. Urbanization may be inevitable, and land disputes are bound to increase, but responsive fiscal policies, effective anti-corruption enforcement, and enhanced social welfare might alleviate the growing pains that economic transition may inflict on developing nations and their people.

2

Property rights, commodification, and land disputes in contemporary socialist Asia

FRANK K. UPHAM

> There is a sense in which rapid economic progress is impossible without painful adjustments. Ancient philosophies have to be scrapped; old social institutions have to disintegrate; bonds of caste, creed and race have to burst; and large numbers of persons who cannot keep up with progress have to have their expectations of a comfortable life frustrated. Very few communities are willing to pay the full price of economic progress.
>
> *Measures for the Economic Development of Underdeveloped Countries*, UN Department of Social and Economic Affairs, 1951[1]

Introduction

China is in its fourth decade of rapid economic growth. Vietnam is close behind. With this growth has come massive social change that, whatever its ultimate net benefits, has created legions of losers: individuals, groups, and communities that have had the framework of their lives destroyed, in many instances through the destruction of their rights in land and homes. As with such people throughout history, the losers in Vietnam and China have not always gone quietly; on the contrary, loss of land, whether farmland taken for expanding cities or urban apartments taken for commercial development, has become both countries' greatest source of social conflict.[2] The reason is simple: more than perhaps any other

[1] Quoted in Artuto Escobar, *Encountering Development: The Making and Unmaking of the Third World* (Princeton University Press, 1995), p. 3.

[2] Two limitations to the chapter bear mention. First, since both Vietnam and China prohibit private ownership of land, these disputes are technically about either land-use rights or ownership of immovable assets, that is, buildings, and in many instances both. For purposes of simplicity and because the consequential differences between a system of indefinite usufruct rights and absolute ownership are minimal in this context, I refer to all

social good, property rights, and especially property rights in land, are radically multidimensional and cannot be easily commoditized. With few exceptions, land not only has economic value – what is seen by the expanding cities and urban developers – but also provides the basis for social relations and in many ways constitutes those relationships through the creation of individual, group, and community identities. Furthermore, when land must be transferred or transformed to allow economic growth, the process implicates not only the mechanism of market exchange, but also the social, legal, and bureaucratic institutions that structure political power.

This chapter tries to deepen our understanding of these contemporary events in two ways. In the second section, I put them into historical and comparative perspective by demonstrating that they repeat patterns of conflict that date at least to the English Enclosure Movement of the fifteenth century and have recurred in periods of rapid economic growth ever since. In the third section, I use property theory to deepen our insight into the nature and persistence of such disputes. Although contests over possession and control of land implicate economic interests, interpreting them primarily through an economic lens is dangerously incomplete. The result of doing so is likely not only to fall short of the economists' goal of market efficiency, but also to engender and at times institutionalize continuing conflict.

In the concluding section, I turn to the disputes described in this volume and attempt to place them in the context of evolving legal systems by analyzing the efforts of the Vietnamese and Chinese governments to respond to the widening social conflict arising from land dislocation. I argue that bureaucratic and judicial responses must address not only the financial impact of land transfers, but also the normative and behavioral changes that are at least as painful and may eventually negate the economic benefits that were the goals of the policy changes that set the process in motion. While adequate compensation may be a necessary element of any effective response, a legitimate process that is flexible enough to address the diffuse non-pecuniary effects of dislocation may be essential to the long-term social harmony that is the rhetorical goal of both governments.

such disputes as land disputes. Second, I draw primarily from Chinese examples with occasional references to Vietnam. There are significant differences between the two situations, but the goal of this chapter is to provide a comparative and theoretical framework that can be profitably applied to both countries.

Historical and comparative perspective

Growth is change, and change means that existing productive technologies and social structures must make way for new ones.[3] Since, as Douglass North put it over three decades ago, "property rights are always embedded in the institutional structure of a society,"[4] growth will require changing property rights. This is precisely what is happening in contemporary Vietnam and China, but they are hardly the first societies to undergo such wrenching social change.

The destruction of common land rights by enclosure in England between the fifteenth and nineteenth centuries substantially increased agricultural productivity, but in doing so it destroyed an established way of life and the property rights that gave it structure and stability. At the risk of oversimplification, enclosure was the process of converting common land to individually owned and controlled land. It ended the rights of village residents to use the land for a variety of purposes, from cutting hay, planting crops, and gathering manure to hunting. Instead, the holder of the newly unified property right could devote the land to monoculture or sheep pasturage. Indeed, it was the social disruption caused by the new owners' turn to wool production that inspired Sir Thomas More's description of the famous man-eating sheep: "Your sheep, which are naturally mild, and easily kept in order, may be said now to devour men and unpeople, not only villages, but towns."[5] While generally credited with accelerating Britain's rise as the first industrial power, the enclosures are also an archetypical example of the destruction of one set of property rights, in this instance the commoners' fragmented rights to use the commons for diverse specific purposes, and its replacement by a unified ownership that recognized the lord's right to dedicate the land exclusively to its most profitable use.

[3] Douglass North recognized long ago that economic growth engenders "immense modern social problems": "Adjustment entails a total societal transformation. Impersonal exchange, minute specialization and division of labour, a radical reduction in information costs, and world-wide interdependence entail a complete transformation of every aspect of societal organisation." He further recognized that it has been the "flexibility of the political and economic institutions of Western economies" that has enabled the West to deal with the social dislocation of growth, noting even that economic change will require "recontracting" that may "sometimes … require an alteration in the rules." Douglass C. North, "The New Institutional Economics and Third World Development," in John Harriss, Janet Hunter, Colin M. Lewis *et al.* (eds.), *The New Institutional Economics and Third World Development* (London: Routledge, 1995), pp. 17, 22.

[4] North, "The New Institutional Economics," p. 5.

[5] Sir Thomas More, *Utopia* (1516).

Although the enclosures did not directly involve industrialization, its iterative process of destruction and re-creation of property rights has been repeated by virtually every society that has evolved from an agrarian to an industrial economy. The case of *Pennsylvania Coal Company* v. *Sanderson and Wife* illustrates the process in nineteenth-century America.[6] In 1868, Mrs. Sanderson bought land along the Meadow Brook specifically intending to use the flow of water for irrigation, fish ponds, and ice. That same year, the Pennsylvania Coal Company dug a coal pit upstream, eventually polluting the stream to the extent that Sanderson could no longer use it. She sued based on the then prevailing water law doctrine known as natural flow, which required that riparian owners preserve the quantity, quality, and impetus of the pre-existing flow of water. The case was not an easy one for the Pennsylvania Supreme Court. The law and the facts were clear: each riparian owner had a property right in the natural flow of a stream and there was no question that the mine had fouled the stream. But the economic and social cost of enjoining coal mining in mid-nineteenth-century Pennsylvania was equally clear. After hearing the case three times over eight years, the court finally concluded that the general social welfare trumped an individual's property rights. After a long opinion that disingenuously distorted the word "natural" to accommodate the digging of the mine and the pollution of the Meadow Brook, the court eventually gave the real reason for its decision:

> The plaintiff's grievance is for a mere personal inconvenience; and we are of the opinion that mere private personal inconveniences ... must yield to the necessities of a great public industry, which, although in the hands of a private corporation, subserves a great public interest. To encourage the development of the great natural resources of a country, trifling inconveniences to particular persons must sometimes give way to the necessities of a great community.[7]

It is important to make clear what the court did here. Sanderson's interest in clean water was not trivial; irrigation, ice-making, and fish farming are central to the agrarian use of land. But even if her complaint had been a "mere inconvenience," it should not have mattered. The essence of a *property* right is that it is not subject to a cost–benefit balancing by the courts, the government, or the neighbors. The classic American statement of this truism is *Jacque* v. *Steenberg Homes, Inc.*,

[6] *Pennsylvania Coal Co.* v. *Sanderson*, 6 A. 453 (1886).
[7] *Pennsylvania Coal Co.* v. *Sanderson*, 6 A. 459 (1886).

where the Wisconsin Supreme Court in 1997 granted US$100,000 in punitive damages for an intentional trespass despite finding no pecuniary damage to the plaintiff whatsoever. That the trespass had been made with no ill will, had caused no harm, and had saved the defendant substantial expense was irrelevant:

> The right to exclude others from his or her land is "one of the most essential sticks in the bundle of rights that are commonly characterized as property" . . . Society has an interest in preserving the integrity of the legal system. Private landowners should feel confident that wrongdoers who trespass upon their land will be appropriately punished.[8]

The difference in these two cases is not politics or a difference in the relative power of the parties; both plaintiffs were individuals suing corporations. The difference was timing. Mrs. Sanderson was suing to enforce property rights that had outlived their economic and social utility. To grant her an injunction would have vindicated her right to exclude, a right which as we will see in the next section has great social and psychological value, but it would have stopped or at least greatly impeded progress. Although the Pennsylvania Supreme Court initially found for Sanderson, and it was not until its third hearing of the case that it reversed and characterized her clear property right as a "mere inconvenience," the court was ultimately not willing to sacrifice perceived economic progress for either Sanderson's lesser economic interests or for the sake of "the integrity of the legal system." By contrast, land in the United States in 1997 was not at the center of a great social transformation, and the *Jacque* court could protect the social and psychological values that property rights protect in stable times.

Each time systemic social change on this scale occurs – and it has occurred innumerable times in human history[9] – property rights must be changed. An example from Japan's nineteenth-century land law reform may be useful since it involves a top-down politically driven change similar to contemporary Chinese and Vietnamese processes, rather than the arguably bottom-up economically driven processes of the enclosures

[8] 563 N.W.2d 154 (Wis. 1997) (quoting the US Supreme Court case of *Kaiser Aetna* v. *United States*, 444 US 164, 176 (1979)).

[9] In Asia as well as the West. See, for example, Thomas Buoye, "Litigation, Legitimacy, and Lethal Violence: Why County Courts Failed to Prevent Violent Disputes over Property in Eighteenth-Century China," in Madeleine Zelin, Jonathan Ocko, and Robert Gardella (eds.), *Contract and Property in Early Modern China* (Stanford University Press, 2004), p. 94 (detailing how this process has occurred often in China).

and American industrialization. Desperate to stave off colonialism, Meiji leaders had to unify the country, mobilize its resources, and create a strong state with the military prowess and patina of modernity needed to convince the West to end the extraterritorial treaties that were not only a constant humiliation, but also substantially reduced governmental power. Law reform was an inevitable choice. It not only promised to intensify central control and increase the now much-needed tax revenues, but it also had the equally important by-product of looking modern in Western eyes.[10]

Central to both goals was the rationalization of ownership to make land flow more readily in commerce and, in a classic example of James Scott's "seeing like a state," increase the visibility of landownership so that it could be taxed more intensively.[11] Despite a high level of commercial activity and sophisticated financial structures, Tokugawa Japan lacked the well-developed formal legal framework considered essential for a modern state. Landownership was often ill-defined and the private sale of land was prohibited, although informal exchanges were common. Thus, a series of legal steps was taken to clarify ownership and commodify land: settling ownership in the farmers rather than their erstwhile feudal lords, legalizing the full alienation of land, granting certificates of title, allowing the eviction of tenants.

At the center of these reforms was the Land Tax Reform Law (*chiso kaiseihou*), which has been called the "single most important reform" of the Meiji period.[12] The law sought to build on the pre-existing system by equalizing the burden and by bringing heretofore untaxed land into a standardized and unified tax roll. The intent was egalitarian, but the net effect of the law and predicate legislation was to benefit large landholders and landlords at the expense of smallholders and tenants. This pro-landlord

[10] Whether the pre-existing Tokugawa legal system needed to "modernize" and become more like the West for any reason other than responding to Western military aggression is quite a different question. John Henry Wigmore, the founder of American evidence scholarship, spent time in Japan ostensibly to help modernize Japanese commercial law. Expecting primitive legal forms, Wigmore famously found "all the expedients and principles of European commercial life" and that "all [the] features of advanced commercial life are seen reflected in the legal records." John Henry Wigmore, *A Panorama of the World Legal Systems* (St. Paul, MN: West Publishing, 1928), pp. 481–482. Advanced commercial practices, however, were no answer to Commodore Perry's gunships.

[11] James Scott, *Seeing Like a State* (New Haven, CT: Yale University Press, 1998).

[12] Kozo Yamamura, "The Meiji Land Tax Reform and its Effects," in Marius B. Jansen and Gilbert Rozman (eds.), *Japan in Transition from Tokugawa to Meiji* (Princeton University Press, 1986), p. 382.

tendency occurred on several levels, beginning with the very act of formally titling land. Valuing uniformity and what we would now call transparency, and lacking any knowledge of the customary law that had governed local land relationships for centuries, the national government resolved disputes by granting deeds to "anyone receiving rents or holding mortgages," which according to one historian of Meiji rural society invariably meant the "richer and more powerful claimants."[13] But it was not only the resolution of contested ownership that was at stake; the urgency and the demand for standardization denied officials the time to understand the nature of tenancy as well. The result was the collapse of dozens of distinct forms of mutual rights in land into arbitrary binary forms borrowed from Western systems, reducing the complexity of customary practice to unitary forms that consistently favored the more powerful party.

My point with these three historical examples is not that property rights should be preserved forever and never transferred involuntarily from one party to another. If we want economic growth and social progress, change will be difficult without modifying the legal structures supporting the preexisting regime, and modifying social structures will almost inevitably mean transforming property rights. Destroying or, to use a common euphemism first used by Harold Demsetz in his classic narrative of changing property rights, "adjusting" changing property rights from a less to a more productive holder does not require legal injustice.[14] In the abstract it is both fairer and more efficient to compensate the holders of existing property rights, but doing so is costly, difficult, and often neglected.[15] But even when the law is followed and compensation is paid, the holder of destroyed property rights may well be left considerably less well off in all but pecuniary terms than before the taking of his property. Thus, in the Vietnamese and Chinese instances described in this volume, more is at stake than just getting the government to pay legally required compensation to the correct persons or households, however desirable that would be. To understand this other dimension of property, therefore, we now turn to what property ownership can mean in other than economic terms.

[13] Ann Waswo, *Japanese Landlords: The Decline of A Rural Elite* (Berkeley, CA: University of California Press, 1977), p. 18.

[14] Harold Demsetz, "Toward a Theory of Property Rights," *American Economic Review*, 57(2) (1967), 347–359.

[15] See Daniel Fitzpatrick, "Evolution and Chaos in Property Rights Systems: The Third World Tragedy of Contested Access," *Yale Law Journal*, 115 (2006), 996 at 1012 (arguing that in many Third World countries property systems are greatly complicated by interactions between legal, normative, and institutional arrangements).

Land law transformations in comparative and historical perspective

Socialist East Asia is not the only place where the destruction of property rights is controversial. In 2005, the United States Supreme Court in *Kelo* v. *City of New London* upheld the use of eminent domain for purposes of economic development.[16] Although the result was hardly surprising to property law scholars or practitioners, *Kelo* has been one of the most politically influential judicial decisions of the last decade, and the reaction against it is credited with sparking a legislative movement that has limited government's eminent domain power in at least thirty-five American states.[17] In contrast to controversial instances of Chinese eminent domain, *Kelo* had this impact without the slightest hint of illegality or corruption; nor were there any allegations that the compensation was inadequate.

The case involved the taking of several private homes in the New London neighborhood of Fort Trumbull by the city under the statutory and constitutional provisions for eminent domain of Connecticut and the United States. As one of many formerly industrial mid-size American cities in economic and social decline, at the turn of the century New London devised a revitalization plan that involved taking private land and transferring it to other private entities, most notably the pharmaceutical giant Pfizer. The city and state followed all the stringent procedural requirements of public hearings and legislative approvals for the location and nature of the development, and there was no question of inadequacy of compensation.[18] The only issue was whether the taking of plaintiffs' property was for a "public use," as required by the federal constitution, a test functionally equivalent to the provisions of the Vietnamese and Chinese constitutions.[19] The plaintiffs argued that the forced transfer of property from one citizen to another solely because the second party would use it more productively could not qualify as "public use" and was therefore unconstitutional. In other words, they argued that New London could not do through the democratic process what the Supreme Court of Pennsylvania did through judicial interpretation

[16] 545 US 469 (2005).

[17] See Ilya Somin, *The Limits of Backlash: Assessing the Political Response to Kelo*, 3, available at: http://works.bepress.com/ilya_somin/2.

[18] *Kelo* v. *City of New London*, 545 US 469, 473–477 (2005).

[19] Constitution of the Socialist Republic of Vietnam, April 15, 1992, Ch. 1, Art. 23; Xianfa amendment 4, §§4, 6 (2004) (China).

when it transferred Mrs. Sanderson's water rights to the Pennsylvania Coal Company in *Sanderson*.

From the perspective of someone who believes that legal text should be applied consistently with its common-sense meaning, in other words, to most non-lawyers, it should have been an easy case. Giving Ms. Kelo's house to Pfizer to use as a research lab hardly seems a "public use," but in fact by 2005 when the Supreme Court decided the case, most legally knowledgeable observers assumed that the court would find for the city, as it did. The reason is that the US Supreme Court had long ago determined that taking property by eminent domain and transferring it to a private party for purposes of economic growth could constitute public use. First, in *Berman* v. *Parker*,[20] in 1954, and then again in *Hawai'i Housing Authority* v. *Midkiff*,[21] in 1984, the court had allowed such transfers. While there is room for an argument that *Kelo* was doctrinally distinguishable from these two cases, to most American property scholars, the facts in *Midkiff*, where the Hawaiian government transferred ownership from individual landlords to their individual tenants, presents a much harder case for public use than *Kelo*.[22] For these scholars the reasons that the latter was much more controversial was the political setting, not any factual or doctrinal niceties.

In the rest of this section, I use *Kelo* to illustrate three factors related to the non-economic meaning of private property, all of which existed in *Kelo* and all of which exist in heightened form in the Chinese and Vietnamese situations: the nature of the parties and the property; the pace of change in contemporary society; and the recurrent abuse of eminent domain by local and state governments.

20 *Berman* v. *Parker*, 348 US 26 (1954).

21 *Hawai'i Housing Authority* v. *Midkiff*, 467 US 229 (1984).

22 Justice Sandra Day O'Conner, who had written the majority opinion in *Midkiff*, wrote a powerful and influential dissent in *Kelo*. Most memorably she argued that the use of eminent domain for purposes of economic growth would inevitably favor the rich and powerful: "The trouble with economic development takings is that private benefit and incidental public benefit are, by definition, merged and mutually reinforcing. In this case, for example, any boon for Pfizer or the plan's developer is difficult to disaggregate from the promised public gains in taxes and jobs." *Kelo* v. *City of New London*, 545 US 469, 502 (2005). Her doctrinal treatment of *Berman* and *Midkiff*, on the other hand, was less persuasive. Her basic distinction was that the eminent domain in those two cases was aimed at ameliorating a harm (urban "blight" and an oligopolistic real estate market, respectively), whereas New London was trying to achieve the benefit of economic revitalization. I leave to the reader to decide the strength of this distinction. For our purposes it is important to note only that the political impact of *Kelo* far outstripped its doctrinal novelty.

The court described the plaintiffs and the property taken in *Kelo* as follows:

> Petitioner Susette Kelo has lived in Fort Trumbull since 1997. She has made extensive improvements to her house, which she prizes for its water view. Petitioner Wilhelmina Dery was born in her Fort Trumbull house in 1918 and has lived there her entire life. Her husband Charles (also a petitioner) has lived in the house since they married some 60 years ago . . . There is no allegation that any of these properties is blighted or otherwise in poor condition; rather, they were condemned only because they happen to be located in the development area.[23]

It is hard to imagine more sympathetic plaintiffs than the Derys: their house has literally and figuratively shaped their entire lives together. Its loss, at 87 years of age in Wilhelmina's case, could kill her, certainly spiritually and conceivably literally.[24] To talk of this loss in economic terms or to argue that monetary compensation could be "just" as demanded by the Constitution is close to insulting to the human condition. But it gets worse once one considers why the Derys are being forced to make this sacrifice: not to provide their community with a school or train station, not because their home had dangerously deteriorated, but so that their home can be razed and presented to a giant drug company.

Of course, most Americans who lose their homes to eminent domain have not lived there for eighty-seven years; they are more likely to resemble Susette Kelo, who had occupied her house for less than a decade, than Wilhelmina Dery. When we think of the many Chinese or Vietnamese farm families who lose their homes, land, and livelihoods to rampant urbanization, however, her situation may actually understate the loss. In the first place, it is very possible that they have farmed land in their village not for a mere lifetime, but for generations, and it is very unlikely that they will have lived and farmed on that land for less than a decade as had Susette Kelo. But there is an even more important distinction: the Derys, for all the pain of their loss, received compensation measured by the fair market price of their home. While there are serious arguments that market price understates an owner's subjective price, it

[23] *Kelo* v. *City of New London*, 545 US 469, 475 (2005).

[24] Wilhelmina Dery died on March 13, 2006, in the home she sought to protect from a government taking in the *Kelo* case. Lynne Tuohy, "Fort Trumbull Plaintiff Dies," *Hartford Courant*, available at: http://articles.courant.com/2006-03-15/news/0603150758_1_takings-wilhelmina-dery-new-london-s-fort-trumbull.

does approximate what their home was worth to others. The Chinese farmers described in this volume, on the other hand, usually get at best the discounted value of thirty years of their harvests, not even a decent fraction of what their property would later fetch the local government after it was sold to a real estate developer.

The Derys and their neighbors had another important advantage over their Vietnamese and Chinese counterparts. They were able to fight the exercise of eminent domain at each step of the process, and the process had many steps. They also had the not insubstantial satisfaction of forcing the city to defend its actions all the way to the US Supreme Court. The Chinese and Vietnamese, on the other hand, had to watch helplessly while the acquiring municipality re-sold their land to the highest bidder for orders of magnitude more than they had received, and this is assuming the affected farmers had actually received their legal due. In other words, the New London, Connecticut, and the United States governments and legal systems paid attention to the Derys and thereby recognized not only the economic value of their possessions, but also their dignity as human beings worthy of social regard. The Vietnamese and Chinese described in this book often get neither.

The second factor behind the influence of *Kelo*, the pace of social change, also has resonance with the Chinese and Vietnamese situations. New London is typical of hundreds of cities in the American northeast and Midwest that have undergone the twin processes of de-industrialization and depopulation. Again the court's opinion describes the situation well:

> The city of New London (hereinafter City) sits at the junction of the Thames River and Long Island Sound in southeastern Connecticut. Decades of economic decline led a state agency in 1990 to designate the City a "distressed municipality." In 1996, the Federal Government closed the Naval Undersea Warfare Center, which had been located in the Fort Trumbull area of the City and had employed over 1,500 people. In 1998, the City's unemployment rate was nearly double that of the State, and its population of just under 24,000 residents was at its lowest since 1920.[25]

The plaintiffs' loss of their homes, therefore, was part of a series of accelerating changes that was already destabilizing their lives. Many of them had likely already gone through the deterioration of their community, the decline in the city's tax base, the departure of their children for better opportunities in other cities and regions, and a diminishing sense of general well-being.

[25] *Kelo* v. *City of New London*, 545 US 469, 473 (2005).

The changes of the last several decades have not been solely for the worse, of course. Concomitant with de-industrialization have come extremely rapid technological advances and new economic opportunities in areas like computer engineering, financial services, and high-end global legal services. For the Derys of the world, however, these changes, while perhaps benefiting their children and grandchildren, have been more disorienting than reassuring, more frustrating than liberating. If, for instance, they now have the capacity to access 193 channels and stream Hollywood movies on their new flat screen television, but cannot figure out how to turn on their roku box or operate any of their four remotes, technological advance can destabilize one's sense of control over everyday life and become a symbol not of additional personal capability, but of becoming one of those "large numbers of persons who cannot keep up with progress [and who] have their expectations of a comfortable life frustrated" as identified by the UN as the victims of "economic progress" over sixty years ago.

The connection between not being able to operate your TV and losing your home of eighty years is indirect, but it is nonetheless real. The former exacerbates the impact of the latter. One of the fundamental roles of property rights is the provision of social stability, not only that you will be made financially whole for the loss of the right to enter the commons and gather firewood in seventeenth-century England or nineteenth-century Japan, or that you will receive the commercial value of clean water in nineteenth-century Pennsylvania, but also that you will be able to continue to lead a "comfortable life." Property rights do not simply ensure that you will not starve or become homeless. They also provide the shared structures that confirm your competence and importance as a member of your community, and that is why the generally positive nature of the change in China and Vietnam still has the potential to destabilize and disorient. It would be silly to ignore the fact that many of the Chinese farmers whose land is taken for industrial parks or urban housing rejoice at the chance to trade a farmer's lot for that of an urban employee, but not all will rejoice even when they receive their legally due compensation. Such will especially be the case when the transformation of your identity from farmer to worker is involuntary and, as in China, when the process barely recognizes your existence and you lack the chance to participate in the process or contest the result. And, of course, this is assuming, contra-factually in many if not most cases, that all procedures have been followed, compensation has been paid, and promises of urban residency, jobs, and homes have been faithfully fulfilled.

The third factor in *Kelo*, what is known as eminent domain abuse, is, like the previous two, even more a factor in current property disputes in China and Vietnam than it is in the United States. Eminent domain abuse in the United States, at least, has the virtue of being legal; in other words, it is an abuse only in the sense that the acquiring government is using its legal power when it should not be doing so, either for moral or political reasons. Brief summaries of two instances, both of which passed legal scrutiny, can illustrate. Poletown was in the early 1980s a stable "lower income and elderly"[26] neighborhood of Detroit. In a desperate attempt to retain the remnants of the automobile industry, the city of Detroit and the state of Michigan took Poletown by eminent domain and transferred the land to General Motors for a Cadillac plant. The primary legal issue in *Poletown Neighborhood Council* v. *City of Detroit*,[27] as in *Kelo*, was whether the blatant preference for large corporations and economic production over private property rights and community stability could qualify as "public use" under the Michigan Constitution,[28] but the sense of abuse comes not solely from the choice of growth over community. The exercise of eminent domain in the United States, at least in major projects such as those described here, is usually preceded by extensive negotiations between the acquiring entity, usually a city as in China, and the ultimate recipient of the property, often a large corporate entity, again just as in China. Even when done with the general social welfare as its goal and free of the petty corruption of bribes and rigged bidding, the process almost inevitably involves such close cooperation between the government and the major recipient of the acquired land that to the public it more resembles a form of legalized corruption on a grand scale than the arm's length bargaining that the law envisions and the market celebrates.

In many cases, moreover, the collusion is not the product of the process, but its genesis. The ongoing expansion of Columbia University in New York City is typical. The main campus is located in northern Manhattan less than a mile east of the Hudson River and on the western edge of the dense residential neighborhood of Harlem. According to the factual findings of the trial court – these exercises of eminent domain are invariably accompanied by litigation – later accepted by the appellate court, the process began when Columbia decided

[26] *Kelo v. City of New London*, 545 US 469, 522 (Thomas J, dissenting).

[27] 304 N.W.2d 455 (1981).

[28] MCLA Constitution, Art. X, §2. The case never reached the US Supreme Court.

that it needed additional space and that the area to the west of its main campus was more suitable than that to the east. There were many factors, but one was the probability that the landowners to the west, a scattered area of small businesses, were unlikely to be able to muster the political clout necessary to oppose a major political power in the city. Acquiring land to the east by eminent domain, on the other hand, meant going up against the politically powerful neighborhood of Harlem.

The university then began to purchase property from willing sellers, leaving such property unoccupied and undermaintained. Meanwhile, the university hired a consulting firm to prepare its case that the exercise of eminent domain in the area and the transfer to Columbia was important to the well-being of the city and, crucially, would improve the condition of what the consulting firm was to demonstrate was a "blighted" area in need of amelioration. Once the city was persuaded to initiate the process, the next step was for it to hire a consulting firm to conduct a survey of the area to determine whether it was blighted and therefore satisfied the requirements of the state Constitution and relevant statutes.[29] Astonishingly, the city hired the same consulting company, which, the reader will not be surprised to learn, determined that the area was indeed blighted. To add salt to the wounds of the recalcitrant owners opposing the project, part of the company's evidence for blight was the deteriorating quality of the buildings purchased earlier by Columbia.

The point of the Columbia story is emphatically not that Columbia is a particularly bad actor or that the NYC government is particularly open to this form of collusion. The point is the opposite: that major government-facilitated projects will as a matter of course involve large-scale preliminary negotiations between the eventual recipients of acquired land and the part of the city bureaucracy responsible for urban planning and land use. Whether the use of eminent domain is necessary for large-scale urban projects is debatable, but the conventional wisdom has been that it is. If that wisdom is correct, eminent domain designed for any goal other than the classic types of public infrastructure will create losers like Wilhelmina Dery, the residents of Poletown, and the small business owners gobbled up by Columbia University. In rapidly growing authoritarian countries like Vietnam and China, the chance of injustice must approach 100 percent, but

[29] *Kaur* v. *New York State Urban Development Corp.*, 933 N.E.2d 721, 725–727 (NY 2010).

even in countries like the United States with endless process and readily available judicial review, the sense of injustice sometimes seems to be just as inevitable.

The multidimensional nature of property rights in land

The owner of a block of shares of General Motors stock equivalent in value to Wilhelmina Dery's home is legally just as protected and economically just as dependent on his property in those shares as she was on her house. The legal system will treat them identically, but the impact on the two property owners is literally incomparable. For Dery, the house was *uniquely* essential to her personal identity. For the GM shareholder, market price will come close to full, if not perfect, compensation. Even if he held the shares because of an idiosyncratic belief in their supra-market value, the refusal to compensate up to that figure will be theoretically just for two reasons: first, because, alas, even our hypothetical investor may be guessing wrong, which is precisely why the use of the crowd-aggregating market price is appropriate; and, second, because his foregone supra-market profit is on the same spectrum of value as his compensation. In other words, he is still the same person.

For Dery, on the other hand, no amount of money can make her whole, literally so in a psychological sense. Her relationship with her husband of sixty years will be different, as will relationships with children and close relatives. Relationships with friends and neighbors will weaken, and those with local merchants will disappear. These cannot be maintained or re-created because they and the Derys' very social existence depended on the spaces and places created and sustained by her house and its physical proximity to other land and structures that defined not only her personal relationships, but also her legal rights, responsibilities, and authority in the community. Exclusion from the type of property that was lost by the Derys means not only exclusion from their particular social networks, but also the loss of the ability to communicate to society more generally because they have lost the tangible property that defined who they were psychologically and culturally.[30]

We cannot know the mix of personhood and pecuniary value embedded in the land lost by the millions of Chinese and Vietnamese described in this volume, but if we take the Chinese farmers of this volume as

[30] Eduardo Moisés Peñalyer and Sonia K. Katyal, *Property Outlaws 26* (New Haven, CT: Yale University Press, 2010).

representative, they are likely to fall somewhere between our GM shareholder and the Derys. In many cases, full market price for their land rights accompanied by urban resident status, substitute housing, and factory jobs will more than make them whole. But in other instances they may not, and the reality is that these quantifiable benefits frequently fail to materialize. Indeed, Chinese farmers are not even legally entitled to the market price of their land-use rights. But the level of compensation is not the only issue; the nature of the process also matters.

Process can matter substantively, that is, it can halt or significantly alter a project. An elaborate procedure for the evaluation, comparison, and approval of a project can reveal flaws in the overall concept or in its concrete application to a specific owner's property. It can also delay the project so long that it runs out of financing or circumstances change such that the underlying rationale or benefit disappears. Even when the process goes to completion as in *Kelo*, the ability to participate has enormous value. Just as successful litigation vindicated the Jacques' dignity versus their corporate trespasser in *Jacque*, the chance to appear at community meetings, to file freedom of information requests, to threaten political retaliation against local politicians, and, if all else fails, to drag the city and state governments into court and force them to justify each decision to a neutral arbiter all give a property right-holder a sense that he or she exists as a recognized member of his or her society. In the words of China's outgoing premier, Wen Jiabao, it gives her dignity.[31] To shift to the international development literature, an ability to challenge formally and meaningfully the authorities that are taking your property constitutes an important capability or freedom as described by economist Amartya Sen, and is an important indicium of a country's level of development.[32]

The process works on two levels. First, it gives the individual the sense of dignity and self-worth described above. The American sociologist Tom Tyler has shown that Americans are most satisfied with an encounter with the legal system when they feel as if they have been listened to.[33]

[31] "Everything we do we do to ensure that the people live a happier life with more dignity." Premier Wen Jiabao at the National People's Congress, May 5, 2010.

[32] Amartya Sen, *Development as Freedom* (Oxford University Press, 1999), pp. 38–39.

[33] See, for example, E. A. Lind and T. R. Tyler, *The Social Psychology of Procedural Justice* (New York: Plenum, 1988); T. R. Tyler, *Why People Obey the Law: Procedural Justice, Legitimacy and Compliance* (New Haven, CT: Yale University Press, 1990).

Having had an opportunity to state their case, legally, politically, and/or morally, is more important to litigants than whether they have won. In other words, an inclusive process can ameliorate substantive loss. Of course, American litigants may be significantly different in this respect from Chinese or Vietnamese farmers who have just lost their land, but the volume of petitions, demonstrations, protests, and aborted litigation over land issues indicate that the Chinese are interested in having at least some say in their own future. Perhaps they are not as mollified by "due process" as Americans, but it would stretch credulity to believe that being treated with respect would not have some level of equivalent effect.

The second function of process works at the societal and political levels rather than at the individual: it can contribute substantially to regime legitimacy. In one sense this second function is the flip side of the first in that citizens who feel respected will be more satisfied with a regime, and a regime that provides procedural justice deserves a higher level of support from those it has injured in some legal way, such as the Derys. In another sense, however, this function is quite different because it operates not on the level of the affected individuals' perception of fairness, but on the level of the whole society's perception of legitimacy. If elaborate and highly visible procedural justice is accorded at least formally and symbolically, it can effectively mask gross substantive injustice. The best explication of this effect is by Isaac Balbus from the 1970s.[34] He looked at the amount of process given to Black defendants arrested in the Detroit race riots, and discovered to his surprise that they were given more scrupulous procedural justice than the average defendant in average times. His conclusion was that the Detroit police were aware that "the world was watching" and that their failure to provide due process in times of crisis would jeopardize their ability to continue to use less protective process during ordinary times. That this procedural masking of mass injustice continues today is best illustrated by the "mass incarceration" of young Black males.[35] The United States leads the world in prisoners, incarcerating fourteen times more people than Japan and six times more than China, but no one notices, and mass incarceration is not an issue in American politics, even on the left.[36]

[34] Isaac D. Balbus, *The Dialectics of Legal Repression: Black Rebels before the American Courts* (New York: Russell Sage Foundation, 1973), pp. 107–164.

[35] Michelle Alexander, *The New Jim Crow: Mass Incarceration in the Age of Colorblindness* (New York: New Press, 2010).

[36] For example, the fact that America imprisons 11 percent of Black males aged between 20 and 35 was not mentioned in the 2012 presidential race.

While it may be true that America's success in making mass incarceration disappear behind a narrative of due process will not translate directly to China's dispossession of its ex- and sub-urban farmers, it may work better than the current equally dramatic denial of due process. Understandably, but perhaps mistakenly, the Chinese government has decided that litigation threatens social harmony and should wherever possible be supplanted by mediation.[37] Their fear, presumably, is that litigation will clarify and sharpen differences, and expose illegality leading to more, not less, social conflict. The demonstrations accompanying administrative litigation described by Xin He in this volume provide superficial confirmation of the wisdom of their choice, but this conclusion overlooks two aspects of this litigation: its largely futile nature and the scale of the conflict behind the protests. If the litigation had a decent chance of success or even of publicly examining the government's actions, perhaps the demonstrators would enter the courtrooms not to implicitly threaten direct action, but to press their legal claims, however weak they might be. And while mediation may be very effective and efficient in resolving individual disputes and avoiding the creation of general rules that can be used against the government in subsequent unrelated disputes, dealing with mass dispossession with case-by-case mediation seems unlikely to address the issues of justice that are at the root of the conflict. What is needed, arguably, is a counter-narrative to that of rich elites bullying poor citizens, and mediation provides no narrative at all except that of a paternalistic government unwilling to grant individual dignity to its enraged citizens. Litigation, on the other hand (the cynical hand), both provides a narrative of procedural justice and of individual agency, and has the potential to run the entire dispute into the limitless sands of administrative litigation and appeals.

China's current efforts do not appear to be very promising in maintaining social stability. Instead of openly acknowledging large-scale conflict, the regime has attempted to submerge it in ad hoc mediation. While superficially attractive if one's goal is the short-term appearance of

[37] The Japanese government has often made the same calculation. When the Meiji land law reform described above resulted in increased tenancy and the tenants took to the courts to find moral, if not legal, justice, the government enacted statutes requiring mediation of such disputes. Similarly, after the success of anti-pollution litigation in the *Big Four Pollution Cases* of the 1970s, the central government established an elaborate and effective system of mediation to avoid further litigation, which it assumed would further de-stabilize society. See Frank K. Upham, *Law and Social Change in Postwar Japan* (Cambridge, MA: Harvard University Press, 1987).

social harmony in a particular locality, denying the commonality of land disputes by the particularistic and opaque process of mediation may result in a treatment more socially damaging than the conflict itself. First, mediation rewards immediately available power and, hence, creates an incentive for coalition-building and expressive violence to balance the greater power of the local government and its real estate developer friends. Second, China's decision to discourage formal judicial involvement may preclude the development of legal institutions that in the long run may become effective means of social and political control. Such was the experience of England, the United States, and Japan in the cases described above. The processes were painful, but one result was the emergence of judicial institutions that contributed considerably to long-term social harmony and, not incidentally, to the long-term stability and legitimacy of the existing political regime.

Conclusion

Economic growth causes problems, and property in land is one of the focal points of such problems, at least in countries moving from agrarian societies to industrialized urban ones. Such is the case today in China and Vietnam, and the problems are materializing in ways reminiscent of other societies at similar stages of development, from fifteenth-century England to nineteenth-century Japan. Existing property structures must be fundamentally transformed and, while it is theoretically possible to compensate property owners for their pecuniary losses, full financial compensation is rarely provided. It is simply too expensive and cumbersome, or the existing bureaucracies are not up to the task for a myriad of reasons. But the message of this chapter is that, even if full financial compensation were possible and achieved, there would still be losers, in the words of the United Nations, those "large numbers of people" whose "expectations of a comfortable life [will be] frustrated,"[38] and that those losers must be attended to if a regime is to achieve social stability.

A comfortable life, after all, is not solely a question of material consumption, even when expanded to include economic security. It is also a question of identity, dignity, and a sense of agency, and land, more than any other type of property, is the foundation of these personal structures. If one is 48 years old and has known only farming, becoming a maintenance worker in a hotel may not provide the same satisfaction as

[38] Quoted in Escobar, *Encountering Development*, p. 3.

tending one's crops or feeding one's pigs, and acquiring legal urban residence in a suburban housing block may not substitute for the loss of the life-long relationships of one's original village. I reiterate that I am not saying that all such transformations are regretted. Quite the contrary is possible. The UN quote references "large numbers of people," not everyone, a majority, or even a substantial minority, but when the pain is inflicted on integrated groups of similarly situated persons and in a manner that ignores the social and psychological values of their pre-existing lives, the cost can be great even to the society in general. It is this type of loss that exacerbates the more visible and recognized material loss that Vietnamese and Chinese property-holders are suffering, but their governments' responses have so far been insufficient and insensitive to Premier Wen's call for more attention to be given to the dignity of individual citizens. Whether their leaders will be overwhelmed and resort to increasingly draconian, but ultimately ineffective, measures or can exploit this traumatic transformation to create the institutions that take these fast-growing societies to the next level of political and social, as opposed to economic, development remains to be seen.

PART II

China case studies

3

Legal and institutional analysis of land expropriation in China

LEI CHEN

Introduction

China has a bifurcated land system, with clear distinctions between urban and rural land-use rights. While state-owned land in urban areas has become commercially transferable, rural land cannot be transferred.[1] This discrepancy has been exploited by property developers, investors, village heads, and local governments, which has caused widespread, large-scale malpractice in relation to expropriation of land. Thus, conflict over expropriation of land has been, and continues to be, a simmering hotpot of social unrest in China.[2] It has been claimed that land disputes over expropriation is one of the most common ways of provoking grass-roots resistance and undermining public confidence in the government.[3]

The last two decades have witnessed exponential growth in China's property and construction sectors, which has also brought about social tensions and innumerable complaints of inequitable treatment. Peasants are perceived to be weak and vulnerable to infringement of their property rights by the local government and property developers. Land expropriation (and the subsequent sale of land to property developers) has become a major source of lucrative revenues and financing for local governments, as peasants are drastically undercompensated for their

[1] It is worth noting that there is no private ownership of land in China. Reflecting its socialist traits, all land in China is owned by the state (urban land) or by rural collectives (rural land). Public landownership has undergone various reforms since the mid-1980s. As a result, there is a separation of land-use rights from landownership. Although all urban land is still publicly owned, rights to use such land may be allocated to, and transferred among, private individuals.

[2] See Yu Jianrong, "Land Issue Became the Focal Point of Peasant's Rights Maintenance," *The World of Research and Study* (调研世界), 8 (2005), 22–23.

[3] See Dang Guoyin, "A Theory on Social Stability and its Application in China's Countryside," *China Rural Survey* (中国农村观察), 3 (1996), 52–61.

expropriated land.[4] More disturbingly, there is increasing media coverage of forced evictions and demolition cases involving violence, sometimes even resulting in death,[5] which have highlighted underlying social tensions and raised public awareness and concern. All in all, most of these problems can be attributed to the dysfunctional bifurcated land tenure system. This chapter argues for the introduction of clearly defined property rights by way of legislation, in view of the mounting number of infringements of property rights via expropriations (formerly known in urban China as "demolition and reallocation").

Lin has suggested that the dichotomy of urban and rural land rights under the bifurcated system is actually a root cause of urban "overdevelopment" and "land hunger."[6] The separate regimes for rural and urban land allow local governments in China to monopolize land supply and thus benefit from converting rural land to urban use at little expense.[7] Many local governments in China have relied on land conversion and allocation charges as an important source of revenue.[8] Ho, on the other hand, argued that China's land tenure system is a "deliberate institutional ambiguity," which allows local governments to adapt and respond quickly to a variety of pressures and rapidly changing conditions.[9] This is particularly the case in relation to the collective ownership of land in rural areas. Hence, there has never been a land

[4] See, generally, Wang Cailiang's blog, "Annual Report of Expropriations in China 2012," available at: http://blog.caijing.com.cn/expert_article-151549-46704.shtml.

[5] In 2010, a forced eviction at a home slated for demolition ended in tragedy when three members of a Jiangxi Province family set themselves on fire outside the Yihuang County house. One died, and two were seriously injured after they doused themselves in fuel and set themselves on fire. Several local Communist Party cadres were later suspended from their jobs in connection with these self-immolations. Yihuang County is certainly not the first community to engage in deadly evictions (血拆). See at: http://english.caixin.com/2010-09-21/100190928.html. In 2004, a local government party chief in Jiahe County, Hunan Province, was among several officials sacked for abuse of power in connection with illegal evictions. Even the State Council was involved, calling a meeting to work out appropriate preventive measures and penalties. In 2009, a Chengdu woman set herself aflame during a standoff with expropriating officials, available at: www.21cbh.com/HTML/2010-12-27/zNMDAwMDIxMjczNA.html. See also the report on this case at *South China Morning Post*.

[6] See George C. S. Lin, *Developing China: Land, Politics and Social Conditions* (London: Routledge, 2009), pp. 27–29.

[7] A. C. M. van Westen, "Land in China: Struggle and Reform," *Development*, 54 (2011), 55–58.

[8] See Jiang Shengsan, Liu Shouying, and Li Qing, *China's Land Policy Reform: Policy Evolution and Local Implementation* (Shanghai: Joint Publishing, 2010), p. 108.

[9] See Peter Ho, *Developmental Dilemmas: Land Reform and Institutional Change in China* (London: Routledge, 2005).

policy that has been "uniform and consistent" throughout China.[10] Interestingly, Merrill and Smith, in their property law textbook, stated that "notwithstanding . . . government interference with property rights, China has had little difficulty in recent years attracting large amounts of capital from foreign investors."[11] For them, the investment influx would appear to be due to the fact that "Chinese administrators in the Post-Mao era have developed a strong norm against interfering with the expectations of foreign investors."[12] As a result, economic growth can still take place notwithstanding lower protection for court-enforced property rights, as various social arrangements may provide alternative forms of protection for property rights underpinning economic activities.[13]

However appealing the above argument may appear, this writer believes that secure property rights formalized by the use/revision of legislation is still the most reliable solution (and should be the ultimate solution) to achieve socially permissible control. Economic growth driven by foreign investment is only one aspect of the myriad issues related to land-use rights. Emphasizing economic development may well further encourage land expropriation, and the increase in the number of cases of land seizures across the country may have been fuelled in part by high housing prices and the government's urbanization policy. Without a properly functioning, comprehensive property law, China cannot accomplish economic development in a sustainable manner. In the past, local governments were able to provide cheap land for foreign investors, but this cannot continue indefinitely.[14] The social norm model worked in the past, but is not feasible nowadays.[15] Today, individual farmers who are subject to unfair

[10] See George C. S. Lin and Samuel P. S. Ho, "The State, Land System, and Land Development Processes in Contemporary China," *Annals of the Association of American Geographers*, 95(2) (2005), 411–436.

[11] See Thomas Merrill and Henry Smith, *The Oxford Introduction to US Law: Property* (Oxford University Press, 2010), p. 232.

[12] *Ibid.*

[13] See Donald C. Clarke, "Economic Development and the Rights Hypothesis: The China Problem," *American Journal of Comparative Law*, 51 (2003), 89–111; Zhang Xiaobo, "Asymmetric Property Rights in China's Economic Growth," discussion paper for International Food Policy Research Institute, 2006, available at: www.aeaweb.org/assa/2006/0108_1300_0204.pdf, accessed August 10, 2013.

[14] See Chen Ruoying, "Divided World: China's Land Tenure System and Implication to Foreign Investment in China," available at: http://ssrn.com/abstract=1665175.

[15] Clarke and Upham cogently argue that they do not mean that property rights are undesirable in China. For example, see Frank Upham, "From Demsetz to Deng: Speculations on the Implications of Chinese Growth for Law and Development Theory," *NYU International Law and Politics*, 41 (2009), 551–600.

expropriation need more than governmental policies and a mish-mash of social norms. They need legal certainty, provided by legislation and enforced by the courts.

While valuing Ho's insightful and context-sensitive theory of deliberate ambiguity, some normative questions should be asked: is allowing local governments to manipulate the land market, albeit subject to local conditions, legitimate and fair?; how should the grievances suffered by the rural farmers be redressed; and how should the Chinese government draw the fine line between economic development and individual property rights? In order to answer these questions, this chapter addresses the root causes of land disputes both from a legal perspective, evaluating the most recent statutory changes, and from the policy perspective, analyzing the national strategy of integrating urban and rural areas (城乡一体化), including the recent local experiments on transforming the inalienability of rural land-use rights.

This chapter is structured into four parts, with this introduction being the first. The second section will review the historical development of the Chinese land tenure system in both rural and urban areas from 1949 to the present. The understanding of historical land institutional changes will provide further insights into the actual implementation of land policies and laws in China today. This section ends by summarizing the key features of the current Chinese land tenure system and identifying the major problems in the current system. The third section describes the current legislative framework in relation to the expropriation of land in China. By discussing the significant reforms in such laws, the major changes between the 1997 and 2011 Regulations will be mapped out. Subsequently, two normative elements of expropriation law are analyzed against the new changes, namely, public interest and fair compensation. The fourth section summarizes the progress and pitfalls of the current land expropriation system and depicts the future outlook of land reform in China.

Historical background and current issues of Chinese expropriation law

Rural land

Shortly after the founding of the People's Republic of China in 1949, China instituted a land collectivization program that replaced private farming under the "tiller owns land" policy of 1947. This initiative in Mao's era was modeled on the former Soviet system.[16] However, under the collective system, and later, the People's Commune system, there was a lack of economic incentives to encourage farming productivity.[17] This unfortunate situation was worsened by the Great Leap Forward (1958–1961). Taking into consideration the outright failure of the People's Commune system, the decentralization of collective ownership to the production team was carried out in the early 1960s. As a result, the *sheng chan dui* 生产队 (production team) became the *de facto* manager of the land in most villages, and this system was retained up to the mid-1980s.[18]

When the Cultural Revolution ended, China steered a new course with dramatic economic and social changes. As an integral part of Deng's reforms, the Household Responsibility System (HRS) was introduced to replace the People's Commune system with a family-oriented farming system in villages.[19] Under the HRS, land is contracted to individual households for fifteen to thirty years. The decentralization of land use from the collective level to the household level improved the peasants' incentives to enhance farming productivity. As a consequence, agricultural production boomed and rural incomes increased rapidly.[20] The HRS was initially conducted as an experiment in several designated areas and, due to its success, was soon introduced nationwide. Under the HRS, households are allocated land-use rights, but not the right to dispose of the land, that is, the right to transfer land or to use it as collateral to obtain a loan. These limited property rights dampened the farmers'

[16] This does not mean that no expropriation occurred in this period. The first statutory instrument at the national level concerning land expropriation was enacted in November 1953 by the State Council, namely, the Expropriation Measure for the Construction of National Projects.

[17] See Wu Jinglian and Bruce L. Reynolds, "Choosing a Strategy for China's Economic Reform," *American Economic Review*, 78(2) (1988), 461–466.

[18] See Chris Bramall, "Chinese Land Reform in Long-Run Perspective and in the Wider East Asian Context," *Journal of Agrarian Change*, 4(1/2) (2004), 107–141.

[19] See James K. S. Kung, "Choice of Land Tenure in China: The Case of a County with Quasi-Private Property Rights," *Economic Development and Cultural Change*, 50(4) (2002), 793–817.

[20] This was so despite the fact that its success was short-lived for various reasons. Some attributed this to the tenure insecurity. See Roy Prosterman, Tim Hanstad, and Ping Li, "Can China Feed Itself?" *Scientific American*, 5 (1996), 90–96. Others thought the reason was due to the low farm-gate price instead of property rights. See James K. S. Kung, "Equal Entitlement versus Tenure Security under a Regime of Collective Property Rights: Peasants' Preference for Institutions in Post-Reform Chinese Agriculture," *Journal of Comparative Economics*, 21 (1995), 82–111. Whatever the reason, this necessitated further rural land reform, which is discussed in the subsequent parts of this chapter.

investment because there was no guarantee that "those who invested to improve the land would be the long-term beneficiaries of such investments."[21] Moreover, under the HRS, land parcels are subject to periodic reallocation at the discretion of the village leaders in view of changes in population and the formation of new households.[22] More to the point, tenure insecurity has worsened due to land expropriation for urban expansion and infrastructure development.[23]

From the mid-1980s to the end of the 1990s, the Chinese Central Government encouraged village collectives to utilize agricultural land for building up township and village enterprises (TVEs).[24] Farmers were encouraged to "leave the land but not the countryside" in order to work in the newly initiated TVEs. This essentially allowed agricultural land to be used for non-agricultural (mainly manufacturing) purposes. Interestingly, TVE land was later used to circumvent the overarching policy of the non-transferability of rural land by way of involuntary transfer: bankruptcy, mergers and acquisitions, and expropriations.[25] There are two reasons for this policy. One reason is that the stimulating productivity effect of the HRS had deteriorated during that period, and the other reason is that there was a huge proportion of the labor force that did not need to personally engage in farming. While the TVE policy shifted resources and discretion to local governments to encourage localized strategies of development,[26] and TVEs have more resources and clout than a single farmer, thus alleviating the fear of land-taking,[27] the law never defined TVEs as a unique secure

[21] See Jean C. Oi, "Two Decades of Rural Reform in China: An Overview and Assessment," *China Quarterly*, 159 (1999), 616–619.

[22] See K Mullan, P. Grosjean, and A. Kontoleon, "Land Tenure Arrangements and Rural–Urban Migration in China," *World Development*, 39(1) (2011), 123–133; Loren Brandt, Jikun Huang, Guo Li, and Scott Rozelle, "Land Rights in Rural China: Facts, Fictions and Issues," *China Journal*, 47 (2002), 67–97 at 74.

[23] Tao Ran and Xu Zhigang, "Urbanization, Rural Land System and Social Security for Migrants in China," *Journal of Development Studies*, 43(7) (2007), 1301–1320.

[24] This policy eventually became a piece of legislation to the same effect. See Arts. 12 and 28 of the TVE Law, 1996.

[25] It should be noted that the number of conversions from rural land to urban land under this method is rather small. The main method is still through government expropriation. See Wang Xiaoli, *Land Law* (Beijing: Law Press, 2003), p. 200.

[26] See Vivienne Shue, "Legitimacy Crisis in China?" in Peter Hays Gries and Stanley Rosen (eds.), *Chinese Politics: State, Society, and the Market* (London: Routledge, 2010), pp. 45–46.

[27] See Donald Clarke, "What Kind of Legal System is Necessary for Economic Development? The China Puzzle," in Tim Lindsey (ed.), *Law Reform in Developing and Transitional States* (London: Routledge, 2007), pp. 71–72.

property-holder. Therefore, the pressing issue of non-transferability of rural land (including TVE land) still persists and calls for further reform. The Rural Land Contracting Law (RLCL), implemented in 2002, aimed to secure households' rights of use and possession by allowing the enforcement of thirty-year land-use contracts in order to prevent large-scale arbitrary reallocations of land and to allow transfers of land between households.[28] Generally, under the current land system, farmers have two use rights over rural land. The first right is the right to contract out the land for agricultural production, and the second right is the right to use the land to construct a residential homestead. Rural land is also periodically redistributed among community members as a result of village demographic changes.[29] Because the right to contract out the management of land is only a limited use right, a holder of such right does not have the power to assign such contracted land.[30] However, the contractor may assign its interests in relation to the contracted management land right, albeit subject to certain limitations, as explicitly allowed by Article 32 of the RLCL. It is clearly stated that such right can be assigned by "subcontract, lease, exchange, or transfer or by other means."[31] This right is, of course, limited to the term of the right-holder's contract, which was specified in the land management contract.[32] The method of transferring the rights is up to the individual rights-holder, not the collective on behalf of the local government.[33]

[28] Li Ping, "Rural Land Tenure Reforms in China: Issues, Regulations and Prospects for Additional Reform," *Land Reform* (special edn.), 3 (2003), available at: www.fao.org/docrep/006/y5026e/y5026e06.htm, accessed August 15, 2013. See also Li Ping and Roy L Prosterman, "From Collective to Household Tenure: China and Elsewhere," in Roy L. Prosterman, Robert Mitchell, and Timothy Hanstad (eds.), *One Billion Rising: Law, Land and the Alleviation of Global Poverty* (Amsterdam: Leiden University Press, 2009).

[29] See Wang Hui, Tong Juer, Su Fubing, Wei Guoxue, and Tao Ran, "To Reallocate or Not: Reconsidering the Dilemma in China's Agricultural Land Tenure Policy," *Land Use Policy*, 28 (2011), 805–814.

[30] Such a limited use right has been a popular subject of debates among scholars as to its legal nature, namely, whether it is a proprietary right or a mere contractual right. The debate was not settled until the introduction of the 2007 Property Law, which defines this land-use right in terms of the civil law concept of usufruct. See Arts. 128 and 129 of the Property Law.

[31] Article 32 of the RLCL 2002.

[32] Property Law, Art. 128: "The holder of the right to the contracted management of land shall be entitled to circulate the right to the contracted management of land according to the provisions in the law on the contracting of rural land. The circulated term shall not exceed the remnant term of the original contract on right to the contracted management of land. Without approval, no contracted land may be used for non-agricultural constructions" (an English translation is available at www.lawinfochina.com).

[33] Article 34 of the RLCL 2002.

Another distinguishing feature of the Chinese rural land tenure system is that in order for rural land to enter the open market, it has to be first converted into urban land by state monopolistic appropriation under the Land Administration Law (LAL).[34] Primarily, both the Urban Real Estate Management Law (UREML) and the LAL require that various structures must be completed on state-owned land. Since the local government is the only authority that may assign a piece of state-owned land to developers, or take collectively owned land and convert it into state-owned land, the government effectively monopolized the supply of land for construction.[35]

Urban land

Initially, there was no provision for private property rights in the 1982 PRC Constitution. With subsequent dramatic changes in economic and social conditions, the PRC Constitution has been amended several times to constitutionally entrench private property rights.[36] The burden faced by the Chinese government to provide enough housing for its citizens was seriously challenged by urbanization and an exploding population. In order to ease the housing burden, China embarked on a new economic policy based on creating wealth by selling land and housing. In accordance with this policy, China amended its Constitution in 1988 to recognize privately owned, transferable land-use rights. This constitutional amendment has far-reaching consequences because it allows the creation of a revolutionarily new form of land-use right. More significantly, the subsequent 2004 amendment of the Constitution places private property on an equal legal footing with state-owned property, such that "citizens' legally obtained private property rights" should not be violated.[37] Furthermore, the amendment requires compensation whenever private property is expropriated. In other words, a limitation of a private property right is permissible, but subject to explicit safeguards or conditions.

[34] Article 63 of the LAL. See more specifically, Art. 8 of the UREML.

[35] See Peter Ho, *Institutions in Transition: Land Ownership, Property Rights, and Social Conflict in China* (Oxford University Press, 2005), pp. 44–48.

[36] See Lei Chen, "The New Chinese Property Code: A Giant Step Forward?" *Electronic Journal of Comparative Law*, 11(2) (2007), 1–24, available at: http://www.ejcl.org/112/abs112-2.html, accessed August 22, 2013.

[37] Article 13 of China's Constitution (amended on March 14, 2004 at the 2nd session of the 10th NPC).

This means that under the Chinese constitutional property clauses, the private property of citizens may be encroached upon only for reasons of public interest and with compensation. Thus, the Chinese Constitution acknowledges the right to private property as a fundamental freedom.

Despite these constitutional amendments, China still lacked a comprehensive and consistently regulated expropriation law. There were numerous divergent property law statutes,[38] administrative regulations,[39] ministerial circulars,[40] and judicial interpretations.[41] Thus, the Chinese expropriation law was fragmented and susceptible to structural weakness, inconsistent treatment, corruption, and an environment generally inconsistent with sustainable development. Before 1994, when housing privatization occurred, the expropriation of urban housing land was aimed mainly at serving the needs of urban regeneration.[42] Expropriations were largely government-oriented and benefited the public by improving living conditions. However, the UREML changed the nature of expropriations of urban housing land. The law creates a number of *de facto* monopolies that render the implementation of just compensation almost impossible. The distinct feature of Chinese land tenure system is the twofold role played by the local governments, that is, the public function of government and as general landlord of all land. Understandably, the entrepreneurial interests of local governments are easily intermingled, but not necessarily aligned, with the

[38] For example, the LAL and the UREML.

[39] For example, the Interim Regulations for Granting and Transfer of Land Use Right on State Owned Urban Land in Cities and Towns of 1990 by the State Council, the Regulations on the Administration of Urban Private-owned Buildings of 1982 by the State Council, and the Interim Regulations on Assignment and Transfer of Rights to Use State-Owned Land in Urban Areas (城镇国有土地使用权出让和转让暂行条例) of May 19, 1990. The regulations issued by the State Council are administrative orders in nature and are ranked lower than the statutes, but they are also applied nationwide.

[40] The *Urban Housing Demolition and Relocation Working Manual* issued by the Ministry of Construction in 2005.

[41] For example, Provisions of the Supreme People's Court on Several Issues Concerning Handling the Cases of Application for Enforcing Expropriation Compensation Decisions of Housing on the State-Owned Lands by the People's Courts; Notice of the Supreme People's Court on Strictly Implementing Laws, Regulations and Judicial Interpretations and Legally and Properly Handling Cases Concerning Expropriation, Demolition and Relocation; Interpretations of the Supreme People's Court about the Issues concerning the Laws Applicable to the Trial of Cases of Disputes over Rural Land Contracting of 2005 issued by the Supreme People's Court.

[42] Decision on Furthering Housing Reform in Urban Areas of 1994, issued by the State Council.

public interest.[43] The UREML allows only licensed developers with the necessary qualifications to construct infrastructure facilities and housing in urban areas, while individuals, organizations, and enterprises are unable to build their own housing.[44] In order to maximize profits from land redevelopment, a private developer buys out the existing residents of a piece of land at a low price, redevelops the area, and thereafter sells the real estate at a much higher price.

In response, the Property Law of the PRC came into effect in 2007.[45] This legislation is intended to secure property rights by clearly defining different types of property rights and safeguarding title security, thus providing greater economic stability in the (real property) marketplace.[46] The effectiveness of this legislation is still an open question as it was introduced too recently for us to assess its impact adequately. Nonetheless, Article 42 of the Property Law of 2007 is commendable as it fleshes out some safeguards for property owners who have had their land expropriated. It provides that:

> Land and housing owned by a collective, juristic persons and individuals can only be expropriated for public purposes or in the public interest; the expropriated land owned by collectives should be compensated to the full extent of the loss suffered subject to law. The compensation includes, among others, compensation for taking the land, a resettlement subsidy and compensation for the fixtures, crops and plants on the expropriated land as well as the premiums for social security for farmers. When the residential houses owned by individuals and institutions are expropriated, compensation shall be provided in order to maintain the legal interest of the expropriated institution or individual. When private housing is expropriated, the accommodation of the expropriated persons should be guaranteed during the removal period.[47]

However, this provision was heavily criticized immediately after its introduction. The main criticism is that the above provisions are skeletal and provide little detail in relation to actual day-to-day, operational practices. First, the term public purpose is not clearly defined and thus

[43] See Sally Sargeson, "Full Circle? Rural Land Reforms in Globalizing China," *Critical Asian Studies*, 36(4) (2004), 637–640.

[44] Article 29 of the UREML.

[45] The enactment of the Chinese Property Law immediately attracted international media attention. See, for example, "China's Clause Four: The Recognition of Property Rights is an Ideological Landmark," *The Times*, March 17, 2007; and "Chinas Volkskongress billigt Eigentumsgesetz," *Frankfurter Allgemeine Zeitung*, March 16, 2007.

[46] See Chen, "The New Chinese Property Code?" pp. 1–24.

[47] Article 42 of the Property Law of 2007. The English translation is a modified version based on the version available at: www.chinalawinfo.com.

remains subject to various interpretations. The ambiguity that surrounds this term opens it to abuse by local governments that are intent on encroaching on private interests. In other words, the vexed problem of what constitutes "public interest" still persists.[48]

Second, does the term "compensation" in the abovementioned provision refer to fair and reasonable compensation? The Property Law contains no concrete yardstick or criteria that measures or determines the fairness or reasonableness of compensation. For example, valuations based on the current use of the property, the history of its acquisition and use, its market value, and the purpose of the expropriation, as well as the change of use, are not mentioned in its provisions. Perhaps more frustratingly, it remains unclear as to who has the authority to expropriate property from collectives and individuals for a public purpose or in the public interest. Can commercial developers take the place of the government in exercising expropriation powers, as regulated by the Regulations for the Administration of the Demolition of Urban Buildings and Relocation (2001 Demolition Regulations)?[49] The amorphousness of this situation leads to potential abuse of the power to expropriate. Accordingly, it can be concluded that read either purposively or technically, the Property Law's expropriation provision is skeletal and obscure. Unsurprisingly, a special, comprehensive statute on expropriation was subsequently been enacted in 2011 by the State Council, which will be analyzed in greater detail below.[50]

Reflections and some persisting issues

The belief that property rights promote prosperity and safeguard against arbitrary intrusion has long been the norm in rights discourse.[51] In China, property rights are weak and vulnerable to the varying dictates

[48] Some Chinese scholars claim that it is beyond the scope of the Property Law to demarcate the meaning of public purpose. They argue that the Constitution should be the proper instrument to regulate the undefined nature of public purpose. See Wang Liming, "The Property Law Cannot Bear the Burden on the Demarcation of a Public Purpose," *Legal Daily* (法制日报), October 21, 2006 (Chinese version).

[49] Article 17 of the Regulations for the Administration of the Demolition of Urban Buildings and Relocation.

[50] The Regulations for Expropriation and Compensation for Houses on State-owned Land of 2011 issued by the State Council.

[51] See Douglass North, *Institutions, Institutional Change and Economic Performance* (Cambridge University Press, 1990); Harold Demsetz, "Toward a Theory of Property Rights," *American Economic Review*, 57(2) (1967), 347–359; Yoram Barzel, *The Economic Analysis of Property Rights* (Cambridge University Press, 1989).

of government policies.[52] Many Chinese farmers learned this lesson the hard way. As stated in the introduction, China employs a bifurcated system of land-use rights, differentiating between urban land and rural land. In the past, while urban land-use rights have been commercially transferable, rural land has been locked and frozen. A village collective is allowed to transfer rural land-use rights to individuals, but such a transfer is subject to the consent of both two-thirds of the villagers' representatives and the township authority.[53] Households who wish to transfer their contracting management rights have to give preference to potential transferees in the same collective.[54] This has changed, albeit in a low-key fashion. In 2007, the State Council (the Central Government) allowed Chengdu and Chongqing to conduct pilot projects in relation to the registration and transfer of agricultural land.[55] Politically, the top leadership has signaled a clear message that it intends to end the bifurcated urban and rural land systems.[56] Since then, Chengdu has been implementing and fine-tuning many concrete policies to set up a legal and institutional framework for markets in rural property rights.[57] Specifically, Chengdu has introduced a decentralized and temporary initial registration system. Village authorities can register a person-based land-use right at the village level for the homestead right (residential construction right), and there is now a household-based registration for the farmland-use right.[58]

Allowing transactions in rural land-use rights would be a major milestone in the economic liberalization of China.[59] Currently, demand for land in

[52] Merrill and Smith, *Oxford Introduction to US Law*, p. 230.

[53] Article 15 of the LAL. [54] Article 33 of the LAL.

[55] National Development and Reform Commission (NDRC), Circular approving Chongqing and Chengdu as the Special Experimental Zones for Coordinated Rural and Urban Development areas (发改经体 [2007] No. 1248). This Notice was dated June 7, 2007. The Chinese version of this Notice is available at: www.sdpc.gov.cn/zcfb/zcfbtz/2007tongzhi/t20100511_346231.htm, accessed August 12, 2013.

[56] Guangdong was actually made a provisional laboratory even earlier than Chengdu and Chongqing.

[57] See Guo Xiaoming, *Coordinating Urban and Rural Development and Rural Land Transfer Reform: An Empirical Study on Chengdu Model* (Beijing: China Science Press, 2012).

[58] Opinion concerning strengthening Agricultural land and Furthering Rural Land and Homestead Rights, Chengdu Municipality, January 2008.

[59] To allow legally recognized transactions of rural land does not amount to total privatization of rural land, as zoning (land planning) ordinances will still apply for the sake of food security and nature preservation as well as the preservation of indigenous people's "family land." I thank Professor Frank Upham for making this point.

rural China is satisfied by state-based models of expropriation converting the legal status of rural land, rather than through impersonal exchanges of property rights. The current model is a cause of widespread land conflicts in China, as state officials appropriate the benefits of transitions to higher value uses of land. The writer calls it "Government gains, farmer pains." Rural land transactions offer a potential alternative to state-based mechanisms of property rights exchange. However, allowing the contractual transfer of rural land-use rights is a sensitive sociopolitical issue in China, not only because of unrest arising from smallholder farmer landlessness, but also because it raises issues of citizens' engagement with the state.

Property rights cannot exist as a social and economic institution without laws that define their content and structure. As stated above, there is a clause in the Chinese Constitution prohibiting the government from taking private property for public interest without fair compensation. But in practice, the public interest requirement is a "black hole" that is open to wide and vague interpretations, and is therefore a toothless provision that is unable to hold local governments accountable for their actions. Moreover, the compensation mechanism does not have to take relevant factors into account: for example, moving costs, the location of the property, the demand and supply situation, and the farmers' employment and social security issues. Therefore, there is a dire need to spell out public interest and fair compensation in more detail in a special statute.

Legislative framework and structural analysis

The new 2011 Expropriation Regulations

The Regulations for the Administration of the Demolition of Urban Buildings and Relocation (2001 Demolition Regulations) was the first statute in China to deal with expropriations (the exact wording used was "demolition and relocation"). Under the 2001 Demolition Regulations, local governments could exercise wide discretionary powers to tear down urban buildings in order to achieve the broadly defined legislative intent of "preserving the smooth progress of construction and urban management."[60] The extensive use (and abuse) of government power to order forced evictions has given the Chinese citizenry (and the rest of the world) the impression that Chinese property rights are very precarious.

[60] Article 2 of the Demolition Regulations.

For years, the word "demolition," entailing residents' grievances and complaints, has been synonymous to urban regeneration in China. However, this changed in early 2011 with the enactment of a new regulation that utilizes the term "expropriations" rather than "demolitions." The new Regulations for Expropriation and Compensation for Houses on State-owned Land (2011 Expropriation Regulations)[61] replaced the 2001 Demolition Regulations, which had in many aspects contravened China's 2007 Property Law.[62]

The 2011 Expropriation Regulations heralded a big leap forward in China's legal framework for state-orientated expropriations. First, for the first time, the different types of public interest that justify and legitimize mandatory expropriation are demarcated. Moreover, before an expropriation decision is made, a cross-department review must be conducted by the local government in order to verify whether the proposed expropriation fulfills the public interest requirement. The expropriation cannot proceed if the cross-department review does not give the green light. The legislative intent behind the 2011 Expropriation Regulations is to regulate the procedure governing expropriation and compensation, while upholding public interest and protecting the legal interests of property owners. This is dramatically different from the 2001 Demolition Regulations, which leaned in favor of the smooth operation of urban development.[63] Second, in relation to compensation, the most contentious part for any expropriation, payment levels would have to take into account the location of the property and market value based on independent third-party assessments. Third, procedure-wise, the 2011 Expropriation Regulations introduce some detailed procedural safeguards, including public hearings, ensuring participation of the property owners affected, the selection of property value appraiser, and dispute settlements during an expropriation process. A homeowner objecting to an expropriation procedure can file an administrative lawsuit. Last, but not least, under the 2011 Expropriation Regulations, it is the housing expropriation department, as a government agency, that signs off on expropriation and compensation agreements with individuals. The implication of this is that the government is the party who

[61] See the Regulations for Expropriation and Compensation for Houses on State-owned Land of 2011 (2011 Expropriation Regulations), issued by the State Council.

[62] See Cui Jianyuan, "Comparing Housing Demolition with Real Estate Expropriation," in Fang Shaokun and Wang Hongping (eds.), *Real Property Expropriation* (Beijing: China Legal Publishing House, 2009), pp. 309–311.

[63] Article 1 of the 2001 Regulation.

enjoys exclusive authority to expropriate, rather than property developers or any other intermediaries, as was provided for in Article 17 of the 2001 Demolition Regulations. In order to provide a graphic and comprehensive overview of the reforms introduced in the 2011 Expropriation Regulations, the major differences between the 2001 Demolition Regulations and 2011 Expropriation Regulations are detailed in Table 3.1. The detailed analysis that follows compares the public interest requirement, measurement of fair compensation, and procedural safeguards.

Structural analysis

Public interest requirement

One of the most controversial issues in expropriation is the requirement that an expropriation must be in the public interest. This requirement prevents expropriation of private property for unlawful purposes and restricts the exercise of the power to expropriate.[64] It is this public interest requirement that legitimizes the compulsory taking of private property rights by the government. Yet there is no clear-cut statutory definition of the term "public interest" to answer the question of whether an expropriation could be undertaken to serve private (commercial) interests. No area of Chinese property law has been more contested in recent years than the use of expropriation to boost economic development initiatives. It has been argued that an inclusive list of specific permissible public purposes must be adopted in order to stave off abuse.[65] However, others contend that it is almost impossible to provide an explicit statutory definition, in an all-inclusive fashion, since the term "public interest" is so dynamic that it does not, and cannot, have an absolute meaning without considering specific circumstances.[66] In practice, this problem is compounded in China by the fine line between public interest and commercial interest, especially in the context of urban redevelopment.[67]

Before the promulgation of the 2011 Expropriation Regulations, the 2007 Property Law and other relevant statutory instruments simply

64 See A. J. Van der Walt, *Constitutional Property Law*, 3rd edn. (Cape Town: Juta, 2011), p. 242.

65 See Liang Huixing, *Commentary on Chinese Property Law Draft* (Beijing: Social Science Literature Press, 1999), pp. 191–193.

66 See Wang Liming, "On Implementation of Property Law and the Improvement on Expropriation System," *Law Science Magazine* (法律科学杂志), 4 (2008), 15–22.

67 See Jiang Ping, "The Ideal and Reality of the Property Code," *Forum of Social Science* (社会科学论坛), 11 (2007), 84–85.

Table 3.1 *An outline of statutory changes between the 2001 Demolition Regulations and 2011 Expropriation Regulations*

	2001 Demolition Regulations	2011 Expropriation Regulations
Legislative intent	To regulate housing demolition and relocation and to offer protection to affected parties, while ensuring development projects can be smoothly carried out (art. 1).	To standardize procedure governing expropriation and compensation, while upholding public interest and protecting legal interests of property owners (art. 1).
Compensation	Adequate compensation is provided to demolition and eviction targets (art. 22).	Fair compensation is provided to evicted persons whose property is expropriated for the public good (art. 2).
Definition of key parties	A demolitioner refers to the authorized unit permitted to demolish and redevelop the property expropriated. A demolitioner refers to a property owner whose property is subject to demolition (art. 4).	The municipal or county level of government is responsible for land expropriation (art. 4). The Housing Expropriation Department (HED) may delegate its power to other organizations, which must not profit from such delegation. The HED shall supervise such organization(s) and remain legally responsible for execution and compensation of the expropriation (art. 5).
Proposal for expropriation	A party delegated with demolition and relocation work shall not carry out any work until it has acquired a demolition permit (art. 6). A demolitioner shall apply to the relevant authority and submit the following the documents: (a) the approval for the construction project;	An expropriation decision should only be made for the following specified purposes: (a) national defense or foreign affairs; (b) government-led construction of energy, transportation, water conservation, and other public utilities;

	(b) the permit for the intended land use for construction; (c) certification of granted land use right; (d) demolition and relocation proposal; (e) certification issued by a financial institution undertaking deposit business to certify compensation for relocation arrangements. The Department shall examine the application and supporting documents and decide whether to issue the demolition and relocation permit to the applicant (art. 7).	(c) government-led construction of science, education, culture, health, sports, environmental, and resources preservation, disaster protection and recovery, cultural relics preservation, social relics, and other civic utilities; (d) government-led construction of government subsidized housing projects; (e) government-led rebuilding of hazardous buildings and obsolete infrastructure in old rural districts as required by the Laws on Urban and Rural Planning; (f) in accordance with laws, regulations and other public needs (art. 8).
Compulsory demolition	If the demolitioner or his/her tenant(s) fails to relocate within the allowed time, the relevant authority shall either carry out compulsory demolition or apply to the court for an order for compulsory demolition and relocation (art. 17).	When an expropriationee fails to apply for administrative review or fails to initiate proceedings within the limitation period, and also fails to relocate within the allowed period, the government may apply to the court for enforcement of the expropriation decision. This application should include the following information: the amount of compensation; the recipient's bank account numbers; address and area of the replacement structure; and transitional housing (art. 28).

Table 3.1 (*cont.*)

	2001 Demolition Regulations	2011 Expropriation Regulations
Appraisal of the property	Monetary compensation shall be calculated based on market value with regard to factors such as the location of the demolished property, the use of the property, and the size of the property (art. 24).	Compensation shall not be lower than the market value of similar housing on the day of the announcement of the expropriation decision. An appraisal should be conducted by a qualified real estate appraisal institution (RAI). A party may challenge the value by applying for a review of the decision. A further and final appeal on the valuation may be lodged at the real estate appraisal expert committee (art. 19). A RAI shall be selected by the expropriationee through negotiation. If the negotiation falls through, the RAI can be randomly selected, or decided by the simple majority resolution (art. 20).

stated that expropriations should be in the public interest, but none of these statutory instruments provide any further detail as to what specific purposes serve the public interest.[68] Local governments were given an unfettered power to determine how public interest is defined, and, consequently, the meaning of public interest expanded to include anything the local government conceived and desired.[69] The constitutional caveat of public interest was rendered a "dead letter," instead of acting as a substantive safeguard on the operation of expropriation.[70] This is because local governments have strong financial incentives to expropriate rural land for low compensation, as the land can subsequently be sold to private developers for high prices once the rural–urban land conversion is completed.[71] It has been argued that such arbitrage opportunities for local governments have caused predatory land grabs to spiral out of control.[72]

The 2011 Expropriation Regulations, however, clearly demarcate the acceptable boundaries of "public interest." Article 8 lists the situations in which the public interest requirement is fulfilled. The local government, at the municipal or county level, shall make a decision to expropriate the private property only when it is necessary for: (1) national defense and foreign affairs; (2) the construction of energy, transportation, water, and other infrastructures initiated by the government; (3) such public utilities as science and technology, education, culture, health, sports, environment and resource protection, disaster prevention and mitigation, protection of cultural relics, social welfare or municipal utilities; (4) the construction of government-subsidized (social welfare) housing; (5) redeveloping a run-down urban neighborhood with dilapidated buildings; (6) any other public interest as prescribed by a law or administrative regulation.[73]

[68] See Wang Cailiang, *The Law and Practice of Housing Expropriation* (Beijing: Law Press, 2008), pp. 26–31.

[69] See Fang Shaokun and Wang Hongping, "On the Normative Model of Public Interest in PRC Expropriation," *Contemporary Law Review* (现代法学), 1 (2006), 68–71.

[70] The phrase "dead letter" is borrowed from Thomas Merrill, "The Economics of Public Use," *Cornell Law Review*, 76 (1986), 61.

[71] See Klaus Deininger and Songqing Jin, "Securing Property Rights in Transition: Lessons From Implementation of China's Rural Land Contracting Law," *Journal of Economic Behavior and Organization*, 70(1/2) (2009), 22–38.

[72] According to an interview with a former party chief of a county government in Hubei Province, the profits arising from land sales could account for up to 60 percent of the entire revenue of the local government.

[73] Article 8 of the Regulations for Expropriation and Compensation for Houses on State-owned Land of 2011, issued by the State Council.

It is clear that the scope of what constitutes "public interest" has been significantly narrowed by the 2011 Expropriation Regulations, with a notable improvement being the prevention of mere private-to-private seizure of land, which no longer constitutes public interest. This helps to reduce the risk that expropriation may operate as a form of private-taking, which is anathema in every jurisdiction worldwide. However, the 2011 Expropriation Regulations do not rule out urban regeneration as constituting public interest.[74] This is understandable as, given the complexity of real economic life, public interest and economic interest are often intermingled and sometimes inextricable. The law should not impose a blanket prohibition on the expropriation of land for redevelopment projects which result in private commercial gain. This is because land, as an institution, embodies a bundle of interactive public and private rights. China is in the process of urbanization, and needs to utilize more land to build factories, shopping malls, and residential housing to develop its economy and accommodate an increasing population of urban residents. Local governments usually interpret public interest broadly to permit an expropriation of a piece of land, before assigning the land to developers for a project that although benefiting private interests, undeniably also brings substantial benefits to the public.[75] The affected parties, if they oppose the expropriation, are often accused of obstructing urban economic development, which is considered by local governments to be in the "public interest." Indeed, establishing a shopping mall or a factory can increase local tax revenues and create more jobs for the local community. Taking the example of constructing an airport, it is commonly accepted that expropriating land to construct an airport fulfills the public interest requirement.[76] However, the airport, which formerly functioned within the public sector, is eventually privatized, and may subsequently even be publicly listed. This casts a question mark over whether this expropriation serves a genuine public interest. Therefore, public interest requirement *per se* cannot tell the whole story, and it functions merely as a gatekeeper. The measurement of compensation and procedural safeguards also need to be taken into consideration.

[74] See Art. 8(5) of the 2011 Expropriation Regulations.

[75] In Germany, the public interest requirement implies that expropriations cannot be taken for improper purposes, such as the general improvement or increase of state property, or to benefit a private third party.

[76] Read Art. 8(2) of the 2011 Regulations.

Nonetheless, the 2011 Expropriation Regulations only cover urban expropriation and do not protect rural land seizures. As long as the state continues to monopolize the conversion from rural land to urban land, local governments will continue to make land development and construction planning decisions arbitrarily.[77] Worse still, many commercial developers engaged in relocation and property valuation businesses are linked to local governments. Further legislative reform on rural land is warranted.

Fair compensation

The 2011 Expropriation Regulations provide that compensation shall not be lower than the market value of similar housing on the day of the announcement of the expropriation decision. This sets up a market value-based mechanism to calculate compensation. In addition, under the new Regulations, an appraisal should be conducted by a qualified and independent real estate appraisal institution chosen by the affected parties. A party has a right to object to the appraisal value by applying for a review of the decision. A further and final appeal on the appraisal value may be lodged at the real estate appraisal expert committee.[78]

However, one may argue that compensation should be determined on the basis of rights that the owner has in the property, not the property itself, as the actual rights held should determine the quantum of the compensation. This is because the approach that takes into account only the market value of the expropriated property leads to under-compensation, for example, loss of community ties or business opportunity. A book kiosk may be peculiarly dependent on its location for its customers, for example, if it is near a university campus. Being forced to move to another place would put it out of business. But how should local governments deal with the actual financial loss caused by the termination of the current use rights of the expropriated land? It raises a concern that local governments would have to incur unnecessary administrative costs to measure it, however difficult it may be. It has been argued that despite disregarding the "subjective premium" of the property, the market value approach is still workable as it deters or discourages owners from making deliberate improvements to their property when it is highly

[77] See Cai Jiming, "Four Major Problems and Their Solutions Regarding Rural Land Expropriation," available at: http://zigong.house.sina.com.cn/news/2012-12-21/1014728452.shtml, accessed August 11, 2013.

[78] Article 19 of the 2011 Expropriation Regulations.

likely that the property will soon be expropriated for a public project.[79] Nevertheless, the market value approach is commendable as it ensures that the expropriated parties are fairly compensated what they deserve.

Once again, the fair compensation rule applies only to urban expropriations. In rural China, the lack of a functioning land market makes this market value approach difficult, if not impossible. The current legal system for compensation in rural expropriations comprises of three parts: (1) compensation for loss of land set at six to ten times the average annual output value of the land for the three years prior to the requisition; (2) a resettlement subsidy set at four to six times the average annual output value; and (3) compensation for structures and standing crops to be determined by provincial governments.[80] The compensation is capped at thirty times the average annual output value for the preceding three years if the above-mentioned statutory standards are insufficient to maintain the affected farmer's original living standards.[81] This production value-based measurement has long been held to be inadequate, and often amounted to "government gains, farmer's pains."

Currently, Chinese lawmakers are deliberating on a new draft Regulation on Rural Expropriation, as well as amendments to the Land Administration Law.[82] Song Dahan, the director of the legislative affairs office of the State Council, admits that problems do exist with respect to rural land expropriation, stating that: "The expropriation procedures need to be improved. The compensation mechanism is flawed: the standards are way too low and rigid. For those whose land has been expropriated, the guarantee for their long-term livelihood is insufficient. The forcible and illegal seizure of farmers' land threatens social stability."[83] It is reported that the draft amendments propose that compensation take more factors into account, including rural residences, relocation allowance, and social security fees.

[79] See Merrill and Smith, *Oxford Introduction to US Law*, p. 250.

[80] Article 47 of the LAL.

[81] *Ibid.* The English translation is taken from Valerie Jaffee Washburn, "Regular Takings or Regulatory Takings?: Land Expropriation in Rural China," *Pacific Rim Law and Policy Journal*, 20(1) (2011), 72–124.

[82] See *Caixin Online*, "Beijing Sets Five-year Target for Laying out Land Use Rights," available at: http://english.caixin.com/2013-02-01/100488774.html, accessed August 3, 2013.

[83] See Song Dahan, "Explanations on the Proposed Amendments of Land Administration Law," available at: www.npc.gov.cn/huiyi/lfzt/tdglfxza/node_19554.htm; "China to Amend Land Administration Law," available at: http://english.cri.cn/7146/2012/12/25/191s740201.htm, accessed August 7, 2013.

Procedural due process

The expropriation procedures under the 2011 Expropriation Regulations are more transparent, and thus increase government accountability. It has been argued that using the word "expropriation" to replace the word "demolition" (which was used in the earlier 2001 Demolition Regulations) illustrates the new emphasis on due process.[84] In this writer's view, the procedural safeguards provided are the biggest breakthrough in the 2011 Expropriation Regulations. The 2011 Expropriation Regulations carefully set out the procedures to notify property owners and solicit opinions. Local governments are now obliged to comply with a mandatory review process before they expropriate. The first step is for the government authority to report its proposed expropriation and compensation plan to the city council after a cross-department examination. The plan must be published so that the public has an opportunity to provide feedback. The period for public feedback should not be less than thirty days. After this period has lapsed, the public's comments and the comments by the city council need to be incorporated into a revised plan. Interestingly, perhaps in view of avoiding vexing social unrest, the local government needs to be cautious and conduct a social stability risk assessment before it reaches a final decision on whether to go ahead with the expropriation. In order to further protect the interests of the property owners affected, the government must deposit the full amount of the proposed compensation into a special purpose bank account. It cannot use these funds for any purpose other than the planned expropriation.

The 2011 Expropriation Regulations require that public hearings must be conducted if a majority of the expropriated residents complain of inadequacies or irregularities in the expropriation and compensation plan. Once adopted, the expropriation decision must be published, in a timely fashion, in an announcement that provides details of the expropriation and compensation plan. Moreover, if there is no compensation agreement reached, the local government can still exercise the power to expropriate, but subject to a "compensate first, demolish later" procedure, meaning compensation must be rendered before the local government can commence relocation and demolition.

Finally, from the work flow chart in Figure 3.1 one can see that the courts are given the power and the duty to revisit the whole expropriation process and to determine whether it was legal, and in the public

[84] See Tu Siyi, "From Demolition to Expropriation: Problems, Solutions and Difficulties in China," *Wuhan University Law Review* (法学评论), 3 (2010), 49–61.

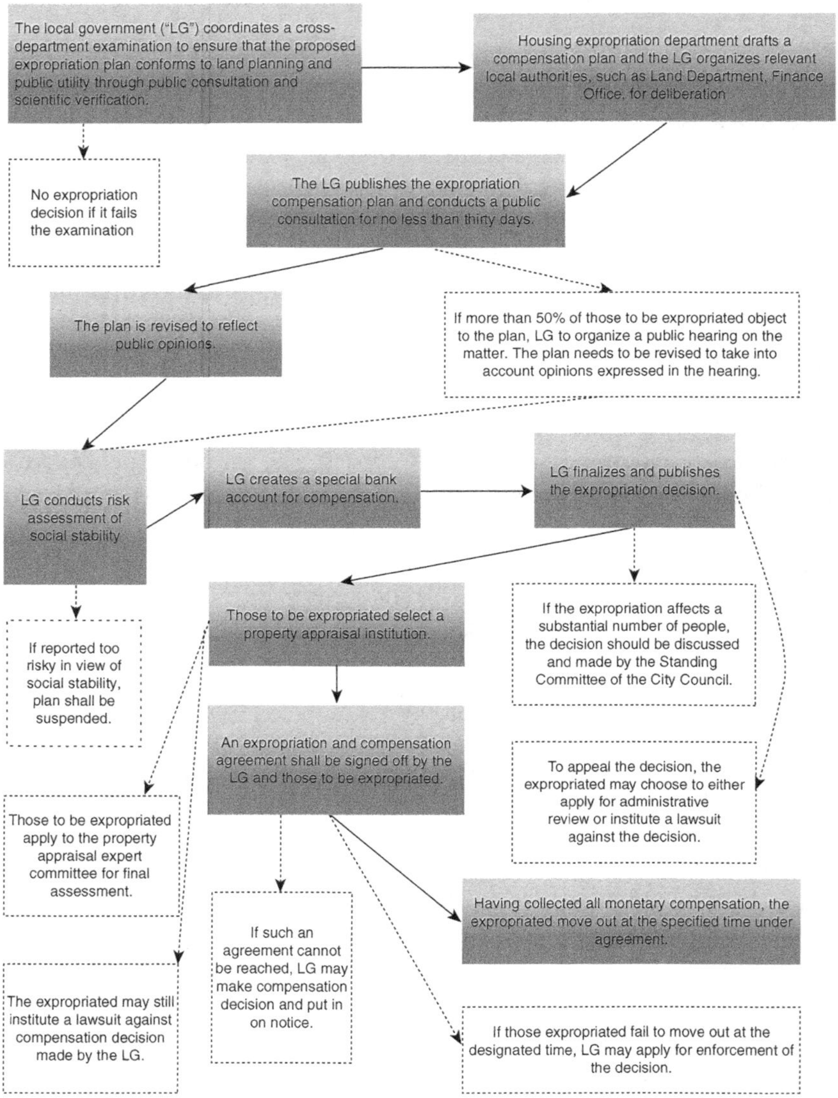

Figure 3.1 Work flow chart of expropriation procedures under the 2011 Regulations

interest. If the court issues an enforcement order, it must notify both the government and the affected parties of its decision. It may even make recommendations to the government as to how it can ensure that the expropriation and compensation proceed smoothly. The Supreme People's Court (SPC) has been gradually restricting the power of local governments to enforce land expropriation decisions in the wake of a number of violent, and even deadly, cases involving forced evictions.

In 2011, the SPC issued the "Notice on Strictly Implementing Laws, Regulations and Judicial Interpretations and Legally and Properly Handling Cases Concerning Expropriation, Demolition and Relocation" (the "Strict Implementation Notice"). In this Strict Implementation Notice, the SPC requested that district courts be careful of issuing court eviction orders sought by developers if they were opposed by local residents, and to suspend expropriations if people resorted to radical protests. The recent 2012 "Provisions of the SPC on Several Issues Concerning Handling the Cases of Application for Enforcing Expropriation Compensation Decisions of Housing on the State-owned Lands by the People's Courts" (the "Enforcement Provisions") set out the factors that courts must take into account when deciding whether or not to issue an enforcement order.[85] The court may refuse enforcement if it finds any of the following conditions to be clearly present:

- absence of a factual or legal basis for the expropriation;
- unfair compensation;
- violation of the owners' legitimate rights;
- failure to guarantee owners' living or business conditions;
- administrative objectives and the public interest are harmed; and
- *ultra vires* found in exercising government's power.

Recently, in April 2013, the SPC issued a "Reply concerning Forced Demolition of Unauthorized Building Works" to restrain itself, and all level of courts, from accepting applications from local government authorities to enforce the forced demolition of unauthorized building works.[86] This is a clear signal that the Chinese courts have gradually refused to be a cause of social unrest resulting from forced evictions and improper expropriations. This is a sign that the judiciary is

[85] See Fa Shi (法释) No. 4 (2012), Provisions of the SPC on Several Issues Concerning Handling the Cases of Application for Enforcing Expropriation Compensation Decisions of Housing on the State-owned Lands by the People's Courts, issued by the Supreme People's Court, March 26, 2012.

[86] See Fa Shi (法释) No. 5 (2013), Reply concerning Forced Demolition of Unauthorized Building Works, issued by the Supreme People's Court, March 27, 2013.

rebalancing its position between a definer and a defender of property rights,[87] given the change of circumstances and public conception of property rights.

Conclusion

The 2011 Expropriation Regulations are a significant step toward the protection of individual property rights. Many of the provisions introduced are much needed and therefore commendable. For example, the 2011 Expropriation Regulations list the situations where land-taking fulfills the public interest requirement. It also strengthens the procedural safeguards against the superior bargaining power of developers and local governments in negotiating compensation for expropriations. This is significant as it makes expropriations in urban China more costly. This is partly due to the Chinese Communist Party's increasing concern to maintain social stability, in view of the sheer number of incidents caused by expropriation disputes. However, this writer believes that these changes arise largely because of the emergence of the middle class, which takes a stand on "my property, my destiny."

However, the 2011 Expropriation Regulations are not applicable to rural land expropriations. Many forced evictions and land disputes are still taking place in rural areas. As highlighted previously, the root cause is the artificial differentiation of transferable urban land and non-transferable rural land. As a result, it is not uncommon to have collusive alliances between the village collective, local government, and commercial developers. Currently, performance assessments of local government officials place a heavy emphasis on factors such as GDP growth, fiscal revenues, and urban infrastructure building. Although local governments are enthusiastically promoting local economic development, land seizures contribute to rural land tenure insecurity. Peasants are prone to forced evictions with inadequate compensation and insufficient provision of social security.

Expropriation is hated by many, particularly when governments trample on property rights by seizing individual property. Land tenure as an institution embodies a bundle of interactive public and private

[87] The phrase depicting the twin roles played by the courts in land-taking as both a definer and a defender is borrowed from Jeremy Paul, "The Hidden Structure of Taking Laws," *South California Law Review*, 64 (1991), 1415.

rights. The question here is: how far should the government forbear from frustrating the owners' expectations about what they can do with their property? Turning this general question to the Chinese context, it appears that there is a trend toward property rights taking root in China. The 2011 Expropriation Regulations are designed to constrain the unfettered power exercised by local government to take urban land. In rural areas, the recent urban–rural coordinated development reform allows rural land to be rented out, or even sold to third parties, thus enabling the privatization of rural land-use rights. However, turning local policies into nationwide law takes time. Against this background, the NPC is reviewing the Land Administration Law, a prevailing statute dealing with land use and management.[88] The proposed amendments aim to streamline the administrative review and civil litigation process for expropriation disputes. In order to avoid the abuse of power, what is needed is to make the expropriation process more transparent, and to allow the general public an easier means by which to seek redress through judicial channels.[89] The draft amendment needs to standardize rural and urban procedures for land expropriation, to set compensation standards, and to build proper channels for handling disputes.[90] Separating urban from rural expropriations is no longer appropriate. However, from a legislative perspective, a piecemeal approach has been taken so far. Therefore, the question remains as to whether the incremental introduction of reforms will be enough to satisfy rural villagers' demands for secure property rights.

[88] According to a conversation with Professor Wang Weiguo on April 15, 2013, a leading expert in land law, the NPC is considering drafting a land law dealing with both urban and rural land systems, which will supersede the Land Administration Law and other relevant land-related statutes.

[89] In the so-called No.1 document, issued by the Communist Party's Central Committee, an effort to map out rural land-use rights in five years has been stated to protect farmers' interests.

[90] Song Dahan, the director of the legislative affairs office of the State Council, admits that problems do exist in land expropriation in China.

4

The judicial role in land-taking cases

JIE CHENG

Introduction

Land disputes in China have attracted growing public attention in the last decades, and have become a major source of resentment against the government. Between 2004 and 2012, the Chinese Communist Party (CCP) has also made issues involving rural areas and land disputes a top political priority.[1] Some economists and legal scholars have advocated for the privatization of rural land in order to improve the security of land rights of individuals or individual households and to improve efficiency.[2] Others try to provide legal content to the concepts of public interest[3] or just compensation.[4] Despite the sensitivity of the topic of privatization and private property rights vis-à-vis public

[1] Nine leading circulars of the Central Committee of the Communist Party (CCPC) in the past ten years have given agrarian policy preeminent emphasis. See "中央一号文件关注土地纠纷 征地条款将修改" ("The No. 1 CCPC Circulars Highlight Land Disputes, Takings Clause is to be Revised"), available at: http://house.ifeng.com/news/detail_2012_02/03/12274601_0.shtml.

[2] Huang Shao'an, Sun Shengmin, and Gong Mingbo, "The Impact of Land Ownership Structure on Agricultural Economic Growth: An Empirical Analysis on Agricultural Production Efficiency on the Chinese Mainland (1949–1978)," *Social Sciences in China*, 26(4) (2005), 48–61; Matthew S. Erie, "China's (Post-)Socialist Property Rights Regime: Assessing the Impact of the Property Law on Illegal Land Takings," *Hong Kong Law Journal*, 37(3) (2007), 919–949, outlining the anti-commons (privatization) model and fuzzy approach (maintenance of a hierarchical order of rights among various players of rural land market) in modeling property law reform in China; Zhu Keliang and Roy Prosterman, "Securing Land Rights for Chinese Farmers: A Leap Forward for Stability and Growth," *Development Policy Analysis*, Cato Development Policy Analysis Series, No. 3 (2007), available at: www.cato.org/publications/development-policy-analysis/securing-land-rights-chinese-farmers-leap-forward-stability-growth.

[3] Hu Jinguang and Wang Kai, "Defining Public Interest in the Chinese Constitution," *China Legal Science*, 1 (2005), 18–27.

[4] Zhang Qianfan, "Just Compensation and Constitutional Control of Takings Power," *Chinese Journal of Law*, 2 (2005), 25–37.

property rights,[5] the government seems to be moving gradually toward the direction of property entrenchment: in addition to the current Land Management Law, the Property Law was promulgated in 2007; and then the Regulations on Demolition of Houses in Urban Areas were abolished and replaced by Regulations on Requisition and Compensation of Real Property on State-owned Land in Urban Areas in 2011. However, the effects of the new laws are not yet apparent, and disputes regarding land-taking have been on the increase.[6] Since there are at least two important statutes and one Constitutional Article laying out the legal grounds for government takings of land, it is no longer plausible to blame all problems on the shortcomings of the statutes. Instead, it is time to review the enforcement of these statutes.

This chapter examines over 200 court cases between 2004 and 2010 that applied certain provisions of the Land Management Law, namely, Articles 46–49. These articles were chosen for examination for several reasons. First, the Land Management Law is the foundational statute for land management and land-taking. Although Article 10 of the Constitution and Article 42 of the Property Law also touch on land-taking, neither contains detailed provisions. Second, Chinese courts generally choose not to directly apply constitutional provisions in their adjudication; therefore, it is difficult to examine the enforcement of Article 10 of the Constitution. Third, the Property Law in China does not deal with disputes between the government and individuals, which are the major parties in land-taking. Therefore, the Property Law has had only a limited impact on regulating land-taking.[7] At the same time, a substantial body of court decisions applying the provisions of the Land Management Law has developed, rendering the neglect of the enforcement and judicial role in land disputes less and less tenable.

The chapter has three parts. The first part introduces the framework of land property law in China, and discusses the data and methodology for the case analysis adopted in this chapter. The cases will be analyzed with

[5] Erie, "China's (Post-)Socialist Property Rights Regime." This article provides a detailed description of the debates of the constitutionality of the new Property Law before its promulgation.

[6] According to a recent statistical study, administrative litigation out of land disputes comprised 15–22 percent of first instance administrative litigations nationwide between 1998 and 2010. See He Haibo, "Fatigued Administrative Litigation," *Journal of East China University of Political Science and Law*, 2 (2012), 86–96.

[7] Mo Zhang, "From Public to Private: The Newly Enacted Chinese Property Law and the Protection of Property Rights in China," *Berkeley Business Law Journal*, 5 (2005), 317.

respect to: (1) the type of litigation (civil, criminal, or administrative); (2) the time and place of the dispute; (3) the land right-holder's identity (village, individual farmers, or other land users); (4) the result of the claim (won or lost); (5) the legal ground of the court's decision; and (6) the judicial policy underlying the court's interpretation of relevant takings' provisions.

The second part summarizes the judicial understanding of the "takings clauses," and highlights various points of consistency and inconsistency in such understanding. Three findings emerge. First, the courts tend to interpret the land right-holders' entitlement narrowly, restricting the compensation of the land rights-holders to mainly direct or original benefits rising from their land. Second, the courts tend to be more "neutral" in adjudicating civil cases than in adjudicating administrative cases, although there seems to be a clear preference for the interests of the rural collective over private or individual claims. Finally, the judicial role in land-taking cases has changed over time because of a changing state policy for addressing land disputes, sometimes without accompanying changes of statutory laws.

The third part then makes several observations with regard to why the courts tend to interpret the takings provisions against certain types of land right-holders, and recent developments from the perspective of judicial policy.

Background and data examined

This part explains the legal background of land rights in China, as well as the empirical methodology and data used in the chapter. While traditional studies of judicial decisions tend to focus on specific cases for analyzing doctrinal issues, the case study in this chapter takes an empirical approach to analyzing how judges apply and interpret the takings provisions in the Land Management Law.

Legal framework of land property rights and the takings provisions

The complexity of land-taking and the controversy over the protection of land property rights cannot be properly understood without an awareness of the history and legal framework of land property rights in China. Indeed, the place of land property rights in the legal system is largely a function of the government's ideology with regard to law and society.

Land property rights have played important roles in modern Chinese history. Before 1949, both the Communist Party and the then-in-power Kuomintang Party advocated the equalization of land rights, which supported private land property rights, but also advocated the redistribution of land property rights according to certain ideological ideals. Immediately upon the establishment of the People's Republic of China (PRC), the Land Reform Law was one of the two statutes promulgated by the new government, which granted farmers land rights based on private ownership. However, the period between 1956 and 1979 also saw socialist reforms and a drastic transformation of property laws. In the early 1950s, the PRC gradually nationalized private property in urban areas and collectivized rural landownership. This system was formally incorporated into the 1954 Constitution. The ensuing years witnessed a disastrous and often violent period of land reform that was characterized by extreme political campaigns of collectivization, and the confiscation and forced conversion of private property into public property.

However, it was not until 1982 that the new Constitution effectively eliminated private ownership in urban areas and established the state's monopoly over urban land. According to Article 10 of the Constitution, not only does urban land belong to the public, but transfers of any kind are also prohibited. This rigid prescription was written into the Constitution at the same time as Shenzhen and other coastal areas began to experiment with land transfers under the name of land-use license, and the Family Responsibility Contracting System was adopted in some rural areas. It was only in 1988 that the Constitution was revised for the first time in order to legalize the transaction of land-use rights in both rural and urban areas.

The Land Management Law was passed in 1986, and Chapter 4 of the law provided for takings of collective-owned land under the title of "Land for National Construction." According to Chapter 4: "The organization the land of which is to be taken should submit to the need of the state, and may not obstruct" (Article 23), and "compensation shall be paid by the organizations who are going to use the land" (Article 27). After the 1988 Constitutional amendment, the Land Management Law was subsequently amended with new provisions to establish land-use rights in urban and rural areas. A series of laws and regulations, such as the 1994 Urban Real Estate Management Law, were designed to exert tighter government control and regulation over the then newly emerging urban property market. In 1998, with rapid urbanization and growing illegal land-taking, following a circular issued by the CCP and the State Council, the original takings provisions were revised to restrain takings powers.[8]

In 2004, Article 13 of the Constitution was revised by the 20th Amendment, which imposed public interest and compensation requirements on the expropriation or requisition of private property. Although the Amendment does not mention land, it is widely perceived as the major target for expropriation and requisition. Three years later, in 2007, the Property Law was passed in response to the public outcry for equal protection of private and public property, and to growing concerns about the insecurity of land property rights in both rural and urban areas.

The seemingly tightened legal protection of land property rights did not stop or slow down the government's active participation in the real property market. Many noticed that because the tax-sharing system, starting from 1994, made local governments' revenue dependent on land sales, land sales revenue experienced an exponential increase,[9] especially after 1998 when the real estate market was formed.[10] According to a 2010 report delivered by the China Academy of Social Science, between 1998 and 2009, revenue from land sales in China increased from 50.7 billion to 1.5 trillion RMB, and the percentage of land sales revenue to national revenue increased from 3 percent in 1998 to 11 percent in 2008. In 2007, land sales revenue rocketed to 1.215 trillion Yuan, comprising at least one-third of the local government revenue, 15 percent of national revenue, at a growth rate of 39.5 percent on the prior year. In 2009 alone, the revenue from land sales increased by more than 63.4 percent over the previous year.[11] Local governments generated more than US$233 billion (1.34 trillion RMB) from the sale of 290,000 hectares of land. Of that, 103,000 hectares were sold to real estate developers, up by 36.7 percent compared with 2008.[12]

This raises the questions: are local governments bypassing the stricter and stricter laws regarding land-taking? What kind of role have the courts

[8] Zhou Yongkang, 关于《中华人民共和国土地管理法(修订草案)》的说明 (Statement of the Draft Bill of Land Management Law Revised), Second Meeting of 9th NPCSC, April 26, 1998.

[9] Xin Bo and Yu Shuli, "Correlation of Land Finance and Local Economic Growth," *Contemporary Finance & Economics*, 1 (2010), 42–47.

[10] 关于进一步深化城镇住房制度改革加快住房建设的通知 (State Council Circular Regarding Further Deepening Urban Housing Reform and Accelerating Housing Construction), No. 23 Guofa (1998). This document is considered to have announced the opening of the Chinese real estate market.

[11] Gao Peiyong, *China Financial Policy Report 2010–11* (Beijing: China Caijing Press, 2010).

[12] "China's Land Sale Revenue Close to $233 Bln in 2009," *Xinhua*, February 2, 2010, available at: www.chinadaily.com.cn/china/2010-02/02/content_9417378.htm.

and judges played in the process? Have they interpreted the laws in ways that are favorable to local governments, and if so, why would they do so? To answer these questions, this chapter has selected cases adjudicated in connection with Articles 46, 47, 48, and 49 of the Land Management Law. These four articles are the major provisions in the Land Management Law regarding land expropriation.[13] Article 46 provides for the procedures to implement the land expropriation scheme; Article 47 stipulates the grounds for calculating land-taking compensation; Article 48 sets forth the requirements for publicity of compensation and for soliciting comments and suggestions; and Article 49 provides for the supervision of the collectives' disposal of compensation fees.

The time frame of the cases examined here, from 2004 to 2011, is chosen for three reasons. First, this is the period during which land property laws began to be enforced. The original 1986 Land Management Law focused mainly on the administrative control of land use. In 1998, the Implementation Regulation for the Land Management Law was passed by the State Council, which laid out detailed procedural requirements for land expropriation and compensation. More generally, more weight was given to compensation for land-taking and the control of government misconduct – especially by local governments – in land administration. In 2004, the Land Management Law was revised after the Constitution Amendments, which echoed the expression of the 20th Constitutional Amendment. The Property Law of 2007 does the same. Finally, in 2011, the Regulation on the Expropriation and Compensation of Houses on Urban State-owned Land replaced the Regulation on the Demolition of Urban Houses. The title of the regulation makes it clear that this is a rights-based real estate regulation.

Second, this period witnessed rapid economic growth and a shift in public policy from a focus on efficiency to more attention to fairness. From 1997 to 2004, the CCP followed the principle of "taking account of fairness while keeping efficiency as the priority."[14] After 2004, however, the policy became "emphasizing efficiency for primary allocation; emphasizing fairness for reallocation."[15] Accordingly, the courts were asked to play different roles over time, alternatively to "protect the sail of the economy" or "to promote a harmonious society." Judicial policies over land disputes changed over time to reflect changing social and economic policies.

[13] See the Appendix to this chapter for the full text of the four articles.

[14] "坚持效率优先,兼顾公平," see Report of CCP, 3rd Session of the 14th Congress, 1993.

[15] "初次分配注重效率,再分配注重公平," see Report of CCP, 17th Congress, 2007.

Third, and finally, this period of time overlapped with the implementation of the Five-Year Reform Outlines of the People's Court. The first five-year reform lasted from 1999 to 2004, and the second from 2004 to 2009. The current five-year reform started in 2009 and will end in 2013. With the five-year outlines, the judiciary set various goals, aiming to transform itself from a bureaucratic organ to a professional and neutral authority. Therefore, examining the courts' practice in adjudicating land disputes during this period provides an opportunity to observe the resolve and reality of the judiciary's commitment to the rule of law and other goals.

Data and methodology

There are many existing case studies of Chinese land disputes, but most investigate one or a few cases in a specific region.[16] Although they enrich our understanding of government (including judicial) practice in dealing with land disputes, it is questionable whether the specific cases are representative and to what degree judges would apply the same rationale behind the cases examined to other cases. There have also been empirical studies of land disputes by economists or political scientists.[17] These help us to understand the social and political background of land disputes, but they do not intend to analyze the variations that lawyers care about: governing principles and rules; the scope of the rights and interests; and rationales behind the judicial understanding of rights and obligations.

This chapter attempts to improve the empirical study of Chinese land disputes by providing a more complete picture of land property rights disputes in China. It does so by examining over 200 cases between 2004 and 2010 available in the public database, Chinalawinfo.[18] From a pure methodological perspective, when compared with empirical research that

[16] For example, see Eva Pils, "Land Disputes, Rights Assertion, and Social Unrest in China: A Case from Sichuan," *Columbia Journal of Asian Law*, 19 (2005), 240–244. See also Zhang Jing, "Uncertainty of Land-use Rules: An Explanatory Framework," *Social Science in China*, 1 (2003), 113–124.

[17] Keliang and Prosterman, "Securing Land Rights for Chinese Farmers"; Loren Brandt, Scott Rozelle, and Mathew Turner, "Local Government Behavior and Property Rights Formation in Rural China," *Journal of Institutional and Theoretical Economics*, 160(4) (2004), 627–671; Klaus Deininger and Songqing Jin, "Securing Property Rights in Transition: Lessons for Implementation of China's Rural Land Contracting Law," *Journal of Economic Behavior and Organization*, 70(1/2) (2009), 22–38.

[18] Available at: www.chinalawinfo.com.

collected cases from media reports,[19] or from one or a few specific regions,[20] the case sample collected here is likely to be less biased and more complete. While there are still many ways in which the sample is not representative – for example, many of the cases are from the same province, while some provinces do not have even one case – we believe that, overall, our dataset improves the representativeness of empirical studies of land property law.

We began by retrieving all cases linked with the Land Management Law, Articles 46–49, from www.Chinalawinfo.com between 1998 and 2011 as of November 30, 2011. But no cases before 2004 and after 2010 were documented as of November 30, 2011. As a result, all the cases were retrieved between 2004 and 2010.[21] Among the cases found, 84 apply Article 46; 108 are decisions applying Article 47; and 6 are based on Articles 48 and 49. Table 4.1 provides an overview of the cases studied. Tables 4.2, 4.3, 4.4, and 4.5 present the more detailed distribution of cases related to the four articles. Two features are

Table 4.1 *Overview of cases analyzed*

	Total	% of total	Article 46 Expropriation procedures	Article 47 Computation of compensation	Article 48 Publicity requirement on the government	Article 49 Publicity requirement on the collective
Total cases	204	100	84	108	6	6
Civil cases	169	83	68	93	2	6
Administrative cases	35	17	16	15	4	0

[19] For example, Liebman collected 223 defamation cases from Internet reports. See Benjamin Liebman, "Innovation through Intimidation: An Empirical Account of Defamation Litigation in China," *Harvard International Law Journal*, 47(1) (2006), 37, acknowledging the obvious problems of reliance on media reports of cases.

[20] Margaret Y. K. Woo and Yaxin Wang, "Civil Justice in China: An Empirical Study of Courts in Three Provinces," *American Journal of Comparative Law*, 35(4) (2005), 911–940.

[21] The Supreme Court Gazette published a couple of cases in 2005, which are not included in the above-mentioned 204 cases. One is 陈清棕诉亭洋村一组、亭洋村村委会 (*Chen Qingzong* v. *Group One of Tingyang Village and Tingyang Villagers' Committee*, No. 10, 2005). Another is 北沙坡村村委会诉西安市高新技术产业开发区东区管委会 (*Beishapo Villagers' Committee* v. *East Administration Committee of Xi'an Municipal High-Tech Industrial Development Region*, No. 40 of Supreme Court Civil Final Adjudication). Both cases are civil cases and the court supported the plaintiffs. No administrative cases regarding land-taking decisions have been published since 1998.

Table 4.2 *Time-spatial distribution of cases based on Article 46*

Article 46	2004	2005	2006	2007	2008	2009	2010	Total
Sichuan		1		1				2
Shandong		1						1
Guangdong	1	1						2
Hainan			2					2
Hubei			1	1				2
Zhejiang			1	2				3
Jiangsu			1					1
Yunnan					60	1	3	64
Henan						3	1	4
Chongqing						1		1
Ningxia						1		1
Hunan							1	1
Total	1	3	5	4	60	6	5	84

Table 4.3 *Time-spatial distribution of cases based on Article 47*

Article 47	2004	2005	2006	2007	2008	2009	2010	Total
Anhui		1						1
Heilongjiang	1							1
Gansu			1					1
Beijing						3		3
Liaoning	2	1		1	1			5
Shanxi		1					1	2
Jinagxi				1				1
Guangdong	2	4	14	2				22
Sichuan		1		1	2			4
Shandong		2	2					4
Fujian				1				1
Hainan		2		18	1			21
Hubei			1	1				2
Zhejiang			1	2				3
Yunnan				7	5	8		20
Henan						7		7
Hebei				1				1
Chongqing		1		2		3		6
Ningxia						1		1
Hunan							1	1
Qinghai	1							1
Total	6	13	19	37	9	22	2	108

Table 4.4 *Time–spatial distribution of cases based on Article 48*

Article 48	2004	2005	2006	2007	2008	2009	2010	Total
Beijing						1		1
Yunnan						1		1
Hubei				1				1
Guangdong			1					1
Zhejiang			1					1
Shandong		1						1
Total	0	1	2	1	0	2	0	6

Table 4.5 *Time–spatial distribution of cases based on Article 49*

Article 49	2004	2005	2006	2007	2008	2009	2010	Total
Henan						1	1	2
Beijing						1		1
Guangxi				1				1
Guangdong		1	1					2
Total	0	1	1	1	0	2	1	6

noticeable. First, most lawsuits were brought after 2006, suggesting the potential impact of the revision of the Constitution and the enactment of the Property Law on the enforcement of a different statute, the Land Management Law. Second, there is no significant difference in the numbers of cases adjudicated in more developed, eastern regions and those in less developed, middle and western regions. This suggests that the stage of economic development does not play an important role in judicial recognition of land property rights, either procedurally or substantively. In other words, adjudications in different regions tend to be "consistent" with each other, which imply the existence of underlying principles or policies behind the judicial behaviors.

Land property rights as shaped by the judiciary

This part discusses the rules and doctrines that may be generalized from the cases adjudicated by the courts, laying the ground for further policy analysis of the judicial decisions.

Overall features: statism, collectivism, and majoritarianism

The conception of "statism" is used in Law's and Versteeg's comparative constitutional study to describe the constitutional arrangement that is in favor of redistribution of social welfare by the state.[22] This characterization appears apt for describing the inclination of the Chinese judiciary when adjudicating land disputes involving government agencies and non-government individuals or organizations. For example, in terms of the distribution of types of litigation, 169 out of 204 cases are civil and only 35 are administrative. Moreover, as Table 4.6 shows, if one compares the plaintiff success rates for the two types of litigation, the likelihood of a plaintiff win in civil litigation (brought against either a collective organization or another individual) is much greater than in an administrative litigation case.

The results of the litigations also have a collectivism color. Consider the following three observations. First, the courts were more likely to reject the claims of the individuals based on Articles 46 and 48 on the ground of lack of standing. According to the decisions, the major reason

Table 4.6 *Plaintiff success rate in litigation*

	Article 46	Article 47	Article 48	Article 49
Number of cases (civil and administrative cases combined)	84	108	6	6
Respective number of civil and administrative cases	68, 16	93, 15	2, 4	6, 0
Number of cases with plaintiff success: civil and administrative respectively	0, 4	53, 7	1, 0	3, 0
Rate of plaintiff success: total	4.7% ?(16%)[(a)]	55%	17%	50%
Rate of plaintiff success: civil	0	56%	50%	50%
Rate of plaintiff success: administrative	25%	46%	0	0

(a) Percentages in parentheses reflect a lower number of total cases when civil cases with the same fact patterns are counted as one.

[22] David Law and Mila Versteeg, "The Evolution and Ideology of Global Constitutionalism," *California Law Review*, 99 (2011), 1163.

for this is collective ownership: the courts believe that landownership in rural areas is collective, so that individuals, even as members of the collective organization, do not have independent standing to claim compensation from the government. Second, even when the courts supported individuals' claims against the government or collective organization, they tend to limit the claims to compensation for young crops and attachments on the land.

According to Article 47 of the Land Management Law, compensation for land-taking comprises four parts: compensation for expropriated cultivated land; resettlement subsidies; compensation for attachments on the land; and compensation for young crops. The total land compensation and resettlement subsidies are not to exceed thirty times the average annual output value of the expropriated land, calculated by reference to the three years preceding such expropriation. However, rates of compensation for attachments and young crops on expropriated land are prescribed by provincial governments, which typically limit this type of compensation to direct damages.[23] As a result, individuals effectively have to rely on the collective to redistribute the compensation for land and resettlement.

Third, and finally, the courts condone practices where a majority of villagers seem to take advantage of the individual households whose lands were actually affected by the expropriation. In one typical scenario, courts support the distribution by villages of compensation to all members rather than to the specific farmers who suffered the loss of land. In another, courts allow the collective not to distribute compensation to some members if that was a majority decision. In both scenarios, courts seem to permit a majority's exploitation of the property interests of a minority.

Substantive review and procedural wrongs

Property rights are considered to be exclusive rights in modern jurisprudence. Although they are not absolute, without due process, government requisition of land property is not justified under Chinese law. Among the four articles in the Land Management Law related to land-taking, three place procedural limits on land requisition and compensation. Article 46 expressly requires that the expropriation be approved through legal procedures, and be announced by people's governments at or above the county level, which government entities are also to implement the expropriation.

[23] This formula is mainly for agricultural land. The formula for compensation for non-agricultural land is similar.

Article 48 provides for the publicity obligations of the local government once the plan for compensation and resettlement subsidies are decided. According to Article 48, the plan must be made available to the general public and the relevant government entities must "solicit comments and suggestions from the collective economic organizations, the land of which is requisitioned, and the peasants." Article 49 imposes another publicity obligation on the collective organization, which is asked to "make known to its members the income and expenses of the compensation received for land expropriation."

However, in practice, the courts rarely invalidate government decisions on expropriation. Nor have procedural wrongs been a ground to overturn the decisions of collectives with regard to the distribution of land compensation. Even in administrative cases where the plaintiffs won claims based on Article 46, courts decided in favor of the plaintiffs mainly because the relevant agencies lacked the proper authorization according to the statutory law. Three of these cases involved local governments that were not authorized to implement demolition of attachments on the expropriated land. According to Article 46, governments above county level are responsible for implementing a requisition, while in the three cases, one street administration[24] and two township governments[25] tried to demolish houses on the expropriated land. The fourth case, in which local government de-registered fourteen people's land-use certificates without authorization, is also more about the agency's qualification than about procedural wrongs.[26]

In a 2009 case adjudicated by Yunnan High Court, forty-one households sought to invalidate a requisition and compensation plan.[27] According to the decision, Dongchuan District Government of Kunming City entered

[24] 裘谢兴诉杭州市余杭区人民政府星桥街道办事处，(2007) 余行初字第32号 (*Qiu Xiexing* v. *Xingqiao Street Administration of Yuhang District*, Hangzhou City, No. 32, First Instance Administrative Trial of Yuhang, 2007).

[25] 周云法等诉台州市椒江区人民政府, (2007) 路行初字第13号 (*Zhou Yunfa and Others* v. *Jiangjiang District of Taizhou City Government*, No. 13, First Instance Administrative Trial of Luqiao Court, 2007). 博罗县石坝镇乌坭湖村民委员会富厚龙富共四个村民小组诉博罗县人民政府及博罗县石坝镇人民政府，(2005) 粤高法行终字第57号 (*Four Villagers' Groups of Wu Ni Hu Village* v. *Shiba Township Government of Boluo County*, No. 57, Final Instance of Administrative Adjudication of Guangdong, 2005).

[26] 王超等十四人诉驻马店市人民政府，(2010) 驻法行初字第1-14号 (*Wang Chao and Thirteen Others* v. *Zhumadian City Government*, Nos. 1–14, First Instance Administrative Trial of Zhumadian, 2010).

[27] 东川区铜都镇深沟村第三村民小组41户村民与东川区人民政府，(2009) 云高行终字第52号 (*41 Households of Shengou Village* v. *Dongchuan District Government of Kunming City*, No. 52, Final Appeal of Administrative Adjudication of Yunnan, 2009).

into the agreement with a village collective (Shengou Village) and compensated the villagers in October 2006 before the Yunnan Provincial Government formally approved the expropriation projected in August 2007. The compensation and resettlement plan was subsequently made public in August and October in 2007. The plaintiffs challenged the requisition and compensation, and asked the courts to invalidate the relevant decisions on the ground of Articles 46, 47, and 48 of the Land Management Law. Both first and second instance courts found procedural wrongs on the part of Dongchuan Government, acknowledging that according to the Land Management Law and its Implementation Measures, Dongchuan Government should have obtained higher government approval and publicized the compensation and resettlement plan for comments before carrying out the requisition. However, both courts declined to invalidate the expropriation decision and the compensation agreement, on the grounds that Dongchuan Government was a qualified agency according to Article 46, and that the procedural wrongs brought no negative consequences to the legal interests of the plaintiffs.[28]

In the few administrative cases where government decisions were invalidated for procedural reasons, substantive review also played a role in the courts' decisions. For example, in *Zhang Guoqi and Others* v. *Zhejiang Provincial Government*, Zhang and other villagers questioned the legality of the government's decision to transfer his land-use right to a developer. The first instance court said that as Zhang was only a member of the collective organization, he did not have standing to sue the government. The second instance court, the High Court of Zhejiang, reversed this decision and invalidated the administrative transfer decision on the ground that it is illegal to apply administrative transfer to the collectively owned land before the taking's procedure, because administrative transfer applies only to state-owned land.[29] In this case,

[28] The plaintiffs argued that Dongchuan Government paid 10,547,265.60 RMB in total to compensate for 105.7 hectares of land in 2006 without completing prior expropriation procedures. It was alleged that Dongchuan Government did so in order to avoid compulsory insurance on expropriated land at 30,000 RMB per hectare, which was required by Kunming City Government starting from January 1, 2007. The compulsory insurance, if applied, would result in 3,171,000 RMB as extra compensation for the farmers. The courts confirmed the procedural problems, but did not support this argument, contending that the insurance should be paid to a unified social insurance account, instead of being distributed directly to the farmers. *Ibid.*, n. 23 *supra*.

[29] 张国其等与浙江省人民政府土地行政复议纠纷上诉案，(2006) 浙行终字第11号 (*Zhang Guoqi and Others* v. *Zhejiang Province Government*, No. 11, Final Administrative Appeal of Zhejiang, 2006).

although a procedural wrong was an important factor to invalidate the government decision, there were also substantive rights concerned.

Collective ownership and individual property rights

As discussed above, the results of the litigations have a collectivist color when disputes between the collective organizations and its members are adjudicated. Table 4.7 categorizes the plaintiffs into five groups: collective organizations; local residents with contracted land (LRC); local residents with no contracted land (LRNC); non-resident with contracted land (NRC); and non-residents no contracted land (NRNC). We also classify the entitlements to land property and rights to compensation upon requisition into the following types: the right to compensation of land; rights to resettlement subsidies' rights to compensation for attachments on the land; and rights to compensation for young crops on the land. Table 4.7 shows the pattern of remedies courts tend to provide to the different categories of plaintiffs.

The basic understanding of the right to land property displayed by the decisions can be summarized as follows. First, only collectives have the right to compensation for land and resettlement. Individuals can have only a share in the compensation. Therefore, no individual farmer in a collective may represent the collective to challenge the overall compensation plan, unless he is the head of the village with proper authorization.

Second, a local resident with contracted land will get compensation for attachments and young crops, which are direct losses due to the expropriation. However, in many cases, local residents with contracted land

Table 4.7 *Pattern of compensation for expropriation*

	Compensation of land	Resettlement subsidy	Compensation for attachments	Compensation for young crops
Collectives	Yes	Yes	No	No
LRC	Yes – share	Yes – share	Yes	Yes
LRNC	Yes – share, but with exception	Yes – share, but with exception	No	No
NLRC	No	No	Yes	Yes
NLRNC	No, but with exception	No, but with exception	No	No

will get only an average share from the compensation for land and resettlement fees. A local resident without contracted land may or may not get a share of the compensation, depending on whether or not he actually lives with the community. For example, a new resident was excluded from a share of land compensation because his actual residence was elsewhere and he did not have any investment in the village.[30] A woman who married out and left her contracted land to her family received 40 percent of the average share as compensation.[31] In another case, the first instance court held that villagers without contracted land did not have the right to land compensation. But the second instance court revoked the first instance decision and instructed the village to distribute the relevant share to the resident villagers.[32]

Third, non-local residents with contracted land will get compensation only for attachments and young crops. The majority of this type of dispute happened when the villages contracted out non-arable lands, such as land for fruit trees, fishponds, riverbanks, or forests. These contracts are not considered household-based contracts, but regular business contracts. Consequently, land-taking will be considered as "changed circumstances,"[33] which leads to termination of the contracts. If the contract contains a provision for this circumstance, the court will respect the agreement. If the contract does not provide for compensation of early termination, courts may ask the village collective to compensate the contractor with a portion of the compensation of land. But the compensation is not considered a remedy for loss of land right, but for breach of contract.[34]

[30] 梁泳仪等与佛山市三水区芦苞镇四联村民委员会君荣村土地补偿费纠纷上诉案, (2006) 佛中法民五终字第372号 (*Liang Yongyi and Others* v. *Junrong Villagers' Committee of Lubao County, Sanshui District of Foshan City*, No. 327, Foshan Intermediate Court, 5th Civil Tribunal Final Adjudication, 2006).

[31] 钟桂常与秦财娣等农业承包合同纠纷上诉案, (2007) 穗中法民二终字第478号 (*Zhong Guichang and Qin Caidi Agricultural Contracting Dispute Case*, No. 478, Huizhou Intermediate Court, 2nd Civil Tribunal Final Adjudication, 2007).

[32] 谷某与屏山镇地多村委会花龙村小组承包土地征收补偿费用分配纠纷上诉案, (2008) 昆民一终字第561号 (*Ms. Gu* v. *Hualong Village Group of Hualong Village, Pingshan County*, No. 561, Kunming Civil No.1 Intermediate Court, Final Adjudication, 2008).

[33] In Chinese, 情事变更。

[34] 魏尤强诉简阳市石桥镇筒车村九组土地征用补偿费分配纠纷案, (2007) 简阳民初字第1049号 (*Wei Youqiang* v. *Tongche Village 9th Group of Shiqiao County, Jian Yang City*, No. 1049, Jianyang Civil First Instance, 2007). Also see 甘肃临洮县辛店镇康家崖村村民委员会与兰州铁路局拆迁补偿纠纷再审案, (2006) 甘民再字第72号 (*Lan Zhou Railroad* v. *Kangjiaai Villagers' Committee of Xindian County, Linyao Township of Gansu*, No. 72, Gansu Civil Retrial, 2006).

Majority rule and minority contractors

Although some villages were expropriated as a whole due to urbanization, in most cases, the government expropriated only a portion of land owned by the collective. If the land acquired happened to be contracted out, the affected farmers would want to get all the compensation for his loss. This always results in legal disputes between the affected farmers (the contractors) and the collective, which owns the land. In a typical dispute, the contractor asks for compensation according to the amount of land that is actually measured and compensated by the government, while the village wants to compensate the farmer only according to the size of land originally described in the contract. The difference in size is usually the result of the farmer's additional effort. However, a court would normally support the village if there was a decision made by the village.[35] As it is either the villagers' meeting or representatives of the villagers that will make the decision, the farmers who are the contractors are viewed as the losing minority in this collective decision. The majorities tend to keep the contractor from getting more than the minimal share prescribed by law, which includes compensation only for attachments on the land and young crops. This allows the majority successfully to allocate the minority's share of compensation according to majority rule.

Summary

Overall, the 204 cases applying Articles 46–49 of the Land Management Law reveal a number of features of land property rights protection in China:

(1) Land property rights do not preclude government from expropriation as a rule, but do provide important legal ground for compensation. Indeed, when the Land Management Law was promulgated in 1986, Article 23 stated that it was farmers' duty to surrender their land.[36] This provision later disappeared from the revised Land Management Law. But almost all legal disputes arising out of land expropriation are

[35] 徐鹏等与晋宁县昆阳镇兴隆村委会三组承包地征收补偿费用分配纠纷上诉案, (2009) 昆民三终字第798–803号 (*Xu Peng and other Five Farmers* v. *Xinglong Villagers' Committee Group 3 of Kunyang County of Jinning Township*, Nos. 798–803, Kunming Civil 3rd Tribunal Final Adjudication, 2009).

[36] Article 23 of the Land Management Law 1986.

confined to compensation rather than the legitimacy or justification of government takings. Even after the Property Law came into force in 2007, Mr. and Ms. Wu, the so-called "most fearless holdout in history," did not seek to keep their house against the taking.[37] They sought to stop the demolition in an attempt to gain higher compensation. In China, this is by no means unique,[38] and makes them different from the plaintiffs in other jurisdictions like the United States, such as the plaintiff in *Kelo* v. *City of New London.*[39]

(2) Procedural violations by government agencies are considered to be less significant than substantive issues such as abuse of power, which does not fall into the realm of the relevant government agency. In practice, neither acts of expropriation nor the distribution of compensation can be challenged successfully on procedural grounds only.

(3) The total amounts of compensation for the collectively owned land are basically determined by government agencies unilaterally for land requisition in rural areas. The determination cannot be challenged in court. In contrast, in urban areas, the law prescribes negotiation and the government will lose the case if it fails to comply with the negotiation and appraisal procedures. Thus, land-taking law in China provides unequal protection of property rights between rural and urban areas.

(4) For land compensation, village members are allowed to claim loss of attachments and young crops, and sometimes resettlement subsidies. But individual farmers cannot challenge the total compensation for the requisition. Plus, individuals or households who claim for a share of the compensation that differs from what is determined by the collective also tend to lose. Since individual farmers do not get compensation for their right to use land at all, it may be said that they actually do not have a right to land.

[37] For example, see "China's Most Incredible Holdout: An Example of Rising Cry for Property Rights," available at: www.nytimes.com/2007/03/26/world/asia/26cnd-china.html?ex=1332561600&en=a821e4ef4e73851a&ei=5090.

[38] In early 2005, collective resistance to proposed demolitions caused large-scale collisions between the villagers and the local government in Dongzhou County of Guangdong and Dingzhou County of Hebei. These protests also did not aim to prevent the government land-taking, but instead sought fair compensation. Many other "property right heroes," such as Liu Zhengyou of Zigong and Qian Huiyun of Leqing, launched long-term resistance against the government through legal or social proceedings for compensation as well. Even in the most recent Tang Fuzhen event, Ms. Tang committed suicide because she disagreed with the compensation rather than the taking itself.

[39] 125 S.Ct. 2655 (June 23, 2005). See Chapter 2 of this book.

Explanations for the judicial approach to land property rights

Many have remarked on weak land property rights in China. Some lay the blame for this on vacuums and vagueness in relevant laws and regulations.[40] Others have commented on the village leaders' incentive to readjust contracting land for rent-seeking purposes,[41] and local governments' incentives to sell or lease land as extra-budgetary revenue.[42] Both provide important explanations for the insecure property system in China. However, the fact that judges tend to be indifferent to the claims of individual land right-holders deserves further investigation for two reasons. First, the courts' lack of sympathy for individual claims may constitute an independent institutional reason for weak property rights. Second, during adjudicatory proceedings, judges do not simply apply rules, but may choose to interpret the same provision inconsistently or even in a distortive way. Consequently, they can promote or curtail individual land property claims.

This section considers three alternative explanations for judges' unsympathetic stance. First, judges may consider themselves mainly as a law enforcement authority. They will apply rules that are expressly prescribed by statute. When rules are absent or unclear, they will look for relevant rules or legal principles from relevant laws as opposed to relying on "judge-made" laws. For example, Article 47 does not articulate how to distribute the compensation among the villagers in the collective organization. When individuals request a share of the compensation, judges may reject those individuals for lack of legal ground. On the other hand, if the affected collective organization files a case, judges are more comfortable in making a decision in favor of the collective according to the collective ownership provision of the relevant laws. Second, judges may consider themselves as part of local governments or are dependent on the other two branches of government. Therefore, judges choose to follow government instructions or political policies. Third, even if judges do not consider themselves as part of the political department, they still do not have the authority for institutional reasons: judges are neither the

[40] Erie, "China's (Post-)Socialist Property Rights Regime"; Deininger and Jin, "Securing Property Rights in Transition."

[41] Brandt *et al.*, "Local Government Behavior." See also Chen Jianbo, "Collective Ownership of Rural Land: Tenure or Principal–Agent Problem?" *Economic Review*, 7 (2006), 83–91 (offering a full account of views from economists regarding the failure of rural land management in China).

[42] Zhu and Prosterman, "Securing Land Rights for Chinese Farmers."

best interpreters of social and economic policy, nor are they in the best position for legal interpretation regarding land disputes. As a result, judges choose not to interfere with government agencies unless the law expressly authorizes it.[43] These explanations are not mutually exclusive and their role may differ across regions.

Judges as pure law enforcement authority hypothesis

There are two reasons why this hypothesis may have explanatory power. First, according to the Chinese Constitution and organic laws, courts are adjudicators not policy makers. Therefore, the role of judges is to apply laws, not to make law. Since both the Constitution and the relevant statutory enactments put great emphasis on collective ownership, and are clearly more sensitive to the protection of public property than they are to the protection of private property, judges should judge in favor of the collective rather than the individuals. Second, as a social policy, distribution of rural land is considered to comprise not just regular alienable property rights, but also implicates social and economic rights: the right to use land is like the right to work; and the allocation of land compensation is like the allocation of social security funds. Consequently, judges should not consider land-taking compensation as merely the price for individual loss. It should be considered as public funds for societal welfare.[44] This explains why judges will examine the relationship between the village and the farmer who claims for a share of the land compensation (as shown in Table 4.7). If the farmer is a dependent member of the village, even if he or she does not farm, he or she will get a share. However, if the farmer does not rely on the land to survive, the courts tend to respect the decision of the village, which is generally unfavorable to outsiders. Even for a contractor who actually farms the land, if that person does not have a dependent relationship with the village, he or she will not get the share. However, if that is the case, this assumption seems unable to explain the judicial preference for substantive review over procedural review, because the Administrative Litigation Law expressly authorizes the courts to invalidate the administrative actions that violate legal procedures, with or without "negative consequences." Indeed, takings,

[43] For example, see 广西壮族自治区高级人民法院关于当前暂不受理几类案件的通知, 桂高法 (2003)18号 (Circular of Guangxi Zhuang Minority Autonomous Region High Court on Several Categories of Cases Not to be Accepted, No. 180, Gui High Court, 2003).

[44] Zheng Shangyuan, "Interpretation of the Right to Survive on the Land: An Analysis of the Nature of Rural Land Contract Management Right," *Tsinghua Law Review*, 3 (2012), 80–95.

or illegal takings without due process, should have been considered the "negative consequence." However, according to our case study, procedural wrongs are not considered sufficient to invalidate administrative actions, unless the actors do not have legal authority.

Indeed, the courts and judges themselves may not support the independent socialist judges hypothesis themselves. For example, in 2003, a guiding instrument issued by Guangxi High Court, "Circular Regarding Cases Courts Should Not Accept," attracted much attention and many comments. Among the thirteen categories of cases, land disputes, especially compensation disputes between farmers and collectives, are considered not suitable in Guangxi Province. When interviewed by curious reporters, the spokesman for the High Court explained that all these cases involve a wide range of people and tend to trigger conflicts. These cases are difficult to deal with because they are complex, vexatious, and costly. Judgments are also difficult to enforce. "For example, cases such as land disputes involving women who have married out, compensations for dam construction immigrants, and disputes over tomb locations for *feng shui* reasons lead to enforcement difficulties even if we accept them."[45] According to the report, the circular was made after an incident caused by a court decision involving illegal fund-raising activities. After that decision was rendered, sixty people were still not able to get their money back from the debtor who was in actual bankruptcy. People who did not get their money back surrounded the court and even harassed the judges, blaming the court for the consequence.

In a typical land-takings case, judges face a similar awkward situation: on one side, a powerful government agency may have demolished houses or occupied land for policy purposes; on the other side, a group of people who are angry and helpless, but ready to demonstrate in front of the court if the court's decision is considered to be unfair. The approach expressed by the Guangxi court circular may be the most rational. Indeed, this self-restraint or "self-effacing" reaction is pervasive among judges and has its root in the court's role in the political system.

Government agency hypothesis

This has been a default understanding for many who study Chinese land disputes, who rarely differentiate court decisions from local government

[45] Gan Bing, "Why Guangxi High Court Rejects 13 Categories of Cases for the Moment," China Youth Daily, August 24, 2004, available at: http://zqb.cyol.com/gb/zqb/2004-08/24/content_935227.htm.

land-taking decisions. Even among legal studies, there are good reasons to believe that local courts may just be a branch of local governments or at least are dependent on local governments. First of all, local judges are appointed by local legislatures in which government officials constitute the majority. The courts will deliver an annual report to the local assembly as a way of accountability. If the local government officials are unhappy with the courts' decisions, they may vote against the court reports and put the courts in a very difficult position.

Second, the presidents and vice-presidents of courts are usually former government officials, or may be promoted as government officials in the future, which creates certain real or potential peer relationships with government officials. Given that court decisions, especially in complicated and difficult cases, will be submitted to the adjudicatory committee headed by the president, and composed of the vice-presidents and some other senior judges, presidents and vice-presidents have a significant impact on court decisions.[46] And if the presidents choose to be prudent when reviewing government decisions, they are authorized to do so through the adjudicatory committee.

Finally, courts are financially dependent on governments at various levels,[47] which have at least two consequences for the courts' attitude to land disputes. First, courts might prefer to reject administrative cases because they do not benefit from the fees collected from administrative cases. Unlike civil cases, from which the courts collect fees according to the disputed amount of money, in most administrative cases courts take a flat rate of 50 RMB.[48] Because many courts still rely on the litigation fees to survive, it is unprofitable to take administrative cases of any kind.[49] Second, local government revenue is the major resource for

[46] According to 最高人民法院关于改革和完善人民法院审判委员会制度的实施意见, 法发 (2010) 3号 (Supreme Court's Implementing Measures Regarding Reform and Improve People's Court's Adjudicatory Committee, No. 3, 2010, Supreme Court), difficult, complicated, and major cases, as well as cases the collegial panels find difficult to deal with should be reviewed or adjudicated by the adjudicatory committee before the court decisions are issued. The president or the responsible vice-president shall decide whether or not a specific case should be submitted to the adjudicatory committee.

[47] 人民法院财务管理暂行办法 (Temporary Measures for Finance Management of People's Courts, 2001).

[48] 诉讼费用交纳办法 (Rules on Litigation Fee Payment, 2006).

[49] Ting Gong, "Dependent Judiciary and Uncountable Judges: Judicial Corruption in Contemporary China," *China Review*, 2 (2004), 33–54. See He Xin, "Insufficient Financial Resources and Judicial Corruption in Chinese Courts," *Twenty-First Century*, 105 (2008), 12–23.

local court funding, and local government revenue is highly dependent on land requisition. As a result, courts indirectly share the benefit that local government receives from land-taking.

The circular by Guangxi High Court, which instructed Guangxi courts to reject land disputes, supports the above hypothesis. The very low success rate in administrative litigation in our empirical study also supports this conclusion. It is especially notable that first instance decisions made mostly by basic level judges tend to support government decisions, while second instance court decisions are more likely to invalidate government decisions or support individual litigants. This makes sense in view of the fact that lower courts are generally dependent on the governments that made the land-taking decisions, whereas the higher courts are not.

However, there is also an institutional argument against this hypothesis. The adjudicatory system in China is based on the finality of second instance review, with unlimited retrial as exceptions. Even if local courts feel that they are obligated to support local government agencies, higher level second instance courts do not share the same degree of solidarity with the challenged agencies of lower level government. This is especially the case when the intermediate courts or high court find that the local government superseded the authority of higher level government agencies or national laws. This made the third assumption more appealing.

Secondary authority hypothesis

The logic of this hypothesis is as follows. According to the Constitution, the National People's Congress Standing Committee (the NPCSC) has authority to interpret law. Although the Supreme Court and the Supreme Procuratorial are also authorized to interpret laws in applying statutes for specific cases, their interpretative authority is considered to be derivative or subordinate to the NPCSC's. This secondary authority was made clear after the NPCSC issued a decision in 2005 that requires the Supreme Court and the Supreme Procuratorial to submit their judicial interpretations for review thirty days after their promulgation.[50]

[50] "司法解释备案审查工作程序" ("Working Process for Record and Review of Judicial Interpretation,", 40th NPCSC Chairs' Meeting, December 2005). Literally speaking, this is not an NPCSC decision, but a decision made by the chairs of the NPCSC. But, in practice, it has a legal effect to subordinate the judicial interpretation. Whether this decision is constitutional or legitimate is another interesting question.

Moreover, since the CCP is the dominant authority in every aspect of Chinese political life, the courts also have to conform their decisions to the Party's policies regarding rural and legal issues. To be precise, the courts and the judges are personally responsible to the Committee for Politics and Law at various levels, especially instructions from the Central Committee for Politics and Law (CCPL). According to the official website of the CCPL, its major function is to unify the minds and actions of respective departments according to the Party's guidelines, roadmaps, and policies, and to deliberate and make policies related to politics and law. The so-called "politics and law departments" include courts and the procuratorials, which therefore are inevitably subordinate to the Party's policies and the specific instructions from the CCPL.[51]

The courts' secondary authority role can be easily demonstrated by the policy shift made by the Supreme Court around 2004. Before 2004, the Supreme Court's basic policy over farmers' claims for land compensation was judicial deference, which in practice meant refusal to review such claims on the basis of lack of standing. In a response to the local high court, the Supreme Court made it clear that only disputes over compensation for attachments and young crops will be accepted, as these are "disputes among equal parties."[52] All kinds of administrative litigation against government agencies, which expropriate lands from the farmers, as well as other claims between farmers and collective organizations, were excluded. Probably due to the amendment of the Constitution in 2004, the Supreme Court extended judicial power to disputes between individual farmers and collectives with regard to land compensation and resettlement the following year. With the promulgation of the 2005 Supreme Court Interpretation Regarding Laws Applied in Adjudication of Rural Land Contract Disputes,[53] courts started to play a more active role in adjudicating land disputes, especially in allocation of land compensation among the villagers' committee and individual farmers.

In a press conference held by the Supreme Court, the then Vice-President Huang Songyou explained the policy concerns and the theory of property rights underlying the new interpretation. According to Huang, disputes over the allocation of compensation for contracted

[51] See, generally, the official website of the CCPL at: www.chinapeace.org.cn.

[52] 最高人民法院关于徐志君等十 一 人诉龙泉市龙渊镇第八村村委会土地征用补偿费分配纠纷 一 案的批复 (2002) 民立他字第4号 (Supreme Court Response to *Xue Zhijun and Other 11 People* v. *8th Villager's Committee of Longquan City Longyuan Township*, 2002).

[53] In Chinese, 关于审理涉及农村土地承包纠纷案件适用法律问题的解释。

land had become a prominent and complicated problem, and petitions of this sort constituted a considerable proportion of farmer-related complaints. Based on the principle set by State Council's Decisions on Deepening Reform and Tightening Land Management,[54] any compensation for land expropriation should be mainly distributed to the farmers. As a result, for the first time the court associated resettlement subsidy and land compensation with the land rights of individuals as opposed to the rights of the collective: resettlement subsidy is considered to be compensation for farmers' land contracting right; and land compensation is considered to be a membership right of the farmers in a collective community.[55]

Since 2008, courts have been considered to be under more political pressures than before after the top CCP leader required the judiciary to apply the "Three Supremacies" in their work. According to this new policy, judges shall always keep in mind of the supremacy of the CCP's course, the supremacy of the people's general interests, and the supremacy of the Constitution.[56] Even though many tried to interpret the three as being in harmony with each other,[57] there is no doubt that judges are expressly required to place politics together with law or even before law.[58] Correspondingly, although the Supreme Court has produced new instructions and guidelines for lower courts to adjudicate land disputes, these should be viewed as responses to the political policies of the new leadership rather than as responses to the claims of farmers. It

[54] 国务院关于深化改革严格土地管理的决定，国发 (2004) 28号 (State Council's Decision on Deepening Reform and Tightening Land Administration, 2004).

[55] 最高人民法院副院长黄松有就最高人民法院《关于审理涉及农村土地承包纠纷案件适用法律问题的解释》答记者问, available at the official website of the People's Courts at: http://old.chinacourt.org/public/detail.php?id=171297.

[56] This was originally presented by Hu Jintao in his address to the All China Politics and Law Representatives Meeting with Senior Judges and Prosecutors on December 26, 2007, and was soon promoted by Chief Justice Wang Shengjun as the guiding principles for adjudicatory works.

[57] See "Further Deepening Theoretical Study of Three Supremacies: A Summary of Scholars' Remarks in the Symposium of Theoretical Guidelines for People's Courts", *People's Court Daily*, June 26, 2009, available at: www.chinacourt.org/article/detail/2009/06/id/363600.shtml.

[58] Wang Shengjun, "Thoroughly Implement the Principles of the 17th CCP Congress, Do All Work of the Courts in a Down-to-Earth Manner," *Qiush*, 16 (2008). Wang was the Chief Justice of the Supreme Court. In this statement, he urged that judges at all levels should keep in line with the socialist path and the CCP's leadership so as to ensure both the political correctness of the people's courts and that the courts serve the larger plan of the CCP and the state.

may be too extreme to conclude that these new instructions will not help in the farmers' land property rights. However, it will not be surprising if the courts judge in favor of the "bigger plan" of the government at the cost of the stability of the land property rights of the farmers, such as development and social stability.

Conclusion

By examining over 200 cases across the country, this chapter finds a pattern of land property protection in judicial practices. The fundamental features of the pattern are:

(1) Land property rights do not preclude government intrusion unless the government agency lacks authorization. This is reflected in the understanding of Article 46, when the Article is mainly understood as a clause to authorize the governments at or above the county level as expropriators, as opposed to a due process of law clause to restrain the government eminent domain power. For the same reason, Article 48 of the Land Management Law is considered to be irrelevant to illegal land-taking. The courts either refuse to examine the proprieties of the land-taking decision or reject the claim on the basis of violation of legal procedures.
(2) Land property rights in rural areas are considered to be a kind of social or economic right distributed among its members. This is reflected in the judiciary's understanding of Articles 47 and 49 for distribution of land compensation, according to which the compensation is paid to the collective organization as a whole to compensate the loss of the collective. Then, the collective will redistribute part of the compensation to the actual affected land users, part to unaffected farmers, and part to the collective organization itself. We can, of course, defend this collectivist redistribution system on the ground of collective ownership. However, with the Land Contracting Law expressly providing for the land-use right of the affected individuals, this interpretation can only be interpreted as the courts' preference for the collective claim to the individual land property rights.

The above judicial perception is consistent with the socialist ideology of collective ownership. But the even more important reason for the pattern may be the self-image of the court as the secondary authority to interpret the law and to enforce state policies.

The conclusion here is mainly descriptive and has focused on the judicial role in adjudicating land disputes through court proceedings. However, it may have implications for land property law. For one thing, the above observation would disagree with the interpretative approach to prevent illegal land-taking. For example, according to this approach, in order to prevent illegal land-taking, relevant statutes should introduce a whole list of items categorized as public interests.[59] This approach is objectionable according to our observation because when the courts apply deference to interpret "public interest," almost any project can be viewed as being in the "public interest." Indeed, this approach has been proved not to be very effective after the Regulation on Requisition and Compensation of Houses on State-owned Land in Urban Areas was promulgated with a relevant provision.[60]

Another implication relates to the idea of privatization. Privatization seems to be a convenient way to address the "tragedy of the commons" in rural areas. However, privatization does not preclude nationalization or the eminent domain power unless an independent authority, such as the judiciary, limits the arbitrariness of state power. Large-scale demolitions of private houses in urban areas illustrate this point, since these are private properties with clear-cut statutory entitlement.

Our empirical study suggests, as a prescriptive matter, that it is important for resolving land property right issues in China to empower the judiciary by cutting the financial and personal ties between the local governments and local judges, giving courts review power of land-takings before the administrative land-taking decisions are enforced, and, eventually, vesting the judiciary with fully-fledged interpretative power of the statutes. The prospective new appointment system is different from the current institutional arrangement in the Chinese Constitution, but it is consistent with the unitary state principle. Other institutional reforms such as authorization of broader judicial review power and interpretative power are both consistent with the current Constitution and will provide the fundamental basis for property right protection.

[59] Hu Jinguang and Wang Kai, "Defining Public Interest in the Chinese Constitution," *China Legal Science*, 1 (2005), 18–27.

[60] Article 8 of the Regulation lays out a list of projects that may be considered as "public interest," but it does not preclude other projects that are not listed in the provision, which leaves room for further interpretation in law enforcement proceedings.

Appendix: Text of Articles 46–49 of the Land Management Law[61]

Article 46 Procedure and Qualification for Expropriation.
Where land is to be expropriated by the State, the expropriation shall, after approval is obtained through legal procedure, be announced by people's governments at or above the county level, which shall help execute the requisition.

Units and individuals that own or have the right to the use of the land under expropriation shall, within the time limit fixed in the announcement, register for compensation with the land administration department of the local people's government by presenting their certificates of landownership or land-use right.

Article 47 Computation of Compensation.
Land expropriated shall be compensated for on the basis of its original purpose of use.

Compensation for expropriated cultivated land shall include compensation for land, resettlement subsidies and compensation for attachments and young crops on the requisitioned land. Compensation for expropriated cultivated land shall be six to ten times the average annual output value of the expropriated land, calculated on the basis of three years preceding such requisition. Resettlement subsidies for expropriated cultivated land shall be calculated according to the agricultural population needing to be resettled. The agricultural population needing to be resettled shall be calculated by dividing the area of expropriated cultivated land by the average area of the original cultivated land per person of the unit the land of which is expropriated. The standard resettlement subsidies to be divided among members of the agricultural population needing resettlement shall be four to six times the average annual output value of the expropriated cultivated land calculated on the basis of three years preceding such expropriation. However, the maximum resettlement subsidies for each hectare of the expropriated cultivated land shall not exceed fifteen times its average annual output value calculated on the basis of three years preceding such expropriation.

Rates of land compensation and resettlement subsidies for expropriation of other types of land shall be prescribed by provinces, autonomous regions and municipalities directly under the Central Government with

[61] This is the official translation provided by the NPCSC, available at: http://law.npc.gov.cn/page/browseotherlaw.cbs?rid=en&bs=30036&anchor=0#go0.

reference to the rates of compensation and resettlement subsidies for expropriation of cultivated land.

Rates of compensation for attachments and young crops on expropriated land shall be prescribed by provinces, autonomous regions and municipalities directly under the Central Government.

For expropriation of vegetable plots in city suburbs, the land users shall pay towards a development and construction fund for new vegetable plots in accordance with the relevant regulations of the State.

If land compensation and resettlement subsidies paid in accordance with the provisions of the second paragraph in this Article are still insufficient to enable the peasants needing resettlement to maintain their original living standards, the resettlement subsidies may be increased upon approval by people's governments of provinces, autonomous regions and municipalities directly under the Central Government. However, the total land compensation and resettlement subsidies shall not exceed thirty times the average annual output value of the expropriated land calculated on the basis of three years preceding such expropriation.

The State Council may, in light of the level of social and economic development and under special circumstances, raise the rates of land compensation and resettlement subsidies for expropriation of cultivated land.

Article 48 Obligation of the Government to Publicize the Compensation. Once a plan for compensation and resettlement subsidies for requisitioned land is decided on, the local people's government concerned shall make it known to the general public and solicit comments and suggestions from the collective economic organizations, the land of which is requisitioned, and the peasants.

Article 49 Obligation of the Collective Organization to Publicize the Compensation.

The rural collective economic organization, the land of which is expropriated, shall accept supervision by making known to its members the income and expenses of the compensation received for land expropriation.

The compensation and other charges paid to the unit for its land expropriated is forbidden to be embezzled or misappropriated.

5

Contending conceptions of ownership in urbanizing China

EVA PILS

The signs of deep contention

Among the incidents drawing attention to the problem discussed here, the self-immolation of a woman named Tang Fuzhen in December 2009 was one of the most widely discussed. Facing the forced demolition of her home, she stood on the roof of the building, doused herself in petrol and, after vainly urging the demolition team to stop beating members of her family, set herself on fire. Her suicide (she succumbed to her injuries a few days later) was captured on camera, and the video clip showing her, a dark, then suddenly aflame, silhouette against the sky, amongst the shouts of shocked observers in the street below, was widely circulated on the internet.[1]

As urbanisation has progressed rapidly,[2] the effects of urban development – to be precise, of urban redevelopment and of the expansion of cities into the countryside – on citizens affected by demolition and expropriation of land or houses has been great in China. While they have no real choice in the face of an order to 'develop' or redevelop their area through urban construction, not all residents actually oppose such measures. Some are glad to accept compensation payments, which can

The author would like to thank Dr. Zhang Yihong, CUHK Faculty of Law, for her excellent research assistance.

[1] Roger Cohen, 'A Woman Burns', *New York Times*, 25 January 2010, available at: www.nytimes.com/2010/01/26/opinion/26iht-edcohen.html; '唐福珍其人 凤凰卫视/' ('Tang Fuzhen as a Person'), Phoenix Television, 15 December 2009, available at: www.youtube.com/watch?v=Pt6cvNq3Umw.

[2] With hundreds of millions having moved to the cities already, Ian Johnson states that according to central government policies, 250 million more citizens are to be moved from the countryside in coming decades in 'Leaving the Land: China's Great Uprooting', *New York Times*, 15 June 2013, available at: www.nytimes.com/2013/06/16/world/asia/chinas-great-uprooting-moving-250-million-into-cities.html. See also Ian Johnson, 'Leaving the Land: Pitfalls Abound in China's Push from Farm to City', *New York Times*, 13 July 2013, available at: www.nytimes.com/2013/07/14/world/asia/pitfalls-abound-in-chinas-push-from-farm-to-city.html.

be substantial and that have given rise to the term 'demolition nabob'.[3] But invariably, some residents are opposed to their removal, and become involved in fights with the government that may cost them far more than just their residences. The experiences of these activist evictees have drawn much public attention, and are among the reasons for continued criticism of the existing regime of ownership and use rights in immoveable property (land and buildings).

The attention that Tang Fuzhen's case generated may have been among the factors stimulating further calls for a revision of the State Council Regulation on Demolition and Relocation. In 2011, a new Regulation on Expropriation of Buildings on State-owned Land came into force; whereas legislative reform of other major laws, such as the PRC Land Administration Law, remains a subject of debate as of this writing. It is doubtful if these recent and currently debated changes can bring significant improvements as long as the basic structure of the land tenure system and resulting property relations remains in place. Nor would it be capable of removing the incentives that drive the urban construction process seemingly 'necessitating' expropriation and demolition under this system. Scepticism on the part of commentators has not been alleviated by publicly available reports on further cases of self-immolation, self-mutilation and suicide,[4]

[3] '拆迁富翁"飞来巨财如何稳健增值' ('Demolition Nabobs: How to Achieve Stable Growth for Wealth Acquired in a Flash?'), 11 August 2010, available at: http://finance.ifeng.com/money/CFP/20100811/2500650.shtml. 'As a financial adviser, I often encounter some old Beijingers who are dressed modestly and who behave with restraint. But these customers are not to be despised, because they may well be already worth a million and own several properties – those are the "demolition billionaires" who got rich through demolition and relocation . . .'

[4] In 2012, Amnesty International produced a report that lists a number of cases of violence and suicides, including self-immolations. See Amnesty International, 'Standing Their Ground: Thousands Face Violent Evictions in China', October 2012, available at: www.amnesty.org/en/library/info/ASA17/001/2012/en (list of self-immolation cases at pp. 56 ff.). Reported cases of self-harm inflicted in protest considered for this chapter include the following. The reports could not be further verified (but see above Amnesty International report). Some of these reports contain pictures or film footage at the links provided: Chinaaid, '湖南:湘潭抗强拆自焚者死亡' ('Forced Demolition Protester Self-immolates, Dies in Xiangtan, Hunan'), 18 July 2013, available at: www.chinaaid.net/2013/07/blog-post_1347.html; Anonymous (佚名), '山东居民不满强制拆迁自杀 官员称拆迁都死人'('Shandong Resident Commits Suicide over Eviction Discontent, Officials say Eviction Deaths Common'), 26 August 2013, Qianlong Newsnet (千龙新闻网), available at: www.tianong.cn/zht/416/view-14318-1-0.html; '北安男子拆迁自焚调查:曾遭殴打 房屋被直接推倒' ('Investigation of Bei'an Evictee Self-immolation Death: Evictee had Suffered Beatings, His Home was Immediately Demolished'), *Xinhua News*, 11 July 2013, available at: http://news.xinhuanet.com/legal/2013-07/11/c_116502753.htm; '安徽农夫拒拆迁自杀村民堵路与特警对峙' ('Anhui

as well as other demolition-related violence[5] in the months since enactment of the Expropriation Regulation (reports available despite censorship), and some experts have commented that there has been no

Peasant Woman Evictee Commits Suicide Resisting Eviction, Villagers Block Road in Clash with Special Police Unit'),' *Legal Weekly* (法制周报), 6 July 2013, available at: http://s.efaw.cn/shtml/fzzb/20130706/6394.shtml; Anonymous (佚名), '我要投诉政府拆迁涉嫌以罚款为由逼迫村民签字 导致一村民自残断四指' ('I Want to Complain Against the Government Demolition and Relocation [office] that Forced Villagers to Sign under Pretext of Imposing Fines, Leading to One Woman Villager's Self-mutilation by Hacking Off Four Fingers'), 24 June 2013, available at: www.ayhlgs.com/Info.php?nid=472; '护家园抗强拆 重庆养殖户点火自焚重伤 ' ('Resistance to Forced Demolition: Case of Self-immolation in Chongqing'), 5 December 2012, available at: www.epochtimes.com/gb/12/12/5/n3745919.htm; '湖南湘潭强拆引村民自焚 行动负责人被刑拘' ('Forced Demolition in Xiangtan, Hunan, Leads to Villagers' Self-immolation, Person Responsible for Action Criminally Detained'), 19 October 2012, available at: http://news.sina.com.cn/c/2012-10-19/034925389671.shtml; 云南妇女引爆炸药疑自杀抗议拆迁 更新时间 2012年5月10日，格林尼治标准时间 10:35, available at: www.bbc.co.uk/zhongwen/simp/chinese_news/2012/05/120510_china_explosion.shtml; '3·15贵州关岭拆迁自焚事件' ('The 15 March [2012] Incident of a Demolition Self-immolation in Guanling, Guizhou'), available at: http://baike.baidu.com/view/8131985.htm; '郑州强拆自焚变成火灾仍有疑点' ('Doubts Cast on Forced Demolition Self-immolation that Became a an Accidental Fire'), 3 March 2012, available at: www.jryaw.com/html/2012/wjj_0303/7668.html; '河南洛阳拆迁自焚一日两起-一重伤一被阻' ('Two Cases of Self-immolation on One Day in Luoyang, Henan: One Seriously Injured, One Intercepted'), *Epoch Times*, 5 January 2012, available at: www.epochtimes.com/gb/12/1/7/n3479170.htm; '山东男子遇强拆房顶自焚' ('A Boy in Shandong Self-immolates as He Faces Forceful Demolition'), 14 December 2011, *Heilongjiang Morning Post* (黑龙江晨报), available at: www.peacehall.com/news/gb/china/2011/12/201112140822.shtml; '武汉强拆,又引发自焚' ('Wuhan Forced Demolition Leads to Self-immolation'), *Boxun*, 8 December 2011, available at: www.peacehall.com/news/gb/china/2011/12/201112082313.shtml; '81-year-old Sets Self on Fire in Protest', *Yahoo*, 16 November 2011, available at: http://news.yahoo.com/81-old-chinese-sets-self-fire-protest-054429415.html; '张家港第二轮强拆 险酿集体自焚' ('Second Wave of Forceful Demolition Leads to Collective Threat of Self-immolation in Zhangjiagang'), *Epoch Times*, 9 November 2011, available at: http://hk.epochtimes.com/gb/11/11/9/146451.htm; '两村民不堪强拆分别自杀身亡' ('Two Villagers Refusing to Accept Forceful Demolition Separately Commit Suicide'), 20 October 2011, available at: http://boxun.com/news/gb/china/2011/10/201110200137.shtml; '南通野蛮拆迁致人自杀，亲属穿状衣讨说法' ('Barbaric Forced Demolition in Nantong Leads to Suicide; Family Dons Complaint Garments, Seeks Justice'), 17 October 2011, available at: http://boxun.com/news/gb/china/2011/10/201110190941.shtml; '辽宁抚顺暴力强拆办公楼 户主父亲欲自焚保财产' ('Violent Forced Demolition of Office Building in Fushun, Liaoning; Owner's Father Intends to Commit Suicide to Protect the Property'), 28 September 2011, available at: http://boxun.com/news/gb/china/2011/09/201109281649.shtml; '湖南株洲村民为阻止强拆自焚 法院称已中止拆迁' ('Villagers in Zhuzhou, Hunan, Self-immolate to Prevent Forced Demolition, Court Says it Has Already Stopped Forced Demolition'), 24 April 2011, available at: www.chinasmack.com/2011/videos/zhuzhou-hunan-self-immolation-protesting-forced-demolition.html and http://news.sina.com.cn/c/2011-04-24/212022349872.shtml.

[5] For example, on 12 November 2011 a man from Nongkou (Hangzhou) was found hanging by the neck in a shrub, dead. His family claim that the day before he had gone

improvement at all.[6] In rural areas, where protests by the villagers of Wukan in China's southern Guangdong province triggered by another death in the context of resistance to eviction drew the attention of the world in December 2011, there has been even less change to the regulatory framework.

This chapter argues that underlying a state-tolerated public debate on certain aspects of urbanisation and property law in China, there is a deeper, less visible contention of different conceptions of property and ownership concerning land and houses. This deeper contention reaches beneath the levels both of textual analysis of current laws and regulations and of reform proposals within the detailed constraints of current constitutional provisions pertaining to land. Deeper, and potentially far more consequential, claims concern historical, political and moral interpretations of this current property regime. Urban activists attempt to call into question the official reading of existing property and ownership rights, arguing against the view that no, or only weak, private ownership rights were left to original urban residents at the beginning of Reform and Opening. Rural activists have on occasion claimed 'full ownership' rights over rural communities' land. But more often, their attack on the existing property regime in the countryside takes the form of implicit disobedience to the rules, for instance, through the mechanism of 'minor property rights' housing, or through resistance to evictions from land and buildings, sometimes described by reference to 'our ancestral land'

to negotiate with the village committee, and had never come back. Police were filmed forcibly removing the body for cremation. See '杭州拆迁再发命案' ('Hangzhou Forced Demolition Leads to Another Death'), 12 November 2011, *Boxun* (博讯), available at: www.peacehall.com/news/gb/china/2011/11/201111121528.shtml. Author conversation (online chat) with local acquaintances, December 2011. See for another report on a suspicious death of an evictee protester after being taken away '屋主反对强拆被带走次日死亡 镇原书记被判' ('Homeowner Who Protested Forced Demolition Taken Away, Dies Next Day'), 5年, 16 February 2013, available at: http://news.sina.com.cn/s/2013-02-16/143926273628.shtml; and for reports of people involved in protests who were crushed at eviction sites, see AFP, 'Fujian Girl, 3, Killed By Bulldozer Runs in Land Dispute,' 30 August 2013, available at: www.scmp.com/news/china/article/1300350/three-year-old-girl-killed-bulldozer-fujian-land-dispute; Patrick Boehler, 'Gruesome Photos of Henan Farmer Killed in Land Grab Protest', *South China Morning Post*, 29 March 2013, available at: www.scmp.com/comment/blogs/article/1202485/gruesome-photos-henan-farmer-killed-land-grab-protest; 'Land Grabs and a Disputed Death in China' (about Qian Yunhui), *The Economist*, 6 January 2011, available at: www.economist.com/node/17859968.

[6] '石山:新拆迁条例无法杜绝暴力强拆' ('Shi Shan: Newly-effective Expropriation Regulation cannot Stop Forced Demolition'), Radio Free Asia, 11 October 2011, available at: www.molihua.org/2011/11/blog-post_7523.html.

or 'our lifeline' and similar phrases. The popular views underpinning such conduct can be usefully juxtaposed with a 'state view' of property and ownership of land and buildings.

The state view described here is extrapolated from the actions of the state as well as from the language adopted by its officials; it is in that sense constructed and does not necessarily represent the views of individuals working for the party-state. Rather, it describes the ideas and principles that the party-state must embrace to provide any – however weak or strong – justification for what it does in the context of urbanisation. Similarly, popular views are also extrapolated from a multitude of forms or popular actions and activism. These range from explicit statements and appeals (as in the case of the rights defenders Hua Xinmin and Yang Chunlin) to statements that unconsciously oppose the state view, and actions that are not accompanied by explicit claims or justifications (as in the case of countless citizens who are ignorant of, or choose to ignore, existing legal rules of the party-state). Thus, not only the citizen composing an open letter opposing the current property and ownership regime, but also the citizen selling or buying a 'minor property right' not recognised by state laws expresses their rejection of the state view.

From the perspective of developers and the government, original residents occupy land without having any moral entitlement to its economic value, and without holding rights of ownership. From that perspective China's socialist system wiped the map clean of private property rights and created a new regime; developing land under this new property rights regime is now vital to China's continued economic growth. The 'state view' described here draws on a positivistic conception of authority, as well as on a utilitarian reinterpretation of the concept of 'socialist public ownership'.

According to underpinning popular protest and resistance, by contrast, the government's decisions and the claim to control over land and buildings underpinning such decisions violate their rights of ownership, understood in a broad and non-positivistic way. In the cities, some argue that the state unfairly took away landownership that had been left untouched throughout China's socialist era, at the very time when it allowed this land to become valuable on the newly created real estate market. In the countryside, from the perspective of rural evictee activists, the state has not only expropriated many collectives without regard to its own rules that are supposed to protect against land-takings. Some also perceive it as having violated a social pact that gave rural residents security of their landholdings, albeit in a context of socialism or collectivism; or they regard it as having destroyed traditional land rights with which it had no right to interfere. Many do not explicitly express criticism, but implicitly reject the hold that the party-state claims to have on 'their' land, for example, by engaging in commercial transactions the state laws do not recognise; and there are many expressions of discontent concerning corruption.[7]

The present study can do no more than attempt to show that deeper contention exists, without attempting to describe contending views in their respective dimensions and weights. It sketches some of the views that can be found represented in contemporary land, housing and property rights activism, showing that they are critical of the state view. To achieve this goal, the chapter proceeds by first describing the land and property rights regime, and the process of expropriation and demolition as they appear from the perspective of the law of the state and its officials. It examines debates devoted to analyses of such existing laws and proposals for reform within the existing constitutional framework and national legislation, arguing that reforms within the constraints of the property regime set by the 2007 Property Rights Law are unlikely to resolve the problems resulting from expropriations, and that officially tolerated reform debates have in recent years been tepid (see section below). The unresolved expropriation problem is what prompts challenges to the state view and more deeply contentious positions on property and ownership, especially on the part of those directly affected by expropriation, eviction and demolition of third section. Some of the arguments used in this context are backward-looking and based in historical entitlement or in the experience of injustice, whereas others are more forward-looking and based in socio-economic rights, such as the right to subsistence and adequate housing. In this context, related changes in the forms and strategies of 'rights defence' activism are also discussed. Especially in urban areas, public evictee rights activism translates easily into political protest and demands, in a situation where public institutions (such as the media or the judiciary) are not at this moment capable of accommodating such debates. Evictee activism may come to play an important role in shaping political activism for a wider right to good government.

[7] On the problem of real estate corruption, see Jiangnan Zhu, 'The Shadow of the Skyscrapers: Real Estate Corruption in China', *Journal of Contemporary China*, 21(74) (2012), 243–260.

Urban development and the current Chinese property regime: the state view

Legal framework and issues

According to the law governing real estate in China today,[8] all land is in 'socialist public ownership', and private individuals or families (households) may only hold use rights granted by the public owner; use or 'usufruct' rights (*yongyi wuquan*) are limited in terms of time and types of land use. In rural and suburban areas the public owner is generally a rural collective. In urban areas, since 1982 or earlier, all land has been owned by the state (i.e., the urban government). Buildings, both in urban and rural China, can be privately owned. In many cases, the residents' rights (e.g., as tenants or owners) are not clearly documented, and they may originate in an historical era whose law is no longer recognised by the state.[9]

The law does not allow the sale and transfer of ownership rights in land, whereas the sale of the various kinds of land-use rights indicated above is legally possible, but restricted in various ways. Urban development, whether it is expansion into the countryside or urban renewal in cities, generally cannot be based in contractual land transactions. Instead, it generally involves expropriation by the state, legal protection against which – in the form of 'public interest demand' constraints and higher level government approval mechanisms, for instance – has thus far been next to meaningless. Compared with other regions in the world, where urbanisation also leads to mass evictions and demolitions of residential dwellings, the process in China is therefore very much driven and controlled by public power exercising rights of public ownership.[10]

[8] For an excellent introduction of the legislative framework (covering immobile property, i.e., the land tenure system), see Chen Lei, 'Private Property with Chinese Characteristics: A Critical Analysis of the Chinese Law on Property of 2007', *European Review of Private Law*, 18 (2010), 983–1004.

[9] Katherine Wilhelm, 'Rethinking Property Rights in Urban China', *UCLA Journal of International Law and Foreign Affairs*, 9 (2004), 227, available from Hein Online at: http://heinonline.org; Amy S. Sommers and Kara Philips, 'A Tragedy of the Commons: Property Rights Issues in Shanghai Historic Residences', *Penn State International Law Review*, 28 (2010), available at: http://papers.ssrn.com/sol3/papers.cfm?abstract_id=1564413; Chinese Human Rights Defenders (CHRD), 'Thrown Out: Human Rights Abuses in China's Breakneck Real Estate Development', 9 February 2010, available at: http://chrdnet.org/2010/02/08/thrown-out-human-rights-abuses-in-chinas-breakneck-real-estate-development.

[10] Yves Cabannes, Silvia Guimarães Yafai and Cassidy Johnson, *How People Face Evictions*, draft, June 2010, available at: www.ucl.ac.uk/dpu/k_s/publications/how_ppl_face_evictions.

Because the land tenure system is bifurcated, the 'urban' and 'rural–suburban' processes terminating in the acquisition of land-use rights for urban construction are different. When urban construction expands into suburban and rural areas where land is in collective ownership, urban governments expropriate the land of the rural collectives (*tudi zhengshou*) and evict rural households on the land, destroying their land-use rights as well as any individually owned buildings on the land.[11] Urban renewal in urban areas, where land is already state-owned, takes the form of 'resumption' or 'recovery' (*shouhui*) of this land and concurrent destruction of any existing land-use rights in this land; it also generally involves the expropriation of the owners of buildings (*fangwu zhengshou*), as well as the demolition and the eviction of the residents (*chaiqian*).

The scope of real estate development in the context of urbanisation in China is enormous, and so, consequently, is the scope of expropriations and demolitions affecting the population. It has been estimated that as of 2007, around 60–65 million rural residents had been affected by rural land expropriation (*tudi zhengshou*) alone; the number of citizens affected by urban expropriation and/or demolition of buildings is not clear.[12] According to a senior researcher from the Ministry of Housing and Urban–Rural Development cited in *China Daily* in August 2010, 'more than half of China's existing residential structures will be demolished and rebuilt in the coming 20 years . . . only those homes built after 1999 are likely to be preserved in the longer term'. China, according to this report, 'annually sees more construction than any other country'. In recent years, 'the nation has had up to 2 billion square meters of development annually', and 'around 40 percent every year is created by the demolition of older buildings'.[13]

Original residents affected by expropriation and/or relocation are entitled to compensation. Legal compensation standards vary. In rural

[11] See for discussions of rural–suburban takings, Matthew Erie, 'China's (Post-)Socialist Property Rights Regime: Assessing the Impact of the Property Law on Illegal Land Takings', *Hong Kong Law Journal*, 37(3) (2007), 919–949; Christopher Heurlin, 'Ruling the Chinese Countryside: Rights Consciousness, Collective Action and Property Rights', University of Washington (draft), available at: www.yale.edu/scr/Heurlin.pdf; Ben James, 'How the Rural Property System Exacerbates China's Urban Rural Gap', *Columbia Journal of Asian Law*, 20 (2007), 451.

[12] Yu Jianrong (于建嵘, editor) '底层政治 – 对话与演讲' ('Subaltern Politics, Dialogues and Lectures'), No. 122 (2009). Yu estimates that of these 60–65 million people, about half do not find new jobs and lack social security, and therefore become destitute.

[13] Qian Yanfeng, '"Most homes" to be demolished in 20 years', *China Daily*, 7 August 2010, available at: www.chinadaily.com.cn/china/2010-08/07/content_11113982.htm.

scenarios, compensation is for land, as well as lost crops and buildings. The law does not provide for 'fair market value' compensation for land; instead, compensation for land is calculated on the basis of lost agricultural income (for houses, there is some orientation towards the market value). In the urban scenario, compensation is for buildings only (see below for the compensation standard under the new Expropriation Regulations);[14] under the new rules, additional costs for relocation are also covered.[15] The new Expropriation Regulations state that 'if any houses have been expropriated accordingly, the state-owned land-use rights are recovered at the same time (Article 13)'. However, urban demolition compensation does *not* include compensation calculated on the basis of the value of land whose ownership is 'resumed' by the government, presumably because such land is supposed to be already state-owned. Yet, especially in urban renewal contexts, the prospective market value of the land can far exceed that of the buildings standing on it. Both in rural and urban cases, compensation packages are supposed to be negotiated with individual households, who are asked to sign agreements with the urban government.

While the law on compensation differentiates greatly between rural and urban land, actually negotiated compensation packages do not necessarily reflect the legally stipulated standards, or 'reflect' these standards only in a very loose sense. Thus, for instance, the compensation for takings of 'rural or suburban' land are to be measured, on principle, in terms of loss of agricultural output; but in some cases, there is no such output, because the land in question has long become part of a *de facto* urbanised area and farming no longer takes place.[16] In such cases, the compensation offered may actually exceed what could be got through farming the land for thirty years, but still fall short of the price of the land

[14] Under the new rules for expropriation of buildings on state-owned (usually urban) land only owners are clearly entitled to compensation, leaving the question open as to what will happen to non-owner residents affected by urban demolitions of the buildings they inhabit. 2011国有土地上房屋征收与补偿条例 (State Council Regulation on Expropriation Of and Compensation for Buildings on State-owned Land), available at: www.gov.cn/zwgk/2011-01/21/content_1790111.htm.

[15] It comprises: (1) compensation for the value of the expropriated houses; (2) compensation for relocation and temporary resettlement arising from house expropriation; and (3) compensation for losses arising from suspended production and business caused by house expropriation.

[16] Eva Pils, 'Waste No Land: Property, Dignity and Growth in Urbanizing China', *Asian-Pacific Law & Policy Journal*, 11(2) (2010), 1–48, available at: www.hawaii.edu/aplpj/articles/APLPJ_11.2_pils.pdf.

on the urban real estate market once it has been formally converted into 'urban' and hence state-owned land.[17] Experience until now suggests that the actual amount of compensation evictees get is decided at least with political considerations (such as concern about popular protest) in mind,[18] and that in some cases, no compensation is paid in retaliation for resistance to the eviction process.[19]

Since evictees are generally required to sign agreements with the government, there is an element of negotiation in the process, and this means that evictees can make some choices; but it does not mean that negotiations are, or indeed, can, be fair in the setting provided by the legal framework, because evictees have little with which to bargain and the process is conducted in a generally coercive environment. Most importantly, evictees have no choice whether they retain their land and/or houses. They will inevitably be dispossessed of these, because the state has decided so and, to varying degrees, they may be weak and intimidated.

It is in fact the formal requirement to obtain 'agreements' regarding eviction and compensation, and the available measure of 'forcible demolition' that – both in urban and rural scenarios – have led to much suffering in the context of the urbanisation process. Threats, intimidation and violence may be used to obtain such 'agreements'. The techniques for this are well known and widely documented. They typically include verbal threats and the cutting of power, gas and water supplies, etc. Such measures have variously involved government officials or their helpers, as well as persons hired by the 'demolition' offices who are usually in charge of the demolition process, as well as by property developers. Reflecting such experiences, the new 2011 Expropriation Regulation states that:

> Article 27(3): No unit or individual may compel the owner to relocate through violence, threat or other illegal means such as suspension of water, heat, gas, power supply and road access in violation of the

[17] Yves Cabannes and Eva Pils, in Cabannes *et al.*, *How People Face Evictions.*

[18] The *Chongqing Nail House* case was the best known example of this phenomenon. See Edward Cody, 'As a House Falls in China, Rights Debate Resonates', *Washington Post*, 4 April 2007, available at: www.washingtonpost.com/wp-dyn/content/article/2007/04/03/AR2007040300542.html.

[19] An example of retaliation is discussed in Eva Pils, 'Land Disputes, Rights Assertion and Social Unrest: A Case from Sichuan', *Columbia Journal of Asian Law*, 19 (2006), 365; reprinted as Hauser Global Law School Working Paper No. 07/05.

regulations. Construction units shall be prohibited from participating in relocation activities.[20]

In individual cases, more original methods, such as releasing scorpions[21] or snakes[22] in a neighbourhood with 'holdout' residents and nailing a live kitten to a neighbouring tree during the night to expose the neighbourhood to its anguished dying meows[23] have been reported.

Demolitions can be carried out forcibly if no agreement can be reached, on condition that forced demolition has been approved. Whereas previously it was possible to obtain a forced demolition decision from the government (in rural as well as urban contexts), the new Expropriation Regulation now requires that a court decision to carry out forced demolition must be obtained in those urban cases governed by the Regulation. In the context of forced demolition (*qiangchai*), particularly serious escalations into violence may occur. Examples include the already mentioned cases of self-immolation by individuals engaged in last-ditch efforts to protest, as well as violent clashes with eviction, demolition or construction teams. Whereas in the context of urban demolitions, conflicts usually take the form of brief, intense standoffs between one or a few resisting families, rural and suburban land expropriation can result in more protracted and much larger-scale violent clashes between eviction and construction teams and villagers.[24] The clash that is internationally most widely known is perhaps that of Wukan Village in Guangdong Province in late 2011 (discussed further below). The well-known eviction lawyer Wang Cailiang published a January

[20] 2011 国有土地上房屋征收与补偿条例 (State Council Regulation on Expropriation Of and Compensation for Buildings on State-owned Land), available at: www.gov.cn/zwgk/2011-01/21/content_1790111.htm.

[21] 'Sting Operation: Shenzhen Developer Scares Residents with Scorpions', 22 July 2011, available at: www.wantchinatimes.com/news-subclass-cnt.aspx?id=20110722000027&cid=1103.

[22] '湖南省衡阳市开发商逼人拆迁放毒蛇、挖大坑(图)' ('Property Developer in Hengyang, Hunan, Releases Scorpions and Digs Pit to Force Out Evictees'), 21 July 2009, available at: www.changzhutan.com/czt-bbsthread-11484.html (contains more pictures); CHRD (维权网), '城镇房屋暴力拆迁问题调查研究报告' ('Investigative Report on Violent Urban Demolitions'), 2 October 2009 (original link unavailable as of November 2009; report remains on file with author).

[23] Author conversation, summer 2011, Beijing.

[24] A well-documented example is that of Baihutou Village in Beihai in Guangxi. A clash in 2009 was captured on camera; it shows the enforcement personnel beating an elderly man with rods. He later succumbed to injuries from the beatings. Yi Ming, 'Defending Rights in Baihutou Village', *China Rights Forum* (2010), available at: www.hrichina.org/content/4960.

2011 report in which he claimed that the previous year, 2010, had been the worst so far for problems with demolitions.[25]

The urgency of these problems, and perhaps also the sense of powerlessness in addressing them through judicial process and the consequent desire to limit judicial responsibility, was poignantly conveyed in an SPC Urgent Notice on Resolutely Preventing Land Expropriations and Building Demolitions From Triggering Bad Incidents, dated 6 September 2011, which the Supreme People's Court addressed to lower courts. It stated with remarkable candour:

> In recent years, grievous incidents triggered by the enforcement of land expropriations and forced demolitions have occurred again and again. Some persons affected by enforcement have opposed [these measures] by self-immolation, jumping off buildings to commit suicide, and self-mutilation, whereas others have tried to disrupt enforcement by igniting gas tanks, spilling gasoline, throwing rocks and other methods. Some have encircled and attacked enforcement officials, creating mass incidents; and some court enforcement officers have inappropriately used weapons and caused casualties, etc.'[26]

A subsequent Judicial Interpretation in 2012 specified that prior to approving forced demolitions, the courts must, *inter alia*, make an assessment of the impact the demolition would have on social stability;[27] and a report in April 2013 suggested that the SPC had interpreted in the laws and regulations in a way that further restricted the courts' responsibility to approve forced demolition of 'illegal' structures.[28]

[25] Wang Cailiang, (王才亮), '2010 年中国拆迁年度报告' ('Annual Chaiqian Report 2010)', available at: www.caing.com/upload/chaiqianbaogao.pdf.

[26] 最高人民法院关于坚决防止土地征收、 房屋拆迁强制执行引发恶性事件的紧急通知 (SPC Urgent Notice on Resolutely Preventing Land Expropriations and Building Demolitions From Triggering Bad Incidents), 6 September 2011, available at: www.lawlib.com/law/law_view.asp?id=360163.

[27] Cf. Article 2(3) of 最高人民法院 关于办理申请人民法院强制执行国有土地上房屋征收补偿决定案件若干问题的规定 (SPC Decision on Handling Compensation for Expropriation in Cases of Applications to the People's Courts to Order Forced Demolitions), 27 February 2012, full text available at: http://news.sina.com.cn/c/2012-04-09/163724242861.shtml.

[28] 最高人民法院关于违法的建筑物、构筑物、设施等强制拆除问题的批复 (SPC Reply Regarding Issues Concerning the Forced Demolition of Illegally Erected Buildings and Structures), 27 March 2013, available at: www.chinacourt.org/law/detail/2013/03/id/146157.shtml; for critical comments, see '中国法院不再受理行政机关的强拆申请案 引发热议' ('SPC Not to Handle any more Cases of Administrative Department Applications to Order Forced Demolitions'), Radio Free Asia (Chinese desk), 3 April 2013, available at: www.rfa.org/mandarin/yataibaodao/renquanfazhi/cq-04032013105224.html.

Through the processes of rural–suburban land expropriation and urban demolition, the urban government ultimately acquires or 'recovers' (*shouhui*) land that is free of occupants and free of prior land-use rights. Such land is sometimes referred to as 'clean' or 'cleared' land.[29] After or prior to the 'clearing' of the land, the Land and State-owned Resources Administration Bureau, representing the state, grants new land-use rights, usually to property developers, and collects land transfer fees from them. The newly granted land-use rights, usually with a limited duration of up to seventy years, become the building blocks for China's urban real estate market.[30] Government revenue from land-use right transfer fees increased from 1.59 trillion RMB in 2009 to 2.7 trillion RMB (*c.* US$527 billion) in 2010 according to the Ministry of Land and State-owned Resources.[31]

The need for, and limits of, state-directed reform

The brief description above has already indicated legal, economic, social, and political problems that have arisen in the context of urban redevelopment and expansion in China.[32] They include coercive methods and violence, compensation, resettlement programmes, corruption on the part of property developers and governments, and denial of access to justice through the courts or through China's indigenous 'petitioning' process. There is also popular discontent about the way gains and losses resulting from urbanisation are distributed. With the exception of petition-related problems, the problems mentioned here also exist in

[29] 'Cleared land' (*jingdi* 净地) is juxtaposed with 'hairy land' (*maodi* 毛地). Chen Yongqing (程永清), 'The Granting of "Hairy Land" Presents Risks for Property Development Enterprises in China' ('毛地出让"中房地产开发企业的法律风险'), Anhui Legal Consultancy Website (安徽法律顾问网), available at: www.fl168.com/Lawyer9374/View/47281.

[30] Gregory Stein, 'Acquiring Land Use Rights in Today's China: A Snapshot from on the Ground', available at: http://papers.ssrn.com/sol3/papers.cfm?abstract_id=942813.

[31] 'China Land Sales Up 70% in 2010', *Straits Times*, 8 January 2011, available at: www.straitstimes.com/BreakingNews/Money/Story/STIStory_622009.html. Yet some experts believe that there is a dangerous real estate bubble. According to Yi Xianrong, an economist at the China Academy of Social Science, there were 64.5 million vacant apartments nationwide as of July 2010. See '64.5 million Homes Lying Vacant: Economist', *South China Morning Post*, 9 July 2010; conversation with Prof Yi, July 2010.

[32] See for NGO reports CHRD, 'Thrown Out: Human Rights Abuses in China's Breakneck Real Estate Development'. Meg Davis, 'Demolished: Forced Evictions and the Tenants' Rights Movement in China', Human Rights Watch, 2004, available at: www.hrw.org/reports/2004/china0304.

contexts in which the property regime is entirely different;[33] but it would be hard to point to a place where the scale of such problems has exceeded that of China. A recent report suggested that the amount of good-quality farmland, which is generally thought to be in short supply, expropriated in China (and eventually built on) amounted to 2.42 million hectares over the past ten years,[34] and it is estimated that nearly two-thirds of rural 'mass incidents' are related to land-takings and evictions.[35]

State-directed reforms for changing the written rules have been confined to what has been deemed realistically feasible. The officially tolerated zone of reform discussion contracted after the enactment of the 2007 PRC Property Rights Law. Prior to this, discussions as to whether ownership of land ought to be privatized were more intense, and included both calls for privatization,[36] and complaints that the consolidation of the then extant regime would violate socialist principles enshrined in the Constitution, as discussed below.

Recent reform proposals directly addressing the issue of urban and rural expropriations and evictions have, predictably, mainly addressed the definition of 'public interest' as a concept theoretically limiting the government's power to expropriate and carry out demolitions; procedures for expropriations and demolitions, for example, 'compensation before expropriation may begin', staying execution by bringing

33 Cabannes *et al.*, *How People Face Evictions*. See especially the description of such cases in Buenos Aires (Argentina), Porto Alegre (Brazil), Durban (South Africa), Istanbul (Turkey), Karachi (Pakistan) and Santo Domingo (Dominican Republic).

34 Bai Chong'en, Cai Hongbin, Huang Haizhou, Li Bo, Ma Jun, Wei Jianing, Wu Ge, Xu Lin, Yuan Li, Zhou Chengjun and Zhou Hanhua (白重恩、蔡洪滨、黄海洲、李波、马骏、魏加宁、伍戈、徐林、袁力、周诚君、周汉华), '土地制度改革与新型城镇化' ('Chinese Land Reform and a New Form of Urbanisation'),'published as a draft for discussion at a gathering of a group known as 'China Forum 40' (CF40), 27 May 2013, available at: www.yicai.com/news/2013/05/2734345.html; also Victoria Ruan, 'Debts Weigh Down New Push for Urban Reform', 6 June 2013, available at: www.scmp.com/business/economy/article/1254145/debts-weigh-down-new-vision-urban-push.

35 See, for example, www.chinadaily.com.cn/cndy/2011-02/18/content_12036442.htm; Cary Huang, 'Farm Seizures Sow Seeds of Social Unrest', *South China Morning Post*, 31 October 2011.

36 See Cao Siyuan (曹思源), 'Revising the Constitution, Protecting Everyone's Legal Rights" ('修改宪法, 保护每个人的合法权利'), September 2003, available at: http://copies.sinoshu.com/copy3054017/. Yale-based Chen Zhiwu argues similarly in 'Returning Land to the Peasants: a Dialogue between Chen Zhiwu (陈志武) and Yu Jianrong (于建嵘)', ('对话陈志武:把地权还给农民'), 14 February 2008, available at: www.infzm.com/review/pltt/200802/t20080204_36453.shtml.

administrative litigation', provisions for compensation for evictees; and expanding mechanisms that allow rural land-use right-holders to transfer land or buildings for the purpose of urban residential use. Even one of the most vocal and independent advocates for change from within the system, Yu Jianrong, has made it clear that he does not support a change that would fundamentally diminish the role of the state in urban expansion and renewal by allowing rural communities or individuals directly to negotiate the transfer of their share in collectively owned land to those willing to buy for non-agrarian purposes of construction. In an interview given in 2012, for example, Yu Jianrong insists that the rights pertaining to land must be 'clarified' (*quequan*), and that such rights included the right to dispose, but he rejects changes that would leave the state out of the process of land transformation from rural into urban land:

> In reality, the problem is not that we need to carve out the Government altogether. The Government should also benefit. We can't refuse to let the Government have one little bit. Since it has interests [at stake] it must also have rights. The problem is . . . rather, that the interests and power of the Government must have limitations/must be of a limited nature.[37]

Recent reforms have included the 2011 Expropriation Regulations,[38] which can be taken as a representative product of the restricted debates of recent years. It has for the first time defined types of construction deemed to be in the 'public interest' (Article 8; see below). It has also prescribed that demolitions must not be carried out before compensation, stipulated a clear requirement that compensation must not be lower than market value (Article 19), provided for evictees' optional right to get 'house property rights exchange' instead of monetary compensation (Article 21), and put the courts exclusively in charge of approving forced demolitions (Article 28). They also state that administrative complaints not only against compensation decisions, but also against the urban government's expropriation as such are allowed 'in accordance with law' (Articles 14, 27).

Through these changes, the 2011 Regulation has shifted bureaucratic responsibilities for the expropriation process away from government agencies in charge of land administration and construction towards the

[37] '于建嵘:'不应高估乌坎事件的意义' ('Yu Jianrong: Wukan Incident Should Not be Overrated'), *21st Century Economic Report* (21世纪经济报道), 8 March 2012, available at: http://news.ifeng.com/opinion/sixiangpinglun/detail_2012_03/08/13054517_0.shtml.

[38] 2011 国有土地上房屋征收与补偿条例 (State Council Regulation on Expropriation Of and Compensation for Buildings on State-owned Land), available at: www.gov.cn/zwgk/2011-01/21/content_1790111.htm.

courts, perhaps in the hope that the courts will be better able to enforce legal provisions intended to protect the rights of evictees. It has also, by specifying instances of expropriations that would not be in the public interest, formally narrowed the scope of legitimate expropriations. It is noteworthy that the new Expropriation Regulation no longer contains provisions for those who are evictees without being the owner of buildings; and at this point it is not clear how these residents are to be taken care of.

This means that the 2011 Regulation has transferred institutional responsibility to an institution that is extremely unfit to bear the burden. Not only are courts responsible for issuing forced demolition orders, but they are also the court police, due to the general institutional structure of enforcement, involved in carrying out forced demolition decisions. Yet courts in China are notoriously weak institutions, under the budgetary control of local governments, and 'receiving supervision' from a variety of institutions including local people's congresses as well as Party organisations such as the political-legal committees. Experience so far suggests that courts are too weak to become involved in the protection of property or other rights of evictees. Even the assessment provided by the Supreme People's Court in its September 2011 Urgent Notice reflects this experience, as it conveys anxiety about the ability of the judiciary to cope with its responsibilities under the new Regulation. Neither is there anything in the new Regulation indicating that this might change. The changes made, which focus on 'public interest', legal definition of compensation standards, and rules concerning the process of expropriation and demolition, are unlikely to be helpful for reasons further specified below.

First, narrowing the definition of 'public interest' to non-commercial purposes can only reduce the volume of expropriations (the number of expropriation decisions as well as the number of people and the amount of land affected) if there is a viable alternative that property developers can choose when they want to build, for instance, office buildings or upmarket residential buildings. Currently, there is often no alternative that is both commercially attractive and legal. Theoretically, property developers may acquire land-use rights through private transactions from already existent urban land-use right-holders. But in many situations, it is easier, cheaper and quicker for property developers to rely on the mechanisms of expropriation and 'resumption of ownership' described above, that is, to rely on public power and its enforcement mechanisms to get land cheaply.

From the perspective of the state and developers, therefore, demolition and relocation *must* be 'in the public interest'. Ren Zhiqiang, the chairman of the board of directors of a real estate company, Beijing Huayuan, was quoted in 2010 as follows:

> There is no such thing as demolition and relocation that is not in the public interest. As long as it is [for the purpose of] urban construction, it is in the public interest.[39]

To judge by the scope of expropriations and demolitions, as well as by the way in which authorities handle complaints against expropriation decisions, Ren Zhiqiang was articulating a widely shared view, and had a clear point. How could any urban construction project ever be judged not to be for a 'public interest demand'? As long as urban construction remains effectively premised on expropriation, denying the legality of a particular expropriation project would effectively block the planned follow-up construction project. Yet should China have *no* (new) luxury compounds, commercial office buildings and shopping malls at all? This does not seem plausible, even though it is not plausible either to declare all these projects to be in the public interest. In this awkward situation, no further definition of 'public interest', however carefully drafted and narrow, is likely to change the current practice of cavalier disregard for this legal requirement. Moreover, the Regulation, in its definition of 'public interest', contains notoriously elastic categories, such as 'renewal of dangerous and dilapidated buildings' (Article 8 clause 5), and envisages the possibility of creating further categories through laws and regulations (Article 8 clause 6).

Second, since, as mentioned, the judiciary is financially dependent on local governments, constitutionally obligated to report to local people's congresses, in fact, answerable to the Party which applies direct influence in some cases, and plagued by problems of corruption, it is unlikely to withstand government pressure. As a result, already existing statutory rules designed to protect citizens against arbitrary government power can be hard to enforce through judicial processes, and the rules and regulations imposing restrictions on any of the actors in the urban construction and renewal process are frequently circumvented.

39 Yang Ming (杨明), Chairman of Beijing Huayuan Group Ren Zhiqiang (北京华远集团董事长任志强☺ says: '不存在非公共利益拆迁 只要是城建都是公共利益', *Oriental Outlook Weekly* (瞭望东方周刊), available at: http://finance.ifeng.com/opinion/zjgc/20100210/1822226.shtml.

Constitutional or international norms[40] that are designed to safeguard individual rights and provide a standard to which other legal rules should conform, do not play any role in legal practice. An example of judicial weakness is the frequent problem of courts refusing to 'file' (accept for litigation) cases submitted to them. Courts come under pressure not to file cases or not to make decisions obstructing the development process. The fact that courts are controlled is well illustrated also by the Urgent Notice, which instructs courts to obtain approval for issuing forced demolition orders in certain cases not only from their superior courts, but also from the local Party committees,[41] affirming a chain of command that everybody knows exists, and at the same time hinting at the Party's ultimate responsibility for the social consequences of expropriation.

A self-published book by a Beijing evictee narrating his own and others' *chaiqian* experiences in recent years quotes, for instance, Beijing western district court division head Judge Yang Ai as saying, on 28 June 1995, that:

> In accordance with directions from above, in handling this kind of administrative litigation cases, our principle is 'to support the administration'.[42]

According to reports, a 'Document No. 106' of the Beijing High Court instructed courts in 1995 not to hear (or file, *li'an*) any cases related to *chaiqian*, and in author conversations similar examples from other cities were mentioned. The 1995 'internal' directive reportedly circulated in Beijing is now obsolete.[43] But to judge by what evictee protesters complain about, court inertia and weakness have remained a problem. For example, a photo of a protest graffiti taken in 2007 in Beijing reads:

[40] See, for example, Office of the High Commissioner for Human Rights (OHCHR), Fact Sheet on the Right to Adequate Housing, No. 21, Rev.1, available at: www.ohchr.org/Documents/Publications/FS21_rev_1_Housing_en.pdf, and in Chinese at: www.ohchr.org/Documents/Publications/FS21_rev_1_Housing_ch.pdf.

[41] SPC Urgent Notice on Resolutely Preventing Land Expropriations and Building Demolitions From Triggering Bad Incidents, Nos. 5 and 6, respectively.

[42] Monograph entitled '我所经历的拆迁' (on file with author), 2010, p. 28.

[43] See for a discussion, for example, 'Shanghai Xuhui District Evictee' (上海徐汇区征地强拆户) blog, '司法、法院、法官在拆迁诉讼中:北京万人诉讼和京高法106号文' ('The Ten-thousand-person Litigation and the Beijing High Court Document No 106'),' 15 January 2011, available at: http://blog.sina.com.cn/s/blog_599b3e430100onzj.html.

> The Courts have turned into demolishers colluding in compulsory purchase and sale. 'Handling matters in accordance with law' is a nice phrase. But they won't look at what's written down in black and white. The laws protect the common people. The courts protect the developers. Homeless in Harmonious Society. Wrong – Wrong –Wrong.[44]

The refusal of courts to file cases in demolition and land-related conflicts, especially, continues to be a great problem. A 2011 campaign by Shanghai activist Feng Zhenghu based on the slogan of 'I Want To File My Case' was themed around the problem of courts refusing to file land-grab and eviction cases.[45]

Third, from the perspective of the state, the problems arising in the context of urbanisation have long been seen as problems of social management and planning, not as problems of protecting evictee rights. The 'planning' state view of land, essentially envisaging plots of already razed to the ground, *tabulae rasae* to be built on,[46] is both utilitarian and authoritarian or positivistic. It assumes unquestioningly the authority of the state to make decisions about the land occupied by its citizens, because the Constitution and further laws have stipulated 'socialist public ownership', and assumes that such decisions will be good ones if they serve in a general way the welfare of all, as understood on the state's owns terms. Problems that arise cannot be fully understood as rights problems from this perspective; and this characteristic of the state view tends to undermine legal concepts that make sense only in the context of rights, such as the right against unlawful expropriation as an aspect of property rights. Instead, evictees will be generally exhorted – for instance, by banners and slogans displayed at eviction sites – to subordinate their individuated goals and interests to those that allegedly serve 'the Nation'. Official slogans displayed at eviction sites read: 'Support the National Construction Project',[47] 'Thoroughly Implement the Scientific Development Perspective, Build a World City with Chinese

44 Picture on file with author.

45 See, for instance, '上海数百人到高级法院抗议' ('A Hundred Shanghai Citizens go to Court to Demand that Their Cases be Filed'), with a photo of protesters holding a banner that reads, 'Thugs are everywhere/No secure residence/Return Our Homes', 19 May 2011, available at: www.epochtimes.com/gb/11/7/14/n3314494.htm.

46 Hua Xinmin (华新民), '城市土地产权 – 从历史到今天' ('Property Rights in Urban Land: History and Present'), 20 October 2007, transcript available at: www.21ccom.net/articles/zgyj/ggzhc/article_201001205159.html.

47 Banner displayed on condemned buildings at an eviction site in Beijing, July 2009 (picture on file with author).

Characteristics!', 'Advance in Solidarity, Revive China, Love the Motherland, Build the Motherland!'[48] and so on.

Social management and planning is today largely determined by two needs: on the one hand, there is the (perceived) need to generate government revenue and GDP growth, and the various planning considerations it introduces. This aspect of the state view is also associated with the notion of a 'scientific development perspective' and with the balancing of needs for growth and the preservation of arable land.[49] On the other hand, there is the (perceived) need for 'social stability preservation', arising more clearly the more that land-grabs and demolitions trigger protest and unrest.[50] Consequently, the state seems willing to address problems to the extent to which it is necessary to prevent instability, but not necessarily beyond that point. For example, a demolition campaign preparatory to urban construction may be temporarily halted or slowed down if it has led to vocal protest and threatens to inflame further 'unharmonious' citizen action.[51] The SPC's Urgent Notice enjoins all courts to 'pay great attention to and strengthen your sense of urgency and crisis'.[52] It goes on to emphasise that cases of expropriation concern 'the masses' vital interests and social stability'.

Further technical implications of the state view explain why the courts are often not capable of protecting the individual rights and legitimate interests mentioned in the SPC's Urgent Notice against certain types of infringement. For instance, courts may invoke Article 12(2) of the Administrative Litigation Law to argue that they do not have authority to review the legality of 'normative documents', that is, general administrative decisions issued by administrative departments;[53] it is unclear

[48] Billboards (Beijing Taoranting), January 2013 (picture on file with author).

[49] In the context of urbanisation encroaching upon formerly rural or suburban areas, this is sometimes framed in terms of a tension between 'preserving the red line' (the total area of farmland that must be preserved) and 'preserving growth', Pils, 'Waste No Land'.

[50] Renewed acknowledgements of the fact that land-grabs and demolitions are a prime cause of such unrest are issued periodically. See, for example, Huang, 'Farm Seizures Sow Seeds of Social Unrest'.

[51] An example for this is the case of a relatively small development affecting over 1,000 households in an inner Beijing district. Author conversations with evictees in an area in Xuanwu district, Beijing, 2009–2010.

[52] SPC Urgent Notice on Resolutely Preventing Land Expropriations and Building Demolitions From Triggering Bad Incidents.

[53] This is one of the problems discussed, for instance, in Pils, 'Land Disputes, Rights Assertion and Social Unrest'.

whether Article 14 of the Expropriation Regulation has brought any change in this context.

Most importantly, the courts are apparently not even meant to be able to *stop* unlawful expropriations. This author is not aware of an entrenched practice whereby the mere discovery that an urban development project was illegal caused a state agency – a court of law, say – to revoke or annul the relevant government decision and order the return of any buildings or land-use rights to the former residents. In some reported cases, decisions of annulment have been made,[54] or building projects have been stopped or even reversed,[55] but no land or buildings were returned to the original owners or residents. A partial explanation for this phenomenon lies in the fact that applications for administrative or judicial review of demolition orders do not stay enforcement of such orders.[56] The 2011 Expropriation Regulation has not clearly changed this (for urban cases, even less for rural ones), even though scholars pushing for genuine improvements were calling for change. As Professor Jiang Ming'an aptly put it:

> If practices continue as before, when the moment an expropriator was sued, it needed merely an application by the government and the court would immediately demolish forcibly [i.e., make an order for forcible demolition], it will remain difficult to restore the rights and interests [affected by the expropriation even if it is found to be illegal].
>
> Therefore the new regulation ought to establish a system of automatic stay of enforcement proceedings by court litigation, with exceptions only for urgent situations. Otherwise, if prior to having got a final decision in the case, you insist on forcible demolition, the person who is affected by the expropriation and who is insisting on their rights may resort to violent resistance or self-immolation. He/she will not, just because you

[54] See, for example, the 2002 decision, 宣懿成等18人诉衢州市国土资源局收回土地使用权行政争议案 (*Xuan Yicheng and 17 Other Residents* v. *Quzhou Municipal Bureau of Land and Resource*), seeking revocation of administrative decision to resume land-use rights, available at: www.lawinfochina.com/display.aspx?lib=case&id=540. It resulted in the annulment of the 'notice of revocation' (*shouhui*) of an urban land-use right, but was not connected with a decision that the land-use right was to be returned to the original resident.

[55] Cf, for example, '北京皇城内四合院祖宅业主砸开围墙要回家/视频' ('Beijing Dongcheng Former Residents Seek to Force their Way into Residential Compound Replacing their Homes'), 26 April 2011, *Boxun*, available at: www.boxunblog.com/2011/04/blog-post_899.html.

[56] But see in detail, 'One Man's Freedom is Hope for Homeowners', *South China Morning Post*, 31 October 2010.

> are a Court, and not a government agency, be patient and compliant. Thus forcible demolition tragedies will remain hard to avoid.[57]

The September 2011 SPC Urgent Notice merely advises that 'on principle', 'advance enforcement' of forced demolition orders ought not be approved in cases where a case against the expropriation or demolition has already been filed, and that approval must be given only with approval from the next higher ranking court.[58] It remains to be seen how 'on principle' will be interpreted by local courts, which remain financially dependent on local governments.

In rural areas, reform has been more halting than in the urban areas, even though a reform of the Land Administration Law is being discussed. On 12 October 2008, the Party Central Committee issued a Decision in which it began to envision a major reform of the existing system for rural land-use rights, and suggested that in the future a rural land-use right for construction might be created and that there ought to be a future 'unified' nationwide market for land-use rights for construction.[59] This could be read as a step towards strengthening rural land-use rights by making them resemble urban land-use rights.[60]

Since the October 2008 proposal up to the time of writing, the state has remained largely intransigent to the option of distributing control over rural land away from the state to the citizens. There are indications that academic debates and experiments about raising the 'market transferability' of rural land-use rights are ongoing, however.[61] Media

[57] Jiang Ming'an, 'Forcible Demolition Must Satisfy Three Preconditions Before "Improvement" Could Happen', *Beijing News*, 17 December 2010 (姜明安,司法强拆实现"进步"须满足三个前提,新京报,2010年12月17日), available at: http://article.chinalawinfo.com/article_print.asp?articleid=57997; see also http://opinion.people.com.cn/GB/13507680.html.

[58] SPC Urgent Notice on Resolutely Preventing Land Expropriations and Building Demolitions From Triggering Bad Incidents. A further issue is that courts may not accept cases for litigation (*li'an*).

[59] 中共中央关于推进农村改革发展若干重大问题决定 (Decision of the CCP on several major issues concerning the promotion of rural reform), 12 October 2008, available at: www.gov.cn/jrzg/2008-10/19/content_1125094.htm.

[60] Wu Bin, 'China's New Blueprint for Rural Reform and Development', December 2008, available at: www.nottingham.ac.uk/Chinese/people/bin.wu.

[61] Professor Zhou Qiren's research on pilot projects undertaken, for instance, in the environs of Chengdu, discussed at a public lecture at Renmin University Conference in 2011, has shown that a variety of mechanisms have been created to allow for (temporary) transfers of rural land-use rights for residential projects, without changing the land into state-owned land (i.e., without expropriation): lease (租用); auction (拍卖); land certificate auction (地票拍卖); consensual transfer (协议转让); transfer within a collective group of villagers (村民小组之

discussion of an 'impending' reform of the Land Administration Law suggests the possibility of letting rural residents participate in land transactions for the purpose of commercial property development, in addition to raising the legally required compensation for rural land expropriation;[62] but no such reform was passed at the subsequent NPC session in March 2013.[63]

The main challenge in so 'liberating' land for 'free circulation' on the nationwide real estate market lies in the fact that it could undermine the viability of collective rural landownership, a constitutional principle; and there is no indication that this form of ownership could be abandoned under the new law. A potential advantage would be that such a new mechanism would present an alternative to state expropriation, as well as to an increasingly complex set of 'grey' market practices, which are discussed below in section three. Yet this alternative, in turn, would become commercially relevant only if it offered better deals to property developers than expropriation, and if the legal scope of expropriation could be effectively limited. Prior to the enactment of the new Expropriation Regulation, a demolition lawyer had submitted a proposal for a new law comprehensively governing expropriations, both rural–suburban and urban. Among other things, this proposal contained a negative definition of projects that ought to be legally defined as not being in the public interest.[64]

In sum, the very proximity of the state to 'demolition and relocation', expropriation and urban construction, the comparative weakness of the judiciary, and the overwhelming interests connected with urban construction make it difficult to prevent or correct wrongs occurring in this context. Legislative or regulatory reforms introduced thus far have not touched the fundamental distribution of property rights that appear to make expropriations and demolitions of urban buildings so easy; even

间转让); minor property right (小产权); waiver of compensation (放弃补偿); construction of several buildings together with rural resident, one of which goes to urban buyer/investor (灭后联建,组内联建), (增减挂钩指标). For details of the conference see at: www.infzm.com/content/59110.

62 '中国土地征收补偿标准或将提高10倍' (Compensation for Land Expropriation May be Raised Tenfold'), 29 November 2012, available at: http://news.163.com/12/1129/02/8HEQ8O1B00014AED.html, quoting Professor Jiang Ming'an, among others. Cf. also Bai Chong'en *et al.*, 'Chinese Land Reform and a New Form of Urbanisation'.

63 Ruan, 'Debts Weigh Down New Push for Urban Reform'.

64 Wang Cailiang (王才良), '不动产征收征用管理法(立法建议稿)' ('Draft Regulation on the Acquisition and Expropriation of Immovable Property'), available at: http://policy.caing.com/2010-10-19/100190257.html.

less do reform proposals concerning immoveable property rights, expropriations and demolitions address the institutional and systemic problems affecting the judiciary and related authorities. Ongoing reform discussion suggests that the state is willing to contemplate certain modifications to the current rules, cemented in the 2007 Property Rights Law, that put it so firmly in control of all land.

Gradual discrediting of the state view? Controlled debates in domestic officialdom, academia and media

The preceding brief exposition of the narrow confines of state-approved reform has already indicated a problem that is also reflected in much of the debates within 'the state' – amongst the officials and institutions of the party-state. These debates tend to portray problems as the result either of individual corruption or of institutional problems with local administration; and so far as they reach beyond recriminations for rule infraction and corruption, they tend to advocate solutions that redistribute responsibilities and powers within the institutions of the (party-) state. The 'solution' to the problem of forcible demolition in urban areas 'by the judiciary' is an example for this strategy. Since it entails merely the internal reorganisation of state power over land in urban areas, it leaves the state view intact – even if the courts, as opposed to the judiciary, are put in control of expropriation processes, the state can continue to see itself as custodian of the land that might otherwise be privately monopolised and/or wasted. As discussed, there is little risk of losing control through a transfer of decision-making power to the judiciary, as long as courts remain weak and largely unable to protect citizens' rights against government agencies.

Perhaps in consequence of its fundamental inability to rectify past expropriation and demolition injustice and to prevent further wrongs, the state view and the laws and regulations that informed as well as reflected the state view have gradually come to be understood to be inherently contradictory. To some extent, reform discussions have themselves had this effect, especially where they have remained abortive.

The most important example of this is probably the discussions prior to the enactment of the 2007 Property Rights Law, a piece of legislation that had been in the making for thirteen years. The adequate protection of private property rights interpreted along liberal lines, both through statutory legislation and constitutional amendment, and both in urban and rural areas, was among the core concerns of liberal reformers for years, as comments made by Professor Jiang Ping of China University of Politics and Law, amongst others, well illustrate.[65] At a 25 February 2006 conference convened by the scholars involved in the process of drafting the new property law, the conference organisers stated:

> It can be said that 1.3 billion people's wisdom and enthusiasm for the *Draft Property Law*, which is soon to come into existence, has already found expression in the process of requesting views and suggestions on the *Draft Property Law* [from the public]. The *Draft Property Law* ... represents the brilliant political decisions of three generations of Party Central leaders[66] ... The facts prove that today, as the *Reform and Opening Up* process has already scored great victories and as the building up of a socialist market economy has swiftly progressed, the *Property Law* must be enacted soon. The *Draft Property Law* is a monument and conclusion to twenty years of *Reform and Opening Up*, to socialist market economy, and to the construction of a democratic legal system, as well as to the Sixteenth [Communist] Party Congress![67]

Yet by the time the Property Rights Law was finalised and ready for adoption by the NPC, it was clear that it would fundamentally be a mere consolidation of the existing property regime, at least as far as rights pertaining to land and buildings were concerned. This meant that it could not be genuinely expected to afford substantially better protection against expropriation. From the perspective of the present discussion, this is at least in part due to the fact that the Property Rights Law is merely pseudo-liberal. It adopts the language of liberal constitutional protections against expropriations, but, as argued above, these protections remain ineffective in the context of the state-centred PRC property regime and lack of judicial independence.

From the perspective of other critics, the root problem consisted in the fact that economic liberalisation had allowed for the creation of property markets in the first place. Conservative Marxist critics, notable among them being Professor Gong Xiantian of Peking University Law School, argued that this violated the Constitution's commitment to the idea of socialist public ownership; so strong were public criticisms of the

[65] In a 2002 interview, Professor Jiang Ping expressed optimism that strict adherence to the principles of legality, to procedural rules, to a public interest criterion, and full compensation in expropriation would provide sufficient protection.

[66] The generations meant here are those of Deng, Jiang and Hu/Wen, leaving out Mao.

[67] Zhao Lei (赵蕾), '辩论物权法' ('Debating the Real Property Law'), *Southern Weekend* (南方周末), 10 March 2006, available at: www.nanfangdaily.com.cn/southnews/jwxy/200603100073.asp.

Property Rights Law draft in 2006 that the enactment of the new law was postponed by a year until 2007. This failure to enact the law must have rattled the authorities, who are little used to such resistance to major legislative projects.

In the author's judgement, by the time the law was finally passed, celebration of this new legislation as a milestone in China's legal development was subdued by an already palpable resentment towards the legal regime it cemented. Even though the thirteen-year reform debate over property law reform had resulted in a piece of NPC legislation, it had failed to address central concerns that had been articulated in the long process of reform debate. Whatever one's views of Marxism, some of Gong Xiantian's comments rang decidedly true – for instance, his wry observation that in a situation where the party-state controlled and disposed of state-owned assets to generate revenue:

> This has led to a situation in which, as some members of the masses have put it, the 'Communist Party' [i.e., in Chinese, 'Communal Ownership Party' or *gongchandang*] has turned into a 'Private Property Party' [*sichandang*]![68]

They rang true, not because the Party had genuinely embraced private landownership, but because it had embraced the idea of putting itself in control of a vast amount of land that, under the new principles established through 'Reform and Opening', could acquire private market value.

Another example for thus far abortive reform debates is the debate over rural land-use rights. In June 2008, the progressive *Southern Weekend* ran an article that questioned whether the central state's proclaimed goals of preserving agrarian land to maintain a national supply of grain, protecting the interests of the rural population, ensuring economic growth could be in tension:

> These three goals [of the Central Government] are to some extent consistent, but there are also inconsistencies amongst them. For instance, maintaining grain supply is a State goal but not a goal of the peasants or of local governments. In a certain sense, preserving agrarian land means

[68] Gong Xiantian (巩献田), '部违背宪法和背离社会主义基本原则的《物权法(草案)》–为《宪法》第12条和86年《民法通则》第73条的废除写的公开信' ('A Draft of the Property Law that is Contrary To The Constitution and the Basic Principles of Socialism', an open letter to denounce the annulment of Article 12 of the Constitution and Article 73 of the General Principle of Civil Law, available at: http://article.chinalawinfo.com/Article_Detail.asp?ArticleID=32266.

> only letting the peasants engage in agriculture and is in conflict with the peasants' desire to participate in industrialisation and urbanisation; moreover, there can be conflict between the goals of preserving agrarian land and increasing construction land.
>
> So far as local governments are concerned, they want to achieve goals of growth and of political performance assessment, that is, both increase construction land to boost their local industrialisation and economic growth, and also to realise financial and profit targets to increase the income of the local revenues and local financing. These goals are completely identical. By speeding up the change of use of agrarian land and increasing construction land they can both boost economic growth and increase their revenue.[69]

The officially tolerated public discussion reflected in these comments was followed by the already mentioned October 2008 Party central decision to liberalise the circulation of rural land-use rights – but then, that decision itself failed to be implemented; and the attitude of the state towards fundamental reform has remained highly intransigent.

In recent years, the central state's focus on GDP growth has come more and more under attack. Even the state's highest ranking officials have begun to question the strong focus on GDP growth of earlier years, as Premier Wen Jiabao did in February 2011 on a widely reported occasion.[70] Yet while this conspicuous criticism of an exclusive focus on GDP growth pushed the boundaries of officially tolerated discussion a little further, it did not demolish the boundaries themselves; and public discussion remains constrained in China's authoritarian political system.

Only occasionally are deep contentions exposed to full public view. One case of controversy, in which the state view's radical utilitarianism was exposed but also defended, involved Professor Yu Jianrong of the Chinese Academy of Social Sciences, who was invited on 11 November 2011 to give a lecture to 700 county cadres in Wanzai, Hunan. Professor Yu chose to discuss the topic of popular protest against forced demolition, reportedly pointing out that the county he was in had a policy of dealing with petitioning in Beijing: such petitioners would be

[69] Zhang Shuguang (张曙光), '如何破解中央与地方土地博弈困居' ('How to Break Through the Impasse of Central–Local Contention Around Land'), 4 June 2008, available at: www.infzm.com/content/12915.

[70] See, for example, 'Premier Wen: China Targets Slower Growth to Focus on People', *China Daily*, 27 February 2011: '"Therefore, I tell local officials, wouldn't it be better if we construct fewer high buildings and spend the funds for expanding the urban scale on raising living standards?" [Wen] said', available at: http://news.xinhuanet.com/english2010/china/2011-02/27/c_13752052.htm.

reprimanded and fined the first time, detained the second time, and sent to 'Re-education through Labour' the third time, in accordance with a local government practice understood to be common. A flustered county secretary challenged the professor during lunch after the lecture:

> "Teacher Yu, you are quite an expert. I didn't know you would come today to talk about these things. It was really bad for me. I told the lowest level village cadres to come."
>
> "This small county of yours will build a 23-square-kilometer development zone. When the people petition you sentence them to labor re-education. This isn't reasonable. Preferably, you should develop a bit slower. It doesn't make any difference."
>
> "Without development, would you have freeways? Could you stay in hotels?" Chen became excited. "If we didn't do it like this, what would you intellectuals be eating?"[71]

Their exchange ended when Professor Jianrong reportedly hit the county secretary in anger, and stormed out in the middle of the lunch. He later commented on the incident on his microblog.[72] It was widely discussed on the Internet because it had clearly touched a raw nerve. Who could have entirely refuted the angry official's rebuke?

After another forced demolition incident in Yihuang County government malfeasance was exposed and punished, an anonymous official from that county wrote a Letter to the Editor in which he made a similar point, complaining that his hometown had been made a scapegoat:

> In truth, it is not the government's aim to force a demolition. The cost of development must be considered ... Urban development requires vast amounts of demolition. If the government pampers individual

[71] 'Everybody has a Microphone', *Southern Metropolitan Daily*, translated by Don Weinland for *China Digital Times*, available at: http://chinadigitalspace.net/2010/12/yu-jianrong. See also Li Yihao, 'My Anger is not Directed Against Particular Individuals', 22 November 2010, available at: www.rmlt.com.cn/qikan/2010-11-22/12584.html.

[72] Weibo: 'Arrived at Wanxian County last night. Gave lecture to more than 700 people today and urged people not to demolish the homes of the commoner. At lunch, a county secretary claimed that demolition must be carried out for the purpose of development. I was furious and said that modern society was built on the foundation of the protection of basic individual rights. He retorted that "if we didn't do it like this, what would you intellectuals be eating?" I was outraged and left the lunch.' ('昨晚深夜赶到万载县,今天给七百多人讲课,号召大家不要去拆老百姓房子。刚才吃饭,县委书记言称,为了发展,就得拆。我怒言,现代社会就是以保障个人基本权利为基础,你们这些人最要做的就是确保个人权利。他说,如果没有我们这些县委书记这样干,你们这些知识分子吃什么。我一怒推椅而起,离席而去。'). Cited, for example, at: http://news.xinhuanet.com/local/2010-11/02/c_12729963.htm.

> homeowners, and increases compensation standards accordingly, then the government cannot afford development . . . To some degree, we could say the Yihuang event is a scapegoat for China's urbanization. When so many are denouncing the forced demolition policy, it seems that we all ignore a basic fact – everyone is the beneficiary of forced demolition policies.[73]

A lawyer's riposte to the anonymous county official was printed in the same magazine:

> My question is, can big government really shape a new China? China's reform and opening up policy is a path toward a market economy, meaning the government gradually pulls out of economic regulation. China is playing catch-up with developed countries and in implementing a national rejuvenation. For that goal, any measures and policies can be justified. The most important of these has been the growth of Local Government Inc. with unlimited power.[74]

As the next section shows, citizen activists campaigning for their own or others' rights in urban renewal processes not only complain about illegality in the narrow terms of existing laws and regulations. They are also increasingly ready to address the deeper, political root causes of property injustices.

Summary

The state view of property and ownership over land is dominated by its self-perception as custodian of national goals with regard to land. The power of the state over how land is used and who has access to it is consequently overbearing. While the state view was once grounded in socialist perspectives on ownership and property, today's formal recognition of individuated property rights, as well as the reality of the urban real estate market, have rendered socialist justifications of the state's control of land unconvincing. Control today is justified to some extent by utilitarian goals of economic growth to which individual rights and interests may be sacrificed, and by political authoritarianism. Growing problems with expropriations have greatly weakened popular acceptance of this regime, however; and they have also weakened the legitimacy of

[73] 'A Local Official Argues for Forced Demolition', *Caixin Magazine*, 12 October 2010, available at: http://english.caing.com/2010-10-12/100187862_1.html.

[74] 'A Local Official Argues for Forced Demolition', *Caixin Magazine*, 15 October 2010, available at: http://english.caing.com/2010-10-15/100188685_2.html.

the state view, even as both the local and central state's dependence on (legal and illegal) revenue from land makes thorough reform of the existing property regime unlikely.

Popular views challenging the state view, and demolition and expropriation practices

Turning to examine the content of actual claims advanced by urban and rural Chinese evictees, one will note that the range of arguments they use extends far beyond the existing framework of statutory and, indeed, constitutional law, and draws on diverse and not necessarily coherent additional historical and political arguments. The context in which such activism occurs is generally referred to as *weiquan*, rights-defending. This general practice has been discussed in a growing body of literature, and *weiquan* practices themselves have developed and changed. While *weiquan* is in some contexts and by some authors viewed primarily as the use of 'authoritatively' condoned rules and rights that can be found in the PRC's many laws and regulations ('rightful resistance', 'rules consciousness'),[75] *weiquan* has increasingly also meant resistance on grounds of political principles and rights-based opposition to government, as citizens have realised that ultimately what would help them would be a better political structure capable of protecting their rights.

The discourses and individual arguments considered in the following sections involve large numbers of people. Some arguments are put forth on the Internet, and it is hard to gauge how many thousands of Chinese readers may be following the discussions they trigger. (Professor Yu Jianrong's twitter account, for example, has over 100,000 followers.) Some other comments considered here consist in lone graffiti that may well have fallen victim to demolition already at the time of writing. Some of the arguments come directly from evictees, whose social background and individual experiences vary greatly, depending on factors such as gender, age, education and income.

The number of persons affected by expropriations and evictions are so great that no easy typologies are possible. Casual comments on the identities of evictee protesters and limited personal observation suggest

[75] This, however, is what Elizabeth Perry and Yu Jianrong have recently argued, characterising Chinese people's opposition, for example, to land-grabs as rules-based more than rights-based. Elizabeth Perry, 'A New Rights Consciousness?' *Journal of Democracy*, 20(3) (2009), 17–20.

a certain prevalence of middle-aged women taking lead roles in protest actions. Some such women's biographies suggest that they started by trying to defend their own homes against eviction, before moving on to helping others to defend their rights:

> I feel that having gathered so much experience with *chaiqian* I need to help other evictees who don't necessarily understand these issues . . . and land is so especially important for the peasants . . . if I can help just one person, I will.[76]

Other comments come from persons not immediately affected by expropriations and evictions, but from rights advocates, lawyers, journalists, scholars and artists interested in understanding their causes and – often – in helping through their own advocacy.

Due to the high price the Chinese political system exacts on organised resistance of any kind, these individuals are in communication with each other, especially in the age of the Internet; and the idea of increasing their influence through organising themselves into groups comes naturally. In village communities, groups are already in place, and resistance can be organised by influential figures within the rural community, as was the case, for example, in Zigong;[77] or it may even draw on the figure of an elected village head, as was the case, for example, in Beihai. In such rural locations, the resisters' identity collects naturally around the place they seek to protect – the village or group of villages. Thus, in Wukan, Guangdong, the villagers displayed banners reading 'The People of Wukan [*Wukan renmin*] Have Been Wronged!'[78]

In urban and suburban communities, groups of evictee resisters may be a little more disparate, but they still begin in one particular location in which, as the case may be, dozens, hundreds or thousands of households may be affected by eviction. Lead figures are very clear about the advantages of organisation, and may use 'public hearings' organised by the authorities to announce demolition and relocation plans to argue for unity:

> When they recognized how they had been cheated, everybody became quite angry and they, too, felt they would like to unite . . . They were angry because we produced a lot of evidence at the hearing, showing that

[76] Author conversation, July 2011.

[77] Pils, 'Land Disputes, Rights Assertion and Social Unrest'.

[78] A picture showing this banner (reading in Chinese '乌坎人民冤枉啊') can be found at: http://mwang141.blogspot.hk/2011/12/tell-you-no-law-in-china.html, accessed 23 October 2012. The expression used for 'people' is the expression generally used by the party-state.

> we ought to have been given accommodation in our original areas [of residence], according to the plans. But they had secretively sold off all the land, and not given us any apartments [there], and they used violence against us. 'And you who moved early, see how little money they gave you, just a few tens of thousand RMB, you needed that mostly for buying new accommodation, and it will soon be spent altogether. What will you live on then? They have acted against the law in so many ways. We can only protect our rights by uniting!'[79]

But due to the Chinese party-state's strict control of civil society organisation of any kind,[80] they do not generally organise in a visible way (e.g., by renting offices, setting up a bank account or similar actions to create organisations of any permanence) or for the purpose of sustained political or legal campaigning. At most, it seems, they take on the form of an 'organisationless organisation' that Chinese scholars have seen emerge in Chinese society.[81]

Arguments based in violations of state rules

Citizens facing eviction from houses and/or land turn to the laws and regulations for protection, but, as mentioned, they generally do not find anything there that could effectively protect them from eviction. Characteristically, two lines in the above-cited graffiti read:

> The laws protect the common people;
> The courts protect the developers.

The view expressed here is typical of what might be called the early stages of protesting expropriation and eviction, stages supported by a belief that the laws as such are good.

To be so classified, however, these laws should prevent iniquitous expropriation and demolition. Under the existing legal regime, the type of argument that could technically prevent eviction/expropriation would therefore need to show that the expropriating decision or the decision leading to eviction was unlawful. Lack of 'public interest' in expropriation contexts

[79] Author conversation, July 2011.

[80] For a discussion of 'graduated control' of civil society, see Fengshi Wu and Kin-man Chan, 'Graduated Control and Beyond: Evolving NGO-Government Relations', in *Locating Civil Society: Communities Defending Basic Liberties,* Special Issue of China Perspectives, No. 3, 2012.

[81] Teng Biao, 'Rights Defence, Microblogs, and the Surrounding Gaze: The Rights Defence Movement Online and Offline', in *Locating Civil Society: Communities Defending Basic Liberties*, Special Issue of China Perspectives, No. 3, 2012.

would be a potential argument ruling out expropriation; another, depending on the case, could be lack of approval from the appropriate higher authority.[82] While the old regulation on demolition and relocation in urban areas contained largely procedural requirements and was silent about the requirement of 'public use demand', the new Regulation on Expropriation of Buildings on State-owned Land contains the same requirement, and provides a detailed definition of 'public interest' for the first time. However, as mentioned earlier, complaints that a demolition or expropriation decision does not satisfy the 'public interest' requirement are generally ineffective, because there is a widespread view that urban development – and hence expropriation and demolition – is indispensable, and because of the institutional weakness of authorities that might enforce the 'public interest' constraint on expropriations. Even if the argument as such works, a judicial decision holding an expropriation decision to have been illegal may well be made only after the property has already been taken and is under 'development', because complaints do not stay the enforcement of demolition and eviction. As discussed, recent legislative and judicial changes do not promise to bring great changes. 'Public interest' arguments do sometimes change the compensation standard chosen in favour of evictees, according to anecdotal evidence.[83]

It is true that evictees often complain about compensation standards and about the fact that actual payments of compensation are not forthcoming. Given this fact, academic observers have stated that demolition and eviction cases are mainly or exclusively 'about' compensation.[84] But it appears that their focus on compensation reflects the perspective of the state preoccupied with development, since from this perspective nothing must stand in the way of creating new real estate, and only criticism of compensation standards is acceptable.

Consequently, public discussion of rule violations is safest if it focuses on the issue of compensation for expropriation. Arguing for this change just prior to the new Expropriation Regulations, and proposing compensation both for buildings and for land, Professor Jiang Ming'an commented that:

[82] In some rural–suburban land expropriation cases this is an argument advanced by the villagers' communities (e.g., Pils, 'Land Disputes, Rights Assertion and Social Unrest').

[83] Author conversations, Beijing, 2010, 2011.

[84] Zhang Rui (张蕊), '全国血拆频现 专家称拆迁补偿是核心问题' ('Bloody Demolition Happens Frequently Across the Country, Expert Says that Compensation is the Core Issue'), *News Weekly*, weekend edition, 新周报, 周末版, 6 November 2010, available at: http://news.qq.com/a/20101108/000702.htm.

> Even though the increase in the value of land is not earned through labour, it is nevertheless related to the land use rights of ordinary people, so why does not the government allow the masses to enjoy the advantages brought by value increase through urbanization?[85]

Jiang Ming'an's view, benevolent in intention, is influenced by the state view: it assumes that the state or the 'government' has the prior authority to decide what residents (including resident owners) should get, and suggests that, since they have not 'earned it through labour', a case has to be made for their entitlement to a share in the increased value of the land. It is, of course, often true that increases in value are not earned 'through labour', and there is a rich discussion about whether fair market value compensation is appropriate in eminent domain cases.[86] But in China, as explained, expropriations functionally replace market transactions. After an initial expropriation making 'cleared' land available as real estate, developers and others can go on to benefit from increases in value through their free participation in the real estate market, a market whose existence is thus largely premised on expropriations. Given this background, compensation below market value would be particularly hard to justify.

Moreover, it is hard to tell, merely from their legal complaints, what evictees feel most aggrieved about, and whether the 'central' problem from their perspective really is the question of compensation. It is especially hard to do so in a legal system that only gives them a realistic chance of complaining about compensation. The system leaves no room for the possibility that residents ought to be 'allowed' not to move at all, or that they ought to be allowed to make their own economic decision about how and when to 'enjoy the advantages brought by increased value through urbanization'. Both in terms of the emotive value of land and its economic value, the system has therefore severely restricted their options from the start.

[85] *Supra*, it continues: 'Professor Jiang also suggested that new laws and regulations ought to clarify the principle of fair market value compensation, let both parties jointly select an evaluation agency; and in addition, they should provide for compensation for the price of the building *and the price of the land*. At the moment everybody only talks about the price of buildings but not about the price of land; that is not reasonable' (emphasis added).

[86] Under the Fair Market Value standard, 'the owner is entitled to receive "what a willing buyer would pay in cash to a willing seller" at the time of the taking'. Katrina Wyman, 'The Measure of Just Compensation', *University of California, Davis Law Review*, 41 (2007), 239 at 242.

Within the framework of the legal rules provided by the state, evictees also complain about procedural violations and violence occurring in the context of evictions. Cases of violence are common enough to have attracted comment from the Supreme People's Court in its 'Urgent Notice'.[87] For example, rights defender Ni Yulan reports about her eviction from a home owned by her husband's family in the Western District of Beijing:

> When the people from the demolition team saw that I really had legal documentation and that my husband really was the owner of this property, and that the six brothers in the family were all named there, they halted the demolition. But the police officer wouldn't let them. That police officer named Xiao Wei, he ordered them, 'don't fucking listen to her. Raze this place to the ground!' He directed them to continue with the demolition, and a plainclothes police officer from the Western Division continued filming the process from close by. When I tried to reason with them the plainclothes police officers ordered the people from demolition team to beat me, at that time I received a head injury, an open wound.
>
> When the emergency response [police] officers came, they clearly saw my head wound. My head was bleeding all over. But they were just like rogues. As they were giving directions to these people demolishing the house, I said, 'if you, the police, act like this, I will go to the Municipal Government and lodge a complaint against you'. That one sentence I spoke plunged me into disaster.
>
> The police officer Xiao Wei, and another named Wen Anwei, took me to the police station. Then they took me to an unofficial detention cell. In that room they had a security guard beat me up . . .'[88]

Complaints about eviction violence and process-related injustices carry a clear risk of further retaliation, as in the case of Ni Yulan. But at times they can be successful in the sense that they may lead to disciplinary measures or criminal prosecution of persons involved, as in the case of the Yihuang incident. Yet such measures cannot rectify unlawful expropriation or demolition. Like compensation, such measures are limited to dealing with the aftermath of injustice, case by case, and are not capable of addressing deeper, systematic aspects of injustice.

In the face of institutional intransigence, seeming official indifference and repression, official understandings of the current legal system ultimately come to be rejected; and where this happens, existing constraints on

[87] For an account from a human rights NGO's perspective, see Amnesty International, 'Standing Their Ground'.

[88] Excerpt from *He Yang* 何杨) 紧急避难场所 (*Emergency Shelter*), independent documentary film (2010).

intra-establishment debates are rejected, too. At the level of 'deep contention' indicated earlier, arguments against the existing property and expropriation regime adopt different argumentative strategies. One kind engages with the past, arguing that there was historic injustice in the creation of the current property regime: of the rules that now shape it, and the expropriations that preceded it in China's Maoist era. The other kind engages with future redress for human rights violations (such as the right to a livelihood), and a broader right to a decent political system to be realised in the future. What is common to both types of argument is that they reject the legitimacy of expropriations and demolitions – even those (if any) that have occurred in accordance with existing rules and regulations. Both types of argument, moreover, require reinterpretations of the meaning of ownership as opposed to the state view and its conception of 'socialist public ownership'. The arguments must trace the 'bifurcation' of the land law regime, and the fact that rural–suburban and urban land have had different recent histories in China.

Reinterpretations of ownership in urban contexts

Prior to 1982, urban land could still be privately owned. Even though the PRC from its inception was committed to Marxism, and although expropriations were not wholly confined to the countryside,[89] but occurred in urban areas too, private ownership in urban land remained untouched as an institution until the 1980s. Urban expropriations after 1949 'only' affected those designated as enemies, traitors of the Chinese people, capitalists and counter-revolutionaries.[90] The 1954 PRC Constitution spoke of socialist public ownership of the means of production; and, beginning in the mid-1950s, the government used

[89] According to the text of the 1950 Land Reform Law, the simple redistribution of control over land to people classified as ordinary 'peasants' constituted an 'abolition of the exploitative feudal system of landlord landownership', and 'realized peasant land ownership'. Article 1, 1950 土地改革法 (Land Reform Law), available at: http://news.xinhuanet.com/ziliao/2004-12/14/content_2331893.htm. See also 1947 中国土地法大纲 (General Principles of Land Law) (used in CCP-controlled areas), available at: www.hudong.com/wiki; Jonathan Spence, *The Search for Modern China* (New York: W. W. Norton, 1990), p. 517.

[90] 政务院关于没收战犯、汉奸、官僚资本家及反革命分子财产的指示 (State Council Directive on the Expropriation of Property of War Criminals, Traitors of the Chinese People, Bureaucrats and Capitalists and Counter-revolutionaries), February 1951, available at: http://policy.yoosoo.cn/Html/AllType/type20/333481.html, Randolph and Lou, ch. 1, pp. 9 *et seq*.

compulsory lease schemes to requisition living space from urban homeowners.[91] As Professor Zhou Qiren explains, until the late 1950s, there was no interference with private landownership. From 1956 onwards, the state implemented a 'socialist reconstruction policy', which led to the state taking over the administration of leases on behalf of building owners deemed to hold too much property of their own; landlords under this *jingzufang* system collected only a part (about one-third) of the rent to be paid to the government.[92]

Further measures and announcements (briefly discussed below) followed during the Cultural Revolution 1966–1976. Their import was to reject private landownership and put the Party in charge of the distribution of land and building use. The nature and legal status of these measures was as uncertain as their implementation was, in some instances, extremely cruel.[93] After the conclusion of the Cultural Revolution, a policy of returning buildings and the land they stood on to the original private owners was implemented.[94]

The 1982 Constitution for the first time stated explicitly that land in the cities was owned by the state, and that land in rural and suburban areas was owned by collectives. The 1982 Constitution and later 1988 Amendments thus prepared the ground, as it were, for 'property development'. Initially, the designation as 'state-owned' had little real effect 'on the ground', since state ownership of formerly privately owned land did not matter, nor was it really much noticed, as long as land use continued unchanged in urban and rural areas. But this was to change with the introduction of land-use rights for construction use only a few years later. Only then did the effects of this urban expropriation through constitutional amendment begin to be felt.

The creation of the new property regime under 'Reform and Opening' is experienced as unjust and illegitimate by at least some evictees. But there is

[91] Each person, including private owners, was entitled to a regulated quota of living space. CHRD (维权网), '城镇房屋暴力拆迁问题调查研究报告' ('Report on Violence in Forced Demolition and Relocation'), October 2009, available at: http://crd-net.org/Article/Class1/200910/20091002094220_17531.html.

[92] Zhou Qiren (周其仁), '城市土地国有化之谜 – 城乡中国系列评论之二十六' ('The Myth of Nationalization of Land Ownership in the Cities: Commentaries of China's Cities and Counties'), available at: http://zhouqiren.org/archives/1329.html.

[93] *He Liren* (何里仁), 大国无私房 (*No Private Home in This Great Country*), independent documentary film (2012). This film contains oral history accounts of 'searches' of privately owned homes undertaken by Red Guards and of struggle sessions affecting homeowners.

[94] Hua Xinmin's account in *He Liren*, *ibid.*

little direct engagement with the political and legal history of its creation. Evictee activist Hua Xinmin has been among a few activists to discuss critically the historical process that is claimed to have led to a gradual appropriation of land by the state. Hua is vehemently opposed to the view that state ownership of urban land is a remnant and expression of China's communist era, and instead suggests that the constitutional and legislative changes introduced from 1982 onwards may have to be understood as an expression of the new state capitalism that then emerged.

Hua argues that any measures to this effect introduced by paramilitary youth groups generically known as Red Guards during the Cultural Revolution were of little legal relevance, not least because they were revoked after the Cultural Revolution.[95] What was crucial were the changes introduced shortly afterwards under 'Reform and Opening'. They laid the legal foundation for the creation of today's real estate market. They enabled the transformation of the Chinese party-state that Gong Xiantian sought to capture in his remark that the Chinese Communist Party had transmuted into a 'Private Property Party':

> The reason why the 1982 Constitution suddenly proclaimed that 'land in the cities is in state ownership' remains a mystery to be solved; but I believe that it is not necessarily related to ideology. It was probably motivated by interests. In this context, Hong Kong property developers played an important role. In Fok Ying-tung's work *My Participation* we can find a detailed account.[96] According to what this book says, Fok Ying-tung submitted suggestions concerning land to the Central Government in 1981. At the time, he ought to have been quite clearly aware of the private nature of land ownership in the cities.[97]

Various reports narrate the story of Fok Ying-tung (in pinyin, Huo Yingdong) providing advice to Deng Xiaoping and the central authorities about how to design their land policies based on his experience with the Hong Kong colonial authorities, which, since almost all land was owned by the Crown, provide most of the Hong Kong government revenue from the granting of land leases. According to these reports, Fok Ying-tung summed up his advice in one famed 'sentence that woke up the dreamers':

[95] This discussion involves a November 1967 document termed '答复关于城镇土地国有化请示提纲的记录' which demands that all private property be transformed into state-owned land.

[96] 霍英东 (Huo Yingdong/Fok Ying-Tung), 改革開放二十年：我的參與 (*Twenty Years of Reform: My Participation*) (Hong Kong: Huo Yingdong Foundation, 1998).

[97] Hua Xinmin's account in *He Liren*.

> Why, if you have land; how can you not have money? You can make money out of the land![98]

Hua points out that just months prior to the passing of these new constitutional provisions, in May 1982, the government issued a call for urban homeowners to register their homeownership by means of obtaining a *fangdichan suoyouzheng*, a 'building and landownership certificate'.[99] It may be difficult to find out how many people were able to obtain such a certificate, as some seven months later, through the December 1982 Constitution, the state took ownership of all urban land:

> Article 10 [of the 1982 Constitution] simply read, 'All land in the cities belongs to the State.' Only eleven characters, concise, clear and forceful, as though it were a statement of an age-old fact.
>
> In fact, it wasn't.[100]

According to Hua Xinmin, the 1982 constitutional redefinition of urban land as state-owned occurred, as it were, by stealth – even though the Constitution was, of course, a public document, she does not think that many ordinary people took any notice of its Article 10. If they had, they could hardly have changed anything about it:

> As to the reason why at the time Article 10 of the 1982 Constitution did not cause any social upheaval; why, I think that it is because private homeowners had just come through the repression of the Cultural Revolution and they were all still facing layoffs; they had been terrified. They did not take any notice whatsoever of this newly created provision, and even less did they realise that it might perhaps threaten their own property. Adding to that was a common-sense perception on the part of the private homeowners: buildings and land could not be separated. Were it not for being forced to confront the issue when they later faced

98 See, for example, 'Zhou Qiren: Fok Ying-Tung with One Single Sentence Started "Land Based [Public] Finances"' ('周其仁:霍英东一句话引发'土地财政'), 24 September 2012, available at: www.w010w.com.cn/htm/wangshangretie/2012/0924/196120.html; '霍英东与中国土地改革:曾建议土地有偿使用' ('Fok Ying-tung and Chinese Land Reform: He Proposed Land Use Rights Against a Fee'), 2 November 2006, available at: http://news.sina.com.cn/c/2006-11-02/101511399728.shtml.

99 Hua Xinmin's account in *He Liren*.

100 Zhou Qiren ('周其仁), 城市土地国有化之谜 – 城乡中国系列评论之二十六 ('The Mystery of the Nationalisation of Urban Land', *Urban and Rural China Review*, No. 26), available at: http://zhouqiren.org/archives/1329.html.

demolition of their homes, they would never have gone on to ask about this problem that had never been a problem before.[101]

Following experimentation with land-use rights grants against compensation in special economic zones such as Shenzhen, in 1988, the Constitution in its then amended form allowed for the creation of new urban land-use rights, also provided for in the 1988 national Land Administration Law.[102] According to Hua Xinmin, it was only then that the state ownership of (urban) land (*tudi suoyouquan*) became transformed into state ownership of urban land *as property with a real estate market value* (*tudi caichan de suoyouquan*).[103] It was this step that led to the large-scale evictions and demolitions, and to the unprecedented urban construction wave of the past twenty-five years.

Hua Xinmin is not prepared to concede that *all* urban land was legally transformed into state-owned land through the 1982 Constitution. In her view, the fact that the state-issued regulations called for the registration of urban state ownership and urban land-use rights by (resident) private homeowners suggests that such a transfer of registration was *required to effect the constitutionally prescribed change*. Yet, she remarks pointedly, it was impossible for people to go through this procedure since, generally, they were never informed about it. Referring to a Supreme People's Court judicial interpretation, she insists that without having undergone a registration change, no change of ownership could take place.[104] In an open letter addressed to the central authorities, Hua and others therefore seek 'clarification' as to the question of whether their families' privately owned urban land was affected by the nationalisation in 1982:

Did you mean to nationalize the ownership of property rights [*caichanquan*]? And if you did mean to nationalize that, were our privately owned land and homes included? If yes, through what procedure and for what reason did you change it into your ownership? You would have had to have an adequate procedure and reason. One procedure and reason would have been if you had purchased the land, right? The 1956 socialist renewal policy affecting industry and commerce also meant that you

[101] Hua Xinmin (华新民), '拆迁律师点评 :土地私有产权从来就没有消失过' ('Chaqian Lawyer Comment: Private Ownership of Land has Never Disappeared'), 4 July 2011, available at: http://news.qq.com/a/20110701/000579.htm.

[102] For the text of the Amendment, 'Constitution of the PRC, Amendment One', 12 April 1988, see at http://english.people.com.cn/constitution/constitution.html.

[103] *Ibid.*, note 9. [104] *Ibid.*

> bought those properties, right, through written contracts? But you haven't bought [our] land. How then can it have changed into State-owned property?
>
> Secondly, another procedure would have been confiscation, right? You must give us a reason, right? And confiscation would have had to be imposed through a judicial procedure. But then you would have to tell us what crime we committed, right? But what crime have all these thousands of people committed?
>
> We have been waiting for a reply since November. Over five months. We have not got a reply yet. This question was raised just by a few old landlords. But the answer may concern the whole people.[105]

State officials would be unlikely to share in this view of continued private landownership rights on the part of the original residents; and in the absence of a legal process allowing for a comprehensive review of evidence and arguments, it is difficult to assess the force of Hua's reasoning. It is certainly possible to read the constitutional provision 'land in the cities is owned by the State' as meaning just that: land in the cities is (from now on) owned by the state. It is possible to understand this sentence as effecting, with the authority of the new Constitution as the formally speaking highest law, compensationless legislative expropriation. This step would no doubt have been counter to the spirit of the Universal Declaration of Human Rights (UDHR) or other norms protecting the right to private property and protecting against arbitrary expropriations.[106] Taking Article 17(2) of the UDHR as the only human rights norm binding the PRC at the time of the 1982 Constitution into account, this provision does not explicitly protect against redefinitions of the scope of property rights through legislation. Hua Xinmin would presumably have to argue, however, that the changes effected through the 1982 Constitution, widely unmentioned and unnoticed and yet so momentous, were equivalent to 'arbitrary' expropriation by means of a constitutional norm.

A different, state-centred reading might draw support from what scholars have described as a gradual erosion of the idea of private ownership in the decades that went before, given that economic markets, sale and transfer of property, and other ways of engaging in 'capitalist' conduct were repudiated and not allowed in China, potentially resulting in punishment and

[105] *He Liren.*

[106] Article 17 of the UDHR, binding the PRC at the time of the 1982 Constitution, is much less detailed than other human rights documents on the topic of expropriation. Its clause (2) reads: 'no one shall be arbitrarily deprived of his property'. It might be difficult to argue that expropriation by means of a constitutional norm was arbitrary.

persecution. It might further adduce the fact that many Chinese citizens have acquired property rights justifiably relying on the property regime created through the legal reforms of the 1980s. In short, a situation has been created in which legitimate concerns, potential complaints and the interests of different groups of citizens, as well as of state agencies, are pitted against each other; and to disentangle and appropriately address the claims of those who have relied on a property regime created, arguably, through historic injustice would be a complicated task.

Yet Hua's impassioned advocacy has great force as a political argument, drawing attention to the basic unfairness of a process that has deprived millions of urban residents of rights in land, while at the same time enriching those able to participate, directly or indirectly, in the state control thus gained over land. Anecdotal evidence, conversations with evictees and a study of the forms of evictee protest certainly suggest the presence of a sizeable group of urban homeowners and residents who object to demolition or expropriation of their land and homes, both because they believe that these measures violate existing law, and because they do not think that these measures can be politically or morally justified. These evictees assert their status as rightful owners in moral and political, as well as legal, terms, and accuse the state and its collaborators of having unlawfully deprived them of their land or homes. Terms used to make this point include 'robbery', 'invasion' and 'injustice', such as, for instance, in a banner reading 'the wrongs of demolition robbery' (*chaiqiang yuan*)',[107] or referring to 'robbery-like *chaiqian*' (*qiangdao ban chaiqian*).[108] In the film *Emergency Shelter*, Jiang Tianyong, a human rights lawyer, comments on the practice of demolition (in urban contexts) as follows:

> What is called demolition and relocation in China occurs in the name of the state, but is actually carried out by individual officials and institutions within the government, along with property developers and including the many people they hire. They make up an interest group of big and small beneficiaries. What you see is superficially the carrying out of 'demolition and relocation', but essentially they're robber bands. In essence, what [they] commit is robbery.
>
> The police, procuratorate and courts [are] merely the tools of those making profit. They have been reduced to nothing more than tools. You can't speak up for yourself. [In the judicial process] they're entirely on the

[107] Picture on file with author, obtained 2007 from Beijing.

[108] Picture of protest poster on the outside wall of a Beijing home threatened by forced demolition (obtained in 2007, on file with author, picture No. 1).

> side of the robbers. We can all see that robbery is wrong, but reduced to mere instruments, the police, procuratorate and courts protect those wrongs. Everybody can see a thing is white, but they will tell you it is black, because they think they have everything under their control. That's why they act like this.

Signs and protest slogans displayed on the outside of buildings often strike a similar note, for example:

> Unlawful *chaiqian* is legally and morally unacceptable. When your home is gone, what meaning does life still have? My family's home is privately owned; the ownership certificate clearly says so: 'The area within this bold line is privately owned property.' It is written in black and white and you can't argue with that. In Harmonious Society the courts should uphold what is reasonable, yet . . . how can it be that if another person wants my things and I don't want to give them to him, that means that I am breaking the law?[109]

There is little indication that homeowners associate the current institution of 'socialist public ownership' or of state ownership of urban land with true socialism. So far as socialism is referred to, what we find are references to the Maoist era and its – according to popular perceptions – more egalitarian conception of justice. Under Mao Zedong, according to this perception, there was a more egalitarian distribution of goods and 'more dignity for ordinary people',[110] when nothing like the current expropriations and demolitions could have happened.

Evictee protesters sometimes associate their acts of defiance with Mao Zedong's revolutionary spirit. Thus, in the film *Emergency Shelter* a petitioner against forced demolition named Zhang Aixiang[111] describes her planned suicide:

> The two of us, we had everything ready. We were going to Tiananmen to jump off a building; I wasn't going to die for nothing. But before I died I was going to remember Chairman Mao, say good-bye to Chairman Mao. 'Long Live Chairman Mao! I am remembering you.'

Since *c.* 2012, a grass-roots group producing 'Citizen Broadcasts' has taken on a number of eviction cases in various locations nationwide, and

[109] Picture of protest poster on the outside wall of a Beijing home threatened by forced demolition (obtained in 2007, on file with author, picture No. 2).

[110] Author interview, Beijing outskirts, July 2010.

[111] For information on her case of forced demolition in Beijing Chongwen district see, for example, www.epochtimes.com/gb/10/3/2/n2832800.htm. According to the description provided here, Zhang Aixiang's home was forcibly demolished in 2002.

has included video footage of a group of citizens holding up two banners and chanting the slogans:

> Lawful Private Property is Sacrosanct and Must Not Be Violated! Return My Home! Rebuild My Home![112]

Urban protesters express a sense of historic or political injustice: of injustice done through past political decisions that cannot be clearly captured as unjust or illegal within the framework of existing laws and regulations. Since, from the perspective of many evictees, the injustice done to them dates back to the beginning of the Reform and Opening era (in urban cases) or afterward, their outrage is not about the overwhelming power wielded by the state and ruling Party under an essentially Leninist political model. Instead, evictees expressing a sense of political injustice and oppression, and 'displace', as it were, their experience to other eras and historical contexts. They make reference to contexts such as 'German invasion', 'Japanese invasion', 'fascism' and 'white terror':[113]

> Our home became their property, their turf. The whole of Xinjiekou had fallen into enemy hands at that time. We were living under a form of White Terror. In winter, the security guards were all clad in grey, with overcoats and red armbands. It felt like we'd been invaded by German troops. From a distance, it looked like an occupation by German soldiers. They were wearing those caps, too. It was very scary. It was as though we were under fascist control.[114]

Reinterpretations of ownership in rural and suburban contexts

Even though the underlying ownership systems differ, rural and urban evictees are increasingly alert to the similarities of their situations, and some evictee resisters have drawn parallels between urban and rural expropriations and demolitions. In a self-produced book distributed by hand amongst petitioners and activists, a Beijing-based activist narrates a story involving Mao Zedong warning, prophetically as it were, against the evils of demolition and relocation. Especially as far as the loss of

[112] Citizen Radio (公民博报), '私有财产神圣不可侵' ('Private Property is Sacrosanct and Must Not be Violated'), 28 May 2013 (was available at: http://v.youku.com/v_show/id_XNTYzOTIwOTQ4.html, accessed 30 May 2013, but link now broken). The report is said to have been produced at an eviction site in Changzhou (Jiangsu Province).

[113] See below; a 2009 protest poster in a different context (photo on file with author) compares the authorities to the fascist German government.

[114] Excerpt from *He Yang*.

homes is concerned, the experience of urban and rural residents is, after all, comparable:

> There was a village in Henan where they wanted to build an airport. They didn't make proper arrangements for the peasants, and didn't explain things in a reasonable way; they just forcefully demolished [their homes] and forced them to move. The peasants said, 'how can you take a stick and beat a bird out of his own nest? If you do that, the bird will cry.' 'Deng Xiaoping, you also have a nest, if I destroy it, will you not also cry out?'[115]

In contrast to urban residents, rural residents have no need to defy the state in arguing that they are owners of their land, because the Constitution protects rural collective ownership of land. Nominally at least, villagers can feel themselves to be members of communities legally entitled to the land now threatened by expropriation, even though rural collective ownership is officially understood to be a form of 'socialist collective ownership', following the rules of socialism as understood under the state view. In an interview in 2011, the economist Cheng Xiaonong commented:

> Before 1978, land was in private ownership for thousands of years of Chinese history. Whether in the imperial, republican or Communist era, right until 1978, the land was in private ownership in accordance with the Chinese Constitution. Of course, land in the rural areas was in collective ownership of the peasants. But 'collective ownership' was still a form of private ownership; it was certainly not 'common' ownership, it was not ownership of the government.[116]

Indeed, one may argue that traditional Chinese landownership was less individuated than in Western traditions; and in allotting land-use rights (*chengbao* rights of agricultural use, and *zhaijidi* rights over residential plots) to households, the current Chinese property regime continues this tradition. The design of the current rural landownership system also draws on the genuinely socialist idea of resource distribution in accordance with needs, however; and the reforms of the recent decades have

[115] Monograph entitled '我所经历的拆迁' (on file with author), 2010, p. 147. A similar narrative can be found at: http://blog.sina.com.cn/s/blog_5041e2ce0100g4wm.html.

[116] Economist Cheng Xiaonong, in a Sound of Hope interview, dates this 'sudden change' to the (third) PRC Constitution of 1978, see '政府为何热衷于拆迁 圈地?' ('Why the Government is So Frenetic about Demolition and Land Enclosure?'), available at: http://soundofhope.org/programs/1017/189857-1.asp. A translation of the 1978 Constitution can be found at: https://commons.wikimedia.org/wiki/File:People's_Republic_of_China_1978_Constitution.pdf.

reflected a struggle between concerns about the equity and security, respectively, of rural household landholdings.[117]

As Chen's comment indicates, the government exercises a high degree of *de facto* control over the legal fiction of the collective under the concept of 'socialist public' collective ownership. Political contention arises typically over the question of how collective ownership rights are to be exercised – in many rural expropriation contexts, villagers feel they have been defrauded or coerced by their own village leadership – and of what such ownership entails for the collective and its individual members: can rural communities dispose of their land? And how are they protected against the state in the event of expropriations? In posing these questions, villagers often expose the thinness – the sometimes merely nominal nature – of their position as collective owners in the context of a legal system that offers only few legal protections against arrogation of control by the government authorities, and is often ineffective against intimidation and other power abuses.

The fact that collective socialist ownership is not supposed to entail the right to alienate is a crucial factor explaining the frequency of rural and suburban expropriations. As mentioned already, according to the perspective of the state, neither rural landownership nor rural land-use rights can be lawfully transferred for the purpose of using the land for construction. Yet the state, represented by urban governments, may expropriate rural collectives 'for public interest demands' and then dedicate that land to the use purpose denied to the rural community. Understandably, members of rural communities feel unfairly left out of a process of property development that almost invariably greatly raises the value of what was once their land; even more so when property development is accompanied by evident or suspected corruption.

It is also on the right, or lack of it, to alienate that contention between state and popular views of rural and suburban landownership often comes into focus. The most frequent form of resistance to existing constraints on alienation is by rule circumvention. The phenomenon of rule circumvention in this context is mostly referred to as 'minor property rights': it concerns a variety of arrangements whereby rural collectives or individual rural households or individuals 'transfer' land or land-use

[117] For studies on this question, see, for example, RDI studies undertaken together with the University of Chicago and Renmin University. Zhu Keliang and Roy Prostermann, 'Securing Land Rights for Chinese Farmers: A Leap Forward for Stability and Growth', Cato Development Policy Analysis Series, No. 3, 15 October 2007, available at: http://papers.ssrn.com/sol3/papers.cfm?abstract_id=1066812.

rights, and sometimes also buildings, to property developers or other buyers. Such transfers are widely deemed to be prohibited under current law and, therefore, the 'right' acquired through such arrangements is a 'minor' or 'small' property right only. Rather like the term *informales* in certain Latin American contexts, this term obscures the fact that according to the state view, no property rights at all can be transferred through minor property right deals. Just like in the case of the *informales* there is a debate about whether the law does in fact prohibit all forms of 'minor property right' transfers, especially with regard to the ownership of houses built on collectively owned 'residential plot' land (*zhaijidi*).

The practice of 'minor property rights transfers' can be interpreted as acts of silent resistance to the existing property regime. These are certainly not acts of resistance in the sense that each and every person engaging in this practice is attempting to make a statement about the inappropriateness of the existing property regime (allegedly) prohibiting (some) minor property rights transactions; but they are in the sense that by undertaking such transactions citizens do not take that system seriously. Since the amount of 'minor property rights housing' created thus far is reportedly quite large, moreover, sellers and buyers are collectively creating *fait accompli* that are hard for the state to ignore, and there has been an ongoing debate about the possibility of legalising 'minor property right' housing. Such a step could be seen as recognition on the part of the state of a practice clearly opposed to the entrenched state view of property rights and ownership pertaining to land.

Due to political constraints and repression, claims that rural residents (or collectives) have the right to dispose of their land and that the state has no rights to expropriate them have rarely been advanced explicitly. One of the few rural landownership declarations demands respect for historically private property rights, arguing that the complex land rights system introduced since the 1980s was little understood by rural residents.[118] The authors of the letter, signed 'in the name of' 250 peasant households in Jiangsu wrote in December 2007 that:

> Shengzhuang, our village, lies on the border of three provinces, Jiangsu, Anhui and Zhejiang. It is a national level travel resort famous for its 'bamboo ocean' and the village reaches back 1,500 years in history. Generation after generation of villagers lived together harmoniously; they

[118] For studies on this question see, for example, RDI studies undertaken together with the University of Chicago and Renmin University. Prosterman and Keliang, 'Securing Land Rights for Chinese Farmers'.

> lived in harmony with the land they had been given by Heaven, and they lived in harmony with the officials of the various ages. Throughout all the dynasties and generations, the peasants had their own land to farm, it was clear to whom the bamboo and the hills belonged, and the peasants respected each others' land rights. Land transactions were carried out in accordance with local custom, which the law of the government protected.
>
> Since the revolution, the new terms of 'villagers' collective ownership' and '*chengbao* land management' have been introduced. But we peasants always thought: no matter what we call it, the land is ours, the peasants'; it has served us for many generations as land to build houses on, to farm, and to develop. Like the old governments, the new government should take responsibility for protecting the land ownership rights of the peasants. It should protect the rights of all the people and help it develop. Only then can it be called a government . . .[119]

Other open letters invoke the promise that was given to peasants at the outset of the Communist Revolution: that all peasants would be given land to farm, often referred to as the slogan *gengzhe you qi di*. This argument was used, for example, in the 2007 Heilongjiang open letter, which according to a version circulated online, has broken the revolutionary promise. Under the current system, the letter observes (again curiously echoing Professor Gong Xiantian's mocking characterisation of the CCP as 'Private Property Party'), local government officials have arrogated the position of *de facto* landowners, while peasants, under this system, have become *de facto* 'serfs' (*nongnu*) on the land.

The Heilongjiang letter 'declared' openly that the landownership of the 150 mu of land in question 'belongs to the peasants belonging to the 72 administrative villages concerned and shall be distributed equally to the peasants'. Ownership, according to the declaration, comprised 'the right to revenue from the land, the right to inherit land, the right to alienate land, and the right to negotiate and ask for a price in case the government and property developers want to develop the land'. Certain plots currently occupied by property developers and the government were to be 'taken back', according to the declaration:[120]

119 '江苏省宜兴市省庄村 250户农民坚持宅基地所有权 要求实现"居者有其屋' ('250 Peasant Households of Shengzhuang village, Yixing City, in Jiangsu Province Maintain Their Ownership Right in Residential Land and Demand Realization of the Policy "Each Resident Should Have a Home"'), 16 December 2007, available at: www.64tianwang.com/bencandy.php?fid-7-id-1153-page-1.htm.

120 Letter entitled '黑龙江72村4万农民宣布拥有土地所有权向全国的公告– 南岗村, 富锦市' ('40,000 Peasants from 72 villages in Fujin City, Heilongjiang, Declare Their Ownership of Land to the Entire Nation'), 9 December 2007, available at: www.peacehall.com/news/gb/china/2007/12/200712091236.shtml.

> We trust that just as peasants then struggled for the right to manage the land and brought about a great change at the beginning of the Reform and Opening era, so we will now achieve an even greater change by struggling for the peasants' ownership right in the land. We peasants have suffered enough deprivation and betrayal. We have had enough of a life of crying to heaven and hearth but not being heard . . . Land is the lifeline of the peasantry, it is the peasants greatest human right. Only when we have obtained true ownership of the land can we live in peace and security, can the Chinese countryside live in peace and security, can the entire country live in peace and security.[121]

When the Shengzhuang and Jiamusi and a number of similar letters were produced not long after the promulgation of the 2007 Property Rights Law, they met with swift and effective repression. Yang Chunlin, the main author of the Heilongjiang open letter, was treated without mercy. According to reports, he was badly beaten in detention and even at the conclusion of his trial; he was sentenced to a five-year prison term for 'inciting subversion of State power'.[122] Several years passed without any indication of other rural communities trying to engage in similarly explicit assertions of rights of full ownership of rural land, even as conflicts over rural expropriations continued and resistance to expropriations remained a much-discussed topic.

The silencing effect of these reactions to explicit challenges to the state view is unlikely to last. In more recent cases, protesting villagers have consistently continued to speak of the government having 'sold our land' and called for the state to 'return our land'; in some cases their protest has been rendered more effective by successful efforts to organise and rally around the common goal of winning land back, even though this did not mean that land, once taken, was actually returned to villagers. Thus, in 2010, villagers in Beihai, Guangxi Autonomous Region, engaged in effective resistance to expropriation after managing to rally round a democratically elected village head. His and their efforts to protect the land of the Beihai villagers triggered violent clashes, in which one person was beaten to death,[123] and ended in the criminal prosecution and conviction of the elected village head, Xu Kun, and other villagers, measures that effectively suppressed local resistance to the expropriation measure.

[121] *Ibid.*

[122] Eva Pils, 'Peasants' Struggle for Land in China', in Yash Ghai and Jill Cottrell (eds.), *Marginalized Communities and Access to Justice* (London: Routledge, 2009), pp. 136–160, with further references.

[123] Pictures of the beatings and of the victim in hospital on file with author (July 2010).

In 2011, collective protests in Wukan village in Guangdong Province drew even more attention.[124] The Wukan protest originated, and to some extent centred, in land transactions carried out with collusion from an allegedly corrupt village head, Xue Chang; but even at the end of many months, after intense efforts to understand the nature of these transactions, it remains unclear what kind of transactions had been undertaken. According to comments offered at a public seminar with Professor Xiong Wei, perhaps the scholar to have gained the deepest knowledge of the case, it seemed possible that the land in question had been sold as 'minor property right' land (i.e., illegally).[125] In any case, it was clear that whatever the nature of the transaction that had taken place, it had not occurred with the consent of the majority of villagers who protested this 'taking' of their land. Incensed at apparent corruption, protesters called for the democratic election of a new village leadership, as well as for return of their land, for example, in posters reading 'Return Our Land So We Can Live!'[126] A democratically elected member of a Provisional Villagers' Representatives Committee, Lin Zulan, described the land conflict underlying the 'Wukan Incident' as villagers demanding 'the land rights they ought to have' (*ying you de tudi quanli*), subtly, and perhaps unconsciously, hinting at the divergence of the property distribution achieved under existing rules, and rules that would be legitimate.[127]

Some ten months later, a wall graffiti in Wukan read, assertively, 'the collective has resumed [ownership of] the land – 12 August 2012'.[128] But in reality, according to reports, most of the land has not yet been returned despite the very unusual degree of public and high level

[124] Willy Lam, 'The Grim Future of the Wukan Model for Managing Dissent', *China Brief* (2012), available at: www.jamestown.org/programs/chinabrief/willyscornercb; Stanley Lubman, 'The Wukan Protests and the Rule of Law', *WSJ Blog* (January 2012), available at: http://blogs.wsj.com/chinarealtime/2012/01/07/the-wukan-protests-and-the-rule-of-law.

[125] Professor Xiong Wei (熊伟), public seminar '烏坎向何处去–解读烏坎民主的困境' ('Whither Wukan?: Understanding Wukan Democracy's Predicament'), University Services Centre, Chinese University of Hong Kong, 20 November 2012.

[126] Heather Stewart, 'Backlash from Beijing Raises Fears that China's Economy is Slowing Down', *The Guardian*, 18 December 2011, available at: www.guardian.co.uk/world/2011/dec/18/backlash-beijing-fears-of-chinese-slowdown.

[127] Ai Xiaoming 艾晓明, 乌坎三日 (*Three Days in Wukan*), documentary film, 2012.

[128] Reuters, 'China Grass-roots Democracy Challenge Awaits New Leaders', 29 October 2012, available at: www.reuters.com/article/2012/10/29/us-china-politics-democracy-idUSBRE89R0JJ20121029.

government attention paid to the case of Wukan.[129] It is also unclear whether land that had been declared to have been 'returned' could actually be accessed by the Wukan villagers.[130] In sum, Wukan villagers' activism neither resulted in a return of 'their' land nor did it lead to a genuine amelioration of village self-rule (democracy) under the village autonomy system.[131]

Generally, once land has been taken it will not be returned for a variety of reasons related to the depth of state–citizen contention over land. No clear process has been created by the state whereby land once taken could be returned to landowning collectives. (It will also be remembered that litigation does not generally stay enforcement procedures when demolition orders have been made. While in the urban context, the issue of staying procedures has been discussed and there have been attempts at improvement, there has so far been no similar discussion or reform attempt in rural contexts.)

It seems that according to the state view, the protection of land rights in the 'vertical' relationship between citizens and the state is premised on considerations of utility that are likely to weigh in favour of the state once a land-taking has been carried out. If this logic holds, then even if an expropriation was at some point unjustified, almost no state consideration would justify restoration of the property, except where the cost of suppressing protest or resistance had spiralled out of control. So far, indeed, it has been generally cheaper to suppress resistance, pacify evictees, for example, by raising compensation payments, and protect the new beneficiaries of land-takings.

Changing arguments and strategies

Evictee protesters, having realised that their resistance is not only legal in nature, but also political, and that the institutions and channels of complaint provided by the state are insufficient, have widened and adapted their lines of argument as well as their strategies of protest.

[129] Stanley Lubman, 'Wukan: Still Unsolved, and Still Significant', *China Real Time Blog*, 19 November 2012, available at: http://blogs.wsj.com/chinarealtime/2012/11/19/wukan-still-unsolved-and-still-significant.

[130] Comments at public seminar with Professor Xiong Wei, *supra*.

[131] Author conversation with expert (anonymous); see also, for example, James Pomfret, 'Freedom Fizzles Out in China's Rebel Town of Wukan', 28 February 2013, available at: www.reuters.com/article/2013/02/28/us-china-wukan-idUSBRE91R1J020130228.

Their arguments increasingly draw on economic and social human rights, such as the right to housing, while their strategies increasingly aim at garnering moral and political support from broad publics.

Evictee activists have increasingly couched their complaints in the language of human rights safeguarded by the Constitution and international instruments. The right to property and protection against expropriation (Article 13), the right to present complaints (Article 41), the right to freedom of speech (Article 35), are among the constitutional rights that are of relevance to the present discussion, because all these rights are under threat in processes of expropriation and demolition when citizens resist these measures. Citizens themselves are also known to have invoked the right of Article 39 of the PRC Constitution: 'The homes of citizens of the People's Republic of China are inviolable. Unlawful search of or intrusion into a home is prohibited,' even though, technically, the constitutional provision of Article 39 is not normally associated with protection against expropriation or demolition.[132] Beyond these rights, rights protecting life and liberty are relevant whenever violence is used to suppress resistance; and, more widely, the right of access to justice, to due process and fair trials are also invoked.[133] In addition to these constitutional provisions, there is also an official state language of 'right to livelihood' (*shengcunquan*) as well as the Sun Yat-sen-based 'People's Livelihood' (*minsheng*) that is occasionally used by evictees protesting their destitution; and even if they do not necessarily make explicit reference to the international instruments and declarations protecting it, evictees also invoke the right to housing.[134]

However, constitutional rights such as provided for in the PRC Constitution cannot, according to the official view, be directly applied in court, and, as is well known, the existing mechanism for reviewing the constitutionality of legal regulations is narrow in scope and not

[132] This provision was invoked, for instance, by an evictee in a case in Hangzhou in 2009 (photograph on file with author).

[133] On the broader topic of access to justice in China, see Jayshree Bajoria, 'Access to Justice in China', available at: www.cfr.org/china/access-justice-china/p15745; Fu Hualing, 'Access to Justice in China: Potentials, Limits, and Alternatives', in John Gillespie and Albert Chen (eds), *Legal Reforms in China and Vietnam: A Comparison of Asian Communist Regimes* (London: Routledge, 2013), pp. 163–187.

[134] Cf. Office of the High Commissioner for Human Rights (OHCHR), Fact Sheet on the Right to Adequate Housing, No. 21, Rev. 1, available at: www.ohchr.org/Documents/Publications/FS21_rev_1_Housing_en.pdf.

necessarily effective in practice. In over a decade since its introduction, only one regulation is known to have been revoked as a consequence of this mechanism having been invoked.[135] Similarly, there is no real chance of successfully invoking international human rights law in judicial processes.[136] The fact that constitutional arguments and treaty-based international human rights arguments are in effect not available to complainants has the effect of 'flattening' the kind of legal arguments that could be presented in court, in those cases in which courts have accepted cases and hear them.

Necessarily, therefore, human rights arguments are presented outside courtrooms. Common ways of invoking them are slogans such as 'No Home To Return To' (*wu jia ke gui*), 'Return Our Human Rights' (*huan wo renquan*),[137] 'Where Are Our Human Rights, Where Is Constitutional Government,' to more complex types of argument that include, for instance, references to specific articles of the PRC Constitution such as quoted above. In addition to quoting Article 39, the condemned house in question also displayed the flowing slogans in August 2009:

> Citizens' rights are sacred and must not be violated.
> Uphold and protect the Constitution, defend Human Rights.
> Give me my land back, protect my home.
> Severely punish violent thugs; safeguard citizens' lives and property.
> The storm may enter, the rain may enter [this house] but the King cannot enter.[138]
> My head may be broken and my blood may be shed, but my property earned through hard work must not be lost.

Amongst these there are also references to the right to housing as a human right, as discussed below. In 2010, for instance, a group of evictee activists organised a 'performance art' action on the occasion of World Habitat Day. Among the slogans prepared for that day was the following text:

[135] Keith Hand, 'Using a Law for a Righteous Purpose: The Sun Zhigang Incident and Evolving Forms of Citizen's Action in China', *Columbia Journal of Transnational Law*, 45 (2007), 114, 159; Thomas Kellogg, 'The Death of Constitutional Litigation in China?' *China Brief*, 9(7) (2009), available at: www.jamestown.org/programs/chinabrief/single/?tx_ttnews[tt_news]=34791&tx_ttnews[backPid]=414&no_cache=1#.UsbcyifvgpY.

[136] Sanzhuan Guo, 'The Implementation of International Law by Chinese Courts', *Chinese Journal of International Law*, 8(1) (2009), 161–179, available at: http://chinesejil.oxfordjournals.org/content/8/1/161.full.pdf+html.

[137] Photo, obtained 2007 from Beijing (on file with author).

[138] In Chinese, 风能进, 雨能进, 王帝老儿不能进. This phrase is adapted from a famous dictum by William Pitt the Elder in the British Parliament in 1763.

I want a home,
A home where the wind may enter, the rain may enter, but no mafia 'emperor' may enter.
9.6 million square kilometres of land – Yet year after year I cannot find a home that belongs to me![139]

The forms of evictee activism have also undergone change, partly in response to increased control. Where evictee activist have not been able to adapt to control, their activism has tended to escalate. Traditionally, forms of activism include petitions in the form of letters; petitioning in the form of 'visits'; litigation (often not allowed); attempts to get state media or international media involved; passive physical resistance (roadblocks etc.); suicide, suicide attempts, for example, through self-immolation; violent resistance (for example, violence against demolition teams, government officials, etc.). These forms of activism, or *weiquan*, have rarely been helpful in actually stopping a demolition or land-grab, although holdouts often succeed in deferring their eviction. Protesters engaging in litigation and petitioning realise that official avenues will not allow them to get justice according to their own understanding of justice. The more they realise this, the more their 'petitioning' activities become expressions of helplessness or anger.

In recent years and months, new forms of activism have emerged. These reflect the main substantive claims that have emerged as activism around these issues has deepened: they are concerned, on the one hand, with documentation of injustices, and, on the other hand, with rallying around what appears to be increasingly political claims.

First, in addition to the now widely practised use of film and photographs to record demolition processes, there have been a number of efforts to create data collections or collections of records and reports about eviction and demolition processes. For instance, there is a form of self-published samizdat monographs;[140] amateur filming and photographing of demolitions and protests (including suicide protests); evictions (explosion of 'citizen documentary' film footage online, for example, footage of Tang Fuzhen's suicide and other similar events);[141]

[139] World Habitat Day action in Beijing, 4 October 2010, document on file with author. In Chinese, 我想有个家, 有个风能进, 雨能进, 黑恶势力"皇帝"不能进的家。960万平方公里的土地 一年又一年找不到属于我的家.

[140] On file with author.

[141] Roger Cohen, 'A Woman Burns', *New York Times*, 25 January 2010, available at: www.nytimes.com/2010/01/26/opinion/26iht-edcohen.html; for footage, see at: http://v.ifeng.com/documentary/society/201008/931a8e4b-ce09-44e5-aacd-2e3441272f88.shtml.

professional documentary film;[142] and the creation of a 'blood properties map' documenting reported violent demolitions.[143] In an interview the creator of the blood properties map said:

> If there is ever a day when we don't have violent demolition [the map] can be there to tell younger generations that there was once a time when things were developing quickly and that some people paid a price in this process.[144]

Secondly, there are new strategies of networking and association, often through the Internet, as well as of mobilisation around 'causes'. These have included the use of micro-blogging (e.g., the 'Yihuang incident');[145] and appeals to international society, in part also making use of new media, for example, by 'petitioning' in front of the UN headquarters in New York.[146] Several of the efforts that have been made in the areas of property and housing rights activism have consciously sought to create loose associations. Such efforts might start from a simple practice of *weiguan* in cases of forced demolitions,[147] to the formation of interests groups, such as a *jingzufang* homeowners' association,[148] and the organisation of collective events, such as a 'collective walk' and 'performance art' organised on World Habitat Day in Beijing and Shanghai, and other 'performance art', including Ai Weiwei's river crab banquet.[149]

142 For example, parts of the Ni Yulan documentary *Emergency Shelter* by He Yang.

143 '血房地图制作者期待换维权方式 号召拒买血房' ('Blood Properties Map Creator Hopes to Change *Weiquan* Method, Boycott Blood-stained Properties'), *Beijing News* (新京报), 27 October 2010, available at: http://money.msn.com.cn/industry/20101027/07141150397.shtml; Josh Chin, 'China's Blood-stained Property Map', 29 October 2010, available at: http://blogs.wsj.com/chinarealtime/2010/10/29/chinas-blood-stained-property-map.

144 Chin, 'China's Blood-stained Property Map'.

145 Oiwan Lam, 'Yihuang Self-Immolation Incident and the Power of Micro-Blogging', 21 September 2010, *Global Voices Online*, at: http://globalvoicesonline.org/2010/09/21/china-yihuang-self-immolation-incident-and-the-power-of-microblogging.

146 'Home Demolished for World Expo, Shanghai Petitioners Seek Just Compensation', *Human Rights in China*, 1 April 2010.

147 Author conversations suggest that in 2009 and 2010 in Beijing, the practice of notification of supporters prior to a demolition or after a demolition had started was perfected, allowing supporters to travel to the demolition site immediately from anywhere in Beijing.

148 For example, '中华经租房主联谊会(筹)致国务院的公开信' ('Open Letter from *Jingzufang* Homeowner Association to the State Council'), available at: www.peacehall.com/news/gb/yuanqing/2011/03/201103181357.shtml.

149 Dave Itzkoff, 'Artist to 'Celebrate' Studio's Demolition', *New York Times*, 4 November 2010, available at: http://query.nytimes.com/gst/fullpage.html?res=9E02EFD91139F937A35752C1A9669D8B63.

Additional efforts, such as video games like the temporarily very popular 'nailhouse game',[150] have further served to popularise the issue in ways that invite sympathy with evictees.

Thirdly, the current decade has seen a more conscious effort to interact with groups and individuals abroad to engage transnational civil society in challenges to the domestic Chinese state view. This is clear from the gradually increasing involvement of international entities, particularly human rights NGOs. Even though their interest in demolition issues has developed somewhat slowly, NGOs have produced reports drawing attention to the issue. The most recent reports of this kind were produced by Amnesty International and by China Human Rights Defenders.[151] In addition, some communities have successfully drawn the attention of the international media and of transnational civil society. In the case of Wukan Village, for example, it was thought that the local community was better able than other villagers to use personal connections with Wukan emigrants living in Hong Kong, and that this was a factor in their ability to attract international attention.[152]

Summary

Popular views confronting the state view are diverse and have found manifold ways of expression. What unites them is that they reject the state positions on socialist public landownership, as expressed in the laws and regulations of the state, and in the reality of practices with regard to expropriations, evictions and demolitions. In urban contexts, challenges take the form of a fundamental challenge to the state's claim of state ownership of urban land as a residual right that may lead to 'resumption' of full ownership, including the right to use the land at any time. In rural contexts, challenges frequently take the form of practices

[150] Tania Branigan, 'China Embraces Web Game Depicting Family's Fight With Demolition Crew', *The Guardian*, 16 September 2010, available at: www.guardian.co.uk/world/2010/sep/16/china-game-family-fight-demolition.

[151] Amnesty International, 'Standing Their Ground'; Centre on Housing Rights and Evictions (COHRE), 'One World, Whose Dream? Housing Rights Violations and the Beijing Olympic Games', available at: www.cohre.org/sites/default/files/mega_events_-_one_world_whose_dream_july_2008.pdf. See also CHRD, 'Thrown Out: Human Rights Abuses in China's Breakneck Real Estate Development'; Cabannes *et al.*, *How People Face Evictions*.

[152] Author conversations, March and November 2012. See also reports available at the iSun Affairs website, entries on Wukan, 23 December 2011, available at: www.isunaffairs.com.

circumventing the prohibition of selling rural land for non-agricultural use purposes, resistance to land-takings perceived as illegal and illegitimate, and – rarely – explicit assertions of 'full' rights of (private) rural landownership. All expressions of these popular views, in particular, those that explicitly reject the state view, carry the risk of repression. Yet as repression increases, so too do insight and a sense of collective grievance.

Conclusion

The great social and political problems that arise in the context of expropriations shed doubt on the appropriateness of the current property regime, and discredit its authoritarian and utilitarian foundations. Popular views discussed here oppose the concept of strict state-controlled 'socialist public ownership' as it is applied in expropriations and demolitions; and some have come to view the state as predatory and corrupt.

The state view of property and ownership has so far remained largely unchanged. The party-state does not engage with substantive demands for changes to the system, as seen above. It limits itself to very moderate reform discussions and crisis management measures; and it mostly treats *weiquan* rights activism as a phenomenon of instability that needs to be repressed, if it cannot be appeased. Even the institutional avenues for redress that ought to be available are often blocked; and even so far as judicial and petitioning mechanisms can be used to bring grievances, these mechanisms themselves are not designed to allow for public challenges to the system.

Since the state does not accommodate them, criticism and activism (*weiquan*) have largely moved outside courtrooms and state-administered avenues of redress. They have also moved beyond conventional forms of – ultimately often violent – resistance to individual expropriations and demolitions on to the Internet and into the arts, literature and documentary film, increasingly addressing and attacking the system that is the basis for individual cases. Activism discussed here indicates a progression from 'rules' and 'rights' consciousness to political consciousness, and perhaps ultimately political activism. People move from protesting abuses and rule violations to questioning the historical and political legitimacy of the property regime that enables so many expropriations and demolitions, and that has so far been unable to stop violence occurring in these processes.

There is no simple way of accounting for these popular views; they are complex and not necessarily fully coherent. It would not work, for example, to suggest that the protesting Chinese masses hold liberal views on ownership and property. Yet, in total, expressions of the popular view studied here suggest a certain tenacity of the belief that homes and land cannot be held merely on the state's sufferance and discretion. What seems common to most protests is that, by rejecting the legitimacy of expropriations for a variety of reasons, people assert themselves as owners (on a variety of political conceptions of ownership ranging from socialist to liberal), and denounce officials and others involved in expropriations and demolitions as bad officials, as lawbreakers, and even as robbers and enemy invaders.

No protest has so far crystallised into a mainstream demand or campaign; but broader public opposition to local and central Chinese governments may come to rally around popular, non-state conceptions of ownership and political rights in the future. Like the current property system, protest has socialist as well as liberal elements; some activists invoke Mao Zedong, while others quote Pitt the Elder and invoke human rights. This lack of unity and coherence among evictee rights defenders is hardly surprising and is a feature of popular protest even in less authoritarian systems than the current Chinese one. It may weaken protest against the system for evictions and expropriations and the wider political and legal system in the short term, making protest easier to control. In the longer term, it can only encourage people to look for solutions in a change of the political system rather than through a change merely of the property regime.

6

What does Wukan offer?

Land-taking, law, and dispute resolution

HUALING FU

Introduction

The villagers' protest against predatory land-taking in Wukan in the southern Chinese province of Guangdong attracted wide attention, both internationally and domestically. Dubbed the Wukan model, the reconciliatory approach taken by the Guangdong government to dilute and divert social tension is highly regarded by the mainstream media and liberal intellectuals. The Wukan event is commonly regarded as one of the most significant rights protection cases in China to date, because it highlights the controversy of land-taking and the potential for reconciliation through dialogue in easing social tension. From that perspective, Wukan offers a path-breaking model to resolve land disputes. As the Beijing University Civil Society Research Center pointed out:

> After the escalation of the conflict, the government, through proactive intervention and disclosure of information, is able to create an effective mechanism for dialogue and negotiation, reconcile the imperative of maintaining order and protecting rights and successfully resolve social contradiction. In doing so, it puts a stop to the tendency of simplistic handling through administrative fiat. The event has profound impact on China's social and political structure when China is experiencing a period of high level social conflict, and also offers a successful model for the government departments to assess and manage conflict scientifically.[1]

At the heart of the Wukan model is the attempt to use law and political-legal institutions to resolve contentious lands disputes. This chapter

The author would like to thank Hilary K. Josephs and Jason Buhi for their valuable comments.

[1] 北大发布2011年度公民社会十大事件 (Beijing University released ten major civil society events of 2011), available at: http://tech.sina.com.cn/i/2012-02-18/02196739262.shtml, accessed March 1, 2012.

investigates whether the legal process can offer effective resolution of land disputes, and does so by placing land disputes and their resolution in the larger context of China's authoritarian decision-making. The principal argument is twofold. First, the Chinese government, in general, is decisive in decision-making, and there is little accountability in the decision-making process. However, this authoritarian decisiveness does not solve contentions, and it merely marginalizes and backloads the inevitable difficulties. A commonly observed irony is that the government encourages citizens to settle their disputes through law, but, at the same time, sets multiple barriers when citizens resort to law to address their grievances. Because of the lack of accountability in the decision-making process, political and legal institutions that are designed to capture and resolve disputes lack the necessary capacity and independence to solve the contention, creating institutional barriers that push individuals whose interests are adversely affected to extra-institutional action.

Second, frustrated citizens, forced to abandon law and take the matter into their own hands, realize that if they can take the matter to the streets and the court of public opinion, and if they can speak unequivocally and act collectively and firmly, it is increasingly likely to force the government to take its own law more seriously. In this alternative model of social mobilization, individuals organize themselves and act forcefully and collectively to bring their private grievances to public attention. In response to the protest, the government is forced to bargain with its opponents and regularly makes certain concessions to protesters' demands.[2] When confronted with disputes that have been publicized and politicized, the government then tries to offer a legal solution and bring contentious matters back to the institutional channels. However, as the Wukan protest demonstrates, law offers a partial solution within the authoritarian context. Legal actions, promised or actual, either stall collective disputes and backload direct confrontations until they erupt again or dissipate them by letting out certain streams among the aggrieved parties. In that sense, law absorbs conflict and protest by taking oxygen out of the fire.

[2] Ching Kwan Lee and Yonghong Zhang, "The Power of Instability: Unravelling the Microfoundations of Bargained Authoritarianism in China," *American Journal of Sociology*, 118(6) (2013), 1475; Hualing Fu, "Politicized Challenges, Depoliticized Responses: Political Monitoring in China's Transitions," in Fergal Davis, Nicola McGarrity, and George Williams (eds.), *States of Surveillance: Counter-Terrorism and Comparative Constitutionalism* (London: Routledge, 2014), 296–312.

Authoritarian decisiveness, mass events, and the limit of law

In Cox's and McCubbins' terms, decision-making in a polity could be decisive or resolute. Decisiveness refers to "the ability of a state to enact and implement policy change," and resoluteness refers to the state's ability to "commit to maintaining a given policy."[3] There are tradeoffs between decisiveness and resoluteness, and a country becomes ungovernable if decision-making is located at either extreme of the spectrum.

Tradeoffs are made according to the effective number of "vetoes" – an institutional device to check and balance powers – that are in place in a political system. Since an increase in the number of vetoes necessitates negotiation among multiple institutions and diverse interests, and causes an increase in transaction cost for policy change, a polity becomes less decisive but more resolute with the increase in the effective number of vetoes.

According to Cox and McCubbins, institutional vetoes have two distinct elements in democratic states. The first is separation of powers as the term is traditionally understood: powers are divided among different institutions that will check and balance each other. A classic example would be the case of executive decisions being subject to legislative endorsement or judicial review. The second element is referred to as the separation of purpose in the sense that divided institutions are not controlled by a single interest. There may be significant policy divergence within the same institution or political party.[4]

China's polity is decisive in the sense that it is able to make quick policy change on significant social and economic issues with few veto points. Power is monopolized in the hands of the Chinese Communist Party (CCP) committee. In this political system, one person in the office, often the secretary of a local Party committee, gains control of all institutions in the decision-making chain. Separation of power and separation of purpose, as Cox and McCubbins define the terms, do not generally apply in China. A decision, once it is made, is not subject to any effective veto. Decision-makers can curb debates, silence dissenting voices, bypass statutory requirements, and fail to inform or misinform the public. Given the lack of effective checks and balances and

3 Gary W. Cox and Mathew McCubbins, "Political Structure and Economic Policy: The Institutional Determinants of Policy Outcomes," in Stephan Haggard and Mathew McCubbins (eds.), *Presidents, Parliaments, and Policy* (Cambridge University Press, 2001), p. 34.

4 *Ibid.*

meaningful external supervision, it is easy to establish a decisive regime. In that polity, one "finds it easy to make decisions; in fact, it is *too* easy."[5]

This does not mean that no formal institutional constraints on the exercise of power exist. Even within the single power there still exists parchment barriers. Decisions on certain policies, especially those affecting the general public's welfare, are subject to congressional endorsement, political consultation, expert advising, and public hearing to allow citizen participation. China has in the past three decades designed multiple devices to make the exercise of power more transparent and accountable, in law at least.[6] Yet these new institutional mechanisms do not evolve into effective veto points and can be, and have been, ignored when decisions are made.

However, a decisive regime is not resolute and is not able to commit to a policy once it is made. This is so for two reasons. First, the monopoly and unrestrictive exercise of power by the Party secretary at different levels alienates other political elites within the system. The constitutional structure permits power-sharing among different state institutions, including people's congresses, political consultative bodies, and competent government departments. Yet political practices allow the Party secretary to bypass the formal institutions and legal processes, depriving other office-holders of their legitimate authority. Stakeholders may be forced into silence during the decision-making process, but would not put their support behind the decision when it is challenged at a later stage. In certain circumstances, the stakeholders may even lead the opposition voices. In some of the major environmental protests, people's deputies or the members in the political consultative conferences played a significant role in supporting public protest.

Second, the general public is kept in the dark about decisions that may affect their property rights and livelihood. Without the proper consultation and prior consent that the law may require, the public stands on higher moral ground in addition to its legal claim when later expressing opposition. In those cases, citizens, armed with a high degree of legitimacy, are easier to mobilize into joining a movement, more confident about their cause, and less fearful about repercussions for their participation.[7]

[5] *Ibid.*, p. 39.

[6] Dali Yang, *Remaking the Chinese Leviathan: Market Transition and the Politics of Governance in China* (Stanford University Press, 2004); Randall Peerenboom, *China Modernizes: Threat to the West or Model for the Rest?* (Oxford University Press, 2007).

[7] Ching Kwan Lee, *Against the Law: Labor Protests in China's Rustbelt and Sunbelt* (Berkeley, CA: University of California Press, 2007).

While a democratic polity with divided institutions and diverse interests may face stalemate and gridlock leading to indecisive government, authoritarian decisiveness "may be plagued by chaos and instability,"[8] and can generate long-term social havoc. In that sense, China trades decisiveness for resoluteness and backloads its social problems, which are simply suspended or postponed. Many commentators have predicted that the true costs of China's authoritarian efficiency will be seen in the future.[9]

Land-related mass protest and, for that matter, environmental and labor protest, has often been a result of China's authoritarian decisiveness.[10] In promoting China's economic growth, the government has marginalized the social concerns of the people whose land and livelihood will be affected. At a policy level, it is well known that principal local officials are evaluated and promoted according to their ability to promote the local economy and increase GDP. Since economic performance provides legitimacy for the authoritarian party-state, development has been the central task of the regime and the priority of any local government. In this political environment, land becomes a significant source of revenue to be exploited for the government. The rights of ordinary residents to their land becomes a marginal concern and, frequently, the government ignores its own law designed for the protection of those rights, leading to predatory land-grabbing and human catastrophes.[11]

This authoritarian decisiveness largely determines the trajectory of land dispute resolution in China. There is a litigation-based trajectory in which the aggrieved residents take developers to courts. There have been significant improvements in legal rules in land-taking cases designed to offer substantive and procedural protection of land rights, luring mostly marginalized groups to the legal system for remedies. The local political economy, however, undermines the institutional capacity, resulting in a systemic failure of the implementation of the law. In reality, courts have only limited power and capacity to enforce land rights in

[8] Lee and Zhang, "The Power of Instability"; Fu, "Politicized Challenges," p. 78.

[9] See, for example, Randall Peerenboom, "Law and Development in China and India: The Advantages and Disadvantages of Front-Loading the Costs of Political Reform," available at: http://papers.ssrn.com/sol3/papers.cfm?abstract_id=1283209; Francis Fukuyama, "The Historical Pattern of Political Development in East Asia," keynote speech at the International Conference on Democracy in Taiwan and East Asia in Global Perspective, National University of Taiwan, August 24–25, 2011, available at: www.asianbarometer.org/newenglish/whatsnew/taiwan100/Francis%20Fukuyama%20keynote.pdf.

[10] Christian Gobek and Lynette H. Ong, *Social Unrest in China* (Europe China Research & Advice Network, 2012).

[11] *Ibid.* See also Chapter 4 in this book.

collective cases.[12] Individual case-based litigation is a painful process, and litigants achieve little in the current legal and political environment. As a result, plaintiffs in land-taking cases have little hope of winning and little confidence in a court in delivering justice.

The institutional design is such that litigation cannot be afforded by the litigants and may not produce effective remedies. Lawyers may not be willing to take on controversial cases against the government; courts may create legal barriers by rejecting a case if there are too many plaintiffs; and judges are unwilling to find for the plaintiff if the verdict may encourage others to sue. While legal rights do exist, the court is not able to enforce them for the benefit of the victims.[13]

The litigation trajectory starts with litigation and ends with tremendous frustration in land and other collective cases. Mass litigation is characterized by power disparity between the parties, taking place largely between private citizens as plaintiffs and developers and governments as defendants.[14] Facing procedural and substantive legal barriers, the majority of the victims simply give in to pressure, give up their rights, and "lump it." However, the litigation trajectory can easily morph into radical self-help. An increasing minority of victims are taking the law into their own hands and pursuing radical measures against developers or the government. In labor cases, workers block highways and commence street actions; in environmental cases, victims sabotage polluting factories, including cutting off power lines or damaging factory property; in land-taking cases, self-immolation, real or threatened, has become a common tragedy. Such drastic actions often lead to direct confrontations with the police and invite state repression, such as beatings, detention, or criminal prosecution.[15]

In China's authoritarian system, the level of political participation in policy implementation is low,[16] and institutional channels for dispute resolution are rigidly restricted.[17] As a result, aggrieved citizens are driven to non-institutional channels and mobilize outside institutions, hence, pursuing/adopting an alternative, mobilization-based strategy.

[12] See Chapter 5 in this book.

[13] Gobek and Ong, *Social Unrest in China*. See also Chapter 5 in this book.

[14] Alex Wang, "Green Litigation in China Today," *Chinadialogue*, July 18, 2011, available at: www.chinadialogue.net/article/show/single/en/4413-Green-litigation-in-China-today.

[15] See, for example, Chapters 5 and 7 in this book.

[16] Tianjian Shi, *Political Participation in Beijing* (Cambridge, MA: Harvard University Press, 1997).

[17] Yongshun Cai, "Social Conflicts and Modes of Action in China," *China Journal*, 59 (2008), 89.

In the mobilization-based trajectory, frustrated citizens organize themselves to demonstrate their dissatisfaction, as well as their power. With the support of a wider community, they may force the government to compromise. Unlike the litigation-based trajectory in which individual victims face powerful entities, mobilization draws upon the collective power of the community and participants from different walks of life who are united through an informal network to fight for a common cause. Social mobilization, rather than individual litigation, is more likely to persuade and compel the government to correct the market and government failures in the related policy areas. Public protest, when combined with lawsuits, elite support, the mobilization of NGOs, and press coverage, has the potential to attract sustained official attention from higher levels and effective responses from the political system.[18] Social and political forces that are generated through mobilization can bring life to the legal system so as to restore its institutional integrity and give the law some credibility.

Through collective action, citizens are mobilized to create or reinforce an institutional veto point in the decision-making process so that the decision makers comply with legal requirements. It is well known that unconventional resistance outside institutions are more effective in achieving their immediate objectives in collective disputes than conventional and institutional mobilization.[19] Citizens who are resourceful and well organized will find sympathizers and supporters in the government and society who will speak out and act on some of the issues. On their own, individual mechanisms, such as congressional supervision, political consultation, media exposure, or expert and public participation, merely represent a "parchment division of power" and do not function as an effective veto in the Cox and McCubbins sense. But when all these forces are harnessed and brought to focus on a single social concern, they are powerful enough to nullify decisions.

Under what circumstances can such a mobilization-based trajectory deliver a positive result for citizens? In environmental disputes, for example, a successful protest depends on the participation of residents from different walks of life, who are united for a brief moment on a single issue of common concern. The principal participants of protests are urban residents who are

[18] Yongshun Cai, *Collective Resistance in China: Why Popular Protests Succeed or Fail* (Stanford University Press, 2010).

[19] Yang Su and Xin He, "Street as Courtroom: State Accommodation of Labour Protest in South China," *Law & Society Review*, 44 (2010), 157–184; Kwan Lee, *Against the Law*.

the key component of China's emerging middle class. They are economically well-off, socially connected, and politically resourceful. It is much easier for these protesters to obtain elite sympathy, media support, and tolerance and the indulgence of local government departments, including the security forces. Can social mobilization occur in rural or more remote settings? Wukan's protest offers a test case.

Land-grabbing and protest in Wukan

Villagers in Wukan experienced the full spectrum of dispute resolution from petition to violent protest between September and December 2011. The village used to have 9,000 mu or 6 km^2 of land, but by 2011 more than 75 percent of the land (6,700 mu or 4.46 km^2) had been sold without either proper authority from, or proper compensation to, the villagers. Allegedly, the village officials illicitly sold the village land to different developers and pocketed a vast amount of the money paid. The villagers, led by the younger generation,[20] had repeatedly petitioned against the illicit land transactions and their struggle gathered momentum in September 2011.[21]

Land-grabbing as experienced by the Wukan villagers is not unique; however, the protest that was unleashed, its level of organization, and the sophistication of its management and leadership during the course of the protest was unprecedented. The protest demonstrated the following characteristics.[22]

First, it was a sustained, and often dramatic, struggle that caught the imagination of the world, and attracted the sympathy and support of people of different political persuasions in China. The villagers adopted a variety of strategies in making their claims and gradually escalated their action, carefully calculated in response to government neglect and repression. They initially occupied local construction sites and demonstrated in front of the villagers' committee offices, forcing out the officials. The villagers then petitioned Sanwei city government departments and took regular street action such as demonstrations and sit-ins.

[20] Zhang Jieping, "乌坎少年" ("The Wukan Kid"), available at: http://zhangjieping.com/1.html.

[21] "Wukan Protest," Facts and Details, available at: http://factsanddetails.com/china.php?itemid=2246&catid=8.

[22] Special Issue, "乌坎与中国基层民主" ("Wukan and Grass-roots Democracy in China"), *iSunaffairs* (阳光时务), 8 (May 16, 2012), available at: www.isunaffairs.com/?p=5672; Al Jazeera, "Wukan: After the Uprising," available at: www.aljazeera.com/programmes/specialseries/2013/06/2013626153044866869.html.

When faced with police attempts to disperse the crowd through force, villagers responded forcefully and even violently by smashing police vehicles, attacking a police station, and beating up police officers. When petitions and demonstration failed to attract government attention, the villagers blocked entrances to the village with trees and wooden boards and forcefully resisted the reestablishment of government control.

Second, Wukan launched a well-organized resistance. Throughout the process, villagers demonstrated their superb capacity for mobilization, organization, and communication. By replacing the Wukan Party branch and villagers' committee (which fled during the protest), the Wukan villagers established their own alternative center of power, the Village's Provisional Village Representatives' Committee (村民臨時代表理事會) and the Women's Representatives' Association (婦女代表聯合會), to lead their protest. The creation of a leadership structure united the otherwise divisive villagers and endowed people like Lin Zulan and other protest leaders much needed legitimacy to act as the villagers' official representatives. This is probably the first time in the history of Communist China when villagers have set up their own governing body to exercise independent political power.

Third, the protest attracted unprecedented international attention as well as coverage in the domestic social media. Surprisingly, the Guangdong authority was tolerant of the extensive on-site coverage by over 100 overseas media outlets, especially those from Hong Kong.[23] The village youth, many of them having returned from cities to participate in the protest, proved to be media savvy and possessed a high level of sophistication in using information technology to tell their story to the outside world.[24] The villagers won the media battle in the court of public opinion before they won the battle with the government.

Finally, under the able leadership of Lin Zulan, the villagers were able to force the provincial authority to the negotiation table.[25] As demanded, the government released villagers who were detained by the police for organizing the protest, and assured them that there would be no

[23] For a study of media presentation of Wukan, see Severo Marta, Giraud Timothée, and Douay Nicolas, "The Wukan's Protests: Just-in-Time Identification of International Media Events," available at: http://jitso.org/2012/12/02/the-wukans-protests-just-in-time-identification-of-international-media-events-revised.

[24] Zhang, "The Wukan Kid."

[25] For a study of the political economy of concession-making on the part of the government, see Cai, *Collective Resistance in China*.

government reprisal against any villagers in future. The provincial government also undertook a serious investigation into the land sales in the village and pledged to punish any wrongdoing. Significantly, the provincial government promised a free election of the village committee so that the newly elected village authority would be able to recover lost land. After a two-hour closed-door meeting between the Deputy Party Secretary of Guangdong Province and Lin Zulan, the villagers declared the end of their three-month resistance on 21 December 2011.

Land disputes and the logic of the Chinese developmental state

Land-taking for development purposes is a straightforward issue for the government despite occasionally fierce and desperate resistance from the individuals and communities affected. For the authoritarian decision makers, those tragedies that land-taking may have caused are temporary, inevitable, and beneficial for national development. As such tragic decisions are made for the national and public interest, they are politically, morally, and, therefore, legally justifiable. After all, all land belongs to the state and all land-taking is justifiable, as long as it is for the national and public interest as the government defines it. It is popularly said that there would be no new China without land-taking.[26]

There is often a high degree of frustration among government officials when their well-intentioned development agenda is not appreciated by the masses. The internal speech by the Party Secretary of Shanwei on the Wukan protest captures that frustration well:

> Year by year, the current central policies have gotten better and more beneficial to the people. And there is only one group of people who feel more hardship year by year. Who are they? They are the officials, me included. Previously a city Party chief could not be so tiring. Everything has now become my responsibility, but day by day, my power is becoming smaller, and measures at my disposal are fewer as the responsibility is getting bigger. And then, day by day, the appetites of ordinary people are getting bigger, the ordinary people are getting smarter and more difficult to control . . . they don't rely on such a good government they have, but resort to a few rotten media, rotten newspapers, and rotten websites in foreign countries . . .[27]

[26] For further elaboration of the statist view, see Chapter 4 in this book.

[27] 汕尾市委书记郑雁雄对乌坎村民讲话的全文 (Full speech by Zheng Yanxiong, Party Secretary of Shanwei City, to Wukan villagers, dated December 18, 2011), available at: http://wenku.baidu.com/view/506d361e6bd97f192279e96f.html.

The general perception from the government is that society has become ungovernable, and that the masses are no longer as obedient as they used to be due to the moral decay and declining governance capacity at the grass-roots level.[28] From the government's perspective, the citizens' demands are often excessive, and the way in which the demands are made is irrational. When the citizens' interests, especially their vital interest in land, are adversely affected, they are able to speak out openly and act out fiercely. Indeed, citizens are determined, and have demonstrated, their clear will and capacity to take drastic measures in protesting their property rights against any encroachment. The well-documented nail-like households in Chongqing and elsewhere, whose owners defy relocation orders and resist to the last moment, have attracted wide international and domestic attention. These public displays of defiance and resistance have inspired many households and individuals to follow their example.[29]

But protest against land-taking is only part of the problem. It is a widely held view among local officials that the government has less effective tools to implement many of its tough decisions. When society is less dependent on the government for their socio-economic livelihoods, the government has less leverage over the masses. Under media scrutiny and enhanced political and legal accountability, government officials often complain, as they did in the Wukan case, that their hands are tied in handling a crisis. It is a risky and costly business to handle a public order event, and as the Shanwei Party Secretary aptly put it, it cost the government a lot of money to use the police to crack down on the protest.[30]

Those financial and political costs notwithstanding, the government is determined to keep any organized protest at bay while simultaneously continuing the same land-taking policy. It is not as if the government is blind to corruption and abuses in the land-taking process. On the contrary, it is well aware of the frustration and tension that land-taking has generated, yet it regards the abuse and corruption as a marginal issue in the economic transitional period. That suffering is an unfortunate yet

[28] Yu Jianrong, 抗争性政治:中国政治社会学基本问题 (*Contentious Politics: Foundational Issues in Chinese Political Sociology*) (Beijing: Renmin Press, 2010).

[29] For an interesting example, see Jeremy Goldkorn, "Property Right: The Coolest Nail House in History," available at: www.danwei.org/bbs/property_rights_the_coolest_na.php.

[30] 汕尾市委书记郑雁雄对乌坎村民讲话的全文 (Full speech by Zheng Yanxiong, Party Secretary of Shanwei City, to Wukan villagers).

unavoidable cost to be paid for China's national development. What underlines the developmental state, as many leftist critics point out, is the determination of the government and the business sector to grow the economy at the cost of peasants, workers, and other marginalized groups.[31]

Facing public protest, the government offers claimants an opportunity to leave the streets and return to the legal and institutional channels, courts in particular, for remedies. Otherwise, the government is entitled to use repressive measures to put protests and street actions to an effective end. The Shanwei government responded firmly when the Wukan villagers marched on the streets. Concerned with the continuous protest, international exposure, and the possibility of a spreading-over effect, the government first mobilized the propaganda machine, alleging the involvement of organized crime. The authority named names in its broadcasting, singling out Lin Zulan and others as the ringleaders of the disturbance. Later, the government took more resolute actions by proscribing the spontaneous organizations and placing five key protest figures under criminal detention for criminal damage during the protest.[32] This series of repressive actions would have ended the protest in normal circumstances.

From a security perspective, the government worried about the political risk that may be posed by the Wukan protest, and linked the protest to the possible infiltration of hostile overseas forces. The Party has been concerned with a potential color revolution in China since 1989, and is vigilant in guarding against any such political risk.[33] The Wukan protest, in its early stage, was seen in the larger context of the Arab Spring.[34] Due to the extensive press coverage of the protest in Wukan, there was a suspicion that overseas forces might use the protest to fan anti-government sentiment. There was also the view that the Wukan protest might be a sequel of the alleged Jasmine Revolution in China in 2011 and part of an ongoing color revolution against the Communist Party. After all, Wukan did create an

[31] For a leftist critique of the Wukan solution, see articles published in www.wyzxwk.com.

[32] One of the villagers later died in police custody, and the death added significantly to the development of the Wukan protest.

[33] Titus Chen, "China's Reaction to the Color Revolutions: Adaptive Authoritarianism in Full Swing," *Asian Perspective*, 34 (2010), 5–51; Hualing Fu, "Responses to Terrorism in China," in Victor V. Ramraj, Michael Hor, Kent Roach, and George Williams (eds.), *Global Anti-Terrorism Law and Policy* 2nd edn. (Cambridge University Press, 2012), pp. 334–356.

[34] Johan Lagerkvist, "The Wukan Uprising and Chinese State–Society Relations: Toward 'Shadow Civil Society,'" *International Journal of China Studies*, 3 (2012), 345–361.

alternative power center, which could be seen as posing a frontal challenge to the established political power. There was a sign that Wukan received sympathy, and the Wukan way was followed by other villages.

The Wukan protest was also connected to the 1989 student movement and the potential of a bottom-up anti-corruption campaign to generate a political crisis. An anti-corruption mobilization could easily morph into an anti-government mobilization, and where the former ends and the latter starts are hard to judge. The level of organization in Wukan and the attention it attracted may have gone beyond what the government was prepared for and could allow. There was the concern that the protest, if uncontrolled, could provoke radical thinking and action, and, if followed by other villages, would escalate into another political crisis.

In a widely circulated internal speech allegedly made by a top CCP official at a stability maintenance conference, the Wukan protest was singled out as a threat that posed a direct challenge to Party rule. It warned that:

> Right now there are tens of thousands of mass incidents [in China each year], mostly happening in rural townships and villages and remote regions, the causes being principally economic. These are convenient for us to independently resolve or break up. But if these spread to coastal cities and are transformed into political demands, the result would be unimaginable. Some comrades lack a real sense of the dangers involved, thinking we are over-reacting. It would be better for a clear directive from the central authorities to over-react than to fall short [of what is needed].

It concluded that:

> The Wukan incident is far from finished. Can challenges to the leadership status of the Chinese Communist Party evade retribution? That is a page we cannot open, that no one dares [to] open.[35]

Well-orchestrated protests against the government must therefore be met with stern responses.

From repression to accommodation

The prolonged and fierce resistance on the part of the Wukan villagers, and the wide coverage in international media, forced the party-state to rethink its crisis management strategy. The Guangdong CCP

[35] Translated in David Bandurski, "The Legacy of Wukan," available at: http://cmp.hku.hk/2012/01/30/18237.

Committee, under the leadership of the liberal-leaning Party Secretary, Wang Yang, modified its position and indicated its willingness to end the matter through dialogue.[36] The significant change in the government's position is its recognition that China's economic success has incurred tremendous social cost to a certain segment of the population, and land disputes in Wukan should first be understood in that particular context. Furthermore, economic deprivation and social inequality, if coupled with political repression, will lead to radicalization and rebellion of the marginalized social groups. From this new perspective, Wukan's protest is seen as a result of the combined effect of economic exploitation and political repression of marginalized peasants.

In a commentary on current affairs, the *People's Daily* reversed the official assessment on the Wukan protest and provided the much-needed legitimacy for the protest.[37] First of all, according to the *People's Daily*, Wukan's claims were legitimate because the villagers were merely demanding transparency and accountability, and, in making the demand, they were exercising their legal rights to know and participate in village governance as the law provides. Villagers sought to protect their economic interests and did not pose any challenge to the political system.

Second, conflict, which is bound to happen during China's economic transition, can be properly and promptly handled. As the *People's Daily* lamented, if the local government "had listened to the peasants seriously, evaluated the claims fairly and acted promptly, a small matter would not have escalated into a big concern threatening social stability which necessitates interventions from higher levels of government."[38] The *People's Daily* was even-handed in pointing the finger. It cautioned against irrational or radical claim-making on the part of the masses and pointed out that people may have a legitimate claim, but that such legitimate claims must be made within a proper legal framework. It then blamed the local government for suppressing the dispute, creating the conditions for confrontation.

According to the new view, the Wukan protest is therefore typical of conflict in transitional China, where individuals are motivated to articulate and protect their social and economic interests. As Guangdong Party Secretary Wang Yang put it:

[36] Chen Jibing, "乌坎标本" ("The Sample of Wukan"), available at: http://blog.qq.com/qzone/622007996/1327030504.htm.

[37] Zhang Tie, "乌坎转机"提示我们什么" ("What Does the 'Turnaround in Wukan' Clue Us Into?"), available at: http://opinion.people.com.cn/GB/16677909.html.

[38] *Ibid.*

> The occurrence of the Wukan incident was both a matter of chance and a matter of inevitability. This is the result of having paid insufficient attention ... to tensions that have been built up in the process of economic and social development ... The tragedy occurred in Wuhan due to management failure on the part of the government who is not able to attend to social problem promptly and effectively.[39]

Law offers the best solution to reconcile diverse interests when disputes occur in these circumstances. Wukan in that sense offered an alternative way of handling social conflict that relies on free articulation, effective remedies, and, in any event, the core principle of legality and the rule of law. The danger lies with the traditional "oppositional stance" that the government takes in suppressing conflict. The solution offered by this new approach is to use legal rules and bring contentious social issues from the streets to the legal process.[40]

Subsequently, the Guangdong authorities softened their position and agreed to meet most of the demands of the villagers. In particular, the Guangdong government agreed to a free election of the governing body in Wukan with the expectation that leaders chosen by the villagers would have more legitimacy and would be able to better manage village affairs. It is interesting to note that the Wukan villagers started their protest with a broad range of demands in relation to the illicit sale of land, but it ended with a promise from the provincial government for a free election of a new village authority.

For liberals, Wukan's demands for a free election and the government's concession represented a "beginning" and a "catalyst" for further constitutional development in China,[41] with the Party chief, Wang Yang, himself stating that the Wukan way has "set a reference standard to reform village governance across Guangdong," that is, to solve the governance crisis through democratic participation.[42] Against all the odds, the election turned out to be a stunning success. In many aspects, Wukan's "wholly transparent, completely open, democratic election"[43] has been heralded as a landmark that defies the doctrinal view on political development.

[39] Cited in Chen Jibing, "The Sample of Wukan." [40] *Ibid.*

[41] See 胡耀邦史料信息网, "'乌坎转机'的时代意义和国家样本意义'" (Historical Information Network on Hu Yaobang, "The Contemporary Significance of 'Wukan Transformation' as an Example for the Nation"), available at: www.hybsl.cn/zonghe/zuixinshiliao/2011-12-26/28051.html.

[42] Cited in Mimi Lau, "Base Reform on 'Wukan,' Party Boss Says," *South China Morning Post*, January 5, 2012.

[43] Malcolm Moore, "Wukan: Rebel Chinese Village Prepares to Hold Extraordinary Elections," *The Telegraph*, January 31, 2011.

The successful election in Wukan is significant in several respects. First, it challenges the proposition that Chinese rural society lacks the necessary social and economic conditions for democratic participation. According to conventional doctrine, democracy requires a prior social and economic condition, including socio-economic freedom, a middle class, and a vibrant civil society. Peasants may suffer and rebel, but there is no support structure, which is necessary for democratic participation. Second, the Wukan success confirms that peasants have enough quality to organize elections and participate meaningfully in democratic politics. There is a long-lasting debate in China on whether the Chinese people have the necessary cultural make-up for democracy. But the Wukan election serves as a powerful rebuttal against the critics' cynical view of the Chinese peasantry. Without achieving conditions that are often regarded as the prerequisites for democracy, Wukan villagers demonstrated their democratic impulse, that is, their strongly felt desire to be free from government corruption and repression, and the desire for autonomy and self-governance. The initial success and the onset of democracy brought hope and excitement for the future. In those few weeks, villagers in Wukan were transformed from members of their clans, caring only for their particularistic interest, into citizens who can be in charge of the destiny of a larger community. In the right circumstances, peasants, like those in Wukan, can develop the political will and capacity to engage in democratic politics.

Third, the democratic process, as demonstrated in Wukan, is both a tortuous and educational one for all who were involved.[44] In Wukan, one witnessed not only the democratic impulse, but also, more significantly, democratic patience and resilience, where villagers were surprisingly passionate about a deliberative and electoral process despite their lack of democratic experiences and exposure.[45] Constitutional learning in Wukan was quick, solid, and, by any standard, impressive. The villagers operated three sophisticated elections within a short time span. They

[44] Al Jezeera, "Wukan: After the Uprising."

[45] In a broad sense, Wukan represents an emerging popular constitutionalism in China. See Michael W. Dowdle, "Beyond 'Judicial Power': Courts and Constitutionalism in Modern China," in Stephanie Palme and Michael W. Dowdle (eds.), *Building Constitutionalism in China* (New York: Palgrave Macmillan, 2009); Keith Hand, "Constitutionalizing Wukan: The Value of the Constitution Outside the Courtroom," *China Brief*, 12(3) (2012), available at: www.jamestown.org/programs/chinabrief/single/?tx_ttnews%5Btt_news%5D=38966&tx_ttnews%5BbackPid%5D=25&cHash=f36abb49170102cf24efa14a1265cd41#.Uhn2qNKBn4s.

elected: 109 members, through an open election in accordance with the legal requirement, to form the Villagers Assembly, which is the representative body; an eleven-member Electoral Committee, which is the body in charge of the election for the Villagers Committee; and, finally, the Villagers Committee, which is Wukan's executive body. Step by step, the peasants, advised by outside experts, learned to participate and they quickly picked up the essence of democratic participation, ranging from nominating candidates, organizing campaigns, making public speeches to balloting and vote-counting. Towards the end, Wukan villagers ran a prefect election that fully complied with legal requirements and fairness in procedures. Democracy is a learning process, and Wukan proved the feasibility of intensive democratic learning within a short time span.

Finally, a more specific contention is whether democracy is possible in a highly clan-based society like Wukan. Wukan may have offered a new path to democratization because the village democratized itself through relying on the traditional social network – institutions that do not fit the definition of the traditional democracy-enhancing civil society and need to be abolished for democracy to arrive.[46] After all, the Provisional Villagers' Representative Assembly was composed of representatives of forty-seven kinships in the village.[47] Wukan built its democracy through creative adaptation of traditional lineage groups, with kinship at the core of village political power providing the necessary organizational framework and trust. To quote Keliher and Wu:

> Wukan is showing that the empowerment of individuals and groups has no set form and no predetermined structure. The democratic means of empowerment do not run through constitutions and political parties, but rather are built from the very materials at hand in the current reality.[48]

The villagers and keen observers of Wukan were well aware of the tension between clan interests and Wukan's larger interests, and the adverse impact that tension may have on Wukan's democratic struggle. The strong clan tradition may shape the institutional design of rural democracy, and in turn the democratic impulse may restrain the distinct clan interests. Clan-based interests surfaced and were well articulated in the electoral process, but in the case of Wukan the clan-based structure

46 Lagerkvist, "The Wukan Uprising and Chinese State–Society Relations."

47 Macabe Keliher and Hsin-Chao Wu, "Trashing the Script: Protests, Democracy, and Kinship Organizations in China," available at: www.possible-futures.org/2012/01/24/trashing-the-script.

48 *Ibid.*

did not divide the village and hinder the democratic process. The common interest of individual voters to reclaim their right to the lost land served to overcome the biases of individual clans. The lesson of Wukan is that village democracy is not a given: it is something that villagers, based on their social, economic, and political interests, have to struggle for and, for some, to die for. Free elections matter a lot to the Chinese peasants.[49] For those who went through the process, democracy with its intrinsic transparency and participatory process, as limited as it is, offers the best starting point to resolve the difficulties they experienced, including corruption and poverty.

The limit of the rule of law and democratic governance

Once the election was concluded and the leadership was in place, the Guangdong government started to downplay the political significance of the Wukan model and assert that whatever happened in the village operated entirely within the existing legal framework. The request for the return of land, therefore, also had to be made in accordance with the law and legal procedures.

When Wukan villagers became aware that land had been sold without their authorization and without proper compensation, their immediate response was to petition the government to resolve their dispute through institutional channels. Interestingly, no attempt was made to bring the case to court and, in the eyes of the villagers, the court was irrelevant in the particular case. The understanding was that land-taking is a highly politicized issue and can be resolved only through political means. When frustrated with the lack of response from the government, the villagers sought self-help by taking to the streets, which led to a sustained and occasionally violent confrontation with the authorities. Eventually, the villagers forced the authorities to negotiate and make the necessary concessions. Villagers were allowed to choose their own leaders with the expectation that the democratically chosen leaders would perform effectively in seeking the return of the stolen land.

Whatever was offered to the Wukan villagers was limited, however, when the Wukan protest is analyzed with the Chinese political system as the backdrop. The election in Wukan took place in a larger context which was hostile to any democratic process. Ironically, while Wukan

[49] See, for example, David Zweig and Chung Siu Fung, "Elections, Democratic Values, and Economic Development in Rural China," *Journal of Contemporary China*, 16 (2007), 25.

was voting for their village leaders, independent candidates for local people's congresses elsewhere were harassed and punished, political dissidents were imprisoned, and dissenting voices were censored and silenced.[50] The government isolated democracy to a single village and, as a "greenhouse" for democracy, its impact was limited.

As many of the critics from both left and the right have pointed out, the Wukan success only tinkered on the margin of the Chinese authoritarian system, and had no impact on the larger political system on which village democracy depends. Indeed, the event did not advance democracy in China because it merely implemented the law that has been in existence since 1987. If it was significant, its significance lay in the fact that it brought life to an electoral system and put a law into implementation. While claiming that the Wukan event is a landmark in developing constitutionalism in China, legal reformers are doubtful that it can be a catalyst for a new round of political reform, realizing that democratic governance and protest of property rights have long been enshrined in the Chinese Constitution and law. Lubman rightly points out that "the protest was resolved, not by law, but by the administrative actions of provincial Party officials." The corrupt officials involved may be punished, but the legal actions "would likely be a fait accompli following a prior Party decision on their punishment."[51] It is ultimately the democracy-deficit that is the root cause of the political problem facing villagers in Wukan and elsewhere. What has been, or is likely to be, achieved will not go beyond the limited existing legal rights under tight political constraints.

Beyond the lack of political reform and its disabling impact on legal institution, there is the political economy of a developmental state looming large in the background. At the end of the day, the villagers, even behind their own democratically elected leaders, would not be in a position to challenge the logic of the developmental state that tips the scale decisively in favor of land-taking for economic growth. The economic logic of the market economy as practiced in China necessitates the continuous expropriation of agricultural land for development purposes. The drive toward privatization creates a high degree of inequality and social tension. The unholy alliance between powerful government

[50] Jean Philippe Beja, Hualing Fu, and Eva Pils, *Liu Xiaobo, Charter 08 and the Limits of China's Political Reform* (Hong Kong: Hong Kong University Press, 2012).

[51] Stanley Lubman, "The Wukan Protests and the Rule of Law," available at: http://blogs.wsj.com/chinarealtime/2012/01/07/the-wukan-protests-and-the-rule-of-law.

officialdom and the resourceful business community has led to both market and governmental failure. As Keliher and Wu argue: "growth has outstripped regulation, allowing those with connections, wealth, and power to exploit loopholes as well as villagers. Here, the lack of legal constraints favours the few and fails the vast majority of the population."[52] The Wukan model notwithstanding, the same difficulties identified by the *People's Daily* and Wang Yang remain.

Within this particular political and economic context, villagers can hardly rely on the rule of law to protect their property rights. They cannot rely on the domestic press to make their claims because there is no press freedom; and they cannot trust the courts for remedies because there is no judicial independence. The implementation of legal rights takes place within a one-party state with authoritarianism at its core. The vast majority of the advocates and reformers are committed to the "system," and are attempting to reform the law within the existing political and economic framework by demanding that the "system" try and live up to its rhetoric. While reformers take the approach of changing the system through piecemeal, incremental, and technical reform, and prioritizing rights that are less sensitive to the party-state, the reform rhetoric should not be accepted at its face value: it is embedded in the same political and economic context, hence, the limit of the model offered by Wukan.

Conclusion

Authoritarian efficiency defines China's developmental state, which tolerates or justifies repressive approaches in land-taking for economic development, and insists on effective state control over land for developmental purposes with only marginal regard to the interests of the people and community. State interest predominates in land-takings, and the imperative of economic growth, which necessitates land-taking, overrides the interest of individuals and rural collectives.

There is also a deeply felt fear that a prolonged protest against land-taking may be contagious and could ignite a large political movement against the party-state. While repression may be necessary to maintain China's economic growth and social stability, resilient and fierce resistance to the developmental state has the potential to undermine the regime's effectiveness and legitimacy.

[52] Keliher and Wu, "Trashing the Script."

Many commentators have seen the Wukan protest as a prototype rebellion in which the Chinese peasantry, when faced with a predatory state, has the will and the capacity to rise up to protect their property rights. The Wukan protest served as a timely reminder that excessive predation and repression has the potential to trigger a larger social movement against the regime, and protests in Wukan and elsewhere have forced the government to take a more cautious approach in expropriating land. Facing fierce resistance and wider support in public opinion, the authorities changed their position and started to see Wukan as offering a unique window of opportunity to use the law to regularize and regulate rural governance. Striking a reconciliatory tone, the authorities became interested in exploring the potential of legal rules and procedures in conflict resolution.

However, the legal solution that was offered to Wukan was a limited one. On the surface, the government made concessions and gave permission to the villagers to enjoy their legal right of self-governance. Upon closer examination, the government successfully used legal rights and the rule of law to tame the democratic or revolutionary impulse that was evident among Wukan villagers, forcing the villagers to take their grievances and claims back to the bureaucratic institutions that failed them in the first place.

7

Protest-supported housing demolition litigation and social change in China

XIN HE

Housing demolition has been a major source of social conflict in contemporary China. With urban renewal and expansion occurring at a breathtaking pace, millions of urban residents have been relocated. Being undercompensated by the government or government-supported developers, homeowners have employed various forms of resistance, including protests, demonstrations, litigation, petitioning higher level governments, and refusing to move out. Official statistics have revealed that twenty-six deaths occurred due to conflicts over housing demolition in the first six months of 2002. Of the 1,730 petitions presented in person to the Ministry of Construction, about 70 percent related to housing demolition.[1]

One recent phenomenon is that more individuals affected by the demolition process have organized themselves and filed litigation challenging the government's decisions. The goal of these individuals is to exert pressure on the decision-making of the courts and other government agencies through protests and demonstrations. In a country where gaining approval to hold a public demonstration is almost impossible to obtain, courtrooms have become a public space for litigants to legitimately voice their grievances, discontent, challenges, demands, and even open defiance. By going to court, negative political labeling is avoided because it is difficult, if not impossible, for the state to say that going to court is politically subversive or incorrect.

The existing literature has rarely addressed how residents organize litigation as resistance. Legal scholars usually focus on the defective procedure that fails to balance the interests of developers and residents,

[1] "The Tragedies and Comedies of Housing Demolition over the Last Decade" ("拆迁十年悲喜剧"), *Southern Weekend* (南方周末), September 4, 2003.

and the collusive relationship between the government and developers.[2] As a result, many social and policy changes have to be inferred from other indicators; for example, some studies have rightly suggested that opposition and protests led to some reforms on housing demolition policy and practice in Shanghai after 2004,[3] but how exactly such change happens remains unknown. The role of Chinese courts in resolving social conflict, and the relationship between state and society, would be much more comprehensive and nuanced if the use of litigation in social movements was explored in the same way as is often done by researchers in the West.[4]

At the same time, students of social protest in China have paid inadequate attention to litigation-related collective action.[5] While some have noted that the filing of litigation is often accompanied by collective action and protest,[6] the dynamics of such trials have rarely been examined. This is understandable because court trials and popular movements have profoundly contrasting logics. Movements have a quick pace and acquire significance from mass public demonstrations and sometimes from a collective defiance of legality. However, court trials follow established procedures and rules, obtaining significance

[2] Matthew S. Erie, "Property Rights, Legal Consciousness and the New Media in China: The Hard Case of the Toughest Nail-house In History," *China Information*, 26 (2012), 35–59; Eva Pils, "Land Disputes, Rights Assertion, and Social Unrest: A Case from Sichuan," (*Columbia Journal of Asian Law*, 19 (2005), 365–392.

[3] Sarah Biddulph, "Justice and Order in Shanghai: The Case of Forced Housing Demolition and Relocation," in Mary Farquhar (ed.), *21st Century China: Views From Australia* (Newcastle-upon-Tyne: Cambridge Scholars Publishing, 2009).

[4] But see Stuart Scheingold, *The Politics of Rights: Lawyers, Public Policy and Political Change* (New Haven, CT: Yale University Press, 1974); Joel Handler, *Social Movements and the Legal System: A Theory of Law Reform and Social Change* (New York: Academic Press, 1978); Frances Zemans, "Legal Mobilization: The Neglected Role of the Law in the Political System," *American Political Science Review*, 77 (1983), 690–702; Paul Burstein, "Legal Mobilization as a Social Movement Tactic: The Struggle for Equal Employment Opportunity," *American Journal of Sociology*, 96 (1991), 1201–1225; Michael W. McCann, *Rights at Work* (University of Chicago Press, 1994); Boaventura de Sousa Santos and Cesar A. Rodriguez-Garavito (eds.), *Law and Globalization from Below* (New York: Cambridge University Press, 2005).

[5] Kevin J. O'Brien and Lianjiang Li, *Rightful Resistance in Rural China* (Cambridge University Press, 2006); Cai Yongshun, *Collective Resistance in China: Why Popular Protests Succeed or Fail* (Stanford University Press, 2010); Ching Kwan Lee, *Against the Law: Labor Protests in China's Rustbelt and Sunbelt* (Berkeley, CA: University of California Press, 2007); Kevin J. O'Brien (ed.), *Popular Protest in China* (Cambridge, MA: Harvard University Press, 2008).

[6] Kevin J. O'Brien and Lianjiang Li, "Suing the Local State: Administrative Litigation in Rural China," *China Journal*, 54 (2004), 75–96.

through individual performances that reinforce existing legalities.[7] In many situations, using established channels may only do harm to the protesters' cause, which is why the government seeks to channel protest into established institutions.[8]

Bringing together the two literatures that tend to move along parallel tracks, this chapter explores how the ideal of the rule of law operates and evolves during the interaction between the courts and protests in a country where state control of civil society remains tight and strong. When faced with mounting numbers of protest-supported cases about housing demolitions, courts can no longer play their original role of mediating and containing social conflicts, which forces them to take decisions that lead to substantial social and legal change. Drawing on court documents and interviews with officials and staff, I examine the pressures the courts face in the litigation process and their actions in response to the litigation and protests. Given that social stability is the paramount concern of the ruling Communist Party, and that decisions favorable to the protestors will invite more litigation and protest, the immediate outcome of the litigation, more often than not, tends to support the land developers or the government. But dealing with protest-supported litigation has led the courts into an embarrassing situation. To relieve themselves from this situation, they have devised strategies to constrain the behavior of the housing authorities. They often do this in the name of the Party's interest in maintaining social stability. Many such actions have proved to be effective, as the housing authorities have altered their behavior and have begun to act in a more transparent and accountable manner.

This chapter is thus an effort to advance understanding on judicial politics in authoritarian states. Until recently, scholars have generally assumed that courts in authoritarian states are pawns of their regimes, upholding the interests of governing elites and frustrating the efforts of their opponents. But as demonstrated by Ginsburg and Moustafa,[9] there is a wide range of governance tasks that courts perform, and courts can serve as critical sites of contention both among the ruling elite and between regimes

[7] Peter P. Houtzager, "The Movement of the Landless (MST), Juridical Field, and Legal Change in Brazil," in Boaventura de Sousa Santos and Cesar A. Rodriguez-Garavito (eds.), *Law and Globalization from Below* (New York: Cambridge University Press, 2005), p. 221.

[8] Yang Su and Xin He, "Street as Courtroom: State Accommodation of Social Conflicts in South China," *Law & Society Review*, 44 (2010), 157–184.

[9] Tom Ginsburg and Tamir Moustafa (eds.), *Rule by Law: The Politics of Courts in Authoritarian Regimes* (New York: Cambridge University Press, 2008).

and their citizens. On the one hand, authoritarian rules often make use of courts to counteract many dysfunctions that plague their regimes. On the other hand, courts also have the potential to open a space for activists to mobilize against the state. Following this line of research, this study expands the scope of the inquiry by examining how movement energy can be converted into pressures inside the courts, and set in motion further conflicts between the courts and administrative cadres. In particular, focusing on the interplay of the Chinese courts, the housing demolition authorities, and the party and government puts courts in a broad political context and draws attention to the inner workings of a far-flung, many-layered state. "What emerges is a state that is less a monolith than a hodgepodge of disparate actors, some of whom have multiple identities and conflicting interests."[10] Disaggregating the Chinese state helps to understand how the conflict in society can be transformed into opportunities for social change. It thus suggests that the causes and consequences of judicial empowerment in authoritarian states could be far more complicated than originally imagined.

The case study

China is a society full of social conflict, and land-taking has been a major source of conflict. With the rapid pace of urbanization in China, large amounts of agricultural land are being converted to new uses and old buildings are being demolished, frequently against the will of those who have built their lives and livelihoods on their entitlement to land and a home. As in other sectors, China has aspired to regulate land-taking using "the rule of law." Starting from the 1980s, the state has promulgated relevant laws such as the Land Management Law (1986) and the Statute Governing Housing Demolition in Urban Areas (1991). For two reasons, however, the laws provide little shield for original homeowners and they are often unsatisfied. First, while the laws and other related regulations provide procedure and compensation for land-taking, these laws often have serious deficiencies. Some legal procedures are not clearly stipulated and the rights of the original homeowners are only vaguely defined. Second, and more important, even these laws are not properly followed because of the strong incentive of local government officials to taking land. Until very recently, economic development and local GDP have been the most important criteria by which to assess the performance of top local officials. And for most cities in China, real estate has been the engine for local economic development. Converting

[10] O'Brien and Li, "Suing the Local State," p. 94.

agricultural land into industrial use, or building luxury housing complexes or shopping malls in urban areas will attract large amounts of investment and bring about plenty of job opportunities. Moreover, local government officials can often benefit themselves by colluding with business developers in these processes. Farmers and homeowners receive only a fraction of the small sum that is their legal due; all too often, the local government and its corrupt officials take the bigger slice. The gross disparity between the affected individuals' losses and the gains of the real estate developers and city officials only exacerbates the dissatisfaction. These are all reasons for the growing number of often violent "mass incidents" in China.[11]

While popular resistance and petition have long been the traditional mode of resistance,[12] recently more of the disputants have also decided to take administrative agencies to court. This is partly due to the regime's own rhetoric in promoting the rule of law. Apart from the nationwide effort to implement administration according to law, "Ruling Jiangsu and Hunan provinces by Law" has been the signature slogan advocated by the party chiefs there. In particular, to remove the original homeowners from their homes, the governments have frequently applied for compulsory eviction permits in court. It is natural for homeowners to attend the court hearings and fight back using legal weapons.

Official statistics show that the number of collective litigation cases over land-taking has recently skyrocketed. In some courts, such cases make up more than 20 percent of all administrative litigation cases.[13] In these cases, the plaintiffs are hundreds, if not thousands, of farmers from several villages, or residents from a block in an old city district. They defend their rights collectively through both legal and extralegal means. Both news reports and fieldwork investigations have found that in Nantong Municipality in Jiangsu Province, the courtrooms are often packed by supporters of the litigants, in addition to many others demonstrating outside. These supporters include family members and other households affected by the state demolition policy and the rulings in such cases. In other cases, cross-neighborhood, and sometimes even cross-provincial, mobilization through the use of the Internet

[11] See, generally, Frank K. Upham, "Reflections on the Rule of Law in China," *Taiwan University Law Review*, 6(1) (2011), 251 at 257–260.

[12] Cai, *Collective Resistance in China.*

[13] "Caseload Pressures in Administrative Litigation Mounted for China's Basic-level Courts" ("中国基层法院面临民告官案件大幅增长诉讼压力"), *Liaowang Newsweek* (瞭望新闻周刊), April 22, 2006, available at: http://news.sina.com.cn/c/2006-04-22/12159690235.shtml, accessed August 27, 2013.

can be observed.[14] As shown in these Internet blogs, this phenomenon is by no means unique to Nantong. According to a government report, in Chongqing before 2009:

> There had been only a few cases in which the householders whose properties had been demolished were coordinated. Coordinating efforts started in some small-scale rural and urban communities and gradually spread to other adjacent communities. In 2009, farmers whose lands had been requisitioned and urban residents whose apartments had demolished started to coordinate themselves, forming relatively large-scale common interest groups. From January to April 2010, the residents in the main urban districts facing demolition started to engage in cross-district coordination. In the land requisition and housing demolition cases heard by Jiangbei District Court, supporters from Yuzhong and Jiulongpo districts and other provinces sat in on the trials.[15]

Drawing on a repertoire of resistance tactics, litigants affected by the housing demolition policies have staged protests and demonstrations. Similar to the environmental justice campaigns in the United States,[16] many of the protests occur in the context of the public hearings required by the law and held by government agencies, but they especially occur

[14] Liu Changfeng, "Forced Demolition: Don't Let the Bullet Fly" ("强制拆迁,不能让子弹飞"), 2010, available at: http://blog.qq.com/qzone/611994212/1285455587.html, accessed August 27, 2013; Liu Yejin, "Compensation Does not Justify Forced Demolition," 2010, available at: http://blog.caijing.com.cn/expert_article-151380-6681.shtml, accessed August 27, 2013; Ma Deqing, "A Critique of Forced Demolition" ("向强制拆迁开炮"), 2010, available at: http://blog.gmw.cn/u/36731/archives/2010/216475.html, accessed August 27, 2013; "Zhang's Trial in Nantong, Jiangsu" ("张永泉拆迁案发回一审南通崇川区法院重审即将开庭"), Forum 0513, 2007, available at: http://bbs.0513.org/thread-144359-1-1.html, accessed August 27, 2013; "Forced Demolition of Ancestors' Home, Fuzhou, Fujian" ("强制拆除我祖祖辈辈居住的房屋"), Forum 163, 2010, available at: http://bbs.gz.house.163.com/bbs/rights/183099835.html, accessed August 27, 2013; "Report of Illegal Demolition in Wuhu, Anhui" ("安徽芜湖发生非法强制拆迁大案 近200 人强拆一民房"), Forum Hexun, 2009, available at: http://xwjdw.blog.hexun.com/44438869_d.html, accessed August 27, 2013; "Report of Complaints by Litigants in Jiangsu" ("南通市崇川区人民法院偏袒被告违规审理 拆迁行政诉讼案件纪实"), Forum Weiquan, 2007, available at: www.weiquan365.com/bbs/index_main.asp?zhuzi=dispbbs&boardid=67&id=14576.

[15] "Trans-local Association among Residents Stands Out in Housing Demolition and Deserves Special Attention" ("基层反映征地拆迁中被拆迁群众"跨区串联"现象突出应予高度重视"), Jiangbei District Stability Maintenance Office (江北区平安办), Chongqing Municipality, May 14, 2010, available at: www.pacq.gov.cn/platform/news_view.asp?newsid=2070, accessed August 27, 2013.

[16] Anna-Maria Marshall, "Social Movement Strategies and the Participatory Potential of Litigation," in Stuart Scheingold and Austin Sarat (eds.), *Cause Lawyers and Social Movements* (Stanford University Press, 2006), pp. 174–175.

during court hearings. Individuals facing the demolition of their homes have filed both civil and administrative cases for reasons ranging from outrageous unfairness and the due process of law to government information disclosure. The plaintiff in a case documented by Erie[17] filed thirteen cases in fighting against the demolition of his home. In some cases, the plaintiffs consist of a group of affected households, while in others, only one affected individual files a case. The latter type of case is also collective because there is a large group of individuals behind the plaintiff, that is, to quote a term used by some judges, "testing the water." The legal representative hired for the plaintiff in such litigation is often collectively paid for by all of the affected households. It seems, therefore, that litigation is not so much an alternative to resistance or protest, but rather one of many strategies deployed in protests.[18] In such contests, resistance takes the form of both direct confrontation and institutionalized resolution. The line between direct resistance and participation in institutional channels is difficult to discern.

An influential media outlet asserted that collective administrative litigation "has become the new trend in citizen versus Mandarin cases."[19] But it is most noticeable in the sector of housing demolition for two reasons. First, housing demolition affects the most important asset most citizens can enjoy; and, second, housing demolition always affects all the citizens in a given community. They all face similar treatment and thus are easier to organize in order to file protest-supported litigation. This type of resistance has also spread to issue areas with similar characteristics such as pensions[20] and environmental disputes.[21]

The analysis below is primarily based on data collected in fieldwork investigations in Nantong, Jiangsu Province, and Taizhou, Zhejiang Province, on the east coast of China during the summer of 2012. These two places were chosen because such protest-supported litigation is widely reported and these places are also known as the pioneering areas in China's legal development. For instance, Taizhou is known for

17 Erie, "Property Rights."

18 Burstein, "Legal Mobilization as a Social Movement Tactic."

19 "Caseload Pressures in Administrative Litigation Mounted for China's Basic-level Courts."

20 William Hurst and Kevin O'Brien, "China's Contentious Pensioners," *China Quarterly*, 170 (2002), 345–360.

21 Benjamin Van Rooij, "The People vs. Pollution: Understanding Citizen Action against Pollution in China," *Journal of Contemporary China*, 19(63) (2010), 55–77.

its innovative practice in administrative litigation, and several administrative cases from Nantong courts on housing demolition are promoted by the Supreme People's Court of China. Economically, these two places represent the most developed areas in China. As one of the first cities opened for overseas investment, for example, Nantong's economy has grown steadily during the reform period. According to official statistics, the city's GNP reached around 287 billion yuan in 2009, ranked twenty-eighth among all Chinese cities and eighth among cities at the prefectural level. Its GDP per capita reached 35,040 yuan or US$5,000 in 2008, surpassing the medium of developed countries, and suggesting that it is one of the most affluent regions of the country. The economy has also been industrialized during the period. In 2008, the agricultural sector accounted for less than 12 percent of its GNP. Construction, textiles, petroleum–chemicals, ports, ship-building, and new energy have become the pillar industries, with the construction industry alone producing more than one-third of its GNP.[22]

The trial dynamics of housing demolition litigation is examined through a close reading of internal documents, including policy deliberations, court reports, judicial suggestions, judgments, and news reports. These documents provide four types of data. First, they detail the rationale and practice of the courts and various government agencies in handling protest-supported litigation; second, they report the concerns and difficulties in resolving collective action incidents; third, they record the actions on the side of the protesters and the reaction of the courts and government agencies; and, finally, they register the outcomes and rationales for some typical cases.

An analysis of documents is complemented by interviews with judges, mid-level court officials, and officials of administrative agencies involved in land lawsuits. I interviewed judges who have adjudicated housing demolition litigation and devised preventive measures for the courts. I asked them what pressures, challenges, and difficulties they faced in adjudicating this type of litigation and what prompted them to initiate further measures. More specifically, I asked them what their concrete tactics were to prevent future litigation and how they dealt with the media. Finally, I asked them about typical litigation cases that had been resolved, and inquired about their concerns and experiences in adjudicating these lawsuits.

[22] Baidu Wenku, "Nantong" (2011), available at: http://wenku.baidu.com/view/796bc41cc281e53a5802ff39.html, accessed May 5, 2013.

In total, I interviewed twenty officials and judges. Each interview lasted between half an hour to two hours, depending on the extent to which the interviewees were involved in administrative litigation and judicial innovation. Most of the interviews were conducted in the offices of the interviewees. Due to the sensitive nature of the topic, I did not record the interviews; instead, notes were taken during the interviews and compiled immediately thereafter. These interviews were complemented by phone interviews with judges from Guangxi, Beijing, and Shaanxi who were experienced in demolition cases. The findings were compared with data collected from other parts of China, such as Sichuan,[23] Chongqing, and Beijing.[24]

Like most qualitative studies, the number of interviews analyzed here is small. Although the small number of subjects requires caution in drawing generalizations, the in-depth approach made possible by small-*N* studies has the potential to reveal considerable nuances and details about the litigation dynamics, the pressures generated, the conflicts between the courts and the government, and their responses. Accordingly, the inquiry presents a theory-building opportunity to examine how legality is politicized and rights are negotiated, as well as how the judiciary is empowered.

Confronting protest-supported litigation

Under regular circumstances, the judge dominates the hearing process and the trial is conducted in an orderly and solemn way, but once litigation is combined with coordinated demonstrations, the dynamics of litigation takes a drastically different form. Turning the court hearing into a stage for protest, the affected households and their supporters exert a tremendous amount of pressure on judges and courts to maintain court order, make decisions, and, relatedly, to prevent the protest from being escalated.

Containing audience number

The presence of a large number of supporters at the hearing is a key characteristic of protest-supported litigation. From the perspective of the affected households, the more supporters they have, the more righteous their cause is and the more pressure they can exert on their opponents.

[23] Pils, "Land Disputes." [24] Erie, "Property Rights."

Also, as will be shown, only with the presence of some supporters in the hearing process will the aggrieved litigants perform effectively. From the perspective of the courts and judges, however, too many supporters may disrupt the hearing process and can sometimes lead to things getting out of control. Many courts thus want to restrict the audience number. The issue of audience number sometimes becomes the first battleground of this type of litigation.

Due to the reforms toward adjudicative transparency, most hearings are now open to citizens with proper IDs. The courts thus have no good reason to limit the audience number in advance without proper justification. In many cases, the supporters of the demolished households have taken advantage of this rule and swarmed the courtroom.

In one case in Luqiao District, Taizhou Municipality, Zhejiang Province in which three hard-nail households fought against the district government because the government had allegedly adopted a compensation standard that was six years out of date (hereinafter, the *Outdated Standard* case), the overall audience number reached more than 400, with people coming from all over Taizhou Municipality. The hearing venue had to be changed three times as more and more supporters turned out. This was completely beyond the court's expectation. Obviously, the organizer deliberately kept this arrangement from the court lest the court limit the audience number.[25]

In an administrative licensing case in which nineteen affected individuals sued the government in Zhabei District, Nantong, Jiangsu Province (hereinafter the *Licensing* case), more than 200 affected individuals and human rights advocates showed up, but the courtroom could only accommodate twenty people. The court thus kept most of the supporters out of the court building. This enraged the supporters, and they immediately blocked the gate of the court building, preventing motor vehicles from getting in or out. The court then had to make concessions, and it allowed the supporters to audit the trial. Due to the small size of the venue, the defendants and the supporters were not clearly separated, even though there was concern that the supporters might physically harm the defendants. Some supporters stood behind the plaintiffs and some stood in the corridor, and as a result, the courtroom doors remained open. The room was so packed that the plaintiffs did not have seats during the whole hearing process and the third party had to sit in the seats designated for the audience.

[25] Author's interview with judges, 2012.

Maintaining court order

Once a large number of supporters get into a courtroom, they do not stay quiet despite the legal requirement to do so. More often than not, they cheer for the affected households and their representatives, and make fun of their opponents.

Applause breaks out for any witty statement that ridicules the defendants or favors the plaintiffs. In the *Outdated Standard* case, the lawyer representing the hard-nail households was greeted with applause at least five times;[26] for example, applause broke out when the lawyer suggested that the Party chief of the economic development zone (the government) should not be introduced as a hearing participant because a party committee, according to the law, does not have any standing. When the lawyer suggested that the land certificate issued by the government might be legally invalid, the crowd roared and the court hearing almost got out of control. In addition to applause, some members of the audience raised banners with short but eye-catching slogans, echoing what was said by the affected households or their representatives.[27]

At the same time, supporters react, both spontaneously or purposely, to place the defendants in a legally and morally unpleasant position. When the defendants or their lawyers are unable to answer the questions raised by either the judge or the plaintiffs, for example, rustling sounds emerge from the audience. In the *Licensing* case, when the defendant was questioned on why their photocopied evidence was not consistent with the original, the defendant lost his train of thought; in response, noise broke out among the audience.

If all of the above behaviors show support for the affected individuals only indirectly, supporters in some scenarios directly participate in court discussions, challenging the statements of the defendants with emotional and confrontational language. According to one official account, "they 'support' (声援) the affected households and 'condemn or denounce' (声讨) the developers and officials. In many situations, they cry out (哭闹) or just act unreasonably to make a scene."

To enhance the effectiveness of support, supporters sometimes wear uniforms and/or display protest slogans in court. This is mentioned in

[26] Author's interview with judges, 2012.

[27] "Trans-local Association among Residents Stands Out in Housing Demolition and Deserves Special Attention."

several official reports.[28] They do these things to show that they are united and determined. These actions also indicate the resolve of the supporters: they are not just willing to participate in the court hearing process; they will also stay together as a block to resist the demolitions. The slogans, depicting the developers as bloodsuckers, or the officials as corrupt, or highlighting the legal clauses protecting property rights, serve to voice their rights and rage, laying the foundations for claiming remedies.[29]

All these behaviors pose a threat to the judges in maintaining a neat court order in the hearings. In the worst cases, they "denounce the judges and adjudicating staff and challenge the sheriffs".[30] In the *Outdated Standard* case, the tension between the defendant and the supporters lasted throughout the trial process; the defendant had to be escorted by the court sheriff as they left the court. In the *Licensing* case, in which the defendant and the supporters could not be separated because the supporters had swarmed the venue, the judge felt nervous throughout the whole hearing process.[31] Supporters sometimes believe that the judges are simply in the same position as the powerful: as the Chinese saying goes, officials and judges alike tend to protect each other. They accuse the judges of colluding with the developers and the demolition authorities, and believe that the judicial process is a sham. Some blackmail the judges and the courts, and some threaten to commit suicide.[32] In the *Differential Compensation* case, the judge told me that at the end of the hearing a supporter told her to "drive carefully."

One may wonder why the judges do not round up some protestors by invoking the contempt of court rule. It is true that in the Administrative and Civil Procedural Laws, the judges are authorized to do so. But in

[28] "Trans-local Association among Residents Stands Out in Housing Demolition and Deserves Special Attention"; Nantong Intermediate Court, "Judicial Suggestions" ("司法建议书"), 2008; Nantong Intermediate Court, "The Experience of Requiring the Person in Charge of Administrative Agencies to Testify in Administrative Litigation" ("推行行政机关负责人行政诉讼出庭应诉制度的经验"), *Nantong Adjudication* (南通审判), 2 (2009), 10–13.

[29] But see John Brigham, "Right, Rage, and Remedy: Forms of Law in Political Discourse," *Studies in American Political Development*, 2 (1987), 303–316.

[30] "Trans-local Association among Residents Stands Out in Housing Demolition and Deserves Special Attention."

[31] Author's interview with judges, 2012.

[32] "Trans-local Association among Residents Stands Out in Housing Demolition and Deserves Special Attention."

reality, this power has rarely been exercised. This is because the judges are required to explain the relevant court requirements to the litigation participants rather than to impose the penalty, which is consistent with the slogan "the judiciary shall work for the people." This is particularly true in this type of case because no judge or court wants to incite protestors who are already agitated.

In a way, the supporters turn the courtroom into a sports stadium. If the litigation parties are the athletes and the judges are the referees, the supporters are the spectators. Defying the legal requirement to stay quiet, the supporters cheer their teams, just as sports spectators do. When their interactions with other court participants are integrated into the court hearing process, the pace and rhythm of the hearing is somehow controlled by the supporters. In this sense, they also turn the courtroom into a theater. Originally, the judge was the leading actor, but the leading role has now been taken over by the supporters. The judges, like the referees, may feel respected and enjoy their positions; but it is also possible that the spectators will turn into mobs if the situation is not properly handled. They thus also feel pressured when conducting hearings.

Tolerating non-legal discourse

According to the civil procedural rules, when litigants or their representatives are making legally irrelevant points, the judge can interrupt them.[33] However, in protest-supported litigation, judges have become extremely cautious about interrupting the litigants because they want to prevent the crowd from becoming agitated. According to one judge with plenty of experience in hearing this type of case, one rule is not to interrupt the representation of the litigation parties. As a result, the plural discourse is allowed in the trial process.

With the presence of the supporters, the discourse of the aggrieved litigants and their lawyers differs from that in regular cases. To magnify their grievances and to expand the scope of the conflict, the claims made by the affected individuals and their legal representatives are always plural: they are not just legal, but simultaneously political and moral. They not only mobilize aspects of the law to challenge the land developers or government, but they also frame their grievances in a moral and

[33] The Supreme People's Court, "The Several Stipulations on the Adjudicative Proceedings of Civil and Economic Cases," issued by the SPC, June 19, 1998.

political discourse.[34] The law is drawn upon as a discourse to build coalitions with other norms, to challenge the assumptions of the Establishment, and to renegotiate the meaning of rights.[35] For example, in the *Differential Compensation* case, in which the villagers who had signed the demolition agreement sued for compensation because the government offered more compensation to the hard-nail households, the claim was that the differential treatment was "outrageously unfair." These villagers further accused the government of not honoring its own words because at the moment they were asked to sign the agreement, the government agreed to increase the compensation it would offer in the future. As a result, the government lost all credibility.

In another case, in which the court agreed to reopen the case after the plaintiff had repeatedly petitioned, the representation made to the court was full of emotional grievance, so much so that legal points were hardly mentioned. The plaintiff was a lady in her fifties who claimed that her home had been demolished without her being duly compensated. It was stated that she had been a volunteer exploring the frontier areas when she was young and that she had contributed her youth to the country. Her son had died in an accident in the frontier area while she was working. Despite this, her home had simply been demolished by the housing authorities at the time when she was about to retire.[36]

In regular cases, the legally irrelevant moral and political dimensions in arguments are easily dismissed. But in this type of case, the judges have to be extremely cautious because once they are invoked in public and are sometimes reported by the media, the courts have to respond to them. The courts thus have to deal with not just legal problems, but also moral and political arguments, making their job more difficult.

[34] But see E. P. Thompson, *Whigs and Hunters: The Origin of the Black Act* (New York: Pantheon, 1975); Martin Chanock, *Law, Custom, and Social Order: The Colonial Experience in Malawi and Zambia* (Cambridge University Press, 1985); Mari J. Matsuda, "Law and Culture in the District Court of Honolulu, 1844–1845: A Case Study of the Rise of Legal Consciousness," *American Journal of Legal History*, 32 (1988), 16–41; Sally E. Merry, "Courts as Performances: Domestic Violence Hearings in a Hawai'i Family Court," in Mindie Lazarus-Black and Susan F. Hirsch (eds.), *Contested States: Law Hegemony and Resistance* (New York: Routledge, 1994), p. 35.

[35] Catherine R. Albiston, "Bargaining in the Shadow of Social Institutions: Competing Discourses and Social Change in Workplace Mobilization of Civil Rights," *Law & Society Review*, 39 (2005), 11–50.

[36] "The Hearing Presentation of the Reopened Huang Shuying Case" ("黄淑英案再审听证代理词"), *Yingke Lawyer*, July 10, 2009, available at: www.yingkelawyer.com/2009/07/10/1333.html, accessed October 10, 2012.

Facing organized protest

The last, but most important, factor that makes this type of case difficult to handle is that the protest is often organized. Epp[37] shows that the most critical variable determining the timing, strength, and impact of rights revolutions is the ability of rights advocates to become organized, which enables them to engage in deliberate, strategic, and repeated litigation campaigns. When properly organized and coordinated, rights advocates can reap the benefits that come from being "repeat players."[38] While Epp's study is concerned with courts in democratic polities, his framework sheds light on the dynamics in litigation backed by organized social movements in authoritarian regimes.

In protest-supported litigation in China, some organizers are simply people affected by the demolitions, but others are seasoned activists. Some have been involved in the opposition to the demolition process and have thus accumulated experience of resistance. Some are simply friends or family members who are hired by the households affected by the demolition policy. Seasoned protestors solicit and persuade families to participate in the efforts to obtain a favorable settlement from the developers; in exchange, they receive a percentage of the settlement or a flat fee.[39] Some of them have even set up consulting firms dealing with housing demolition issues.[40]

Organizers coordinate with other affected households, organize protests outside and inside the courtroom, educate the family on the laws and policies related to urban housing demolition, feed the media with stories, and help to hire experienced lawyers. Some seasoned protestors even either directly coach the plaintiffs or act as their representatives themselves, thus improving the performance of the plaintiff in the litigation process. They are also the people behind the petitions to upper-level governments. All this

[37] Charles Epp, "Connecting Litigation Levels and Legal Mobilization: Explaining Interstate Variation in Employment Civil Rights Litigation," *Law & Society Review*, 24 (1990), 145–164.

[38] Marc Galanter, "Why the 'Haves' Come Out Ahead: Speculations on the Limits of Legal Change," *Law & Society Review*, 9 (1974), 95–126.

[39] But see Benjamin Liebman, "The Media and the Courts: Towards Competitive Supervision?" *China Quarterly*, 208 (2011), 833–850; "Court in the Shadow of Protest: Medical Malpractice Lawsuits in China" (2012), manuscript on file with author.

[40] "Trans-local Association among Residents Stands Out in Housing Demolition and Deserves Special Attention"; "Several Phenomena of the People Affected By Land Requisition and Housing Demolition Need Attention" ("征地拆迁中被拆迁人的几种表现值得研究"), CCP News Net (中国共产党新闻网), July 14, 2010, available at: http://djxt.yzjsj.gov.cn/showArticle.jsp?id=9525&partyId=50, accessed August 27, 2013.

requires that the courts and judges must be extremely cautious in conducting the hearings and making decisions.

In the *Outdated Standard* case, in order to ensure that all the supporters could get into the courtroom, the number of supporters was not revealed to the court in advance. The representing lawyer was hired from Shanghai and was known for his expertise in demolition cases. At the time of the adjudication, numerous reports and blog articles were put up on the Internet. In another case (hereinafter, the *Ultra Vires* case), when a pig-rearing ranch was demolished, a video-recording of the savage demolition process was put up on the Web, and this soon aroused sympathy within society and the attention of the media, including some national media. The effectiveness of such a strategy was easy to verify. In response to society's sentiments about the case, the court decided for the plaintiff, citing *ultra vires* and undue process, in the amount of more than 5 million yuan, an extremely high amount for this type of case.

Embarrassed courts

Although the courts have been placed in a position to adjudicate disputes between private parties and administrative agencies, their autonomy from the political hierarchy remains weak. The promulgation of national laws and directives on administration in accordance with the law does not alter the fact that the Party and the government at the same administrative level have the final say on the appointment of senior court officials. Also, despite some indications that the Central Government might take over the costs of running local courts, court funding remains largely controlled by the local government. Given such institutional arrangements, the courts often face a dilemma: they are required to vigorously exercise judicial review according to the national law issued by the Central Government, but they also have to avoid colliding with locally more powerful political actors. If, under regular situations, the courts are still capable of mediating and containing social conflicts, the mounting housing demolition cases backed by coordinated protest places the courts in a difficult and embarrassing position in performing their traditional dispute resolution role.

Faced with an increasing number of cases,[41] the courts first responded with some temporary techniques. To reduce public pressure, for

[41] The number of mass plaintiff cases has increased rapidly: there were 538,941 cases nationwide in 2004, up 9.5 percent from 2003. See Randall Peerenboom (ed.), *Judicial Independence in China* (New York: Cambridge University Press, 2010), p. 193.

example, courts across the country have broken plaintiffs up into smaller groups, provided spokespersons to meet with them, and encouraged conciliation, settlements, and even withdrawal.[42] To maintain courtroom order in open trials packed with supporters, some courts have deployed all available court sheriffs and, when this proved to be inadequate, sought help from the local police. Sharing his experiences, a veteran judge said: "The key is to choose a courtroom which is large enough to accommodate the supporters. This will prevent the supporters from turning emotional and getting out of control. A corresponding number of court sheriffs should be present so as to establish a psychological deterrent against the supporters."[43]

But these short-term measures have not rescued the courts from embarrassment. Of course, it would be best if the courts did not have to take on any of these disputes, a practice not uncommon in some regions, as documented by Wang and Yin,[44] but as the formal dispute resolution organization, it is not easy for them to reject all the petitions because for some petitions with a clear legal basis an outright rejection would only lead to an appeal to the upper-level courts and the eventual return of the petitions to the courts. For other petitions, the Communist Party and the government require the courts to resolve the disputes in order to reduce the pressure on the party-state.[45] Once a public trial has commenced, however, it is difficult for the courts to control subsequent events; everything is then under the close scrutiny of the media.[46] At the same time, preventing death or violence is the priority of the top officials in the regions. All these protests and pressures have made adjudication difficult and could result in judges being held liable for mishandling

[42] Feng Chen and Xu Xin, "'Active Judiciary': Judicial Dismantling of Workers' Collective Action in China," *China Journal*, 67 (2011), 87–107; Li Li, "Strategies for Judicial Restraint in Chinese Group Action Cases: A Realistic Reaction to Judicialization," (2011), available at SSRN: http://ssrn.com/abstract=1789564 or http://dx.doi.org/10.2139/ssrn.1789564, accessed August 27, 2013.

[43] Author's interview with judges, 2012.

[44] Qinhua Wang and Xin Yin (eds.), *An Empirical Study of Administrative Dispute Resolution in Grassroots China* (中国基层行政争议解决机制的经验研究) (Shanghai: Shanghai Sanlian Press, 2010).

[45] Su and He, "Street as Courtroom."

[46] Although the Chinese media may not be allowed to report on protests in the street, they do frequently report actual court cases. See Donald C. Clarke, "Lawsuits as Criticisms," Commentary, *New York Times*, June 2, 2009, available at: http://roomfordebate.blogs.nytimes.com/2009/06/02/chinas-new-rebels, accessed October 10, 2012; Benjamin Liebman, "Watchdog or Demagogue? The Media in the Chinese Legal System," *Columbia Law Review*, 105 (2005), 1–157.

cases. As one judge recalled: "In dealing with hundreds of litigants in one day, my throat was hoarse. In hearings, emotional speeches were delivered by the victims of the demolitions and their lawyers; the courtroom had been occupied by supporters from all over the country. They were there to see how the court decided on these thorny issues. It is hard to imagine the pressures that fall upon us."[47]

To make things worse, mediation, the normally effective way of dispute resolution for such cases, has become extremely difficult when litigation is accompanied by coordinated protest. When litigants are not organized, the courts can coordinate with the developers and determine a compensation arrangement that is acceptable to both sides. A key to success is to require the litigant to sign a non-disclosure clause for the negotiated compensation. Once litigants are organized and coordinated, however, this becomes extremely difficult. When a few litigants ask for a prohibitive price, others will never accept a lower, though realistic, offer. If the hard-nail households or those who refuse to sign the compensation agreement often get a better deal, coordinated protests in the litigation process only make a settlement more difficult. Originally, the courts could deal with litigants individually. Now that the litigants stand together in a united front, sharing every bit of information, little room is left for negotiation. Moreover, the extreme behavior of affected households is fueled by coordinated protest because when like-minded people get together, they tend to end up thinking a more extreme version of what they thought before they started to talk.[48] Often, the more radical one becomes, the more support one gets. At the end of the day, however, extreme or strategic behavior only increases the difficulty of reaching a settlement either inside or outside the court.[49]

When mediation becomes less available, the courts have to award a judgment, either supporting or rejecting the claims of the plaintiffs, but coordinated litigation pushes the bid higher and makes a fair or acceptable decision difficult to reach. More often than not, a coordinated group refuses to accept any special treatment for some members; instead, they ask for equal protection. On the other hand, some affected households dare not accept a relatively low compensation price due to the pressures

[47] "Caseload Pressures in Administrative Litigation Mounted for China's Basic-level Courts."

[48] Cass R. Sunstein, "Deliberative Trouble? Why Groups go to Extremes," *Yale Law Journal*, 110 (2000), 71–119.

[49] Robert Mnookin and Lewis Kornhauser, "Bargaining in the Shadow of the Law: The Case of Divorce," *Yale Law Journal*, 88 (1979), 950–997.

inside the coordinated group, even though they would have been prepared to accept it under normal circumstances.[50] Some litigants, due to personal or historical reasons, are entitled to preferential treatment, but this has become difficult to realize because now every litigant asks for the same treatment. In the *Differential Compensation* case, for instance, the government, in persuading the villagers to sign the demolition agreement, promised in various scenarios that any increase for those who signed the agreement later would be applied to those who had signed earlier. Most of the households in the area signed, except for nine hard-nail households. In order to complete the extended line of a highway as planned, the government later agreed to give each of the nine hard-nail households an extra 80,000 yuan compensation. This enraged the households who had signed earlier; they claimed for the same treatment in court and sent petitions to Beijing. A judge in Nantong told me that in one case, a plaintiff should have been compensated more because the demolition company had indeed cut into his land without authorization, but the judge had dared not offer the plaintiff the compensation in case other households protested. As a consequence, the plaintiff appealed and made various petitions.

More often than not, the courts support the positions of the government and the land developers when social stability is at stake. O'Brien and Li[51] argue that with petitions and other tactics of resistance, the likelihood of winning litigation tends to increase, but my interviews suggest a less clear-cut picture. This is because in protest-supported litigation, a decision favoring the plaintiffs only opens the floodgates to more litigation. In response to a group of petitioners fighting for more compensation, a vice-president aptly made the following comment: "If we [the court] award the case for you, all the Chinese people will come to us for justice." As a consequence, the court in this case adamantly refused to offer any help, even though it admitted that the demand was not unreasonable and the amount requested was comparatively small. In another case documented by Erie,[52] the plaintiff was awarded appropriate compensation, but this never appeared in the court decisions because the authorities did not want to set a precedent. Another judge in Nantong said: "I was willing to compensate a victim of demolition if his extra compensation was not disclosed. But how could I be assured of

[50] "Several Phenomena of the People Affected By Land Requisition and Housing Demolition Need Attention."

[51] O'Brien and Li, "Suing the Local State." [52] Erie, "Property Rights."

that? Victorious litigants all want to spread the news." While many judges from the developed areas said that the government or the Party rarely instruct the courts in detail on how a case shall be decided, the judges are still concerned with the consequences or the social impact of their decisions: can their decisions withstand the scrutiny of the test of both the law and the political requirements of social stability? How should they respond if the government and the Party raise questions about a case? Another female judge specializing in administrative law said: "We cannot do much to the macro political environment. So in many cases we are adopting a temporary treatment approach (姑息疗法), staying in line with the government regardless of the long-term impact." Another judge in Beijing said that in one case, the court was held hostage by the government because the unlawful practice of the government was so widespread and declaring it illegal would definitely cause social instability.[53]

However, making decisions favoring the government will not let the courts off the hook. For one thing, this type of protest-supported litigation continues to occupy the courts, creating a vicious circle; for another, such decisions may trigger escalated collective protestations. In one case involving thousands of plaintiffs and several petitions in May 2001, an intermediate court in central China dared not issue its judgment favoring the government immediately after the hearing. Instead, it worked very hard to convince other government agencies to provide tangible remedies for the litigants in advance. On the day the judgment was to be issued, detailed preemptive actions were implemented to prevent mass incidents.[54] While this is reported to show that the court did a good job in resolving social conflict, it betrays the embarrassing situation of the court. Furthermore, more than 30 percent of such cases have been appealed, which is much higher than the figures for other types of administrative litigation. These cases also take a much longer period of time to be closed;[55] it is not uncommon for them to last two to three years despite the fact that the statutory adjudication period is normally six months. In the *Outdated Standard* case, six months after it had been appealed, the adjudication committee of the appeal court discussed the case three times, the responsible judge wrote numerous

[53] Author's interview with judges, 2012.

[54] "Caseload Pressures in Administrative Litigation Mounted for China's Basic-level Courts."

[55] *Ibid.*

reports to relevant authorities, and the court president in charge of the case met with the district Party head on several occasions, but at the time of writing this chapter, the adjudicating judge still had no idea how and when a decision would be made.[56]

While in many of these cases the courts still support the cause of the housing demolition authorities, it is clear that the courts have different concerns. Originally, the conflicts existed between the households being affected by the demolition policy and the developers or the housing demolition authorities. Litigation, however, shifts the blame. In taking the litigation, the courts have become a target of the protesters. Losing the case pushes the protesters to depict the courts and judges as corrupt and incompetent, or simply "wearing the same underwear as the government." The same picture is depicted in most media reports. While many media outlets are still controlled by the ruling party, more leeway is given to them. To attract audiences and the accompanying advertising revenues, many local newspapers and TV stations have been sympathetic to the families whose properties are being demolished. The courts are often depicted as opponents, rather than the arbitrators, in the conflicts. As a result, the courts and judges are blamed for the hatred that has accumulated in the conflicts with the developers and the housing authorities.

But the courts and the judges are not the beneficiaries of the housing demolition policies and activities. They are not the decision makers who approve the projects and determine the compensation plans and prices. They may not even have anything to do with the demolition activities or the developers. Since in many projects the affected families may not take the issues to the courts, the courts and the judges are unlikely to benefit from the projects, but they are responsible for doing the most difficult part of the job once conflicts arise. In cases involving the mishandling of demolition projects, it is the courts and the judges who have to bear the responsibility. Nowadays in China, the number of collective protests and other vicious incidents have been a paramount measure of the career performance of local officials, including the judges.[57] In brief, the housing demolition authorities take the benefits, but push the courts and judges to the frontline in handling the litigation. Being placed on the

[56] Author's interview with judges, 2012.

[57] Carl Minzner, "Riots and Cover-Ups: Counterproductive Control of Local Agents in China," *University of Pennsylvania Journal of International Law*, 31 (2009), 53–123.

erupting volcano of conflict and responsibility, the judges feel that they are being taken advantage of and unfairly treated. One judge said bluntly: "We are clearing the shit left by the demolition authorities and the developers! They take away all the carrots, but we are asked to use the sticks and bear the responsibility in case of incidents."

Social change

The conventional treatment of the housing demolition issue focuses on the outcome of individual cases. Focusing narrowly on case outcome, however, prevents us from appreciating the long-term social and legal change brought about by protest-supported litigation. This section shows how the courts have turned their embarrassing situation into tactics to empower themselves, rein in state actors, and elicit social change toward fairness and transparency.[58]

With short-term measures failing to resolve the problem, long-term strategies have surfaced. Realizing that administrative agencies such as the housing demolition authorities are powerful and the courts alone may not be able to constrain their behavior, the courts need to borrow the authority of the more powerful institutions. Since the local Party committee holds the highest position in local political hierarchy, the first thing that the courts tried to do was to seek Party support. In Nantong, Jiangsu Province, for example, the courts lobby the Party committee to strengthen the administrative litigation system by emphasizing its impact on social stability, the biggest concern of the Party. In a letter to the Party committee, they state:

> With the deepening of reforms, various social contradictions become salient, and state–society conflicts have become a crucial factor contributing to social instability . . . Taking the initiative in sharing the worries of the Party and in bearing social responsibility for the government, the courts have already resolved and settled many state-society conflicts and this effort shall be further beefed up.

[58] I understand that litigation of this type will also generate a symbolic impact on social change, which does not depend on a successful outcome of the case. But here I focus only on the policy and institutional changes brought about by the courts because they are directly related to the conflicts between the courts and the housing authorities intensified by the protest-supported litigation. See Michael W. McCann, "How Does Law Matter for Social Movements?" in B. Garth and A. Sarat (eds.), *How Does Law Matter?* (Evanston, IL: Northwestern University Press, 1998).

It continues:

> In a few regions, for example, administrative disputes arising from the demolition of urban housing and the requisition of rural land have easily triggering collective incidents and already seriously impacted social harmony and stability.[59]

Since social stability has been the central concern of the local Party committee, the court request met with a positive response: both the vice-chief of the municipal Party, charged with law and politics affairs, and the municipal mayor, who was another vice Party chief, endorsed the Opinions and forwarded them to all the government and Party agencies in the region. In front of the forwarded Opinions, it states that: "the administrative agencies being suited shall fulfill the duty to respond to the litigation, enforce the judgments of the courts, and shall not unlawfully interfere with administrative litigation."[60]

With the municipal Party behind them, the courts have taken more courageous and innovative steps. One widely reported development has been to require the chief official of administrative agencies to take the stand in administrative litigation. The appearance of chief officials in administrative litigation has markedly facilitated the process of administration in accordance with law. In China, the chief leader in an administrative agency, or any state organizations, is pivotal on almost all fronts. The fact that such a leader takes the stand indicates his or her willingness to engage in administration in accordance with law. Moreover, realizing the importance of laws in the process, many of them reorient the operation of the agencies not only in accordance with law, but also in a way acceptable to the public. As reported, one county in the region demolished tens of thousands of square meters each year, displacing thousands of families, but for many years no large-scale petitions ever occurred. It is said that the lack of large-scale petitions there is closely related to changed pattern of the government toward the administration in accordance with law and fair legal enforcement.[61]

59 Internal court document, 2006.

60 Du Mong, "Government Directives Pressure Officials into Taking on the Stand, More Than One Thousand Judicial Suggestions Facilitate Officials to Take on the Stand: Why Can Plaintiffs Meet the Officials in Citizens vs. Mandarin Litigation in Jiangsu Province?" ("政府发文将出庭率纳入考核"逼"官出庭,法院千余件司法建议"促"官出庭 – 解读江苏"告官见官"为何成常态"), *Legal Daily* (法制日报), September 19, 2007, available at: http://news.sohu.com/20070919/n252232641.shtml, accessed August 27, 2013.

61 Mong, "Government Directives Pressure Officials into Taking on the Stand."

Another important step taken by the courts is to make use of judicial suggestions to rectify the agencies' unlawful behaviors. If a carefully crafted constitutional review proposal can push authorities to move related reforms forward,[62] a carefully crafted judicial suggestion will not only expose the flawed administrative practice, but also exert pressure and provide guidance for the agencies to make adjustment. In its judicial suggestions, for example, the court always makes it clear which administrative practice is unlawful and what the legal basis is. This is because only with clear legal basis will the agencies realize the flaw of their practice. A judicial suggestion involving a housing demolition license, for instance, states that the authorities, violating Article 47 of the Administrative License Law, did not inform the affected private parties of the hearing before issuing the land planning and demolition license, and thus infringing their lawful rights. With all the facts and related legal regulations clearly specified, the agencies have few excuses not to comply.

In some cases, although the courts award the decision for the government, they explain the reasons for such a decision, but clearly suggest the right way. In a case concerning the demolition of a public hospital located on the site of a cultural relic, a judicial suggestion provided explanations for the case outcome: "Considering the fact that the demolition applicant has reached agreement with the majority of the affected individuals, and the local government has sought approvals from upper-level government with regard to the demolition of the public hospital, this court rejected the petition of the appellant, largely due to the concern of social stability. But with regard to the cultural relic, your Bureau must strictly follow the reply of the Jiangsu Provincial Government." Underlying the message was a threat that future cases like this would be struck down.

The courts have further expanded their powers by sending such reports both to the administrative agency in question and to institutions that have control over the agency: the government immediately above the agency, the legal department of the municipal government, and, most importantly, the Party Disciplinary Department. *Shuanggui* (双规), a form of detention imposed exclusively on Party officials and operated by

[62] Keith J. Hand, "Citizens Engage the Constitution: The Sun Zhigang Incident and Constitutional Review Proposals in the People's Republic of China," in Stephanie Balme and Michael Dowdle (eds.), *Building Constitutionalism in China* (New York: Palgrave Macmillan, 2009), p. 222.

the Party Disciplinary Department, results in immediate termination of their career,[63] so it remains an important brake on state officials. Of course, it is not the court's task to investigate corrupt activities in the process of administrative litigation, but a judicial suggestion indicating irregular behavior by the agency may send a signal to the Party Disciplinary Department, and this is dreadful enough.

On the basis of these tactics, more general policy changes have been initiated. To relieve the courts from embarrassment in protest-supported litigation, the courts do not approve any compulsory eviction permits if the demolition authorities cannot reach a compensation agreement with urban residents, or the hearing process on setting the compensation price is not transparent.[64] The Nantong Municipal Government further announced that it is forbidden to use force in demolishing housing before the residents move out, or before all the required papers are completed. It also prohibits the use of savage behavior, such as cutting off the gas, running water, and electricity to force residents to move out. In response to the practice that thugs are hired to beat the residents, it states that those who have no permanent jobs in the city cannot be hired to participate in the demolition work.[65] In Taizhou, the municipal government, urged by the courts, is working on an annual standard for housing compensation in order to fill a legal vacuum in this area in which a lot of disputes and controversies have occurred. As a result of the pressures by the courts, some housing demolition authorities have streamlined their procedures and increased the transparency of the decision-making process.

These social and legal changes are not at all limited to Nantong and Taizhou, the field sites for this chapter. A search on the Internet finds similar regulations in various parts of China, especially in more developed areas. On the national level, the government has responded both by holding individual officials accountable and by introducing more laws. In January 2011, the State Council promulgated the Regulations for Expropriation and Compensation for Houses on State-owned Land, replacing the notorious 1991 Urban Housing Demolition Statute. Despite the fact that many issues remain unaddressed, the Expropriation Regulations impose greater

[63] Flora Sapio, "Shuanggui and Extralegal Detention in China," *China Information*, 22(1) (2004), 7–37.

[64] The author's interview with judges, 2012.

[65] "New Stipulation in Nantong: No Compulsory Demolishment before the Evictees Move out" ("南通市规定:被拆迁人未搬出的不得强行拆除"), *Xinhua News*, September 08, 2010, available at: http://xh.xhby.net/newxh/html/2010-09/08/content_273808.htm, accessed August 27, 2013.

constraints on the administrative action of expropriation, including defining public interest, standardizing the expropriation process, guaranteeing due process, and requiring that compensation be according to market value. It is widely regarded as an advancement in this area of legal reform. On September 9, 2011, the Supreme People's Court issued the "Urgent Notice on Firmly Guarding Against the Triggering of Vicious Incidents by Land Expropriation and Forced Housing Demolition and Relocation." Of course, there are many reasons behind this policy change on the national level, but the concern for social stability brought about by protest-supported litigation and the pressure exerted on the courts is definitely a crucial one.

Conclusion

This chapter has demonstrated that the legal battles involving popular movements in China play out not as a total shutdown of the government response, but as a series of reactions that, at times, leads to more transparent and accountable social change. Since the courts are a relatively weak institution within the local political structure, they rarely render decisions against the powerful and the rich, especially when such decisions will arouse further social instability. But when faced with mounting numbers of protest-supported litigations, local courts can no longer play their stereotypical role of mediating and containing social conflicts, which forces them to take innovative steps that lead to substantial social and legal change. The chapter specifies the rationale of the court responses, and the mechanism by which the ideal of the rule of law operates and evolves during the interaction between the courts and protests in a country where state control of civil society remains tight and strong.

This Chinese case has allowed us to better understand the evolution of rule of law in China and the relationships between the state, courts, and social change. The rule of law has been adopted in reforms in China, but its trajectory is not self-evolving or solely determined by the political center. It is evolving, at least in part, because of the forces from the bottom and the dynamics between the grass-roots efforts and various judicial and political players. This chapter helps us to understand how social and policy changes occur at the grass-roots level and also the evolving tactics of both the state and the protesters.[66] More often than not, it is

[66] But see Doug McAdam, "Tactical Innovation and the Pace of Insurgency," *American Sociological Review*, 48 (1983), 735–754; Doug McAdam, Sidney Tarrow, and Charles Tilly, *Dynamics of Contention* (Cambridge University Press, 2001).

difficult for courts to bring about social change, even in democratic societies.[67] But judicial institutions embedded within authoritarian systems could enjoy an expanded role because such change will ultimately help to deliver social stability, the paramount need of authoritarian rulers. This study appears to attest to the extraordinary level of willingness displayed by the Chinese government to allow for such changes.

Indeed, a legal system is functional only when it is mobilized by ordinary individuals. Ultimately, the driving force for the development of the rule of law comes from grass-roots demands for such reforms. Some existing studies have already pointed out that despite the stiffness and inertia of the authoritarian regime, a popular form of constitutionalism is emerging in China: the courts have come to be seen as more trustworthy among citizens, and the majority of citizens who have settled a dispute in court would do so again;[68] courts and judges, even in rural China, are increasingly willing to engage in protecting the rights of the people.[69] Dowdle argues that referring more and more to the law and the courts indicates a change of discourse, and more "juridification" suggests that courts will play a significant role in China's constitutional development.[70] Echoing these existing studies, this chapter captures the detailed mechanisms whereby the courts and state institutions respond to the popular use of the law, and eventually how the rule of law or constitutionalism is evolved.

This Chinese case thus shows a trajectory of judicial empowerment in authoritarian regimes. When law is highly politicized and controlled by the central state, legal conflicts, particularly when they are backed by social mobilization, are bound to cause tension between courts and the local governments and officials which are one of the sources of such conflicts. In reducing the amount of litigation backed by collective

[67] Gerald Rosenberg, *The Hollow Hope: Can Courts Bring About Social Change?* (University of Chicago Press, 1991); Tomiko Brown-Nagin, "Elites, Social Movements, and the Law: The Case of Affirmative Action," *Columbia Law Review*, 195 (2005), 1436–1528.

[68] Pierre Landry, "The Institutional Diffusion of Courts in China: Evidence from Survey Data," in Tom Ginsburg and Tamir Moustafa (eds.), *Rule by Law: The Politics of Courts in Authoritarian Regimes* (New York: Cambridge University Press, 2008), pp. 218–219.

[69] Stephanie Balme, "Ordinary Justice and Popular Constitutionalism in China," in Stephanie Balme and Michael Dowdle (eds.), *Building Constitutionalism in China* (New York: Palgrave Macmillan, 2009), pp. 179–198.

[70] Michael W. Dowdle, "Beyond 'Judicial Power': Courts and Constitutionalism in Modern China," in Stephanie Balme and Michael Dowdle (eds.), *Building Constitutionalism in China* (New York: Palgrave Macmillan, 2009), pp. 199–220.

action, the state could inadvertently move toward a more transparent and accountable system. This is conspicuous in this part of China because of its particular fragmented political system, the profound principal–agent problems that come with it, and the willingness of the local Party committee to empower the courts. The laws representing the will of the central state could easily clash with the behavior of the local officials; the courts required to adjudicate litigation based on laws would soon find themselves in an uneasy relationship with the local administrative agencies. The particularities of China's political and legal structure suggest this process may not necessarily be generalized as a pattern, but it does provide an example of how the judiciary is empowered and how this type of judicial politics may exist in other authoritarian states with similar characteristics.

This chapter thus also sheds light on the relationship between the judiciary and social development. The law and development movement has emphasized judicial reforms and judicial independence as necessary for economy growth, poverty reduction, the protection of human rights, social justice, and the consolidation of democracy. Judicial independence has long been regarded as essential for the establishment of the rule of law in transitional countries.[71] Yet the debate on how judicial independence should be understood has never been settled, and this case has provided further fuel for the debate. On the one hand, this chapter illustrates the difficult position of the courts when confronted with socio-economic issues that they may not be capable of handling and to which they cannot propose feasible solutions.[72] On the other hand, it also suggests that the Chinese judiciary can, at this stage of development, be used as a public forum for social and legal development. The social conflicts may drive them to be more independent from the administrative agencies and to take a more active and significant role.

[71] Thomas Carothers, "The Rule of Law Revival," *Foreign Affairs*, 77(2) (1998), 95–106.

[72] Randall Peerenboom, "Economic and Social Rights: The Role of Courts in China" (2011) 12 *San Diego International Law Journal* 303–331.

8

Courts and political stability

Mediating rural land disputes

SUSAN H. WHITING AND HUA SHAO

Introduction

In March 2013, the First Session of the Twelfth National People's Congress recorded 605 votes (more than 20 percent of the 2,948 votes cast) opposing the Work Report of the Supreme People's Court.[1] This vote, of little substantive significance, is symbolic of the challenge facing the Chinese court system. The tally represents the most "no" votes for any report of the session, reflecting widespread dissatisfaction among the delegates with the work of the courts – particularly, dispute resolution and social control.[2] The conflict resolution and social control functions of courts are closely related.[3] Indeed, disputes arising from violations of citizens' rights – especially rural land rights – have contributed to a marked increase in public unrest,[4] unrest that courts have failed to contain. Moreover, some of the most contentious issues of China's

1 See "Supreme Court's Work Report Gets Lowest Number of Votes," March 18, 2013, available at: http://english.sina.com/china/2013/0317/572328.html.

2 The distinction of receiving the most "no" votes is not new for the Supreme People's Court. For example, it also characterized the voting at the five sessions of the Eleventh National People's Congress between 2009 and 2012, where the report on the work of the court received opposing votes ranging from 15 to 18 percent of the totals.

3 See Martin Shapiro, *Courts: A Comparative and Political Analysis* (University of Chicago Press, 1986), p. 18. Beyond the basic functions (dispute resolution, social control, rule-making) identified by Shapiro, Tamir Moustafa and Tom Ginsburg add regime legitimation, control of administrative agents of the state, and providing a foundation for economic growth, particularly in authoritarian regimes. See Tom Ginsburg and Tamir Moustafa (eds.), *Rule by Law: The Politics of Courts in Authoritarian Regimes* (New York: Cambridge University Press, 2008).

4 Public unrest is often referred to as "mass incidents" ("群体事件"). See Yu Jianrong, Speech before the Beijing Lawyers' Association, available at: http://chinadigitaltimes.net, accessed March 24, 2010.

economic transition occur in rural areas, where professionalization of the courts poses some of the greatest challenges.

This chapter examines the process of dispute resolution in rural land disputes with particular focus on the place of mediation and the role of the courts. It argues that the state's paramount political goal of ensuring stability has driven a shift away from recent, Western-style civil procedure reforms[5] toward renewed emphasis on mediation, both inside and outside the courts. We also argue that the renewed emphasis on mediation, justified variously on pragmatic, historical, and philosophical grounds, has the effect of undermining the place of codified law and weakening the norm-applying function of the courts. As a result, rural courts in their handling of land disputes fail to provide predictable, determinant, and legally defined norms to guide dispute resolution. Ironically, in their mission as state agencies tasked with maintaining stability, courts inadvertently embolden villagers to use violence, leave local government behavior unchecked, and privilege customary over formal state law. Finally, we stress that disputes and the role of courts in resolving them must be understood in context, reflecting the institutional settings in which disputants and courts are embedded. Overall, these findings have important implications for interpreting the nature of the "rule of law" and the vast new investment in laws, lawyers, judges, and courts in China.[6]

The chapter is organized as follows: the first section examines the renewed emphasis on mediation in Chinese policy, particularly with respect to land disputes. The second section puts the courts in a local administrative context. The third section presents empirical evidence of the role of mediation in handling rural land disputes drawn from a representative sample survey, case records, and in-depth interviews – all from rural Hunan Province. The fourth section provides an explanation of the patterns of dispute resolution identified in the chapter. It explores the conflicting roles of the courts in contemporary Chinese society and polity. The final section concludes with an analysis of the tension between mediating for political stability and upholding legal norms.

[5] See Guo Xinghua, "Understanding the Logic Behind Rule of Law in China," *Chinese Sociology and Anthropology*, 41(2 (2008), 3–6; Hualing Fu, "Access to Justice in China: Potentials, Limits and Alternatives," in John Gillespie and Albert H. Y. Chen (eds.), *Legal Reforms in China and Vietnam: A Comparison of Asian Communist Regimes* (London: Routledge, 2010), pp. 163–187; Carl Minzner, "China's Turn Against Law," *American Journal of Comparative Law*, 59 (2011), 935–984.

[6] See Fu, "Access to Justice," who refers to the great number of laws passed, the increase in training of lawyers, and the growth of the judiciary since the initiation of reform.

Mediation in policy and policy discussions

Since the early years of the twenty-first century, the party-state has promoted multiple channels for mediation outside and inside the judiciary as a means of maintaining political stability, particularly at the rural grass roots. This section documents the pressure, facing local officials and judges alike, to use mediation to maintain stability. It demonstrates the revival of Ma Xiwu-style trials that, historically, relied heavily on mediation to consolidate Chinese Communist Party (CCP) rule in the countryside in the 1940s. It suggests that political pragmatism rather than resurgent traditional values is the core motivation for this renewed emphasis on mediation. Finally, it documents the introduction of still other models for local governments to follow in promoting mediation, including "comprehensive mediation." Mediation is intended to limit direct petitions to the government, precede or replace litigation in the courtroom, and prevent protest ("mass incidents").

The party-state hierarchy governing leading cadres at the local level has put increasing emphasis on maintaining the stability of rural society, preventing disputes, and containing disputes at the local level explicitly through mediation. In 2004, the State Council Office promulgated an "Urgent Notice on Appropriate Resolution of Current Rural Land Contract Disputes," pointing to the increasing number of "mass incidents" involving disputes over rural land that have undermined stability at the grass roots.[7] This document assigns particular responsibility for proactively mediating such disputes to township and village leaders: "Township People's Governments, villages, and small groups must conscientiously take responsibility for mediating rural land contract disputes."[8] It calls on local leaders to quickly and thoroughly address petitions to all government offices, and mandates that all disputes should be resolved in the local community before they escalate. From the perspective of a village or township official, escalation entails local residents' directly petitioning county government agencies, filing suit at the county's basic-level court, or holding protests large enough to necessitate a response from county government agencies.[9] Indeed, Zhou Yongkang, Secretary of the Central Party Political-Legal Committee from 2007 to 2012, promoted the slogan "small matters don't leave the

[7] See 国务院办公厅, "关于妥善解决当前农村土地承包纠纷的紧急通知 (2004)" (State Council Office, "Urgent Notice on Appropriate Resolution of Current Rural Land Contract Disputes"), No. 21, April 30, 2004.

[8] *Ibid.* [9] Author's interviews, August 2007.

village, large matters don't leave the township, and conflicts do not rise to higher authorities" ("小事不出村，大事不出镇，矛盾不上交").[10] He called upon local leaders to develop the mediation system in order to reduce confrontational litigation, conserve judicial resources, and to promote a harmonious society.[11] A key directive calls for the use of mediation in order to prevent individual disputes from becoming "mass incidents." In practice, maintenance of public order has become a primary criterion in job performance measures for local party leaders.[12]

Central elites attribute part of the breakdown in stability to a failure of the courts. The Petition Office of the National People's Congress Standing Committee estimates that about 40 percent of petitions are made against the legal system, and that the vast majority of these complaints have some justification.[13] Yu Jianrong, drawing on interviews with 632 petitioners, finds that more than 60 percent had attempted to use the courts before resorting to petitioning to Beijing.[14] Plaintiffs' dissatisfaction, according to Yu, stems from three sources: courts' refusal to accept cases; unfavorable court judgments; and, in only a handful of cases, failure to implement favorable judgments. Rural concerns are front and center: Yu and petition officials alike identify land appropriation, village governance, and peasant burdens as grievances commonly motivating petitioners.[15] Thus, the focus on stability maintenance and resolving disputes at the local level poses a direct challenge to the courts.

Courts have been under pressure to place renewed emphasis on the practice of judicial mediation. In 2003, some scholars in judicial policy

[10] See "周永康要求地方把问题解决在当地做到矛盾不上交" ("Zhou Yongkang Requests that Problems be Resolved Locally; Disputes Not be Passed Upwards"), November 25, 2008, available at: http://news.ifeng.com/mainland/200811/1125_17_894187.shtml.

[11] *Ibid.*

[12] Author's interview, August 2007. On the evaluation of leading cadres at the local level, see Susan H. Whiting, *Power and Wealth in Rural China* (New York: Cambridge University Press, 2001) and Susan H. Whiting, "The Cadre Evaluation System at the Grass Roots: The Paradox of Party Rule," in Barry J. Naughton and Dali L. Yang (eds.), *Holding China Together: Diversity and National Integration in the Post-Deng Era* (New York: Cambridge University Press, 2004), pp. 101–119. On the role of similar incentives in the court system, see Minzner, "China's Turn Against Law."

[13] See Hualing Fu and Richard Cullen, "From Mediatory to Adjudicatory Justice," in Margaret Woo and Mary Gallagher (eds.), *Chinese Justice: Civil Dispute Revolution in China* (New York: Cambridge University Press, 2011), p. 45.

[14] See Yu Jianrong, "The Defects of the Petition System and its Political Consequences," as cited by Fu and Cullen, "From Mediatory to Adjudicatory Justice."

[15] See State Petition Bureau, "Eighty Percent of Petitions Have Grounds," *Banyue Tan*, November 20, 2003, as cited by Fu and Cullen, "From Mediatory to Adjudicatory Justice."

circles denounced the decline in court-sponsored mediation relative to adjudicated outcomes that followed the implementation of civil procedure reforms begun in the late 1970s.[16] In September 2004, the Supreme People's Court issued "Provisions Regarding Several Questions on Civil Mediation Work in the People's Courts," creating new incentives to privilege mediation in dispute resolution.[17]

The renewed emphasis on court-based mediation is also evident in the revival of old models for judicial behavior, including the "Ma Xiwu trial mode." Ma Xiwu (1898–1962) was a judge in the Shaan–Gan–Ning (Shaanxi–Gansu–Ningxia) Communist Base Area during the revolutionary war and rose to become vice-president of the Supreme People's Court in 1954. Based on a 1955 account written by Ma Xiwu, his method entails five key characteristics: active investigation by the judge; holding the trial in the local community; conducting the trial in public; public participation in the decision; and mediation.[18] This method was promoted in CCP newspapers at the time, including a *Liberation Daily* article, published in 1944, highlighting Ma's handling of rural land disputes based on extensive consultations with the local community, including both party cadres and local residents.[19]

While the Ma Xiwu trial method is closely associated with the Maoist notion of the "mass line," it also represents a pragmatic approach to resolving political tensions in the CCP's rural governance. Ma Xiwu's trial mode allowed the judge to balance tensions between formal law and community values, and between implementation of formal law and

[16] See Su Li, "司法解释, 公共政策和最高法院" ("Judicial Interpretation, Public Policy and Supreme People's Court"), *Law Science* (法学), 8 (2003), 27.

[17] See Announcement of the Supreme People's Court of the People's Republic of China (Interpretation No. 12 of the Supreme People's Court, 2004), September 16, 2004, The Provisions of the Supreme People's Court about Several Issues Concerning the Civil Mediation Work of the People's Court), available at: http://209.200.107.14/english/law2_disp.asp?sublawcode=SUB1652449610111514&lawcode=LAW39494751115131017&country=China, accessed March 29, 2013.

[18] See 马锡五, "新民主主义革命阶段中陕甘宁边区的人民司法工作" 《政法研究》 ("People's Justice Work during the New Democratic Revolution in the Shaan–Gan–Ning Base Area"), *Political and Legal Research*, vol. 1, 1955, available at: www.21ccom.net/articles/lsjd/jwxd/article_2012030955203_2.html, as cited by Xiao Ma, "Understanding 'Rule by Law' in China: A Historical Analysis of Ma Xiwu Trial Mode," unpublished paper, Yale University, May 2, 2012.

[19] See 1944 年3月13日《解放日报》评论:马锡伍同志的审判方式, ("Commentary: Comrade Ma Xiwu's Method of Judging"), *Liberation Daily*, available at: www.21ccom.net/articles/lsjd/jwxd/article_2012030955203_3.html, accessed March 29, 2013.

consolidation of party rule. Mediation ensured outcomes were in line with community norms, and privileged stability and harmony over formal law. According to a widely cited analysis of the Ma Xiwu style by Fan Yu:

> The social function of civil actions is to solve disputes, and individual cases are treated individually to solve disputes. It works in conjunction with other social regulation (or dispute-resolution) mechanisms (even including policies and morals), focuses on the application of various types of "living laws" in practice, capitalizes on the positive effects of mediation, strives for reasonable trial results (substantive justice), relies on local dispute-resolution modes and local authority (relies on the masses) and attaches particular importance to the social impact of dispute resolution . . .[20]

Hence, Ma Xiwu-style adjudication emphasizes "active and personalized judges"[21] who mediate on the basis of local values, seek to provide substantive justice, and minimize threats to social stability.

With the renewed emphasis on court-based mediation in the 2000s, local courts began to adopt the Ma Xiwu trial mode, a practice actively promoted in the *People's Court News* and the *Supreme People's Court Bulletin*. Several examples are illustrative of the return to Ma Xiwu-style adjudication: in 2008, Henan Province High Court President, Zhang Liyong, promoted the concept of "justice for the people," suggesting that judges actively adopt a new "Ma Xiwu-style of handling cases," by taking mediation and judicial initiative as key features. Similarly, in Long County, Shaanxi Province, in 2008, the judiciary adopted the principles of mediation first, integrating mediation and judgment, and establishing "a judge for each village."[22] As a result, in September 2009, the *Supreme People's Court Bulletin* explicitly promoted the Long County experience; the report trumpeted "protecting social stability and social harmony" as the successful outcomes of this approach. Finally, in 2010, the *People's Court News* published a front-page article praising the adoption of the Ma Xiwu trial mode in Hainan. While these examples are not exhaustive, they reflect the prominence accorded to court-based mediation.

20 See parenthetical comments in the published translation: Fan Yu, "简论马锡五审判方式" ("A Brief Analysis of the Ma Xiwu Trial Mode"), *Tsinghua Law Review*, 2 (1999), trans. Irene Lee in *Chinese Sociology and Anthropology*, 41(2) (2008), 78 at 81.

21 See Fan Yu, "A Brief Analysis," p. 82.

22 See "法官驻村主动审案陕西陇县司法改革引同行关注" ("Shaanxi's Long County Judicial Reform of Judges Trying Cases in the Village Draws the Attention of the Judiciary") May 31, 2009, available at: http://news.xinhuanet.com/legal/2009-05/31/content_11460169.htm.

National court data show that, after reaching a low in 2003, the percentage of court-mediated outcomes as a share of all outcomes of civil cases began to rise after declining steadily for two decades, nearly doubling in four years from 31 percent in 2004 to 59 percent in 2008. In 2013, outgoing Supreme People's Court President, Wang Shengjun, reported that, if combined with withdrawn cases (often attributed to the mediation efforts of judges), 65 percent of civil cases in courts of first instance were mediated as of 2012.[23]

While there is no question that the courts have returned to the practice of judicial mediation, there is debate about the root motivation for their active embrace of this approach. The debate centers on the role of traditional Confucian values as opposed to more pragmatic considerations of maintaining political stability and CCP rule. Zhang Mingshan argues that the embrace of Ma Xiwu-style adjudication in particular stems from its emphasis on human sentiment.[24] In traditional Chinese culture, human sentiment is not only a model for behavior, it is also a measuring rod for justice. However, as discussed below, we find little support for this perspective in our interviews with judges or disputants.

A second perspective suggests that courts have a political motivation for embracing judicial mediation. Some commentators have linked Hu Jintao's and Wen Jiabao's populist emphasis on a harmonious society with the Maoist notion of the mass line. A 2002 commentary in *Seeking Truth* states that: "the fundamental guarantee of the CCP as a ruling party is maintaining flesh-and-blood links with the people" (i.e., the mass line).[25] The revival of Ma Xiwu-style trials harks back to the "mass line." The Supreme People's Court considers judicial mediation to be appropriate for rural society, appropriate to the "mass line" promoted by the ruling Party, and consistent with the goal of pragmatism. The renewed emphasis on judicial mediation is part of the larger agenda promoting political stability (维稳). The practice of judges actively mediating local disputes is in response to calls from the center for local officials to resolve disputes at the earliest stages before they can escalate

[23] See Wang Shengjun, "Work Report of the Supreme People's Court," available at: www.china.com.cn/news/2013lianghui/2013-03/10/content_28191634.htm.

[24] See Zhang Mingshan, "人民法院推行马锡五审判方式是时代的需求" ("Ma Xiwu-style Adjudication Advanced by People's Court is the People's Demand"), available at: http://hnfy.chinacourt.org/public/detail.php?id=73918.

[25] See *Seeking Truth* (February 2002), as cited in Willy Wo-Lap Lam, *Chinese Politics in the Hu Jintao Era: New Leaders, New Challenges* (New York: M. E. Sharpe, 2006).

(把纠纷消灭在萌芽状态).[26] Indeed, as Stanley Lubman has suggested of mediation under Mao, "the political functions of mediation are so pervasive that they frequently overshadow the settlement function . . ."[27] Similarly, Philip Huang draws a distinction between the CCP promotion of judicial mediation and the societal tradition of community mediation.[28]

The court system has also advocated another model: the "comprehensive" approach to mediation. The goal of "comprehensive mediation" is to bring together people's mediation (by people's mediators), administrative mediation (by government agencies), and judicial mediation (by judges) in order to resolve disputes at the grass roots. Although the 2009 Work Report of the Supreme People's Court did not refer explicitly to "comprehensive mediation," in proposing a renewed emphasis on mediation, it called for the bringing together of people's mediation, administrative mediation, and judicial mediation for dispute resolution. Local judges we interviewed referred to the same approach of integrating all mediation channels, suggesting that judicial mediation is an important part of this renewed emphasis on mediation. The official goal, once again, is to resolve disputes at the lowest possible level before they can escalate.

The administrative status of the courts

Basic-level courts and other local government agencies face significant pressure from both society and the state to resolve disputes. However, the judiciary is particularly constrained in performing its dispute resolution function by its subordination to political goals and political authority. Although the Chinese Constitution (Article 126) states that courts "shall exercise independent judicial power and are not subject to interference by administrative organs, public organizations, or individuals," in reality, courts are simply one bureaucratic agency of the state, and judges are regarded as agents of the Party.

26 See "河南法院全面推行马锡五审判方式", 河南法院网 ("Henan Courts Comprehensively Promote Ma Xiwu's Method of Judging"), Henan Court Network, available at: http://hnfy.chinacourt.org/public/detail.php?id=72518 as cited in Xiao Ma, "Understanding 'Rule by Law' in China."

27 See Stanley Lubman, "Mao and Mediation: Politics and Dispute Resolution in Communist China," *California Law Review*, 55(5) (1967), 1287.

28 See Philip C. C. Huang, "Court Mediation in China, Past and Present," *Modern China*, 32(3) (2006), 275–314.

This principle was later reinforced by President Hu Jintao, who articulated the policy of "The Three Supremes," referring to the supremacy of the Chinese Communist Party, the people's interest, and the Constitution (in that order of priority) in all judicial work. Similarly in 2009, a justice minister called upon lawyers to "above all obey the Communist Party and help foster a harmonious society."[29] As state agencies are subordinate to the Party, courts are tasked by the CCP with assisting the government in controlling society and maintaining stability through mediation. For example, in the context of rural land disputes, a 2007 State Council document sets the explicit goal of establishing mediation mechanisms within existing dispute-resolution channels, including litigation, arbitration, mediation, and petition agencies.[30] The courts, like other local government agencies, are responsible for preventing petitions from reaching higher authorities, resolving disputes where they occur, and ameliorating tensions at the grass roots.[31] Courts commonly receive instructions not to accept certain types of cases, face pressure to mediate rather than to adjudicate, and push citizens out of litigation to seek administrative mediation or to petition relevant government bureaus for redress.[32] As legal scholars publishing in both English and Chinese highlight, basic-level courts are merely one part of the state apparatus without real independence.

The preceding sections have demonstrated that basic-level courts are treated as agents of the Party in promoting political stability and doing so through mediating disputes. They also show that some of the most acute concerns about stability occur around rural land disputes. As we will demonstrate below, the politically motivated embrace of mediation undermines the role of the court as an entity that upholds legal norms. In the next two sections, we use empirical evidence from rural China to explore the actions of local courts, among other local agencies, in responding to conflicts over land.

[29] See Elizabeth Lynch, "I Pledge Allegiance to the CCP: Chinese Lawyers' New Oath Requirements," *China Law & Policy*, March 22, 2012, available at: http://chinalawandpolicy.com.

[30] See 国务院七部委关于开展全国农村土地突出问题专项治理的通知,国务院2007 (State Council/Seven Ministry Commission Notice Regarding Launch of Specific Governance, State Council, 2007, [Procedures] Nationwide for Prominent Rural Land Problems).

[31] *Ibid.*

[32] See Huang Jialiang, "Logic of the Practice of Law in Grass-roots Courts," *Selection of Master's Dissertations in Sociology of Peking University, Tsinghua University, and Renmin University* (Shandong People's Press, 2006), pp. 1–55, trans. Irene Lee, "How are Laws Practiced? A Sociological Analysis Based on a Judicial Case in China," *Chinese Sociology and Anthropology*, 41(2) (2008), 41–77.

Empirical evidence of mediation in rural Hunan

As demonstrated above, local government agencies, including courts, have been tasked with addressing the threats to political stability that arise as a result of disputes over rural land. This section examines rural land disputes from the perspective of both the aggrieved farm households and the local officials, particularly judges, charged with containing and resolving household grievances at the local level, in the context of renewed emphasis on mediation.

Attempts by aggrieved households to resolve rural land disputes typically involve one or more of the following possible actions, beyond "lumping it" (doing nothing) and direct negotiation among the parties themselves: third-party mediation, petition for administrative action, litigation in the courts, or protest. In practice, following the state initiatives to promote mediation documented above, every one of these actions is likely to involve attempts at mediation. The following paragraphs report on our effort to document disputes and analyze the process of dispute resolution.

In 2007–2008, we selected two counties in Hunan Province in which to conduct a representative sample survey of households regarding their experiences with land disputes. The survey sought detailed information regarding respondents' experience with disputes, and found that 14 percent (n=89/638) of respondents had, in the last ten years, been involved in disputes relating to land. Here we distinguish four types of land disputes: disputes over compensation for land-takings; village reallocation of landholdings; contracts over abandoned or transferred land; and boundary disputes among villagers (see Table 8.1).

A brief summary of the distinguishing features of land disputes reveals the actors and interests involved. *Land-takings* involve the requisitioning

Table 8.1 *Most recent land disputes*

Most recent land dispute, by type	Frequency	%
Land-taking compensation	26	29.2
Land reallocation	23	25.8
Abandoned/transferred land	12	13.5
Boundary/other	28	31.5
Total	89	100.0

of village collective land – either cultivated land or residential land – for conversion to state-owned land for non-agricultural uses. The land-taking disputes identified in this study challenge the level of compensation that farm households receive for land they had contracted from the village collective, although disputes may also challenge the procedural legality of the taking itself. Compensation disputes can have high stakes, since compensation can be large relative to annual household income. *Land reallocation* disputes focus on the village's distribution of contracts for arable land among households. The length of land contracts between the village or village small group, on the one hand, and the farm household, on the other hand, are intended to be stable for thirty years. However, villages reallocate land among households for a variety of reasons, including redistributing contracted land in the wake of land-takings; assigning more land to more productive households; and assigning more land to households that have increased in size through marriage, birth, or death. *Abandoned or transferred land* disputes occur when households challenge involuntary transfers of land from one household to another entity or challenge the terms and conditions under which land has voluntarily been transferred. Finally, *land boundary* disputes involve encroachment by one villager upon the arable or residential land of another.

Fully 60 percent of survey respondents who reported experiencing land disputes felt that the dispute had a great or very great impact on their lives. Moreover, of those reporting land disputes, nearly 60 percent initiated action to resolve the dispute. Another 12 percent took action in response to someone else's initiative; in total, nearly three-quarters of respondents reporting land disputes were involved in some kind of action to resolve the dispute. Land is a valuable asset for rural residents. It can produce an income stream and, until recently in the PRC regime, has served as the main source of social security for rural residents. Because of the high salience of land to the livelihoods of rural residents, they are unlikely to "lump it" (i.e., do nothing) in the face of a land dispute. This behavior is consistent with the emphasis placed on rural land disputes by higher authorities as highly contentious issues in rural communities.

Attempting direct negotiation is a natural first response in the face of a grievance. Fully half of all respondents taking action over a land dispute attempted direct negotiation (see Table 8.2). Nearly as many respondents with land disputes participated in mediation (44 percent), and in virtually all cases (with only a single exception) a village cadre

Table 8.2 *Approach to dispute resolution for respondents in most recent land disputes* (n=*89)*

	%[a]
No action	31.5
Direct negotiation	50.6
Mediation	43.8
Petition (government)	28.1
Litigation	6.7
Local People's Congress contact	3.4
Protest	6.7
Media contact	2.2

[a] Percent of respondents attempting any given action, multiple responses allowed.
Arbitration is not included here, because in the Hunan survey counties land arbitration commissions (mandated under the auspices of the county agriculture bureau) had not been established.

served as the first mediator, highlighting that village cadres are on the "front line" in rural land disputes. Mediation that takes place in other fora, like courts and petition offices, is reflected in the figures for petition, litigation, etc. Twenty-eight percent of respondents attempted to resolve their dispute by going to the government for help (petitioning). Seven percent sued in court, and an equal percentage participated in a protest. Only a handful of respondents sought out their Local People's Congress representative or the media in response to a land dispute.

Distinct patterns emerge when we examine the dispute resolution mechanisms employed in different types of land dispute. Mediation remains an important channel for dispute resolution across types of land dispute. However, in disputes over compensation for land-takings and land reallocation, mediation is less common than for other types of dispute. In land-taking compensation cases, the highest stakes dispute reported in the sample, petitioning government agencies and suing in court are more common than for other types of disputes (Table 8.3). Of all the types of land disputes examined here, compensation for land-takings involves government agencies, directly or indirectly, most closely

Table 8.3 *Percentage of respondents reporting land disputes in past ten years* (n=*89) with dispute resolution mechanism by dispute type*

	Land-taking compensation	Land reallocation	Abandoned/ transferred land	Boundary/ Other
Percent attempting:				
Mediation	39	50	39	50
Petition (government)	46	8	17	29
Litigation	19	0	0	4
Other	19	0	4	11
Percent resolved	35	83	52	64
Percent extremely dissatisfied	78	56	17	15
Number of cases	26	23	12	28

Note: Percentages do not sum to 100, since multiple actions are possible.

in the dispute. Land reallocation involves local village cadres most closely, with – in some cases – direction from township or county authorities. Therefore, disputants seek what they consider to be more authoritative venues to address the dispute. Indeed, "authoritativeness" is given as a major reason why respondents choose to petition government agencies.

In addition to the survey, we conducted in-depth, follow-up interviews with respondents who experienced actual land disputes. Consistent with the survey findings, the interviewees indicated that they would go to the village to mediate first when they tried to settle their disputes. If mediation failed, they would petition, go to court, or give up, due to the time and money involved in filing suit in court. Most of them expressed the view that litigation could protect their rights better than mediation, because mediation meant having to compromise with the authority of the village (or higher level) cadre. Indeed, for the 53.5 percent of survey respondents for whom the dispute had been resolved (n=49), 65 percent were dissatisfied or very dissatisfied with the result. For 46.5 percent of the survey respondents detailed above, the dispute was still on-going at the time of the survey.

In interviews, respondents indicated that, on the one hand, they mediated disputes in reality. On the other hand, they express a longing for the ideal that the law can bring about justice and equality. As one respondent commented in a follow-up interview: "Law is more important than emotion, and law can remedy unreasonable events and bring equality for us."[33] Survey respondents consistently identified local courts as being more trustworthy than other local government agencies, including mass organizations, the media, the village committee, the county and township governments, the petition office, and the police.[34]

The following section examines in-depth four land disputes from rural Hunan in order to reveal the tensions between containing conflict and maintaining political stability, on the one hand, and upholding legal norms, on the other.

Cases

Mediation is not only promoted in official policy; it is also a low cost and convenient dispute resolution mechanism. Based on the survey data reported above (Table 8.2), it is the most common form of dispute settlement apart from direct negotiation. However, it does not necessarily provide a principled or normative set of rules that are consistently applied at the grass roots. The results depend on the parties' power and interests.[35] Dissatisfied parties may try to take their cases to court, but, even here, courts are too constrained to adhere consistently to a set of legal norms through which cases can be resolved, preventing the development of bargaining under a predictable shadow of the law. Basic-level Chinese courts operating under political constraints refuse to accept many land lawsuits because of the sensitivity of the issues involved and the difficulty of enforcement. If the court refuses to accept lawsuits, one party may petition or give up. Nevertheless, the conflict still exists, even though it may be suppressed temporarily.

33 Liang Zhiping describes this sentiment in his discussion of what the rule of law means in China. Traditionally, the Chinese have used law to help them to resolve disputes. At the same time, they are pragmatic; if legal procedures hurt their interests, they abandon them without hesitation. See Liang Zhiping, "法治:社会转型时期的制度建构" ("Rule of Law: The System in Transition China"), in Liang Zhiping (ed.), 法治在中国:制度、话语与实践 (*Rule of Law in China: System, Dialogue and Practice*) (Beijing: Chinese Politics and Law University Press, 2002), p. 142.

34 Courts were the most trusted institution among eleven local agencies. Trust in the courts was uncorrelated with reported personal contact with courts or court personnel.

35 See also Changdong Zhang, "Power Structure and Access to Justice," paper presented at the ACLS Workshop on "Sending 'Rule of Law' to the Countryside: Development Theories and Chinese Realities," University of Washington School of Law, May 6–7, 2010.

Case 1

In Hu Village of County N, Hunan, approximately 60 mu of relatively low-quality land was abandoned/fallowed by the holder of the land-use contract some time before 2004 (but after the second round of land contracting). In 2004, the village reallocated the abandoned land to a new party, with whom it signed a new land-use contract. The new contract-holder started a crayfish farm and within several years had generated a significant economic return. Recognizing the increased value of the land,[36] and jealous of the new land user's success, the original contract-holder sought to regain control of the land in 2008, provoking a conflict with the village small group leaders. In essence, the first step taken by the aggrieved party was to negotiate directly with the small group – the issuer of the original contract. The second step taken by the aggrieved party was to petition the local government; the original contract-holder, collectively with other members of the small group, petitioned the township government for return of the land. In response to the petition, the township government sought to mediate the dispute. In protracted mediations, the township requested that the new contract-holder pay the value of all government agricultural subsidies to the original contract-holder. Moreover, the township requested that the new contract-holder pay to repair the irrigation system of the small group. In exchange, the new contract-holder would continue to operate his fish farm on the land in question. The new contract-holder, in order to avoid further conflict and to protect his economic interest in the land, reluctantly agreed to the mediation plan. Ultimately, therefore, the case was resolved through mediation by the basic-level government.

Analytically, we can see that the mediation recognized and acted on multiple competing norms in a way that a strict interpretation of the law might not allow. First, it partially recognized the legal right of the original contract-holder to the land by awarding him compensation equal to the value of state subsidies. However, the Rural Land Contracting Law (RLCL), which came into effect in 2003, prior to the issuance of the new contract in 2004, indicates that existing contracts should remain in force (Article 62) for up to thirty years (Article 20), and that the contracting party – the village small group – may not unilaterally abrogate the existing contract (Article 26) as it did in this case. Moreover,

[36] Multiple factors may have affected the value of the land, including the abolition of the agricultural tax, the provision of new agricultural subsidies, as well as investment.

State Council Office Document No. 21 (2004) not only reaffirms the RLCL, it also explicitly states that abandonment or fallowing of cultivated land by a household does not constitute grounds for reallocation of land contracts, and that where the contract for abandoned land has been reallocated, it should be returned to the original contract-holder.[37] Second, the township government as mediator recognized the collective governance interests of village small group leaders. It did not change the fact of the land reallocation, which may have generated certain fees for the village small group.[38] The township called for a collective benefit to the small group in the form of investment in irrigation infrastructure. Third, the mediator – in this case the township government – recognized the economic interest of the new contract-holder by allowing him to continue to operate and profit from his fish farm.

Case 2

During the second round of land contracting in County A, Hunan, in 1995, a father and son together contracted 9 mu of land from the village small group. They subsequently subcontracted 4 mu to a relative to cultivate. The relative then further subcontracted the 4 mu to a third party. No written contracts were used in any of the subcontracting arrangements. In 2000, the village conducted a small reallocation of arable landholdings and, in the process, issued a land-use contract to the third party cultivating the 4 mu of land.[39] In 2007, the original household contracting the land demanded that the third party return the 4 mu. The third party, citing the large number of people in his household, refused to return the land. Hence, the first step was an

[37] The township may have understood the village's act of reclaiming abandoned land as being informed by a local reading of Article 37 of the 1998 Land Management Law, which states – in apparent conflict with the 2002 RLCL – that: "Whereas a unit or individual that has contracted for land use has abandoned cultivation and allowed the land to go to waste for two successive years, the original contracting-out party shall terminate the contract and recover the land contracted out for cultivation." Authoritative commentators in the central government have explained Article 37 of the LML as applying only to rural land abandoned in the process of development for non-agricultural uses (as by township- and village-run enterprises).

[38] Interviews indicate that, even after the abolition of taxes on agriculture and agricultural sidelines in 2004, villages continued to collect certain fees, at least through to 2007. Village/village small group may also collect rental fees on land.

[39] There is no indication that the reallocation was approved by two-thirds of village households as mandated in the Land Management Law.

attempt at direct negotiation. The second step was an attempt at mediation by members of the village party committee, but without success. The original contract-holder filed suit in the basic-level court – the third step – seeking return of the 4 mu of land. The court accepted the case. Upon discovering that the original contract-holder had been issued a land-use certificate in the second round of contracting in 1995, the court found in favor of the original holder. Fourth, following the judgment, the original contract-holder applied for court enforcement. On two occasions, the court dispatched officers to enforce the judgment without success. There are multiple reasons for the failure to enforce the judgment. First, the land was intercropped, and forcible leveling would harm production. Second, at each attempt at enforcement, the entire family of those occupying the land would threaten to violently resist eviction. The court officers felt there was nothing they could do; however, the plaintiffs continued to seek compulsory enforcement of the judgment. Ultimately, the court returned 2,000 yuan in enforcement fees to the plaintiffs, notifying them that the judgment was unenforceable. Following this episode, the court in County A issued an important internal regulation, stating that the court would no longer accept this kind of land contract dispute, guidance apparently followed by the court subsequently. Moreover, the court instructed the parties to seek out a government agency to mediate the dispute. In essence, the court resorted to "comprehensive" mediation, after it failed to enforce the judgment and thereby avoided a violent confrontation, suggesting that a mediated outcome would be more readily enforceable and less likely to provoke a mass incident.

In this case, the formal legal rights of the plaintiffs were, in principle, fully recognized by the court. However, two other principles – agricultural production and political stability – are evident in the failure to enforce the court's judgment and in the lack of support for the court from any other agency of the state. The threat of a mass incident in the local community by the defendant's family posed a threat to political stability, a key performance criterion for the local officials. There is also a reference to the impact on agricultural production. Clearly, enforcing the court's judgment was not a political priority. Another interpretation suggests that "might makes right," or that local bullies commonly prevail in rural communities. But given the repressive capacity of the local state, the idea that other priorities simply trump enforcing a court judgment is more plausible. Most significantly, the court – as a policy matter – responded by closing off its docket to this entire class of cases, ending the possibility for similarly situated plaintiffs to pursue recourse through the courts, and making outcomes in accordance with formal legal norms even less likely.

Case 3

In 2008, a village in Township T, County C, requisitioned more than 100 mu of basic agricultural land for the development of a commercial plant nursery. The land-taking, however, did not follow the necessary legal procedures. Moreover, a number of villagers were dissatisfied with the compensation they were to receive, since it could not provide adequately for their future livelihood. They planned to file a collective administrative suit challenging the legality of the taking, but this initiative was suppressed by the township government. After various attempts, this group of villagers let the matter drop. Among the villagers was a woman who had married outside the village, but whose household registration was still in the village; hence, she was entitled to the same compensation as other villagers. However, when the distribution of compensation funds took place, she received resettlement compensation, but no land compensation.[40]

On this basis, the married-out woman sought to sue the village small group over the distribution of land compensation. Her lawyer went to the County C basic-level court to file a civil suit on her behalf. The court refused to accept the case, despite entreaties by the lawyer directly to the president of the basic-level court and despite appeals to the intermediate- and high-level courts. The basic-level court gave the following reasoning: although judicial interpretations clearly state that the court should accept the case, there are too many cases of this kind in County C; even if the court accepted the case, it would be hard to implement. The court indicated that it would be better for the plaintiff to seek a remedy through government mediation, even though the government itself was complicit in the illegal taking by allowing it to go forward.

Neither the villagers who sought to challenge the legality of the land-taking itself, nor the married-out woman who sought to challenge the unfair compensation were able to bring suit in court, despite their efforts. Courts

[40] Another aggrieved party was a college graduate who had already worked for several years for a private company in the provincial capital; however, shortly before the land-taking occurred, he paid 10,000 yuan in exchange for the approval of the village small group to return his household registration to the village. He received only resettlement compensation, but no land compensation.

themselves are highly constrained actors in dispute resolution. Case 3 provides another example of legal norms in competition with political and other interests. It also highlights the political function of "comprehensive" mediation. In this case, the land rights of married-out women are protected by the RLCL; however, as the judicial authority, the court cannot help them to defend their rights. Similar to the other cases described above, the law failed to serve as the victims' weapon for rights protection. This situation demonstrates the gap between rights on paper and rights in action. The results of dispute resolution mostly depend on the extent to which people admit the effect of law. It is a constitutional principle that women have the same land rights as men;[41] however, many rural communities do not recognize this principle in practice. If the village is unwilling to accord women equal rights to land compensation, they may pass such a vote, relying on the principle of village self-governance.[42] Rural communities oppose the equality principle by claiming village autonomy, although even village autonomy is limited in the RLCL by the stipulation that the approval of a two-thirds majority is necessary to approve decisions involving land (Articles 18 and 27), and that all collective decisions must comply with existing laws (Organic Law of Villagers' Committees). In the absence of a conflict of law, the court should deal with the complicated interests involved with local government support in enforcement. In this case, anticipating a difficulty they could not resolve, the court suggested that the victim seek help directly from the government. The government, in turn, used comprehensive mediation to defend its own administrative power. What the court did was to relieve pressure by avoiding a situation in which it had to return the litigation fee, as happened in the second case, above. The Supreme People's Court has recently indicated that the basic rights of women are superior to village autonomy, but it is not clear what the effect of this Supreme People's Court clarification will be, in light of the emphasis on mediated outcomes at the grass roots.

Case 4

In 2006, the land bureau in County A took 29.9 mu of land by eminent domain from a village near the county seat for the purpose of road-building. The taking encompassed 0.9 mu belonging to villager Han, for

[41] Article 5 of the Chinese Constitution.

[42] The Organic Law of Villagers' Committees states that actions of village committees cannot violate other laws.

which he anticipated compensation totaling 25,000 yuan. The village refused to distribute the compensation funds to Han, because the rights to the 0.9 mu of land were disputed by Han's former wife's younger brother. Both the village committee and the township made repeated attempts to mediate the dispute – the first step in the dispute resolution process in this case – but they were not able to get the parties to come to an agreement. Han's next step was to file suit against the village for failing to pay him the land compensation.

After investigation, the county court found that, although Han did not have a land-use certificate, he did have rights to the land in question. Han had married in 1989. After the second round of land contracting in 1995, Han's father-in-law, Zen, had transferred 1.8 of his 3.95 mu of land to his daughter and son-in-law. They, in turn, cultivated the 1.8 mu and undertook responsibility for all land-related fees and obligations. The court interpreted Han's land rights as established by inheritance (division of land within the family). The father-in-law (Zen) and his son cultivated the other 2.15 mu of the family's landholdings and took responsibility for the fees and obligations on that parcel of land. These arrangements did not change after the father-in-law's death or after Han's divorce from the daughter in 1998. Moreover, the younger brother made no effort to challenge Han's occupation of the land prior to the land-taking. The county court found for the plaintiff and instructed the village committee to pay the land compensation for 0.9 mu to Han.

The village appealed the decision to the intermediate court and presented several reasons in court for withholding payment. First, at the time of the second round of land contracting in 1995, Han's household registration was not in this village; so the village did not consider Han to be eligible for compensation. Second, Zen's own son had married in 1994 and had produced a grandson in 1995; so, by rural custom, the village already considered Zen's son to be the household head. Moreover, before Zen's death, he had transferred the land-use certificate for all 3.95 mu to his son. Therefore, the son had decision-making rights regarding the disposition of the land.

After the county court issued its ruling in the first trial, the village had solicited the opinions of the deputy county executive, the county court vice-president, several township cadres, and members of the community, and, with their implicit approval, had proceeded to give the compensation funds to Zen's son in contravention of the county court's ruling. Despite these political signals, the intermediate court upheld the basic-level court's ruling.

It subsequently became clear that the village leaders' own job performance ratings (for facilitating completion of the road and maintaining political stability) were also factors in their handling of the land compensation funds. Zen's son, in demanding that the compensation be given to him and not to his former brother-in-law, had repeatedly blocked construction work on the road. Removing this literal roadblock may have motivated the village leaders to resist the basic- and intermediate-level courts.

In interviews regarding this case, divergent opinions have been expressed. One view is that the plaintiff did not hold the land contract, and therefore the court made a mistake in its ruling. The other view is that the court withstood political pressure and provided access to justice. In addition, the case involves a conflict of law. Article 5 of the Rural Land Contracting Law indicates that members (成员) of the village collective may contract village land, and Article 9 protects the rights of contractors from any interference by individuals or organizations. The village committee thought that Zen and his son held these rights. Article 15 of the Rural Land Contracting Law indicates that the rural land contracting system is based on family household (家庭) contracts, and family household contracting of agricultural land is also a constitutional principle (Article 8). The court regarded Han as a member of the family (家庭) and as the one who cultivated the land in question, and therefore, Han held these rights.

The fourth case raises several important theoretical questions. First, if local courts in China are not empowered to resolve conflicts of law, then perhaps mediation is a reasonable way for local courts to resolve disputes involving such conflicts. Second, if courts regularly face political interference from local officials, then mediation may be a reasonable way to prevent the de-legitimization of the court.

The four cases described in detail in this section highlight the difficulties in the resolution of land disputes and shed light on the patterns identified in the first part of section three. Rural households do seek recourse through the courts, particularly in land-taking disputes involving relatively high monetary stakes. Rural households also report high levels of general trust in local courts as compared with other local institutions. At the same time, high-stakes disputes often go unresolved and leave rural households extremely dissatisfied. In Case 1, the court was not involved. Government mediation resulted in land contracted during the second round not being returned to the contract-holder, but being left in the hands of an economically productive new user, with partial compensation to the contract-holder. In Case 2, the local court made a ruling based on a strict interpretation of the law, upholding the claim of the contract-holder, and the court's attempts at enforcement resulted in a violent backlash. The court's response was to block further cases of this kind from its docket. In Case 3, the court declined to accept a sensitive case involving land-taking compensation, and pushed it into mediation by the government. In Case 4, although the court itself withstood political pressure in its judgment, local leaders gave in to physical force. In these cases, the effectiveness of courts was limited by the institutional environment. At the same time, the courts may have attempted to maintain their legitimacy and comparatively high trust among the public by shielding themselves from the most politically sensitive and difficult-to-enforce cases. However, if drafters of the Rural Land Contracting Law intended to strengthen the rights of rural land contract-holders, this goal of the law has not necessarily been realized. Moreover, the disposition of the courts may have inadvertently emboldened villagers to use violence, left local government behavior unchecked, and privileged customary over formal state law. These circumstances reflect the institutional challenges facing local courts and, at the same time, shed light on the negative evaluation of courts by NPC delegates.

Explaining the patterns: role play and role conflict

As the survey and interviews evidence suggest, there is active interest in law and courts as a means of dispute resolution. Respondents are more likely to try the courts in high-stakes disputes involving land-takings compared with other land disputes, as shown above. Survey respondents also express greater trust in the courts than in other local government agencies. At the same time, the case studies demonstrate the political constraints on the courts, which affect the roles courts play in accepting, handling, deciding, and enforcing cases. High-stakes land-takings compensation cases are least likely to be resolved, leading to popular dissatisfaction.

Deflecting cases, combining adjudication with mediation, and combining court-performed mediation with comprehensive mediation are conscious choices within the court system in this study. This behavior is driven by multiple factors, including the impact of politics on the courts, the court's desire to improve its capacity to resolve disputes, and the court's effort to break through the pressure to play different roles. The

2010 Work Report of the Supreme People's Court highlights the objective of combining mediation and adjudication, and complementing litigation with alternative dispute resolution.[43] Mediation has become a core part of court-based dispute resolution.[44] In light of the judicial reforms of the past twenty years, why have comprehensive mediation and Ma Xiwu-style adjudication taken center stage? This section employs the concept of roles and role conflict to analyze this issue.

The sociological concept of roles describes the anticipated behavior of people in specific statuses. According to Linton, a person plays a role while occupying a certain status.[45] In every highly structured social interaction, the community provides a script to guide the behavior of the person in each role. Everyone in society must inevitably occupy multiple statuses, corresponding to multiple roles, with the potential to experience conflict among them. Chinese courts and judges occupy many roles in the state system. Most importantly, they perform the function of dispute resolution. Moreover, they represent, in principle, judicial organs' exercise of independent judicial power not subject to interference by administrative organs.[46] In reality, however, there is no separation of powers, and courts are not independent of the ruling party or executive. The opinion of former president of the SPC, Xiao Yang, cited above, clearly reveals the constraints on the status and function of the courts.

In their roles as judicial organs, courts are simultaneously regarded as party and state organs, and judges are regarded as officials of the party-state. Internal administrative management in the courts, including budget, equipment, and staff, is the same as in other government organs, and judges' ranks are parallel to other officials.[47] Article 107 of the Constitution stipulates that local people's governments shall be the ones to conduct judicial administration in their respective administrative areas. Moreover, the lower

43 See 2010 Work Report of the Supreme People's Court, Pt. V.

44 According to the 2010 Work Report of the Supreme People's Court, 62 percent of civil disputes in basic-level courts were mediated in court-performed mediation.

45 See Ralph Linton, *The Study of Man* (New York: Appleton-Century-Crofts, 1936).

46 Article 126 of the Chinese Constitution.

47 While courts adopted another judges' rating system after the "Law on Judges" was enacted, judges' wages are still in accord with their administrative rank. See CPC Organization Department, Personnel and Supreme Court on Issuance, "PRC Judges Grade Interim Provisions," Notice, December 12, 1997 promulgate (《法官法》实施之后,法院采用另一套法官评级制度,但法官的工资有对应的行政级别。参见:《中共中央组织部、人事部、最高人民法院关于印发<中华人民共和国法官等级暂行规定>的通知》, 1997年12月12日颁布).

the level of the court, the fewer resources it can control, the more it is constrained by the local government, and the more pressure it has to face. For example, the judges in basic-level courts are tasked with maintaining stability for local governments and must participate in public propaganda about the official role of law and courts.

To relieve the pressure from role conflict and to maintain their legitimate legal status, courts seek ways to balance their different role requirements. Therefore, since 2007, local courts have been exhorted to promote judicial initiative and to undertake comprehensive mediation.

The difference between adjudication and mediation in the context of this study is that adjudication strictly implements the law, while mediation flexibly employs it.[48] In principle, mediation can also take place within the shadow of the law. However, Huang, focusing specifically on Chinese history and culture, argues that there is no uniform understanding of courts mediating similar disputes.[49] In some instances, we can explain the varied resolution of land disputes by identifying the protection of various local interests rather than by making reference to law. Judges in basic-level courts face difficult challenges in resolving disputes while at the same time balancing law and policy. Mediation, which allows them to resolve disputes through compromise, provides flexibility when enforcing the law. Ultimately, courts employ mediation to achieve the "unification of legal effect and social effect," as indicated by former SPC President Wang Shengjun.[50]

Sociologist Zhang Jing argues that the choice of norms by parties to a dispute is based on interests, not on rules of law.[51] Political power and social structure determine one's ability to assert one's interests as primary. A dilemma, which courts face if they employ court-performed mediation to resolve disputes, arises when the parties feel that the law is flexible according to their differential power levels; as a result, courts may lose their ability to make the law the normative rule.[52]

[48] See also Gary Friedman and Jack Himmelstein, *Challenging Conflict: Mediation Through Understanding* (Chicago, IL: American Bar Association, 2009).

[49] See Huang, "Court Mediation in China, Past and Present."

[50] Wang Shengjun, former president of Supreme People's Court, speech.

[51] See Zhang Jing (张静), "The Uncertainty of Land Use Rules: An Interpretative Framework," *Social Sciences in China*, 1 (2004), 36–46.

[52] 法院除了纠纷解决,另外一个功能是规则之治。(Besides dispute resolution, courts also have the function of governing norms.) See 苏力, "农村基层法院的纠纷解决与规则之治," 北大法律评论, (Su Li, "Rural Basic-Level Courts' Dispute Resolution and Norm Governance", *Peking University Law Review*, 1 (1999), 80).

One way in which local courts may seek to protect their long-term legitimacy is to deflect at least some types of sensitive cases that attract political interference. In the short term, however, the rule of law appears to be undermined. This result occurs at the same time that constitutional revisions rhetorically emphasize the role of law in governance.[53]

Conclusion

This chapter has documented the official promotion of mediation as a key form of dispute resolution for use by courts and other local government agencies in addressing rural land disputes. The promotion of mediation was linked to the goal of maintaining political stability. This study demonstrates that, in general, rural residents in Hunan had relatively high trust in local courts and that, specifically, they turned to the courts in high-stakes land disputes. At the same time, the study also suggests that instances of adherence to formal land law by local courts exacerbated conflict in some cases. Indeed, the outcomes most acceptable to powerful or vociferous interests in rural communities were not consistent with the courts' interpretation of relevant land law in the cases detailed above. Local courts in the study responded by refusing to accept certain cases and grappling – sometimes unsuccessfully – with the challenge of enforcement in other cases. Courts may seek to protect their legitimacy by avoiding cases in which their role as an institution tasked with upholding formal land law and their role as part of the local government administration tasked with maintaining political stability come into conflict. However, courts' refusal to accept cases is a major source of dissatisfaction. Similarly, although rural residents in this study did turn to the courts in high-stakes cases, the cases in the survey had a low resolution rate and a high dissatisfaction level. Thus, it is not clear whether the strategy of deflecting cases threatens or protects the relatively high trust overall that survey respondents reported in local courts.

When courts deflected cases to other venues for mediation, in some cases, land rights ended up in the hands of more productive and more powerful users who could share benefits with the state and collective; in other cases, land rights ended up in the hands of those willing to provoke "mass incidents"; and, in still other cases, in the hands of traditional power-holders. None of these claimants was explicitly intended to

[53] Establishing a "socialist rule of law state" was a key element of the 2004 constitutional revision.

benefit from stronger property rights in formal land law. While, in principle, mediation by trained mediators can be conducted in the "shadow of the law," in these cases, in which mediators were village cadres and local government officials tasked with maintaining political stability, law does not appear to have cast a very long shadow. The land claims of the returned migrant worker holding a land-use certificate from the second round of land contracting and of the married-out woman whose equal rights to land are enshrined in law – were partly or wholly rejected.

The multiplicity of roles played by local courts may vary over time. According to comments from the Legal Committee of the National People's Congress, over the past several years, high quotas for judicial mediation of cases in basic-level courts have over-burdened local judges, suggesting that high mediation rates should no longer be emphasized as an evaluation criterion for judges. Following the confirmation of new Supreme People's Court President Zhou Qiang at the First Session of the Twelfth National People's Congress in 2013, discussions in legal circles suggest that these political pressures on courts may ease or change form.[54] Under the Hu-Wen administration and during Wang Shengjun's tenure as SPC President, judges were to favor mediation even in the litigation process, to be proactive in directing the dispute resolution process, and to give precedence to the Party according to the Three Supremes. These slogans and policies may be allowed to fall by the wayside, suggesting the possibility of a change of course in the role of mediation in the judiciary.

[54] See He Bing, "Heard Friends at the Supreme People's Court Say, the Following Three Slogans Will be Dropped: Three Supremes; Pro-active Judging; Mediation First. The Supreme People's Court Wants to Change Course" ("听最高法院的朋友说,以下三个口号寿终正寝:三个至上;能动司法;调解优先。最高法院要调整航向了"), April 10, 2013, 5:47, Weibo.

9

Power and rule by law in rural China

State-initiated mediation in land disputes

CHANGDONG ZHANG AND CHRISTOPHER HEURLIN

Introduction

In a village outside Fenghua City, in Zhejiang, a group of villagers felt that the local government had given them insufficient compensation for land that the local government was expropriating. When the villagers negotiated with the village cadres to no avail, they began petitioning the local Land Resources Bureau. After their petitions and demands for administrative reconsideration went nowhere, the villagers went to the Provincial High Court, sued the Zhejiang Province Legislative Affairs Office, and won.[1]

Land disputes like the Fenghua case have become extremely common. As China has urbanized and industrialized, land has become an increasingly valuable resource, especially on the urban fringe. The abolition of the agriculture tax, increasing government subsidies, and the rising prices of agricultural commodities have all made farming much more profitable than it was in the 1990s. Even remote rural land has become much more valuable. Consequently, land has become a major source of disputes: disputes between villagers; disputes between villagers and the government; and between villagers and the village committee.[2] As Yu finds, since the 2004 abolition of agricultural taxes, land disputes have replaced taxation disputes as the main

The authors want to thank Susan Whiting, Hualing Fu, and Kathinka Furst for their valuable comments.

1 China News Network, "浙江农民讲述"民告官:'用法律为政府部门纠错'" (Zhejiang Farmer Talks About 'People Suing the Government': Using Law to Rectify Mistakes of Government Departments"), available at: http://news.xinhuanet.com/lianzheng/2007-04/12/content_5965170.htm.

2 The village committee is an organization of grass-roots self-government that is not legally speaking a part of the government. In practice, however, it is often tightly integrated with the township government through the village Communist Party branch.

source of rural unrest.[3] Yet the Fenghua case is unique because courts are seldom involved in the resolution of rural land disputes. Indeed, despite Central Government commitments to rule by law, local governments have progressively closed off access to the courts. Given the Central Government's professed commitment to "rule by law" (*yifa zhiguo*), why have local governments undermined efforts to build the rule by law by emphasizing government-led mediation and shutting off access to the courts?

We argue that mediation has become the preferred mode of resolution in rural land disputes because of the institutional incentives officials and judges face to resolve conflicts and maintain a "harmonious society," especially when the state has direct stakes in the dispute.[4] Local officials have issued instructions to local courts – which are dependent on the local government – to refuse to accept cases in which the local party-state is involved. Far from standing on the sidelines as observers, officials actively attempt to draw villagers into mediation. State power thus forces villagers to pursue mediation instead of litigation to resolve their disputes. Our analysis of three different kinds of land dispute, however, shows the limitations of local governments' mediation strategy. Mediation is least effective when local government interests are directly implicated in the dispute. In these cases, villagers have frequently resisted mediation and turned to petitioning or even rioting in an attempt to gain leverage over local officials.

This chapter is organized in five sections. First, we will review alternative explanations for the emergence of mediation and rule by law in authoritarian states. In the section that follows, we offer conceptualizations of state power in the legal system and an illustration of the argument. Subsequently, we will discuss three types of land dispute – land lease disputes, abandoned land disputes, and land-taking disputes – to analyze how state interests influence both the choice to emphasize mediation, but also the efficacy of this strategy in resolving disputes. In the conclusion, we summarize the findings and discuss the theoretical implications.

Rule by law, mediation, and authoritarianism

The law, it would seem, is on the move. In Europe, politics are becoming judicialized to the point that states are argued to be "governing with judges."[5]

[3] See Yu Jianrong, "土地问题成为农民维权抗争的焦点," 调研世界, 2005年03期 ("Land Has Been the Focus of Peasants' Protests," *World of Investigation*, 3 (2005), 22–23).

[4] The term "harmonious society" has become the hallmark of the Hu Jintao administration. The term carries with it a strong connotation of social stability.

[5] See A. Stone Sweet, *Governing with Judges* (Oxford University Press, 2000).

Nor is this trend confined to Europe. Rather, the "judicialization" of politics is sweeping the world.[6] Authoritarian states have not been excluded from this trend. In recent years, many authoritarian regimes have invested a substantial amount of effort into building, if not a rule *of* law system, at least rule *by* law.[7] China is no exception in this regard, as the state has invested heavily in establishing and strengthening judicial institutions.[8]

In explaining the puzzle of the judicialization of politics in authoritarian regimes, Ginsburg and Moustafa argue that independent courts in authoritarian regimes serve five basic functions. First, courts allow the state to establish and exercise social control. Second, courts generate legitimacy for the regime. This is because courts can give the regime a veneer of democratic legitimacy. Propagating laws – and empowering courts to enforce them – allows the state to claim that it is bound by the law. Third, courts are a tool of administrative control. By empowering courts to accept administrative lawsuits, the Central Government can use the courts as a "fire alarm" to warn it about deviations from national laws by state agents. Fourth, courts can help to provide a credible commitment to businesses. A court that is empowered to resolve property rights disputes independently of the state may help authoritarian rulers to build confidence in the quality of the business environment, thereby spurring economic activity. Fifth, courts can be used to depoliticize policy-making. In this sense, courts can accept legislative deferrals from the state: reforms that are too politically or ideologically difficult for the regime to adopt on its own. Crucially, Ginsburg and Moustafa argue that these five functions of the rule by law in authoritarian regimes are mutually reinforcing.[9]

In this chapter, we call into question this argument by examining how local officials have responded to efforts by the Central Government to build rule by law in ways that have undermined these functions. The conflicting political goals of local officials – particularly between maintaining credible commitments to property rights to encourage economic growth, on the one hand, and maintaining social control, on the other – have led local officials to progressively undermine Central Government

[6] See C. Neal Tate and Torbjorn Vallinder, *The Global Expansion of Judicial Power* (New York University Press, 1995).

[7] See Tom Ginsburg and Tamir Moustafa, *Rule by Law: The Politics of Courts in Authoritarian Regimes* (New York: Cambridge University Press, 2008).

[8] See Tom Ginsburg, "Administrative Law and the Judicial Control of Agents in Authoritarian Regimes," in Tom Ginsburg and Tamir Moustafa, *Rule by Law: The Politics of Courts in Authoritarian Regimes* (New York: Cambridge University Press, 2008), pp. 58–74. See Randall Peerenboom, *China's Long March Toward Rule of Law* (New York: Cambridge University Press, 2002).

[9] See Ginsburg and Moustafa (eds.), *Rule by Law*.

attempts to build a rule by law system. Instead of following Central Government mandates to provide credible commitments to land contracts and access to administrative law to control state agents, local officials have emphasized mediation based not primarily on legal norms, but on Party power. Local governments' obsession with maintaining social control has progressively weakened the four other functions of rule by law, particularly the legitimacy-generating functions.

The emergence of mediation as a form of dispute resolution has often been linked to societal norms. Ellickson, for example, argues that social customs have led neighbors in the mountainous areas of California to settle disputes through negotiation and mediation.[10] In Illinois, Engel found that social norms discouraged lawsuits in personal injury disputes as an abdication of personal responsibility.[11] Similar arguments have been put forward with regard to China, as Zhu also argues that local knowledge and customs are important in resolving disputes in remote areas of China.[12] Fu and Zhang suggest the tension between formal rules and informal customs in the formation and resolution of disputes.[13] However, a major finding of this chapter is that mediation has been institutionalized as a state practice instead of a social practice.

With regard to the Chinese case, scholars have offered two explanations for the prominence of mediation. First, they have argued that mediation has become commonplace because of disputants' distrust in the courts.[14] This explanation is consistent with the argument that mediation is a social practice. The most insightful work on disputing in rural China has been conducted by Landry and Tong, as well as by Michelson, who use large surveys of rural disputes. Landry and Tong find that individuals who trust the court are more inclined to bring their disputes to court. Landry argues

10 See Robert Ellickson, *Order without Law* (Cambridge, MA: Harvard University Press, 1991).

11 See David Engel, "The Ovenbird's Song: Insiders, Outsiders, and Personal Injuries in an American Community," *Law & Society Review*, 18 (1984), 551–582.

12 See Zhu Suli, 送法下乡 (Send the Laws to the Countryside), (Beijing: Chinese University of Politics and Law Press, 2000).

13 See Hualing Fu, "Access to Justice in China: Potentials, Limits, and Alternatives," in John Gillespie and Albert H. Y. Chen (eds.), *Legal Reforms in China and Vietnam: A Comparison of Asian Communist Regimes* (London: Routledge, 2010), pp. 163–187; Jing Zhang, "二元整合秩序:一个财产纠纷案的分析", 社会学研究 2005年03期 ("Order of Dual Integration Mechanisms: A Study of a Property Dispute Case," *Chinese Sociology Review*, 3 (2005), 1–19).

14 Our fieldwork also finds some counter-evidence for this argument: some farmers choose not to litigate because they are afraid that, if they lose the suit, higher-level governments will refuse to accept subsequent petitions.

that social networks are important in the diffusion of legal mobilization for two reasons. First, networks facilitate communication of legal knowledge and therefore improve trust in the court. Second, connections with the courts and government enhance trust in the court.[15] This explanation, which is focused on litigants, largely neglects the active role that local officials have played in shaping and restricting access to the courts.

Second, scholars have also attributed the low levels of legal mobilization to the lack of a "support structure."[16] Fu finds that the short supply of lawyers limits citizens' access to justice, especially in rural areas.[17] Even in urban areas, Michelson finds that the dependence of the lawyers on the state makes them an "obstacle to justice."[18] Lawyers are particularly unwilling to accept administrative cases.[19] The dependence of lawyers on the state points to the importance of considering the role of the state in shaping patterns of dispute resolution in China. Yet the influence of the state extends far beyond simply the pressure placed on lawyers not to accept controversial cases. Much more important, we argue, is how local officials both actively initiate mediation and use their control over local courts to prohibit judges from accepting cases.

The role of the state has been largely neglected in explaining the prominence of mediation. Both local governments and local courts operate in an environment that is heavily regulated by the Party. In particular, the cadre evaluation system – or nomenclature system – plays a very important role in providing incentives to the behavior of local officials.[20] Within the Chinese system, officials are heavily dependent on their superiors, who give them clear evaluation criteria that motivate their behavior. While in the 1990s these criteria concerned primarily economic development, in the 2000s social stability became an increasingly important component of evaluations. Therefore, what is largely missing from accounts of disputing behavior in China is an

[15] See Pierre Landry, "The Institutional Diffusion of Courts in China: Evidence from Survey Data," in Tom Ginsburg and Tamir Moustafa (eds.), *Rule by Law: The Politics of Courts in Authoritarian Regimes* (New York: Cambridge University Press, 2008), pp. 207–234.

[16] See Charles R. Epp, *The Rights Revolution: Lawyers, Activists, and Supreme Courts in Comparative Perspective* (University of Chicago Press, 1998).

[17] See Fu, "Access to Justice in China."

[18] See Ethan Michelson, "The Practice of Law as an Obstacle to Justice: Chinese Lawyers at Work," *Law & Society Review*, 40 (2006), 1–38.

[19] See Yongshun Cai and Songcai Yang, "State Power and Unbalanced Legal Development in China," *Journal of Contemporary China*, 14 (2005), 117–134.

[20] See Maria Edin, "Remaking the Communist Party-State: The Cadre Responsibility System at the Local Level in China," *China: An International Journal*, 1 (2003), 1–15; Susan H. Whiting, "The Cadre Evaluation System at the Grass Roots: The Paradox of Party Rule," in Barry J. Naughton and Dali L. Yang (eds.), *Holding China Together: Diversity and National Integration in the post-Deng Era* (Cambridge University Press, 2003).

approach that emphasizes how local politics, especially the interests and actions of local officials, can lead them to actively undermine the rule of law and intervene in disputes to force mediation.[21] It is to this that we now turn.

In the context of the institutions of rule by law in China, local governments reign supreme at the grass roots. While the Central Government has legislated a wide variety of laws and administrative regulations, the majority of litigation and contestation takes place at the grass roots. As the following sections will show, local courts are under the administrative leadership of the local Party and government. This limits the extent to which Central Government efforts to build rule by law can function at the grass roots. Local officials have strategically institutionalized mediation as a way of strengthening the local Party and government at the expense of both local courts and central laws.

The nature of local state involvement in the dispute critically influences the degree to which local officials attempt to channel disputes into mediation and their efficacy in doing so. When local officials are not directly a party to the dispute, villagers have been less constrained in their ability to engage in legal mobilization. The case of land-lease disputes most closely resembles the mediation as a social practice model, as villagers have often proactively sought out the village government for meditation and have sought to go to court only when mediation fails. In these cases, the state typically succeeds in mediating disputes. In abandoned land disputes, however, the local government's interests – in this case in tax collection – are more clearly implicated. As a result, local officials have attempted to emphasize mediation and close off the courts. Local government success in mediation has been moderate, although local officials have been less successful than in land-lease disputes. Yet in land-taking conflicts – which typically pit villagers against the township and county government – the immediate involvement of the local state as a party to the dispute has severely undermined the efficacy of mediation. Villagers in these cases view mediation as unlikely to yield positive results and instead turn to more confrontational strategies, such as protests or collective petitions to higher levels of government, to improve their bargaining power. The influence of state interests on the prevalence and efficacy of state-initiated mediation is described in Table 9.1 below.

[21] Susan Whiting's work is an exception. She argues that the fiscalization of land explains the emergence and resolution of land disputes. However, our chapter provides a more comprehensive examination of the institutional context of dispute emergence and the resolution of land disputes. See Susan H. Whiting, "Values in Land: Fiscal Pressures, Land Disputes and Justice Claims in Rural and Peri-urban China," *Urban Studies*, 48 (2011), 569–587.

Table 9.1 *Patterns of dispute resolution by land dispute type*

Dispute type	State interest	Court independence	Relative frequency of strategies for resolving disputes	Success of mediation
Land-lease dispute	Low	High	Litigation: medium state-initiated Mediation: low	High
Abandoned land dispute	Medium	Medium	Litigation: low State-initiated mediation: high Petitioning: high	Medium
Land-taking dispute	High	Low	State-initiated mediation: high Petitioning: high Protest: medium	Low

Data

This chapter relies primarily on qualitative data collected by one of the co-authors (Zhang) during fieldwork conducted in two counties in Hunan (A and B) during 2007–2008, two counties in Chongqing (C and D) in 2009, and a county in Zhejiang (E) in early 2010. The methodology used in selecting these counties is that they represent counties in central, western, and eastern China with differing levels of economic development. As Bernstein and Lü find, local governments in rural areas of these three regions face different fiscal pressures: in central China governments must rely on limited local revenue sources, while governments in western China receive fiscal transfers from the Central Government, and governments in eastern China rely on abundant local industry revenue sources.[22] While there is significant regional variation in economic development and the fiscal situation of the local governments, we find that the dispute resolution mechanisms work similarly in these regions.

Data collection methods included interviews with government officials (including judges), lawyers, village cadres, and villagers. The data sources also include documentary records, such as court cases, village rules (*Cungui Minyue*), government records, and publicly available government documents from government websites and libraries. Other materials are drawn from incidents reported widely in the media.

[22] See Thomas P. Bernstein and Lü Xiaobo, *Taxation Without Representation in Contemporary Rural China* (New York: Cambridge University Press, 2003).

State power and legal institutions in China

In examining the role of state power in rule by law in China, we focus on two overlapping institutions: the legal system and the cadre management system. In particular, we focus on how officials and judges in the politics and law system (*Zhengfa Xitong*) are embedded in the cadre management system. The cadre management system, in turn, offers a lens on the relationship between the local and central state. Courts are state agents that play an important role in shaping access to the law. Yet the role of the court is paradoxical. On the one hand, the Party wants to promote the rule by law as a legitimation strategy. The Party can point to the growing body of law to claim that the Party itself is constrained by the law and that citizens can "use the law as their weapon" to protect their rights.[23] The Party and the Central Government have also used courts as a tool in implementing political reforms that emphasize rule by law. Seen in this light, courts can help the central state overcome principal–agent problems in monitoring far-flung local government agents.[24] This enables citizens to use the courts to contest state actions, although the chances of winning remain relatively low.[25] On the other hand, however, the courts remain dependent on the Party at the grass roots, and the Party has many conflicting goals. The pursuit of economic growth by local officials, for example, may lead the very authorities charged with enforcing labor laws to violate those same laws.[26] Under certain conditions, therefore, the pursuit of rule by law falls by the wayside. Furthermore, courts often suffer from limited institutional capacity, frequently falling short of staff and funding, further weakening rule by law.

Institutionally, the Party's Politics and Legal Committee (*Zhengfawei*) has the power to intervene in court judgments. The committee consults with the court in any cases that it deems to be "major and complex," and intervenes in cases that touch upon the interest of the party-state (particularly administrative cases).[27] The Politics and Law Committee typically draws its membership from the court, procuracy, police

[23] See Mary Gallagher, "Use the Law as Your Weapon!," in Neil Diamant, Stanley Lubman, and Kevin O'Brien (eds.), *Engaging the Law in China: State, Society, and Possibilities for Justice* (Stanford University Press, 2005).

[24] See Ginsburg and Moustafa, *Rule by Law*.

[25] 行政案件立案难 (in administrative cases, plaintiffs also often have difficulty getting their cases accepted by the court).

[26] See Ching Kwan Lee, *Against the Law: Labor Protests in China's Rustbelt and Sunbelt* (Berkeley, CA: University of California Press, 2007).

[27] See Mei Y. Gechlick, "Judicial Reform in China: Lessons from Shanghai," *Columbia Journal of Asian Law*, 19 (2006), 97–137; He Xin, "Why Do They Not Take the Disputes?

department, Justice Bureau, and the State Security Department. Although the head of the local court might serve on the committee, he serves only in the role of an ordinary member, while senior Party officials from the local party organ or the government chair the committee. In some cases, the chair is the chief of the local police.[28] The "interference" by the Politics and Law Committee may not be purely at the initiative of the committee. Rather, local courts often proactively seek out the committee to solicit its opinion on sensitive cases.[29]

In county A, the head of the court is nominated jointly by the municipal Party Organization Department (a Party organ charged with personnel control) and the Politics and Law Committee.[30] The municipal Party Standing Committee, meanwhile, approves the nomination. The county government provides a recommendation on the nomination, while the municipal intermediate court investigates the process and the county local people's congress holds the final vote that confirms the nominee. This system of appointment constrains judicial interference by county officials only to a small degree. The county government's control over court personnel (other than the head of the court) further facilitates local government control. As a result, even personnel officials in the court admit that the "court's dependence on the county party-government is very strong."[31]

Within the court, judges are evaluated on the basis of several criteria, including how many cases they handle and the quality of their decisions. Judges are also evaluated, however, based upon how many of their cases are overturned on appeal. This gives judges an incentive to pay attention to the preferences of higher courts when deciding potentially sensitive cases. More importantly, judges are evaluated on the basis of how many cases they resolve through mediation instead of giving a verdict. Judges themselves, therefore, have strong incentives to pursue mediation. As one lawyer in Hunan emphasized to us, the mediation targets can be understood as a social stability target.[32] When disputes are resolved through mediation

Law, Power, and Politics in the Decision-making Process of Chinese Courts," *International Journal of Law in Context*, 3 (2007), 15–37.

28 See He, "Why Do They Not Take the Disputes?"

29 See Gechlick, "Judicial Reform in China."

30 In theory, the head of the court is jointly nominated by both the Politics and Law Committee and the intermediate court. The Organization Department, meanwhile, is tasked with vetting the nominee. Our interview with the vice-county court head, however, indicated that the Organization Department took a more active role in the process.

31 Interview with vice-county court head HN080723.

32 Interview HN070723.

neither party "loses" the dispute. Mediation targets, therefore, are a way of trying to reduce the number of petitions and disputes generated by verdicts that villagers see as "unfair." In some areas, judges are even evaluated on social stability much more directly: on the basis of the percentage of their cases that generate petitions and repeat petitions.

Short of funding and staff for grass-roots courts, the local police and the local branch of the Justice Bureau may also limit access to the courts. This occurs for two reasons: (1) limited resources make the judiciary unable to effectively resolve all disputes; and (2) "customers" have to pay for public services. Especially in poor areas, the police are unable to meet all their expenditures through the regular budget and are required to raise funds by themselves. To raise funds, the police may charge for mediation. Consequently, poor villagers may not even have access to mediation – unless it is in the state's interest to provide it. In a township of county A, the head of a police station told us that according to the national policies, they should have five policemen but in fact were only allocated three. Moreover, fines and fees collected by the police constitute two-thirds of their operating budget. This makes it difficult to provide mediation and other services, especially for those who cannot pay the fees.[33] Courts face a similar situation and also need to raise funds to support their operations.[34] As a result, courts tend to accept suits that are more "profitable," creating incentives for corruption.[35]

Grand mediation

Mediation has also emerged as a local government response to changes in the Central Government's priorities. In the last decade, maintaining social order (*Weiwen*) has become a very important goal of the Chinese Communist Party (CCP). As a result, reforms to the cadre evaluation system have made social stability an increasingly important indicator.[36]

[33] Interview HN080725. [34] Interview HN080723.

[35] In general, economic disputes between businesses tend to involve the most "profits" for the court, while administrative disputes and small claims tend to offer little in the way of revenue. Fu and Cullen argue that the court is not powerful enough to solve many disputes because of its limited power and capacity (Hualing Fu and Richard Cullen, "From Mediatory to Adjudicatory Justice," in Margaret Woo and Mary Gallagher (eds.), *Chinese Justice: Civil Dispute Revolution in China* (Cambridge University Press, 2011).

[36] All government officials in both poor and rich areas think social stability is very important, as they argue that "development is the goal and [social] order (*wending*) is the precondition." In their expenditures, government spending on maintaining social stability accounts for as large a portion of the budget as government officials' salaries.

Local governments have responded through innovative institutional arrangements that resolve or "hide" disputes through other means, such as "Grand mediation" (*da tiaojie*).[37] Officials in county A explained that under the policy of Grand mediation, disputes are resolved through mediation coordinated by several government departments at the township level. The Office of Comprehensive Social Order Maintenance (*Zongzhiban*) initiates administrative mediation. The Bureau of Justice (*Sifasuo*) also initiates administrative mediation. Finally, the police station initiates mediation. This system is known as "three mediations working together (*santiao liandong*)."[38] Grand mediation coordination centers have been established at the city, county, and township levels. In Sichuan Province, for example, nearly 150,000 mediation working groups have been established at all levels, with over half a million personnel assigned through double postings to these groups.[39] What is important to note here is that Grand mediation is a strategy of administrative – not judicial – mediation. Instead of emerging as a way of resolving court cases without having to resort to a verdict, Grand mediation is a local government strategy for resolving disputes through the administrative power of the party-state, while at the same time preventing disputes from even reaching the court.

The local state's overriding concern with maintaining social stability prompts the party-state – through the Politics and Law Committee – to interfere with the judiciary when the Central Government's political goal of rule by law comes into conflict with the local government's responsibility to maintain social stability. As a result, the court's role in solving different types of disputes varies with the type of dispute; as we will show, the court is much more constrained in handling disputes with higher levels of local state involvement than disputes in which the local state is only marginally involved.

[37] In county A in Hunan, local cadres told us the mechanism of "Three Mediation Work Together": administrative mediation (the Office of Comprehensive Social Order Maintenance or *Shehui Zhi'an Zonghe Bangongshi*), judiciary mediation (township branch of the Bureau of Justice, or *Sifasuo*), and police mediation (police station, or *Paichusuo*). There are also informants at the village level, who will report disputes to the township government in time.

[38] Interview HN070803. In some areas, the three mediations may also be people's mediation conducted by the People's Mediation Committee, administrative mediation conducted by the Bureau of Justice, and judicial mediation by the court.

[39] See Xinhua News Agency, "An Eye-Witness Account of the Establishment of a Complete 'Grand Mediation' Work System in Sichuan" (2010), available at: http://news.xinhuanet.com/politics/2010-03/22/content_13222368.htm.

Land-lease disputes

Land-lease disputes most frequently occur between villagers over land that one villager has leased to another, but may also occur between a township government or village committee and a company or individual who lease the publicly owned land. Most often these disputes are about unilateral changes in the conditions of the lease or when one party breaks the lease before the contract expires. Land-lease disputes are comparatively easy to resolve because both parties – typically common villagers – are relatively equal in power and they usually have a well-written contract. More importantly, the local state's[40] interest in these disputes is relatively limited. As a result, the state rarely restricts access to the courts, giving villagers much more flexibility. Social networks, however, also often influence both the dynamics and outcomes of disputes. This is particularly the case because much "contracting" activity between villagers relies upon the thick interactions and dense ties of village life. Instead of relying on legal contracts to govern leases, villagers often strike bargains with one another based upon their reputations and trust. When these agreements become contested, the legal ambiguity of these agreements facilitates mediation.

According to cadres in county C's Bureau of Justice and several villages, most land-lease disputes were resolved primarily through negotiation. Villagers have relatively little land and mostly lend their land to people they know well, such as neighbors or relatives. In such circumstances interpersonal relationships are more valuable than the income from land rents. "I rent a lot of land from many people," one village cadre reported, "they only ask a little for rent." The cadre rented land to grow feed for his hog farm. "If someone comes back [from the city to the village], I will send him some rice and vegetables so he can use them during his stay. Most of them will not ask for anything else in return. If he really wants to get the land back, we can sit down and talk. It will not cause any trouble."[41]

When negotiation fails, villagers commonly turn to mediation. In most cases, one party approached the village committee for mediation. At other times, however, the breakdown of negotiations leads to melees between

[40] Here we discuss the "state" as government at the county level or above. The county in China has the lowest level of court under its control.

[41] Interview CQ082109. His fellow villagers confirmed this, without his presence. When there were contracts signed by both the lessor and the lessee or the village committee, it is much easier to solve the dispute because the contract lists all the conditions clearly. In the absence of contracts, as we will show later, the outcome of disputes varies widely.

villagers. Under these circumstances, the village committee steps in to initiate mediation and to restore order, preventing the dispute from escalating into a criminal case of assault. Village cadres often try to persuade the two parties to reach some agreement by explaining the policies and emphasizing the possibility of criminal charges, as well as using their own personal relationship with the villagers to resolve the dispute ("please give me face, stop making troubles for me").[42] In some cases, the villager may not trust the village committee, and therefore will not seek village mediation. In other cases, the village committee cannot solve the dispute.

When mediation by the village committee fails, local officials initiate Grand mediation in order to prevent the dispute from escalating further. It is at this point – when land-lease disputes might threaten social stability – that the local state attempts to initiate mediation. The township government Justice Office or police, or sometimes even the township head or party secretary, steps in to mediate. Yet village governments rarely fail to mediate settlements in land contract disputes, meaning that Grand mediation occurs very infrequently.

Social stability evaluation criteria have given officials incentives to institutionalize mediation efforts. Many township governments have implemented "Letter and Visits Days" every week, a practice known as *xiafang*.[43] This offers villagers a chance to meet directly with township and county officials. The efficacy of such mediation is limited, however. Since it is difficult to find hard evidence, "the common tactics are to persuade them by reasoning, or even threaten them by exaggerating the consequences," a township party secretary of county A in Hunan told us.[44]

The dispute may also be resolved through the intercession of higher levels of government. Some villagers choose to petition to the land-related bureaux (i.e., the Land Resources Bureau and Agriculture Bureau) to solve their disputes through arbitration. But these bureaux have no direct power to resolve the disputes even though they are empowered to arbitrate land disputes. All the bureaux can do is to ask the township government to intercede and mediate. Even petitioning, therefore, tends to end in mediation.

If land-lease disputes are not particularly prevalent in the area, villagers are more likely to be able to both file a lawsuit and win their case. This is

[42] Interview HN072107.

[43] It is known as *xiafang* because government officials go "down" (*xia*) to "visit" (*fang*) the grass roots; instead, the villagers go "up" (*shang*) to "visit" (*fang*) the government. *Shangfang* is the Chinese term for petitioning.

[44] Interview HN090407.

because the courts are less likely to have standing orders prohibiting them from accepting the case. In the court records of county A, we found several cases of lawsuits against the township government and village committee. A township government of county A rented marshland to several entrepreneurs from the village. The contract allowed the entrepreneurs to renew the contract as long as they offered to match the highest bid. In the end, however, the township government rented the land to another party even though the entrepreneurs offered a matching bid at renewal. The entrepreneurs sued the township government and won the case. In this dispute, the level of the government involved was critical. Courts are under the jurisdiction of local governments at the county level. Had the defendant been a county government department (instead of the township), it is unlikely that the plaintiffs would have prevailed.

The local government also initiates mediation when land-lease disputes degenerate into riots. In one case in Jiangxi, rising lumber prices and predatory logging sparked a dispute between villagers and a logging company. After villagers began stealing trees from the forest they were beaten by employees of the logging company. Villagers retaliated by ransacking the office of the logging company. Alarmed by the riot, municipal officials stepped in and mediated the dispute.[45]

To summarize, mediation has emerged as a common form of dispute resolution in land-lease cases due to the relatively high cost of litigation compared with the small stakes, but also because of local officials' fears that disputes will escalate into feuds between villagers that undermine social order. The state – initially in the form of the township government – becomes actively involved in these disputes only if they begin to threaten social stability, in which case Grand mediation is initiated. In areas where land-lease disputes become more common or cause violence, the state may identify them as politically sensitive "social problems" (*shehui wenti*). This alters the dynamics of the disputes as the state's interests in maintaining social stability become activated. Consequently, courts become sidelined and play a very marginal role in the resolution of disputes that devolve into riots. Yet, as we will see in the next section, the state's interests may also become activated for reasons entirely unrelated to social stability.

[45] The case was widely reported. See, for example, http://news.sina.com.cn/c/2008-10-26/195716528546.shtml, www.wyzxsx.com/Article/Class22/200810/55471.html, and www.caijing.com.cn/2008-10-27/110023495.html. What happened in Tonggu county is not unique. A similar riot occurred in Menglian, Yunan, in the same month.

The emergence and resolution of abandoned land disputes

We begin by offering a brief overview of abandoned land disputes in county A, a primarily agricultural county in Hunan. Abandoned land became a serious problem in the late 1990s in county A. In 1998, farming became unprofitable because of heavy tax burdens.[46] More and more villagers migrated to coastal cities, especially Guangdong, typically failing to pay their land taxes and fees. This caused serious challenges for the township government, which relied on agriculture taxes and fees as their major source of fiscal income. In order to meet their tax quotas, the township government encouraged village committees to assign the abandoned land to villagers who stayed in the village. These villagers farmed the abandoned land and paid the taxes and fees. In most cases, the farmers did not sign contracts with the former land users. Some villagers who farmed the abandoned land even made substantial investments in the land, converting them from rice fields to orchards. Sometimes a single plot of abandoned land was transferred many times, involving more and more actors and making contractual relations increasingly complicated. By actively reassigning land contracted to migrant workers, the state laid the seeds for the abandoned land disputes that would begin to emerge a few years later.

After 2005, the Central Government abolished the agricultural taxes and some fees nationwide. At the same time, the salaries of migrant workers in Guangdong had not grown over the previous decade. In the years that followed, the Central Government started to increase public expenditures in rural areas and to subsidize farming. As a result, more and more migrant workers wanted to go back to their home towns and resume farming. When they came back, these villagers found that their abandoned land had been (often informally) re-contracted to other villagers. This caused many disputes in almost every township, if not every village, in county A. This also happened in county B, but not in the other three counties.[47]

When these disputes first began to emerge and negotiations between villagers failed, some villagers turned to the courts and filed suit. In one

[46] See Bernstein and Lü, *Taxation Without Representation in Contemporary Rural China*, for a detailed description.

[47] Outgoing migrant labor was less common in some of these counties (county B, Zhejiang), or people have little and therefore not very valuable land (in county C, Chongqing), making abandoned land disputes less prevalent. Another important reason is that the local governments in east and west China did not rely heavily on agriculture taxes in the 1990s, meaning that the abolition of the agricultural taxes had a limited effect on farmers.

case, the court did not want to accept the suit at first, but reconsidered after the plaintiff (the farmer who had abandoned the land) offered to increase the filing fee from 200 to 1,200 yuan. The farmer who had abandoned the land won the suit because he was able to provide the land certificate. But the court found the verdict hard to implement because the current land user refused to return the land. He demanded compensation for all the taxes and fees he had paid for it over the last several years. Popular opinion sided against the returned migrant worker, as most villagers sympathized with the farmer who had paid the taxes while farming remained unprofitable. The villagers helped the current user to block the implementation of the verdict. Unable to implement the verdict, the court then mediated a settlement in favor of the current user. The court asked the defendant to pay the 1,200 yuan filing fee, but he was too poor and refused to pay.[48]

When there was no contract between the former landowner and the village committee or the current user, or the former user cannot find the land certificate, the disputes became much more difficult to resolve. In a suburban village in county A, the deputy village Party Secretary told us that most of the disputes of this type could not be resolved.[49] When mediation initiated by the village committee failed to resolve the disputes – as it frequently did because the village committee is implicated in the disputes – the township government often had to step in and initiate Grand mediation. Township-sponsored Grand mediation is therefore much more common in abandoned land disputes than in contract land disputes, where village committee-initiated mediation is often sufficient to resolve disputes. Some villagers who refuse to accept Grand mediation turn to the court. Evidence from county A, however, indicates that even under these circumstances the court emphasizes mediation instead of litigation. In the court records of judicial mediation, the outcome of the successfully mediated cases generally involved returning migrants paying compensation to the other party.

If mediation failed, the court generally refused to accept these cases as formal lawsuits. Initially, the court refused these cases because the verdicts were too difficult to implement in the face of popular opposition from villagers – who typically took the side of the farmers who had stayed behind and informally farmed the land. Over time, however, this local court practice became formalized as a local policy, because the local government came to fear that litigation would lead to more social

[48] Interview HN070813. [49] Interview HN070810.

instability. The lack of litigation over abandoned land is also influenced by villagers' unwillingness to go to court. Seeing that the village government has been complicit in the creation of these disputes, villagers are leery of taking the disputes to court. As a result, the failure of mediation generally means that the dispute will go unresolved, as a senior official in the county judiciary bureau told us.[50]

The same government official also told us that some villages, even township governments, were trying to assign new land certificates to the peasants to endorse the *de facto* land distribution. This is illegal, however, and does not fundamentally resolve the disputes. As the official told us, "how can farmers who have lost their land get by if they don't get their land back?" The official viewed abandoned land disputes as a very serious problem and a potential source of social disorder. More importantly, it was a problem that the government had thus far been unable to resolve.[51] Subsequent fieldwork proved him right, as one year later another government official from a neighboring county told one of the authors that two-thirds of the criminal cases in his county were caused by the abandoned land disputes that escalated into melees between villagers.[52]

Land-taking disputes

Land-taking disputes involve the transformation of farmland into non-agricultural uses. Land-takings are conducted under land expropriation laws granting the state the right to take land from villagers for projects that are in the public interest. In practice, land-takings occur not only for projects that are strictly in the public interest, such as dams, roads, or schools, but also for projects that would be considered to further "private" interests, such as manufacturing, commercial and housing projects.[53] Land-taking disputes are essentially distributional conflicts. The legally mandated compensation given to villagers is relatively low compared with the land transfer fee that the state charges to the end-users of land. Typically, villagers' compensation will only account for 5–10 percent of the entire land transfer fee. The remainder of the fee is retained by the state. Proceeds from land-takings have become an

[50] Interview HN080821. [51] Interview HN080821. [52] Interview HN090713.

[53] See Christopher Heurlin and Susan Whiting, "Villagers versus the State: The Politics of Land Takings in China," paper presented at the American Political Science Association Annual Conference, 2007.

important source of revenue for local governments. In some eastern counties, such as county E, revenue from land-takings accounts for about two-thirds of all local fiscal income. In central China's county A, land-taking revenues account for more than half of local fiscal income. The tremendous revenues that the state can realize through land-takings have made land-takings not only very common, but also very contentious. This distribution of proceeds from land-takings has sparked many conflicts between villagers and the state.[54]

The Central Government has emphasized in particular that Grand mediation should be used to resolve land-taking disputes. In order to give local officials an incentive to conduct mediation and comply with these policies, recommendations from the Central Government have emphasized that the mediation of disputes should become an indicator in cadre evaluations, and that cadres who perform this mediation work poorly should be investigated, criticized, given formal warnings, and even have all their other work performance vetoed (*yipiao fojue*) (National Network Anti-Corruption Center).[55] The involvement of county and municipal governments in land-takings, however, has greatly limited the efficacy of Grand mediation because county and municipal governments outrank and (in the case of the county) directly supervise township governments.

Judges also attempt to dissuade would-be litigants from taking their cases to court in the first place. This phenomenon is well known by court staff and lawyers alike. "The court told us," a lawyer informed us, "abandoned land disputes and land-taking disputes will not get registered. If you guys insist on suing, we can register the case and possibly give you a favorable verdict. But be aware that we cannot implement it. So, be wise and don't waste your time."[56]

In some counties, before accepting lawsuits, courts require villagers in land-taking disputes to go through two rounds of mediation, first with village leaders and – if this fails – with township officials. If villagers do manage to take the local government to court, judges – under pressure from local officials – attempt to resolve the case through mediation rather than issuing a verdict. The following statement from a provincial

[54] See Christopher Heurlin, "Responsive Authoritarianism: Protest and Policy Change in Rural and Urban China," PhD dissertation, Department of Political Science, University of Washington, 2011.

[55] Officials whose performance is "vetoed" receive no bonuses or promotions in that year and may even be disciplined or fired.

[56] Interview HN080724.

research group in Zhejiang comprising judges and academics illustrates well the pressures faced by the court:

> When the defendant's concrete actions are in error, the court does not give a verdict according to law, instead it uses mediation methods (*xietiao fangshi*) to get the plaintiff to withdraw their suit. Especially in cases of land takings, housing demolitions and other mass disputes, the local government in the general name of economic development and stability puts pressure on the court, demanding that the court uphold the defendant's concrete behavior. In this situation the court falls into a difficult spot where it doesn't dare to issue a verdict saying the government lost, and also cannot fail to take the legal interests of the plaintiff into consideration. In a situation in which it is under pressure from both sides, the completely safe plan is to begin a multi-sided mediation between the plaintiff and the defendant in order to make the plaintiff withdraw their case.[57]

At the same time, judicial mediation can effectively prevent any future resort to the courts, as disputes that are judicially mediated cannot be appealed.

When administrative or judicial mediation fails, villagers draw upon a repertoire that includes petitioning, rioting, appealing to the media, and legal mobilization. As social stability has been given more priority by the Central Government since the late 1990s, maintaining social order has become an important cadre evaluation indicator.[58] As a result, local officials are very much afraid that villagers will riot. This makes protest more effective, providing that villagers can overcome their collective action problems. Collective petitions and protests against land-takings are usually organized on the basis of social networks within the village. In this section, we will use some cases to examine how the configuration of power at the local level and its manipulation can influence people's access to the courts.

The Longquan land-taking case is a good example of how villagers may successfully resist a land-taking.[59] In June 2003, the government of Longquan City tried to "reclaim state land" totaling 2,000 mu from 1,300 farmers in the Longyuan Street (*jiedao*).[60] The villagers, however,

[57] Zhejiang Provincial High People's Court Research Group, 2007.

[58] See Chen Xi, "Power of Troublemaking: Chinese Petitioners' Tactics and Their Efficacy," *Comparative Politics*, (2009), 451–471.

[59] Villagers very rarely succeed in preventing land-takings. Longquan is the first case in which citizens have won an administrative reconsideration claim against a provincial government since the founding of the PRC.

[60] A "Street" (*jiedao*) is the urban equivalent of a town-level government.

refused to allow the land-taking to proceed. The local government responded with heroic efforts to mediate the dispute. Over the three years that the dispute dragged on, the government held over forty meetings with the villagers. Officials also paid 6,000 visits to the homes of the villagers to mediate with individual villagers, a practice known colloquially as conducting "ideological thought work" (*sixiang gongzuo*) on the villagers. Yet these efforts at mediation almost completely failed. Instead of accepting mediation, the villagers continued to petition for three years.

Unsatisfied with concessions offered by the Street government, the villagers once again petitioned to the provincial government in Hangzhou. The city government finally decided that the villagers would never willingly relinquish their land and began to prepare to forcibly take the land. In early March, the municipal government sent out two bulldozers with about 300 officials to take the land coercively. Hundreds of villagers fought back, carrying large pictures of Mao and Deng. Villagers hoisted banners proclaiming "The nation cannot go without peasants, land belongs to the peasants."[61]

The protest placed severe pressure on local officials, especially since the protest was covered by several Xinhua reporters who published a widely read internal reference article on the event. As a result, local officials postponed the land-taking. In May 2005, the government of Longquan City posted a bulletin announcing that the Zhejiang Provincial Government made the decision to reclaim the land and that the land had been reclassified as being worthless for farming. The farmers were not convinced by the Provincial Government decision and filed for an administrative reconsideration to the provincial Legislative Affairs Office, which was subsequently denied.[62] The farmers then hired a lawyer to file an administrative review of the decision.[63] The lawyer took the case to the State Council, which sent two teams to investigate in May and December of 2005. The State Council handed down its

[61] See Haiping Pan and Lie Fang, "暴力征地危及基层政府权威 – 龙泉市土地纠纷的警示" 浙江内参, 2004 ("ViolentLand Takings Endanger the Authority of Grass-Roots Governments: The Warning of the Longquan City Land Disputes," *Zhejiang Internal Reference*, 11 (2004), 6–11).

[62] Administrative reconsideration is a non-judicial process in which Legislative Affairs offices review the actions of other government departments for breaches of the law.

[63] Lawyer Zhang was the only lawyer who dared to accept this case. He is not from Zhejiang but from Beijing. This makes him less vulnerable to retaliation from Zhejiang officials, who do not control his lawyer's license.

verdict in February 2006 and corrected the local governments' designation of the plots as wasteland. The villagers won their claim for reconsideration against the provincial government. Throughout the four-year dispute, however, the villagers never went to court.

Land-taking disputes display the limits of the state's mediation-centered strategies in resolving land disputes. As the case of Longquan illustrates, villagers frequently reject the efforts of local state officials to mediate land-taking disputes. At the same time as the local state is using its authority to seize land to use for industrial development and local government revenues, the local state is also attempting to present itself as a mediator standing between the interests of villagers on the one side, and developers on the other. Villagers – rightly – see local officials as attempting to act as both a player and a referee in land-takings. As such, villagers frequently spurn local officials' efforts to mediate and instead turn to petitions or protests. Likewise, the local government's supervision of the courts has enabled it to close off avenues for judicial redress. Rule by law has played relatively little role in the resolution of land-taking disputes. Instead, villagers have attempted to gain leverage over the local state primarily through petitioning and protests. As a result, land-takings have become one of the most prominent sources of petitions to both local governments and the Central Government.[64]

Conclusion

As the primary source of disputes in the countryside, land disputes are important to our understanding of the rule of law in China. The manner in which the state, courts, and villagers have interacted to resolve these disputes provides insights into how state institutions and society mutually transform each other in China. On the one hand, the state's interests and actions shape the patterns of dispute resolution. Mediation has been transformed from a social practice into an institutionalized state practice. As Grand mediation shows, the local party-state plays a central role in the initiation of mediation. Since the court is dependent on the local government and lacks the necessary personnel and funds, litigation can be effective only in purely civil cases where no, or few, state interests are involved. The local party-state intentionally limits the court's role in solving abandoned land and land-taking disputes because it fears that positive rulings may have demonstration effects that compel others to

[64] See Heurlin, "Responsive Authoritarianism."

challenge state authority. Arbitration by the Agricultural Bureau or the Land Resources Bureau also plays only a very limited role in land disputes, as arbitrators lack training and are dependent on the township government for implementation.

Societal explanations for the emergence of mediation have only limited explanatory power. Mediation is a state-sponsored tactic to resolve land disputes. In a broader sense, the emphasis placed on mediation – as seen in Grand mediation – has emerged because the party-state wants to maintain social stability in the face of a rapidly changing society. Mediation is emerging as a strategy to defuse or even hide disputes while forgoing policy or institutional changes that might prevent these disputes from occurring in the first place. Mediation can therefore be seen as a "muddling through" strategy that seeks to avoid changing the existing power relations in the countryside – especially by empowering courts and other legal institutions, or by empowering peasants to constrain the local government's predatory behavior. Instead, the local state's focus on mediation enfeebles rule by law, particularly in cases in which the interests of the state are implicated.

To push our argument further, state power not only shapes access to the courts, but also generates major disputes. The Chinese case suggests that we should be less optimistic about how the various functions of rule by law in authoritarian regimes interact. We suggest that when the state is disaggregated, the functions of authoritarian rule by law proposed by Ginsburg and Moustafa may conflict as often as they are mutually reinforcing. It is only in the case of land leases, where local state interests are minimally implicated, that the functions of the courts are mutually supportive. In abandoned land disputes, local officials trample villagers' property rights – and thereby undermine their credible commitment to protect them – in order to generate revenue and enforce social control. In land-taking disputes, meanwhile, local governments likewise undermine their credible commitments to land property rights by engaging in illegal land-takings to provide land to investors at low cost as a means of attracting investment. When villagers attempt to use the law to restrain the administrative agents (i.e., local officials) of the state, they find that the local state blocks them from doing so, as local officials interfere with rule by law in order to exercise social control. This has, in turn, also undermined the legitimacy-generating functions of the law as villagers become progressively more disenchanted with the law and the courts. The prevailing interactions between the local state, the courts, and the villagers therefore are unlikely to strengthen rule by law. Instead, local officials have consciously undermined several functions of the rule by law – legitimation, credible commitments, controlling state agents – in order to achieve another function of rule by law: social control.

The emergence of social stability as a policy priority should be understood as a Central Government reaction to the rural unrest and legitimacy crises provoked by local governments.[65] This represents a dynamic mutual transformation between the state and society in rural China, a Chinese-style "double movement": predatory local governments try to extract from society thereby causing socially destructive consequences, while the "benevolent" Central Government reacts to such destruction through policy and institutional initiatives.[66] This chapter contributes to an emerging body of literature on the Chinese-style "double movement." Xu Wang argues that the Central Government popularized village elections to empower the villagers to restrict the predatory village committees from overtaxing them, thereby achieving mutual empowerment of the Central Government and the villagers.[67]

Lee argues that the local government follows the logic of accumulation, thereby generating labor disputes, while the Central Government follows the logic of legitimization and tries to solve the disputes. She argues that legal reform is a crucible for the intersection of two dynamics: a fractured authoritarian state marked by contradictory goals and interests, and a populace interpolated by the law to become citizens rather than subjects.[68] However, Lee mischaracterizes the situation by placing too much emphasis on the achievements of the CCP's legal reforms in building rule by law. As this chapter has shown, the CCP has turned not to the legal system, but to

[65] Other major efforts include the initiation of village elections, the abolition of agriculture taxes, and the "Constructing a New Socialist Village" campaign, which significantly increases government investment in rural areas.

[66] Some scholars argue that the central government's 1994 taxation reform is the cause of local governments' predatory behavior. The central government took a larger share of taxes than previously, but still left local governments with the same amount of responsibility – if not more – for providing public services. These "unfunded mandates" pushed local governments to extract heavily from rural society. Therefore, it is wrong to blame only the local government for state predation in rural China. For a recent study on the urgent importance of reforming the current fiscal system as a means of solving social problems in China, see Xu Wang, "Mutual Empowerment of State and Peasantry: Grass-roots Democracy in Rural China," *World Development*, 25 (1997), 1431–1442.

[67] *Ibid.*

[68] See Lee, *Against the Law*. However, the Party's Third Plenary Session of the Seventeenth Central Committee did not amend the Land Contract Law to give the villagers individual land property rights, as many had expected.

mediation to resolve social disputes. The rule of law or rule by law is being sacrificed in the name of maintaining social order.

The question that emerges is: which is a more effective long-term dispute resolution mechanism, rule of law or mediation? In the authoritarian context of one-party rule, mediation has won out not only because it is more effective in the short run, but also because it strengthens – instead of weakens – the party-state's power. This happens, however, at the cost of weakening the court system and reversing the process of building the rule of law. This path-dependent dispute resolution method strengthens the party-state's re-penetration into society and blocks the progress of a rule by law that might empower peasants with political and economic rights. As our research shows, compared with using the courts to resolve disputes based on laws and rights, mediation utilizes state power and may reinforce power inequalities between state and society. The transformative power of mediation for villagers is therefore rather low, and it is unlikely that mobilization through mediation would further deepen the rule of law. Instead, the patterns of dispute resolution emerging at the grass roots are strengthening the party-state and weakening rule by law. Without greater judicial independence, it is unlikely that rule by law will be effective at restraining local state power.[69]

[69] See Yongnian Zheng and Xu Wang, "论中央地方关系中的集权和民主问题",战略与管理, 2001年03期 ("On the Centralization and Democracy between the Central and Local Governments," *Strategy and Management*, 3 (2010), 61–70), for a discussion on the limits of the Party's organizational and disciplinary power, and their proposal for building an independent court system to rebuild central control of the local governments.

PART III

Vietnam case studies

10

An historical overview of Vietnamese land law and dispute resolution

TOAN LE AND NGUYEN HUNG QUANG

Introduction

After decades of a socialist land regime, land disputes are a highly sensitive issue in Vietnam.[1] According to government reports, complaints involving land acquisition and compensation made up 70 percent of all complaints to governmental agencies received from July 1, 2004 to 2011.[2] Recently, a series of land disputes, many of which involve the use of violence, erupted in cities and provinces across Vietnam.[3] Significantly, the increase in land disputes has occurred following land reforms that have strengthened land-use rights and public accountability for land administration.[4]

In this chapter, it is argued that land disputes in Vietnam are not a new development, but rather a recurring feature of Vietnamese history. As discussed in Chapter 1, "land disputes are not only attributable to economic and demographic changes, but they are also anchored in

[1] Chris Brummitt, "In Vietnam, Rage Grows Over Loss of Land Rights," *AP The Big Story*, January 31, 2013, available at: http://bigstory.ap.org/article/vietnam-rage-growing-over-loss-land-rights, accessed March 9, 2013.

[2] Report of the Government No. 304/BC-CP to the National Assembly on October 26, 2012 (on implementation of laws and policies for settlement of citizens' complaints and denunciations against administrative decisions relating to land), p. 6, available at: www.na.gov.vn/htx/Vietnamese/C1396/C2094/C2164/default.asp?expandaction=subexpand%26khoaQH=11%26intkyhop=266%26#x0023;Hoo5i0fTkL1B.

[3] "Shootout Makes Land Disputes Vietnam's Priority: Southeast Asia," *Bloomberg News*, July 11, 2013, available at: http://www.bloomberg.com/news/2012-07-10/shootout-makes-land-disputes-vietnam-s-priority-southeast-asia.html, accessed on March 9, 2013; Murray Hiebert and Phuong Nguyen, "Land Disputes Stir Political Debate in Vietnam," Centre for Strategic and International Studies (CSIS), July 24, 2012, available at: http://csis.org/publication/land-disputes-stir-political-debate-vietnam, accessed on March 9, 2013.

[4] See Chapter 1 in this book. See also Dang Hung Vo, "Improving Land Acquisition and Voluntary Land Conversion in Vietnam," Policy Note 51942 (Hanoi: World Bank, 2009).

historical contests that reflect long-standing beliefs and practices." This chapter points to the social fault lines and incompatible land systems that are currently generating ambiguous and multi-layered dispute resolution practices. As noted in Chapter 1, it is the fragmented modes of regulating access to land and dispute resolution that are responsible for the most intractable disputes.

In exploring the reasons leading to fragmented land regulation, this chapter draws upon the discussion in Chapter 1 about the interaction between different regulatory communities. As explained there, one way of understanding this interaction is through system theory. To recapitulate, system theorists posit that society is divided into different epistemic communities (or land communities as they are described in Chapter 1), and each community has its own mode of thinking about regulation, comprising norms and epistemologies that prioritize the relevance and value of external communication.[5] Effective communication requires different epistemic communities to share a mutually compatible conceptual language. For example, if government and local communities share common or compatible ideas about access to land, they are likely to communicate effectively with each other and form a common understanding about appropriate regulatory responses. Conversely, disagreements are likely to occur where different modes of thinking limit or remove the decision-making powers of the landholders to make decisions in relation to their land.

Before examining contemporary land communities, it is useful to consider briefly the historical origin of the different regulatory approaches to land in Vietnam.

The regulatory regime in pre-colonial times (1428–1887)

In pre-colonial times, land use in Vietnam straddled the two social interfaces of imperial–village and village–family. The emperor owned all land, and he granted land to the village for state purposes. Under this tenure system, land was first allocated to villages, and then village authorities allocated land to families living within the village.[6]

[5] Gunther Teubner, "Legal Irritants: Good Faith in British Law or How Unifying Law Ends up in New Divergences," *Modern Law Review*, 61(1) (1998), 11. For a discussion of how to apply system theory to analyze legal transfers, see John Gillespie, "Towards a Discursive Analysis of Legal Transfers into Developing East Asia," *New York Journal of International Law and Politics*, 40 (2008), 657.

[6] Nancy Ann Wiegersma, *Vietnam – Peasant Land, Peasant Revolution: Patriarchy and Collectivity in the Rural Economy* (New York: St. Martin's Press, 1988).

The administrative organization that underpinned the pre-colonial tenure system resulted in the existence of three important players: the emperor, the village, and the family.[7] The emperor, as the owner of all land, had an interest in ensuring that land was used for state purposes. Further, the "Heavenly Mandate" obligated the emperor to ensure that land was allocated on an equitable basis that maximized food production.[8] Under this system, village authorities were responsible for paying tax and providing labor to the emperor. Concurrently, they were interested in preserving village autonomy over land and more generally in protecting their powers from imperial encroachment.

As in imperial China, Vietnamese emperors were preoccupied with protecting taxation revenue. Until 1720, public land underlay the fiscal system of the state.[9] Another of the emperors' interests was to ensure that communal land did not fall into private hands and provided tax revenue. The ability of emperors to protect communal land depended on their political power, which was generally strongest at the beginning of the dynastic reign. For example, the first emperor of the Le Dynasty (1428–1527) – Le Thai To – was able to ensure that his laws on distribution and redistribution of land were followed.[10] This system was closely modeled on the Ming Dynasty (1368–1644) land system developed in China. However, later Le emperors encountered civil conflicts as the Nguyen, Mac, and Trinh families undermined imperial control over land.

Emperors encouraged the registration of land, as this enabled the landholder to be identified, and facilitated the collection of agriculture and the head tax, which were the main sources of revenue for the government.[11] At this juncture, it should be noted that land was granted to the family, and the head of the family name is recorded in a land register called the *dia bo*.[12] The *dia bo*, however, was not a title

[7] See Lê Code, Arts. 342–387 (1428–1788). See also John Whitmore, "Social Organisation and Confucian Thought in Vietnam," *Journal of Southeast Asian Studies*, 15 (1984), 296 at 301.

[8] Wiegersma, *Vietnam – Peasant Land, Peasant Revolution.*

[9] Stephen B. Young, "The Law of Property and Elite Prerogatives During Vietnam's Le Dynasty 1428–1788," *Journal of Asian History*, 10(1) (1976), 1.

[10] Wiegersma, *Vietnam – Peasant Land, Peasant Revolution.*

[11] Young, "The Law of Property and Elite Prerogatives During Vietnam's Le Dynasty 1428–1788."

[12] John Louis Bassford, "Land Development Policy in Cochin China under the French (1865–1925)," PhD thesis, University of Hawaii, 1984, p. 107.

registration system, as its primary purpose was to collect tax. The corollary is that specific details of the dimensions of land were not provided in the *dia bo*, and a general description sufficed.

This system led to the village custom that land occupation equated to ownership.[13] The custom was reinforced by the Hong Duc Code (Luat Hong Duc) issued by the Le Dynasty. The Code confirmed the emperor's ownership of public land (*công thổ*) and private ownership for a household's land (*tự điền*). The Code recognized private ownership, including women's ownership over land, and provided principles for settlement of private land disputes.[14] Historical records do not discuss specific cases or provide statistics about land disputes, but the provisions in the Code recognize the existence of disputes.[15]

Villages played a significant role in managing land through customary rules. To enhance central control, the emperor used the village as an intermediary between the central state and the people.[16] Village authorities had responsibility for allocating land, collecting tax, and settling disputes. Over time, the regulatory functions resulted in the development of a perception among villagers that the laws of the emperor yielded to the customs of the village, as reflected in the Vietnamese adage *phép vua thua lệ lang* ("the laws of the king yield to the customs of the village"). In reality, the state–village relationship was more complex. Most writers agree that the village operated under the supervision of the central government.[17]

The preceding discussion shows that, during pre-colonial times, Vietnam had a well-established system of land regulation. At this time, the emperor, the village, and the citizens each had different roles and interests in land. The discussion further shows that there was a bifurcation between imperial and village land regulations; echoes of this cleavage continue to influence land tenure into the contemporary period.

[13] Bassford, "Land Development Policy in Cochin China under the French (1865–1925)," p. 114.

[14] Available at: http://vksbacninh.gov.vn/index.php?option=com_content%26view=article%26id=904:luat-hong-duc%26catid=77:cac-linh-vuc-khac%26Itemid=131.

[15] See Hong Duc Code, Arts. 532, 357.

[16] Nola Cooke, "Regionalism and the Nature of Nguyen Rule in Seventeenth-Century Dang Trong (Cochinchina)," *Journal of Southeast Asian Studies*, 29(1) (1998), 122–161.

[17] The Anh Nguyen, "Village Versus State: The Evolution of State–Local Relations in Vietnam until 1945," *Southeast Asian Studies*, 101(1) (2003), 101–122 at 101.

Introduction of statutory rights-based property rights and title regime under the French colonial government (1887–1940)

French colonial occupation of Vietnam occurred during the second wave of European colonization during the mid- to late nineteenth century.[18] France saw Vietnam as an underdeveloped nation. Land was considered as being ripe to establish a capitalist market serving French interests.[19] As discussed above, in capitalist markets, land needs to be disembedded from village relational controls and treated as a marketable commodity. The French introduced a Torrens title registration system by a decree of July 31, 1925 to realize this objective.[20] The law provided landowners with individualized, private property rights, and the government employed a concessionary land policy to accelerate the development of urban cities and rural towns.[21] A French Inspector of Native Affairs expressed confidence that the new land system would be well received:

> The establishment of property ownership will be the prosperity of the country: the rights to sell, to buy, to mortgage – to execute all the conveyances of property will augment the country's wealth in circulating the capital which is now frozen by many cultivators.[22]

In practice, the penetration of the new regulatory system was limited in certain regions of Vietnam.

For much of their rule in Vietnam, the French used a dual legal system. In the south (Cochin-China), the French system was more deeply entrenched as this region was under direct French rule and the Vietnamese could voluntarily elect to be bound by French law.[23] In the center and the north of Vietnam, the people remained bound by the imperial codes, and voluntary election was possible only in limited circumstances. The result was that, while the introduction of the Torrens law system was widespread in the

[18] Martin J. Murray, *The Development of Capitalism in Colonial Indochina (1870–1940)* (Berkeley, CA: University of California Press, 1980), p. 10.

[19] Guy Gran, "Vietnam and the Capitalist Route to Modernity: Village Cochinchina, 1880–1940," PhD thesis, University of Wisconsin, 1975.

[20] See, generally, M. B. Hooker, *A Concise Legal History of South-East Asia* (Oxford: Clarendon Press, 1978), pp. 153–161; M. B. Hooker, *Legal Pluralism: An Introduction to Colonial and Neo-colonial Laws* (Oxford: Clarendon Press, 1975), pp. 232–235.

[21] See Bassford, "Land Development Policy in Cochin China under the French (1865–1925)," p. 129.

[22] *Ibid.*

[23] See Minh Quang Dao, "History of Land Tenure in Pre-1954 Vietnam," *Journal of Contemporary Asia*, 23 (1993), 84 at 85.

south, this system appears not to have proceeded beyond major urban centers in the north by the end of French rule in 1954.

Further, French land and economic development fragmented the long established pre-colonial modes of land regulation. A small, educated elite connected to the French bureaucratic structure prospered from the Western rights-based land policies. Most people remained outside the French system, and did not understand abstract ideas such as title by registration. Some lost their land in swindles or were displaced by large-scale industrial plantations.[24]

In 1928, a famous land dispute case known as the Noc Nan Affair highlighted the conflicts between the traditional and colonial modes of land regulation. The case involved a piece of virgin land of 9.46 hectares in Noc Nan, Bac Lieu Province, South Vietnam. The land was first cultivated prior to 1900.[25] In 1908, Huong Chanh Luong inherited the land and applied for a land registration certificate. The government accepted the application and issued a receipt in 1910. In 1912, a French official, *Arboratie*, completed the measurements, and Luong was given a land registration certificate. Unfortunately, this certificate was lost in a burglary. This gave Tang Van D an opportunity to claim that a portion of land that Luong was cultivating actually belonged to him. Although D did not win the case, the village chief ordered Luong to provide D with 798 m^2 of the land to settle the dispute. Luong was given temporary certificate No. 303, dated August 8, 1916, pending the issuance of a final certificate. Luong died, however, and the land was passed to Bien Toai, his eldest son.

In the meantime, a Chinese resident, Ma Ngan, alias Bang Tac, knew that Luong and his sons were cultivating unregistered land. When the owner of the adjoining land died, Tac paid the owner's widow to sell not only her husband's land, but also a portion of the land held by Luong.

Bien Toai made a complaint to the Chief Executive of South Vietnam (Thong doc Nam Ky). The district chief Ngo Van H was assigned to resolve the dispute. Although H was required to conduct a thorough investigation, he only discussed the case with Tac. Based on this account, H ordered that the disputed land be divided between Tac and Bien Toai. Sensing injustice, Bien Toai appealed the matter to various local bodies without success. On April 4, 1926, the office of the Chief Executive of South Vietnam officially sold the 8.9 hectares of land in dispute to Tac. Bien and his family, including siblings,

[24] See Bassford, "Land Development Policy in Cochin China under the French (1865–1925)," p. 154.

[25] Son Nam, *Lich Sử Khẩn Hoang Miền Nam (History of the Southern Expansion)* (Ho Chi Minh City: Van Nghe Publisher, 1984).

were ordered to vacate the land. He refused, and a bloody standoff ensued. Three members of Bien's family and a French soldier, Tournier, died in the struggle. Bien Toai and his siblings were detained and criminally charged.

The criminal trial acquitted Bien and the siblings of the crime. It was subsequently revealed at trial that H had a business association with Tac. The French-administered trial was as much a trial of Bien as it was a trial of the colonial land system. In his closing statement, the French defense advocate, Tricon, submitted that Bien Toai suffered many injustices caused by the complicated land regime. This case highlights the fragmentation in viewpoints that arose when different systems of land regulation clashed.

In summary, the French land reforms transformed the pre-modern land regime, which relied heavily on customary land rights, into a statutory rights-based regime, regulated by formal law and judicial procedures. Prior to French colonization, Vietnam had a strong tradition of recognizing ownership based on occupation and community knowledge. The introduction of legal concepts such as title by registration disrupted the traditional regulatory modes, and, in the process, alienated the community, resulting in disagreements in determining access to land.

The revolutionary group the Viet Minh was able to exploit this conflict to stage a revolution that relied on the slogan *nguoi nong co ruong* – the promise to return ownership of land to the lower-class peasants.[26] The revolution that ousted French rule and Japanese occupation was achieved in August 1945. The next section discusses changes made to the land regimes under socialist rule.

Changes to the land regulatory regime under socialist rule (1945 to present)

Vietnam has undertaken major reforms to the land regime during the socialist period. This section outlines how the changes fragmented regulatory thinking that resulted in land disputes.

Early revolutionary period (1945–1954)

The August revolution led to the establishment of the Democratic Republic of Vietnam led by Ho Chi Minh. From 1945 to 1954, war continued between the Vietnamese anti-colonial forces and French troops. The defeat of the

[26] Trường Chinh and Võ Nguyên Giáp, *The Peasant Question, 1937–1938* (New York: Southeast Asia Program, Department of Asian Studies, Cornell University, 1974).

French in Bien Dien Phu led to the Geneva Conference of 1954 and the partitioning of Vietnam along the 17th parallel. Ho Chi Minh's Democratic Republic of Vietnam controlled the North, and the Ngo Dinh Diem Republic of Vietnam (RVN) controlled the South.

In North Vietnam, the revolutionary government laid the foundations for transforming the land regime, and to establish a new political and social culture. Socialist reforms swept away the colonial land titles and village household ownership and introduced class-based access to land.[27] The national parliament passed the key land law in December 1953. The Agriculture Land Reform Law 1953 authorized government officials to confiscate (*tich thu*), requisition (*trung thu*), or acquire (*trung mua*) the land of colonists, large landlords, rich peasants, and reactionaries of former governments.[28] The land and properties confiscated in Hanoi from colonialists, traitors, and reactionaries, or managed "on behalf of" those Vietnamese who had fled to the South in 1954 was reallocated to North Vietnamese cadres and veterans of the French War of Resistance. Other land was transferred to form agriculture cooperatives.

A key notion underlying the formation of agriculture cooperatives was to create a cohesive military and economic force.[29] The manner in which land was confiscated and land trials were conducted under the land reform, however, caused great social conflicts. During this period, family members were encouraged and pressured to denounce other family members as rich landlords, capitalists, or exploiting peasants.[30] According to some commentators, many individuals who lost their lives in this period were wrongly classified as rich landlords.[31]

In the period of land reallocation, class and personal relationship replaced land titles and legal procedures in determining access to land.[32] In 1955, Decree No. 600 on class demarcation in urban areas was circulated internally to provide instructions for the allocation of land to cadres and veterans based on "need."[33] In practice, officials described

[27] See Edwin Moise, "Land Reform Errors in North Vietnam," *Pacific Affairs*, 49 (1976), 70 at 72.

[28] See Gareth Porter, "The Myth of the Bloodbath: North Vietnam's Land Reform Reconsidered," *Bulletin of Concerned Asian Scholars*, 5(2) (1972), 8–12.

[29] Bernard Fall, *The Viet-Minh Regime Government and Administration in the Democratic Republic of Vietnam* (Westport, CT: Greenwood Press, 1956).

[30] Porter, "The Myth of the Bloodbath." [31] *Ibid.*

[32] John Gillespie, "Land Law Subsystems? Urban Vietnam as a Case Study" *Pacific Rim Law & Policy Journal*, 7 (1998), 555–567.

[33] This internal guideline was never published and is on file at the Ministry of Justice Information Center. See Gillespie, "Land Law Subsystems?"

a less orderly process of decision-making based on relational obligations occurring in this period.[34]

Land collectivization followed the land reforms of 1953–1956. By 1959, this process was largely completed according to rather optimistic government statistics from 1960: 86 percent of peasants worked the land on 41,401 collectives and 97 percent of private businesses had been nationalized.[35]

Few land disputes were reported following the nationalization of land. In 1959, the Communist Party issued a statement warning that any private owner who opposed socialist reform was an enemy of the state.[36] Following these warnings, open resistance diminished. The loss of life and turmoil created by the land reforms forced the government to admit that "mistakes" were made.[37] It should be noted that, even at the height of collectivization, land was routinely, but illegally, sold, and the state did not, and could not, entirely supplant local customary land practices.[38]

In summary, revolutionary land reform from 1953 to 1959 generated deep social conflicts as the state sought to use class, rather than title, to determine access to land. Opposition to socialist reforms was suppressed because land reallocation and collectivization were linked to winning the war and liberating the country.

High socialist period (1954–1986)

During the high socialist period, private ownership of agricultural land was actively suppressed.[39] Agricultural output steeply declined.[40]

[34] See Phan Huu Chi, former Chief Legal Advisor to the Ministry of Justice in Hanoi (1992–1994), and Nguyen Thu Bao, former Director of the House and Land Department (pre- and post-1954).

[35] Huy Duc, *Ben Thang Cuoc: I Giai Phong (The Winning Side: In Liberation)* (OsinBook Smashwords, 2012).

[36] *Ibid.*

[37] *Ibid.* For a different account from that of Huy Duc, see V. T. Sơn, "Cải Cách Ruộng Đất: Giai đoạn đấu tranh sắt máu sau 1954" ("Land and Land Reform: Period of Bloody Battle following 1954"), available at: www.vlink.com/caicachruongdat/ccrd03.html, accessed March 9, 2013.

[38] Adam Fforde, "Law and Socialist Agriculture Development in Vietnam: The Statute for Agriculture Cooperatives," *Review of Socialist Law*, 10 (1984), 315–317.

[39] Huy Duc, *Ben Thang Cuoc: I Giai Phong.*

[40] Martin Rama, "Making Difficult Choices: Vietnam in Transition, Based on Conversations with H. E. Vo Van Kiet with Professor Dang Phong and Doan Hong Quang," Working Paper No. 40, Commission on Growth and Development, p. 16, available at: www.finance.tvsi.com.vn/Handlers/DownloadReport.ashx?ReportID=301, accessed March 9, 2013.

The peasants responded to collectivization by devoting their efforts to the family-controlled land and not working productively on the collective land. As peasants withdrew their labor, local chiefs responded by introducing fence-breaking (*pha rao*) measures to quietly resist central measures. In 1966, Mr. Kim Ngọc, the Party Secretary of northern Vinh Phuc Province, was the first to break protocol by allocating land to farmers and contracting with them at prices above those set by the government.[41] Upon hearing of this secretive experiment, Truong Chinh, the chairman of the National Assembly and Central Committee on Socialist Theory and a senior member of the Politburo, convened a meeting of all key Party leaders to denounce the Vinh Phuc experiment. Kim Ngọc was severely criticized because of his support for "illegal" contracting and jailed, and the experiment was terminated.[42] By the middle of the 1960s, the choice by key political leaders to align Vietnam closely with the USSR[43] led to the adoption of a high-level technocratic planning approach from the Soviets.[44]

In contrast to the socialist land regime that applied in the North, the Republic of Vietnam (RVN) continued to follow the French rights-based land and capitalist regime until reunification in 1975.[45] It would appear from the circulation of French title certificates at the time of reunification that the French title-by-registration system had made inroads in the large urban centers in the South.[46] Following reunification, Vietnam became the Socialist Republic of Vietnam, and the government pressed on with socialist land reforms and transferred the socialist model of the North to the South.[47] This precipitated a tense standoff in the South as landowners protested against the reallocation of their land.[48]

[41] *Ibid.* [42] *Ibid.*

[43] Jack Woddis (ed.), *Ho Chi Minh's Articles and Speeches 1920–1967* (New York: International Publishers, 1969).

[44] See Chapter 1 in this book. See also William S. Logan, "Russians on the Red River: The Soviet Impact on Hanoi's Townscape, 1955–90," *Europe-Asia Studies*, 47(3) (1995), 443.

[45] Nguyen Anh Tuan, *South Vietnam, Trial and Experience: A Challenge for Development* (Athens, OH: University Center for International Studies, Center for Southeast Asian Studies, Ohio University Press, 1987).

[46] M. B. Hooker, *The Laws of Southeast Asia, vol. I: The Pre-Modern Texts* (Singapore: Butterworths, 1986), pp. 449–451.

[47] Rama, "Making Difficult Choices: Vietnam in Transition," p. 14.

[48] Brian J. M. Quinn, "Legal Reform and its Context in Vietnam," *Columbia Journal of Asian Law*, 15 (2002), 219 at 268.

Reforming the socialist system (1980–2003)

From the early 1980s, the land regime underwent a new phase of reforms as Vietnam embarked on economic revival. The 1980 Constitution broke with the past by formally abolishing private ownership. Article 19 stipulated that land belonged to the people. Article 20 then stipulated that all land was to be exclusively planned and managed by the state. The effect of these provisions was to nationalize land. The 1980 Constitution was, however, careful to reassure households that occupants could continue to reside on their land.

According to interviews conducted by Toan Le[49] and others,[50] the 1980 Constitution did not provoke immediate protests from the people. Despite the prohibition against land transfers, land officials at the local level continued to recognize the French land titles and handwritten land transfers. As Le Trong, a land broker at this time, recalled, a covert housing and land market operated during the high socialist period (1954–1986) with the knowledge, and acquiescence, of local officials.[51] Participants in the covert market used handwritten documents to sell (*sang tay*) land and traced ownership through a chain of transfers dating back to the colonial titles.[52] The transfers of land were made on the tacit assumption that long-term, cross-generational land transfers conferred full ownership of the land. Trong's account suggests that urban Vietnamese trusted the French title system. Further, although the Vietnamese may not view ownership of land merely in the abstract terms of title by registration, they appeared willing to use the French title to bolster their claim to cross-generational ownership of land.[53]

The Revolutionary Government indirectly facilitated land transfers by making "distribution decisions" that were equated to land titles. People used handwritten papers to sell land without any certification in *hoa hong* transactions. Although buyers did not have their names on the "title," courts recognized their claims. However, when the first Ordinance on Residential Housing was introduced in 1991, *hoa hong* transactions were no longer recognized.

[49] Personal interview, Nguyen Khanh Son, law partner, Ho Chi Minh City, February 15, 2013.

[50] John Gillespie, "Exploring the Limits of the Judicialization of Urban Land Disputes in Vietnam," *Law & Society Review*, 45(2) (2011), 241 at 253–254.

[51] *Ibid.* [52] *Ibid.* See also Quinn, "Legal Reform and its Context in Vietnam," p. 267.

[53] Gillespie, "Exploring the Limits of the Judicialization of Urban Land Disputes in Vietnam," pp. 253–254.

The 1988 Land Law closely followed the parameters set by the 1980 Constitution. Although the law prohibited all land transfers, individuals and economic organizations were granted rights to occupy land. The government soon realized that the law did not allow it to regulate the large self-regulated land market. The 1993 Land Law was introduced to regulate land more effectively. It contained some important changes that recognized a private land market. Party leaders were unwilling to recognize an open market and gave the government powers to set land values for allotments and transfers. The law allowed landholders rights to exchange, transfer, lease, inherit, mortgage, and guarantee land-use rights; however, it stopped short of granting full ownership rights. Article 12 went on to give the state powers to compulsorily acquire land at a compensation level established by the state.

Although it brought the law closer to the self-regulating market, the 1993 Land Law unleashed a new set of problems. First, the law did not give local officials sufficient discretion to allow land users to convert pre-existing land tenure rights based on colonial and revolutionary land rules into land-use rights.[54] The recognition of pre-1980 land titles provoked a rush of claims from local and overseas Vietnamese attempting to reclaim ownership over land and houses commandeered by the government during the high socialist period. Eventually, the state had to limit these claims to avoid dispossessing the high-ranking officials residing in these premises.

Second, the law gave rural land users limited rights to agricultural land, provoking large-scale social unrest. For example, in 1997, villagers throughout the Thai Binh Province took over government offices and fought pitched battles with security police in the streets.[55] In addition to systemic official corruption, villagers protested the lack of *cong bang* (popular fairness or justice) in the distribution of tenure rights connected with rural land.[56] A year later, the General Department of Land in Vietnam reported that 11,097 land dispute complaints had been reported to its officials for resolution.[57] Most of the disputes

[54] Quinn, "Legal Reform and its Context in Vietnam," p. 269.

[55] See Zachary Abuza, *Revolutionary Politics in Contemporary Vietnam* (Boulder, CO: Lynne Rienner, 2001), pp. 83–85; Trần Thị Thu Trang, "State-Society Relations and the Diversity of Peasant Resistance in Viet Nam," in D. Caouette and S. Turner (eds.), *Agrarian Angst and Rural Resistance in Contemporary Southeast Asia* (London: Routledge, 2009), pp. 159–179. See also Chapter 11 in this book.

[56] See Benedict Kerkvliet, "Agricultural Land in Vietnam: Markets Tempered by Family, Community and Socialist Practices," *Journal of Agrarian Change*, 6(3) (2006), 285–305.

[57] "Complaints and Denunciations Overload Cadastral Department," Tuổi Tre, December 3, 1998, at p. 1.

concerned land-taking cases and the amount of compensation paid for land acquired.[58]

These disputes underscore the ongoing fragmentation in state and non-state understandings about just land tenure regimes. The 1993 Land Law is riddled with contradictions. On the one hand, the government continued to treat land as a special commodity that was not subject to market prices. At the same time, it permitted private land transfers. This disjunction between regulatory ideology and market practices continues to animate land disputes.

The Party and state have responded to land disputes both politically and legally. Politically, the Party views *tu tap* (crowd gathering) and other spontaneous expressions of civil protest as a threat to its monopoly of power and uses anti-assembly laws to break up land demonstrations.[59] In practice, the security police tolerate small-scale public demonstrations, such as the daily protests by farmers outside courts and other government buildings. In sensitive protests, for example, claims by members of the Catholic Church for recovery of land from the state, the government uses sedition powers in the Penal Code to detain and jail activists. In 2008, church members were jailed on charges of "destroying public security" by organizing public demonstrations in Hanoi to reclaim land surrounding the former bishop's palace.[60]

The government also used legislation to resolve land disputes. The 2003 Land Law and the implementation decrees that followed created land-use rights that can be bought and sold (*quyen quan ly*). Concurrently, the government grappled with the issue of compensation for the compulsory acquisition of land. The new law also increased the opportunities for investors to form alliances with the government to develop urban centers and industrial parks.[61] Initially, the alliances were biased toward the protection of developers. Article 9 of the 2003 Land Law, supplemented by Decree No. 181/2004/ND-CP, gave

[58] See also Quinn, "Legal Reform and Its Context in Vietnam," p. 267.

[59] See "Four Vietnam Land-rights Activists Appeal Sentences," *Intellasia*, August 20, 2009, available at: www.intelasia.net/news/articles/society/111337038.shtml.

[60] See Nga Pham, "Prayers and Protests in Vietnam," BBC News, September 2, 2008, available at: http://news.bbc.co.uk/1/hi/world/asia-pacific/7593251.stm; "Vietnam: End Crack Down on Catholics," Human Rights Watch, October 6, 2008, available at: www.hrw.org/news/2008/10/06/vietnam-end-crackdown-catholics.

[61] Gillespie, "Towards a Discursive Analysis of Legal Transfers into Developing East Asia."

the government extensive powers to compulsorily acquire land for the public interest and defense security. If land was acquired for economic development, the law provided investors with an option to negotiate directly with landowners or to work with the land compensation and settlement team of the district people's committee to compensate landowners. Under Decree No. 22, compensation was based on the value of economic production, giving district authorities considerable discretion to assist developers to pressurize farmers into selling cheaply.[62]

Far from resolving the problems, land disputes intensified following the introduction of the 2003 Land Law. The alliance of the government and private developers increased, as did land abuses and outright corruption. The growth in land protests forced a rethink, and, in 2004, Decree No. 197 directed the district authorities "to settle citizens' complaints, denunciations related to compensation, support and resettlement" and "to guarantee impartiality and equity when considering and deciding on the compensation, support, and resettlement."[63] Further, it provided for provincial government oversight of compensation and resettlement. By 2007, Decree No. 123 had brought compensation rates into "alignment with market prices."[64] Legislation could not overcome the lack of functioning land markets. There is evidence to suggest that increased compensation is not the only solution, as it does not provide the landholder with the ultimate right to decide who has access to their land.

The Doan Van Vuon land dispute in 2011 revealed ongoing divisions between state and community approaches to land regulation.[65] In this case, fish farmers had reclaimed marginal coastal land near Hai Phong. The legal basis for the claim was never clearly determined, but the farmers and local community recognized customary rights acquired through long-term use. As previously discussed, occupation rights to land developed in pre-colonial times have subsisted in an uneasy relationship with colonial land titles and socialist collectivization. The

[62] Annette M. Kim, "Land Takings in the Private Interest: Comparisons of Urban Land Development Controversies in the United States, China, and Vietnam," *Cityscape*, 11(1) (2009), 19–32 at 28.

[63] Article 43 of Decree No. 197/2004/ND-CP.

[64] See also Decree No. 69/1999/ND-CP on Providing Additional Clarification for Land Use Planning, Land Prices, Land Recovery, Compensation, Support and Resettlement, August 13, 2009.

[65] See David Marr, "Vietnam's High Profile Land Dispute," *Inside Story*, March 23, 2012, available at: http://inside.org.au.

"fuzzy property rights" (see Chapter 1) that emerged after decollectivization freed up space for the state to recognize occupation rights. In this case, local authorities reclaimed the land for their own benefit, prorogating a violent land dispute that received widespread mass and personal media attention in Vietnam.

This and other land cases are increasingly showing the limits to the state land regime. It was superimposed over, but did not entirely displace, the pre-existing land regimes. Two decades of land law reform have not reconciled the fundamental discrepancies between state and community approaches to land regulation. It is at the interface between different land regimes that most land disputes arise.

Conclusion

This chapter shows that the history of land reform in Vietnam is best understood as a cycle of foreign borrowings and local adaptations – the new overlaying and interacting with, rather than displacing, the old. It argues that the most serious land disputes occur when there are fundamentally different modes of regulatory thinking in society. It also presents problems caused by the mismatch between state law that represents the "aspirations of ruling elites, both spatial and social, and omit or blur the inconvenient or resistant to control."[66]

As Chapter 11 explores in more depth, the incremental movement toward full landownership reveals few indications of correcting the problem. Recent government land reforms have drawn heavily on Demsetz's hypothesis that self-interest is the primary motive for land disputes (see Chapter 1).[67] Yet findings from a recent World Bank survey suggest that market reforms are not the only solution.[68] The state compulsorily acquired approximately 400,000 hectares of farmland for residential and industrial purposes between 2001 and 2005. During this five-year period, objections to land compensation and clearance increased from 30 percent to 70 percent of the total number of administrative complaints received by the state.[69] Significantly, this increase

[66] See Chapter 1 in this book.

[67] See T. W. Merrill, "Introduction: The Demsetz Thesis and the Evolution of Property Rights," *Journal of Legal Studies*, 31 (2002), S331–S338.

[68] See World Bank, *Compulsory Land Acquisition and Voluntary Land Conversion in Vietnam* (Hanoi: World Bank, 2011), pp. 16–18.

[69] *Ibid.*

occurred when the government incrementally brought land compensation levels into alignment with market prices.[70]

In Chapter 11, John Gillespie explores in more depth why changes to the land law do little to reduce the problems underlying land disputes in Vietnam. He argues that disputes occur where land communities cannot agree about the ground rules for land access and the most appropriate regulatory solutions.

[70] See Decree No. 123/2007/ND-CP on Amendments and Supplementation of Decree No. No 188/2004/ND-CP, November 16, 2004. See also Decree No. 69/2009/ND-CP on Providing Additional Clarification for Land Use Planning, Land Prices, Land Recovery, Compensation, Support and Resettlement, August 13, 2009.

11

Narrating land disputes in three Vietnamese communities

JOHN GILLESPIE

Introduction

For twenty years, legal, economic, and social reforms have unleashed land disputes across Vietnam.[1] The most acrimonious conflicts, which occasionally escalate into violent confrontations, concern the compulsory acquisition of land by the state.[2] In a recent dispute in Tien Lang in northern Vietnam, a family used homemade weapons to repel riot police taking possession of their fish farms.[3] This case attracted unprecedented attention from the media and bloggers, sending the prime minister and other senior leaders into damage control to prevent further demonstrations. Such is the current intensity of land disputes in Vietnam that confrontations are not confined to public land-takings and have recently erupted between the developers and residents of luxury apartments in Hanoi and Ho Chi Minh City.

From the perspective of the orthodox property law theory, the escalation in the number and complexity of land disputes in Vietnam is puzzling. For two decades, the Vietnamese government followed advice from

[1] There are no publicly available statistics giving the precise numbers and types of land disputes. From 2003 to 2007, the number of complaints concerning land increased approximately 70 percent, and grievances about the compulsory acquisition of land amounted to about 70 percent of all land complaints. See World Bank, *Compulsory Land Acquisition and Voluntary Land Conversion in Vietnam* (Hanoi: World Bank, 2011), p. 16.

[2] See Ministry of Justice, *Chu De Tranh Chap Khieu Nai To Cap ve Dat Dai va Giai Quyet Tranh Cahp Khieu Nai To Cao ve Dat Dai (Disputes, Claims and Land Denunciation Settlement of Land Disputes)*, Coordination Council Report on Dissemination and Education of Government Law, Hanoi 1–20 (2009); Thanh Nhien, "Golf Drives Hanoi Farmers Off their Land," *Look at Vietnam*, August 18, 2009, available at: www.lookatvietnam.com/2009/08/golf-drives-hanoi-farmers-off-their-land.html, accessed May 15, 2013.

[3] See David G. Marr, "Vietnam's High-profile Land Dispute," *Inside Story*, March 23, 2012, available at: http://inside.org.au/vietnam-high-profile-land-dispute, accessed May 9, 2013.

international donors, such as the World Bank and Asia Development Bank, predicated on this theory. The government clarified and registered property rights, decentralized land administration, and incrementally recognized private land markets – reforms that were supposed to take the heat out of land disputes.[4] Although legislative and administrative shortcomings remain, land tenure rights and land administration have unquestionably moved toward this ideal since the enactment of the Land Law in 1993.[5] Rather than reducing land disputes as predicted, reforms have coincided with a dramatic increase in disputes. Not only have land reforms failed to control disputes, as we shall see, new types of property rights have created opportunities for dispute where none previously existed. In this chapter, it is argued that orthodox land theory[6] promoted by international donors in Vietnam makes an unrealistic distinction between state regulation and self-regulation of land. This is because the multiple regulatory approaches to land in Vietnam[7] are not easily reduced to an overarching set of exclusive property rights. Frank Upham makes the analogous point in Chapter 2, "property rights in land are radically multidimensional and cannot be commoditized."

This chapter argues that state legal regimes rarely displace pre-existing regulatory orders, but rather compete and cooperate with each other. What this suggests is that, rather than monopolizing land regulation, the state is often only one of many regulators seeking to order particular geo-political spaces. From this pluralistic perspective, land regulation resembles a continuum along which there are many points representing different degrees of state and non-state/hybrid regulation. Increasingly, private corporations and urban elites look to land titles and property rights to secure their assets. At the other end of the regulatory continuum, rural and peri-urban populations are ambivalent about state land regimes and turn to self-regulatory systems to determine what they can and cannot do with their land.

This chapter aims to show that, where land communities (state, non-state, and hybrid) share common assumptions about access to land and

[4] See World Bank, *Revising the Land Law to Enable Sustainable Development in Vietnam* (Hanoi: World Bank, 2012).

[5] See Sun Sheng Han and Kim Trang Vu, "Land Acquisition in Transitional Hanoi, Vietnam," *Urban Studies*, 45(5/6) (2008), 1097–1117.

[6] See Hernando de Soto, *The Mystery of Capitalism: Why Capitalism Triumphs in the West and Fails Everywhere Else* (London: Black Swan, 2000), pp. 47–62; Harold Demsetz, "Toward a Theory of Property Rights II," *Journal of Legal Studies*, 31(2) (2002), 653–672.

[7] Discussed in Chapter 10 in this book.

the optimal solutions to disputes, they can reconcile differences and identify common objectives. Where communities do not imaginatively engage with each other, hybrid actors emerge who mediate disputes in multiple epistemic settings both within and beyond the state orbit. They blur distinctions between formal state law and community regulation to find mutually acceptable solutions.

Land communities as regulators

State land communities are distinguishable from other land communities by their use of statutory and prerogative powers to secure objectives (see Chapter 1). Non-state regulators are not so readily identifiable because they use discourse to control behavior. In this chapter, land communities are treated as regulators. The guiding assumption is that people interpret and regulate land disputes from the particular sets of beliefs, practices, and goals – the regulatory histories – in which they are embedded (see Chapter 1). Three different types of land communities have been selected to demonstrate how different regulatory histories produce different responses to land disputes.

The first case study discusses a traditional village community outside Hanoi. Members of this village drew predominantly on sentimental and spiritual connections to the land to oppose the acquisition of farmland for an industrial park. The second case study examines a spontaneous community that emerged in peri-urban Da Nang to oppose the acquisition of land for a large residential housing development. The residents in this case were more prepared to accept compensation to move from their land than members of the traditional community. The third case study explores a planned community residing in luxury apartments in peri-urban Hanoi. Despite living in an orderly law-defined world, members of this community selectively relied on law and relational connections to resolve their dispute.

The following questions about the interaction between the state and regulatory communities are posed in this chapter via the case studies:

1. Does the state pay attention to the internal structures and needs of communities when applying the law?
2. Do members of the communities behave like hybrid regulators in selectively drawing on the law and other regulatory traditions to resolve disputes?

Traditional community case study: Đông Dương village dispute

This case study explores how farmers in Đông Dương village, located in Thai Binh Province near Hanoi, responded to the compulsory acquisition of their farmland.[8] With government support, Neo-Neon, a Chinese investor, constructed a factory on their land in 2007. Many farmers in the village supported government modernization and industrialization policies, but questioned the magnitude and finality of the sacrifice they were expected to make for national development. They drew extensively on internal traditions and spiritual beliefs to resist efforts to be moved from ancestral land. In this regard, the villagers resembled a traditional community; they functioned as a cohesive group united by ideology, spiritual beliefs, and village regulatory traditions.[9]

The legal framework governing land clearance

To promote economic growth, the government gave provincial governments powers under Article 9 of the Land Law 2003[10] to convert farmland into industrial parks. Private investors, such as Neo-Neon in this case study, work closely with provincial governments to classify their projects as "nationally significant."[11] This classification enables provincial authorities to use state powers to negotiate compensation rates and fast track projects. A dispute arose in this case study when farmers rejected the compensation and resettlement package offered by the provincial government for land that was compulsorily acquired to build a factory near Đông Dương village.

[8] This case study is based on interviews conducted by the author with representatives from the land construction company, lawyers working for the investor and construction company, and the main village representative. The interlocutors preferred to remain anonymous. Interviews took place in Hanoi and Đông Dương village in March and October 2011, and in Hanoi in April and September 2012.

[9] For a discussion about land communities, see Amnon Lehavi, "How Property Can Create, Maintain, or Destroy Community," *Theoretical Inquiries in Law*, 10(1) (2008), 43–76.

[10] The detailed provisions governing this area are found in Decree No. 181 2004/ND-CP implementing the Land Law 2003.

[11] See Andrew Wells-Dang, "Promoting Land Rights in Vietnam: A Multi-sector Advocacy Coalition Approach," paper prepared for presentation at the Annual World Bank Conference on Land and Poverty, Washington, DC, April 8–11, 2013.

Mapping a traditional community

Đông Dương villagers trace the foundation of their village to the tenth century, when nearby Hanoi was established by the Ly Dynasty.[12] For 1,000 years, including the French colonial period (1884–1954), the village organizational structures and land management practices remained largely intact.[13] Villagers lived in a densely built settlement surrounded by a bamboo hedge and worked the surrounding rice fields. Radical change took place in 1954 when most villagers enthusiastically participated in the land reform program led by the Viet Minh (see Chapter 10). Although the revolutionary government displaced the mandarins and "rich peasant" class from positions of power in the village, the clan structure remained relatively intact.

Following decollectivization in the late 1980s, most village households received land-use rights that corresponded to their pre-1954 holdings. Even where records from this period were missing, *chu ho* (clan heads) could recall old boundaries and lobby officials for an equitable share of the land.[14] Only land confiscated (*tich thu*) from "collaborators" and "rich peasants" was not returned to the previous owners.

As *doi moi* liberalizations took hold during the 1990s, villagers began to reassert pre-revolutionary village traditions.[15] The village clans refurbished their *dinh* temples to venerate ancestors. In addition, they fastidiously attended to village deities and other rituals that promoted a spiritual attachment to "place."[16] These beliefs forged a sense of solidarity and shared purpose – a collective identity. For example, villagers talked about country customs (*quan the nong thon*) and the "sentiment of their home-village"

[12] Hanoi or Thang Long as it was then known became the capital of Dai Viet under Emperor Ly Thai To in 1010.

[13] French administration rarely fundamentally disrupted village organizational structures. See Martin Grossheim, "Village Government in Rep-Colonial and Colonial Vietnam," in Benedict Kerkvliet and David G. Marr (eds.), *Beyond Hanoi: Local Government in Vietnam* (Singapore: Institute of Southeast Asian Studies, 2004), pp. 58–73; Minh Quang Dao, "History of Land Tenure in Pre-1954 Vietnam," *Journal of Contemporary Asia*, 23(1) (1993), 84–92.

[14] Most of the *dien-bo* (register of fields) upon which land tax was assessed showed landholdings before collectivization.

[15] This phenomenon has been observed elsewhere in northern Vietnam. See Benedict Kerkvliet, "Agricultural Land in Vietnam: Markets Tempered by Family, Community and Socialist Practices," *Journal of Agrarian Change*, 6(3) (2006), 285–305.

[16] This phenomenon has been observed in the general literature. See Philip Taylor (ed.), *Modernity and Re-Enchantment: Religion in Post-Revolutionary Vietnam* (Singapore: Institute of Southeast Asian Studies, 2007).

(*tinh cam que huong*) that bound them to the village. Most thought the "village cultural character" (*ban sac van hoa lang xa*) had strengthened during the decades leading up to the land dispute in 2007.

Bound up with sentimental and spiritual connections to the land were economic considerations. Studies in Vietnam suggest that land acts as a social safety net in a society lacking other forms of income-smoothing insurance.[17] Farmers have long considered land as an inalienable form of property on which they can safely rely if conditions are tough.

A major point of contention between the government officials and the villagers concerned the conceptualization of land rights. The state system rests on imported notions of exclusive property rights that were grafted onto state management principles borrowed from the former Soviet Union.[18] As previously noted, following decollectivization, many villagers reasserted traditional land claims that recalled pre-socialist land rights.[19] Their moral and spiritual claims to the land contradicted the exclusive tenure rights granted to investors under the Land Law 2003. Villagers in this case based their claims on long-term land occupation – a principle encapsulated by the proverb "what my grandfather owned, I own."[20] This claim is predicated on small contingent commonalities between villagers and spiritual connections with "place" without a grand abstracted idea about rights to land.

A feature of this case study is the way in which the dispute brought about a convergence of views within the village concerning the compensation and resettlement plan. Although the village population was relatively homogeneous, fewer than 10 percent of the residents came from other areas and many residents worked in non-farm occupations outside the village. Interaction with Hanoi and regional centers had rapidly increased during the 1990s, and most village households were enmeshed in relational networks that brought news about land disputes in surrounding areas. This interaction gave rise to heterodox views about the land project.

Divisions within the village about the merits of the industrial park primarily, although not entirely, followed generational lines. Most

[17] See G. Promsopha, "Land Ownership as Insurance and the Market for Land: A Study of Rural Vietnam," preliminary version, unpublished paper (2011).

[18] See Janet Sturgeon and Thomas Sikor, "Post-Socialist Property in Asia and Europe: Variations on 'Fuzziness,'" *Conservation and Society*, 2(1) (2004), 1–17.

[19] For a discussion about this connection to land and place, see Hy Van Long, "State, Local Associations, and Alternate Civilities in Vietnam," in Robert Weller (ed.), *Civil Life, Globalization, and Political Change in Asia* (London: Routledge, 2012), pp. 123–147.

[20] See Chapter 10 in this book.

villagers supported the party's economic development goals in principle, but some – mostly younger villagers – saw opportunity in development to improve their pay and working conditions. Younger villagers were also more likely to question superstitious land practices.

Villagers born between the 1930s and the 1950s were the most active in organizing resistance to the project. They established a protest committee to negotiate with the provincial people's committee and the construction company to relocate the project away from the village. Members of this group lived their formative years during the revolutionary period (1953–1986) when socialist ideas engaged with pre-modern traditions. Their opposition to the project drew extensively on ideas from these traditions.

The land dispute

In 2007, Neo-Neon hired Techconvina, a Vietnamese construction firm, to build a factory complex on a 40-hectare site close to Đông Dương village. The Thai Binh Provincial People's Committee compulsorily acquired the land, and the *Hoi Dong Den Bu* (Council for Compensating Damage for Ground Clearance) negotiated with the chairman of Đông Dương Commune, clan heads, and householders regarding compensation payments. Neo-Neon paid land clearance compensation to the Provincial People's Committee based on the fifty-year land-use right issued for the industrial park. Instead of passing this payment on to the farmers, the Provincial People's Committee reduced the compensation, claiming that under the Land Law 2003 farmland is allocated for a twenty-year period and villagers were only entitled to a pro rata payment. The Provincial People's Committee retained the balance of the compensation funds.[21]

On discovering that the Provincial People's Committee had appropriated their compensation, the villagers were outraged and attacked state officials and the construction workers, setting their machinery ablaze.[22] In desperation, the investor paid provincial authorities to protect the construction

[21] See M. Tuấn, "Rắc rối ở khu Công nghiệp Gia Lễ, Thái Bình: Khi 'thảm đỏ' . . . đổi màu" ("Trouble in the industrial area of Gia Le, Thai Binh: When the 'red carpet' . . . changes color"), *Thaibinhonline*, July 31, 2010, available at: www.thaibinhonline.com.vn/News/tinthaibinh/2010/07/3136.aspx, accessed July 31, 2012.

[22] See Lao Dong, "Vì sao trở thành 'điểm nóng' về an ninh?" ("IZ Family Feast: Why Become a Security 'Hot Spot'?"), *Thai Binh News*, November 3, 2010, available at: http://baothaibinh.net/chuyen-dong/phap-inh/570-kcn-gia-le-vi-sao-tro-thanh-diem-nong-ve-an-ninh.html, accessed May 10, 2013.

site, but the villagers were undeterred and fought pitched battles with the police. At the height of the conflict, more than 500 police struggled to secure the construction site.

To end the deadlock, the villagers appointed Mr Tuan (not his real name), a retired state official, to negotiate with the investor, the construction company, and the Provincial People's Committee. It soon emerged that the villagers entertained fundamentally different understandings about how to resolve the dispute from the other parties.

Conceptualizing state and community approaches to land

What arises from this case study is a conflict between two profoundly different ways of regulating land. The first disagreement concerned the conceptualization of land disputes. For the Provincial People's Committee, the Land Law 2003 and sublaws stipulated clear dispute resolution procedures.[23] Complainants were required first to attend district-level conciliation councils, and, failing agreement in this forum, to lodge petitions with district- and then provincial-level people's committees.

To comply with these procedures, the village protest committee wrote many petitions (*đơn kiến nghị*) and denunciation letters to the responsible authorities. They used state-sponsored anti-corruption narratives to frame the dispute within officially sanctioned parameters. For example, the petitions accused the provincial authorities of mismanaging the land, corrupt practices (*sự tham*), harboring bureaucratic and authoritarian attitudes (*tác phong quan lieu hách dịch*), and being distant from the masses (*xa rời quần chúng*). Villagers borrowed these terms from Party-orchestrated anti-corruption campaigns aimed at corrupt land officials.

When it became clear that the Provincial People's Committee was ignoring the petitions, the village protest committee decided to take direct action. To justify this tactic, they drew on storylines circulating within the village that glorified opposition to corrupt officials. In 1997, villagers across Thai Binh Province shocked the central government by occupying the offices of local authorities and fighting security police in the streets.[24] Village stories

[23] For a detailed description about dispute resolution procedures, see World Bank, *Compulsory Land Acquisition*, pp. 176–187.

[24] See Zachary Abuza, *Renovating Politics in Contemporary Vietnam* (Boulder, CO: Lynne Rienner, 2001), pp. 83–85; Trần Thị Thu Trang, "State–Society Relations and the Diversity of Peasant Resistance in Viet Nam," in D. Caouette and S. Turner (eds.), *Agrarian Angst and Rural Resistance in Contemporary Southeast Asia* (London: Routledge, 2009), pp. 159–179. See also Kerkvliet, "Agricultural Land in Vietnam."

promoted violent protest as a "righteous struggle" (*Đấu tranh chính nghĩa*) – a legitimate way in which to restore popular fairness or justice (*cong bang*) and the equitable distribution of land.

As the dispute progressed, young villagers who initially supported the factory project increasingly viewed the dispute in moral terms as a betrayal by the authorities. They were shocked when the police took the side of a foreign investor. Although the young villagers did not invoke spiritual claims to the land, they agreed with their parents and grandparents that the compulsory acquisition by the state trampled on the values the villagers had fought for during the anti-colonial and wars of resistance against the Americans.[25] Especially after the violent confrontation with the police, high emotions transformed a land claim into an anti-government conflict.

Negotiating a settlement

During settlement negotiations, the investors and provincial officials initially dismissed the villagers' sentimental and spiritual claims as a "peasant way of thinking" (*cach suy nghi cua nong dan*). Instead, they viewed property rights as entitlements that flow from the law. This "seeing like a state" perspective attempted to define out of existence customary property claims.[26] The Land Law 2003, for example, created exclusive rights that secured tradable commodity rights and did not recognize any customary land claims. Village- (*Xa*) level officials were more in sympathy with the villagers' claims, but played a subordinate role in the negotiations.

Representing the village protest committee, Mr. Tuan could not simply articulate the villagers' claims, which fundamentally contradicted the law. Instead, he acted like a cultural intermediary in transforming the highly figurative and sentimental language used by the villagers into the technical, bureaucratic language understood by the officials. He tried to draw the authorities into a dialog that stood outside state law and procedures. The villagers' sentimental and spiritual claims to land were not recognized by the law as either valid land rights or grounds for compensation.

[25] See, generally, Luong, "State, Local Associations, and Alternate Civilities in Vietnam," pp. 136–137.

[26] See Chapter 1 in this book.

To reach a settlement, Mr. Tuan needed to shift the conceptualization of land away from rights and commodities to consider the underlying morality of compulsory acquisition and compensation. This shift required a refocusing from the substantive and procedural justice in the Land Law 2003 to popular notions of distributive justice. He invited the disputants to use *thoa dang* (situational validity) – a traditional Vietnamese decision-making technique that emphasizes distributive justice.[27] *Thoa dang* encourages disputants to treat the law as just one of many sources of authority, and to balance competing claims against a broad range of norms derived from "reality processes" (*qua trinh thuc tai*).

To deflect attention away from substantive and procedural justice, Mr. Tuan drew attention to *cong bang* (popular fairness or justice) and the unequal participation in the profits generated by the land project. He also argued that the compensation payments were insufficient to enable farmers to buy new farmland, and that the investor did not provide the skills villagers needed to work in the factories built on their land. To support this argument, he tapped into a rich narrative that attributes rising social inequality in Vietnam to the commodification of land,[28] and reminded the officials of their duty as party members to assist the poor. He encouraged the officials to apply the law flexibly and to draw solutions from a wide range of economic and social principles.[29]

Eventually, the provincial government and the investor agreed to increase the compensation and to retrain the farmers for factory work. Yet, in the end, the villagers failed to secure what they wanted most – the right to remain on their ancestral land.

In summary, Mr. Tuan acted as a hybrid regulator. He drew on sets of norms and epistemic assumptions from both state and village regulatory

[27] This form of decision-making was interwoven during the high socialist period (1954–1986) to form the doctrine of "reason and sentiment in applying the law," which courts still use to resolve land use disputes. See John Gillespie, "Exploring the Limits of Judicial Review in Urban Land Disputes in Vietnam," *Law & Society Review*, 45(2) (2011), 241–275.

[28] See the interview with a retired former deputy chief justice of the Supreme Court, Even Lin, "Phỏng vấn LS Trần Lâm, nguyên Thẩm phán Toà Án Nhân Dân Tối Cao" ("Interview with Chen LS, former Judge Supreme People's Court"), *Viet Studies*, December 8-9, 2009, available at: www.viet-studies.info/kinhte/TranLam_RFA_pv.htm, accessed May 30, 2013.

[29] For a general discussion about these issues, see Nguyen Van Suu, "Industrialization and Urbanization in Vietnam: How Appropriation of Agricultural Land Use Rights Transformed Farmers' Livelihoods in a Peri-Urban Hanoi Village," EADN Working Paper No. 38, 2009.

traditions to create a new conceptual framework for resolving the dispute. This regulatory technique broke the impasse between the officials and developers, on one side, and the farmers, on the other side. But it failed to persuade the officials to recognize sentimental and spiritual claims to land. Such claims were based on highly localized narratives about spiritual identity and connection to "place" that did not connect with official discourse about *Nha nuoc phap quyen* (law-based state), modernization, and industrial development. Ultimately, the farmers lacked the resources, both financial and political, to build a campaign that might have convinced central and provincial authorities to force the investor to relocate the industrial park.

Spontaneous communities: the Golden Hills case study

With residential property prices reaching unaffordable levels in the larger urban centers of Ho Chi Minh City and Hanoi, developers turned their attention to the relatively less expensive land in Da Nang. Following a lavish ground-breaking ceremony, work began in April 2011 on the 400-hectare Golden Hills residential development in peri-urban Da Nang.[30] To clear land for this luxury development, the People's Committee of Hòa Vang District sent compulsory acquisition notices to thousands of residents living in Hòa Lien Commune. Simmering hostility to the forced relocation erupted into violence in late August 2011 when thousands of residents blocked access to the construction site and destroyed the developer's offices. Although this case and the Đông Dương dispute both involved compulsory acquisition for private commercial projects, they differed in two important respects. Đông Dương village is a traditional community, whereas Hòa Lien Commune in this case study experienced urban transition and is more accurately described as a spontaneous community. In addition, the authorities in these cases responded to the disputes in different ways.

Mapping a spontaneous community

Hòa Lien Commune first appeared in Vietnamese records as a farming community annexed from the Champa kingdom in the late fifteenth

[30] This case study is based on cited newspaper articles and interviews with journalists from *Tuoi Tre Phap Luat* and *Sai Gon Tiep Thi* in Ho Chi Minh City in September and October 2011, and September 2012, respectively.

century. Industrial and residential development began to transform the area during the American war in the 1960s and 1970s, and then more rapidly after the *đổi mới* reforms in the 1980s. By the mid-1990s, Hòa Lien Commune had been absorbed into the urban fabric of Da Nang.

One visible sign of rapid urbanization is population growth, which increased by 50 percent between 2003 and 2009.[31] Many of the new residents were permanent migrants who came from the inner city and from neighboring rural districts. Residents increasingly diversified their livelihoods, and less than one-third were still engaged in agriculture when the Golden Hills development commenced. They also transformed the built environment by subdividing rural land for residential and industrial purposes.

When the dispute began, the residents lacked the strong clan and relational networks that bound the Đông Dương villagers together. Decades of population movements and loss of farmland had severely eroded, although not entirely displaced, village structures and regulatory traditions. Most residents were brought together by a shared opposition to the development, rather than by pre-existing relationships – a key characteristic of spontaneous communities.

The dispute

Residents began complaining about the project soon after construction began. A central concern related to the inadequate and unfair compensation payments. The Hòa Vang District People's Committee negotiated compensation payments with the residents on behalf of the developer. The initial compensation rates of 29.5 million *dong* (approximately US$1,500) per *chao* reflected market prices for peri-urban farmland in 2009. Facing pressure from the residents, the developer subsequently increased the payments to 35 million *dong* (approximately US$1,700) and finally to 42.5 million *dong* (approximately US$2,020) per *chao* – well above the market price for rural land, but well below the value of comparable urban land.[32] This multi-staged negotiating tactic incensed the residents who had accepted the initial compensation payments.

[31] See Hoi Vang Government website, available at: www.hoavang.danang.gov.vn/node/85.

[32] A problem in this case was that Hòa Lien Commune was designated a rural *huyen* under the state price frame and was valued at a lower rate than contiguous land in the urban *quan* across the city boundary.

Causing further aggravation, the construction of the first stage of the project took place during the dry season. Dust and noise from trucks affected the remaining residents, who complained that they had to "eat and sleep, together with the dust."[33] Attempts by the residents to negotiate a settlement with the developers failed. In frustration some residents took direct action by blockading the access road to prevent trucks from entering the construction zone.

On August 29, 2011, five men associated with the developer arrived at the house of Nguyen Van Tuan, a leader of the residents action group, and attacked him with iron pipes and swords, causing serious injuries.[34] Later that night, more than 1,000 residents stormed the construction site, destroying computer equipment and smashing windows. On the following night, the residents again clashed with police.

Negotiating a settlement

Lacking the tight-knit organizational structures that bind traditional communities, the residents initially negotiated as individual households or in small groups with the Hòa Vang District People's Committee. They were told that the compensation rates were confidential and not to discuss them with neighbors. At first, this tactic succeeded because community members lacked the networks to communicate with each other. Eventually, when rumors about unequal compensation payments spread and the dust from the construction disrupted people's lives, some prominent and articulate residents agreed to form a protest committee to represent the residents and petition the people's committee.

The protest committee depicted the Golden Hills development in glowing terms, as a beautiful new residential area. For them, the development epitomized the bright urban future they aspired to join. In contrast to the Đông Dương village case, the development was not seen as an assault on the residents' traditions and identity. Instead, the chief complaint concerned the inadequate compensation, and later, as the emotional intensity increased, residents felt betrayed by the officials.

[33] See Dang Nam, "Đà Nẵng đối thoại với dân vùng giải tỏa" ("Da Nang Dialogue with Regional Releases), Tuoi Tre, September 7, 2011.

[34] See Nguyen Tu, "Five Arrested in Attack on Pollution Protestor in Central Vietnam," *Thanh Nien Online*, September 2, 2011, available at: www.thanhniennews.com/2010/Pages/20110902133855.aspx, accessed June 29, 2013.

Dang Tan Do, a member of the protest committee, summarized the residents' concerns: "We are ready to move if we get reasonable compensation. But the land for our relocation is not even available, so where do they expect us to move to?"[35] To ensure that residents received similar levels of compensation, the protest committee demanded that "democracy and public policy apply to compensation for all the people so that they can know, check and monitor payments."[36] Residents also complained that the resettlement package did not include training to enable farmers to find work opportunities outside agriculture.[37] As the dispute became more confrontational and violent, the residents refocused their animosity toward local authorities. Residents complained that it was unfair that only developers and officials profited from land re-zoning and development. Ngo Kinh, a resident representative, voiced these concerns when he said: "We always disagree with the planning policy of the city, because it simply hands over our land to investors."[38] The residents' representatives also depicted the dispute as a betrayal by the state. Like the Đông Dương villagers, they stressed the "righteousness of the struggle" (*Đấu tranh chính nghĩa*) by drawing attention to the many local people who had supported the revolution and fought against American forces stationed in Da Nang and Hue. They described Hòa Vang District as a "cradle of the revolution," and urged the Party and state to protect the workers. This revolutionary narrative remains potent today despite fifteen years of state socialization policies that have sought to shift responsibility for housing and employment from the state to the people. Chinese land protesters have also invoked revolutionary rhetoric to legitimize their disputes.[39]

[35] See "Boss's Brother Seized for Assaulting Protester," *Tuoi Tre Online*, September 10, 2011, available at: http://123.30.128.29/cmlink/tuoitrenews/society/boss-brother-seized-for-assaulting-protester-1.43868, accessed June 24, 2013.

[36] See Hữu Trà, "Dân bức xúc về đền bù trước Bí thư Thành ủy Đà Nẵng" ("People Pressing for Compensation before the Da Nang Party Secretary"), *Thanh Nien Online*, July 9, 2011, available at: www.thanhnien.com.vn/Pages/20110907/Dan-buc-xuc-ve-den-bu-truoc-Bi-thu-Thanh-uy-Da-Nang.aspx, accessed May 30, 2013.

[37] See H. Khá and Đ. Nam, "Chính quyền Đà Nẵng đối thoại khẩn cấp với dân" ("The Da Nang Dialogue with Emergency"), *Tuoi Tre Online*, August 31, 2011, available at: http://tuoitre.vn/Chinh-tri-Xa-hoi/453843/Chinh-quyen-Da-Nang-doi-thoai-khan-cap-voi-dan.html, accessed May 30, 2013.

[38] See Le Phi, "Khoi to hai vu an lien quan den Golden Hills" ("Khoi Case Related to Golden Hills Case), *Soha Online*, September 1, 2011, available at: http://soha.vn/thongtin/khoi_to_hai_vu_an_lien_quan_den_golden_hills-v58FQXSNW.htm, accessed May 30, 2013.

[39] See Chapters 5, 6, 7, 8, and 9 in this book. See also Kevin J. O'Brien, "Rightful Resistance," *World Politics*, 49 (1996), 31–55.

Journalists from national daily newspapers, such as *Thanh Nien* (Youth) and *Tuoi Tre* (Young), supported the residents by highlighting their claims to fair compensation, work opportunities, and resettlement accommodation. They also argued that the state should do more for its revolutionary heroes. Journalists were less direct in voicing the residents' feeling of betrayal, but nonetheless reported that the district people's committee acted unfairly in distributing compensation and failing to prevent pollution.

In a dramatic intervention, the Da Nang Communist Party called a meeting with the residents on August 31, 2011 to resolve the dispute.[40] Dressed in white, the party chairman, Nguyễn Bá Thanh, and his aides addressed a crowd of approximately 2,000 residents and supporters. Thanh quickly distanced the Party from the Hòa Vang District People's Committee and the developer. He accused the Chairman of the People's Committee of "lacking resourcefulness, reacting too slowly to the residents' complaints and slowly releasing compensation payments, which resulted in the people laying siege to the developer and a situation that was not good for both sides."[41] He also agreed with the residents that the project lacked proper community consultation and transparent compensation payments.

Nguyễn Bá Thanh attempted to defuse the emotional intensity of the conflict by acting as a mediator between the residents and the government. He acknowledged the community's sense of injustice and assured them that the Party did not want the project to make the people "poor and hungry." His figurative and vernacular language was in contrast to the precise and technical narratives associated with land governance. It reflected his regulatory approach, which drew on pre-*doi moi* statecraft where the party led society through morality rule. This mode of governance stressed sentiment and reasonableness, rather than legal and procedural solutions, to social problems. He sought pragmatic solutions that did not directly reference the law, such as instructing the District People's Committee to speed up the payment of compensation and the resettlement program. Above all else, Thanh drew on charismatic rhetoric to "get close to the people" and resolve the dispute. Obeying Party instructions, on September 6, the Da Nang City People's Committee

[40] See Dang Nam, "Đà Nẵng đối thoại với dân vùng giải tỏa" ("Da Nang Dialogue with Regional Groups"), *Tuoi Tre*, May 15, 2011.

[41] *Ibid.*

began urgent talks to relocate the residents and to reduce dust from the construction site.[42]

To resolve this dispute, Thanh stepped outside the law-based regulatory framework. Like Mr. Tuan in the Đông Dương case, he acted as a hybrid regulator in finding creative solutions in a wide range of regulatory traditions. Thanh has been promoted to chair the Central Party Anti-Corruption Committee, but his record of governance in Da Nang remains controversial. To the acclaim of farmers, Thanh revived a revolutionary style of governance that cut through the thicket of regulations that profited developers and local officials. But this ad hoc popularism has been criticized for undermining the technology of land governance that the central authorities have been constructing over the last twenty years of land law reform.[43] Although the Party is given a role along with the state to resolve land disputes, it is not supposed to displace the state.[44] To prevent large-scale social unrest, Thanh appealed to the residents' emotional grievances without addressing systemic shortcomings in the law.

Planned communities: the Manor case study

At first glance, the residents of the Manor luxury apartments in Hanoi have little in common with the previously discussed land communities. Some commentators argue that, in buying luxury apartments, Vietnamese "nouveaux riches" signal their desire to leave traditional Vietnam and join a cosmopolitan planned community that provides security, comfort, and legal certainty.[45] This case study shows that residents of planned communities have not entirely broken from the regulatory traditions that order

[42] See "H. Kha and D. Nam Chính quyền Đà Nẵng đối thoại khẩn cấp với dân" ("Da Nang Government Dialogue with Civil Emergency"), *Tuoi Tre Online*, September 1, 2011, available at: http://tuoitre.vn/Chinh-tri-Xa-hoi/453926/Chinh-quyen-Da-Nang-doi-thoai-khan-cap-voi-dan.html, accessed May 30, 2013; "Boss's Brother Seized for Assaulting Protester," accessed May 30, 2013.

[43] See Chapter 10 in this book.

[44] See Ministry of Justice, "Chu De Tranh Chap Khieu Nai To Cap ve Dat Dai va Giai Quyet Tranh Cahp Khieu Nai To Cao ve Dat Dai" ("Disputes, Claims and Land Denunciation Settlement of Land Disputes"), Coordination Council Report on Dissemination and Education of Government Law, Hanoi, 2009, pp. 35–36.

[45] Michael Waibel, "The Production of Urban Space in Vietnam's Metropolis in the Course of Transition: Internationalization, Polarization and Newly Emerging Lifestyles in Vietnamese Society," *Trialog*, 89 (2006), 43–48. See also Michael Douglass and Liling Huang, "Globalizing the City in Southeast Asia: Utopia on the Urban Edge – The Case of Phu My Hung, Saigon," *International Journal of Asian-Pacific Studies*, 3 (2007), 1–42.

traditional and spontaneous communities. This case study explores protests organized by residents of the Manor to claim ownership over car parking spaces in the development. This is not an isolated case, as residents in many luxury apartments in Hanoi and Ho Chi Minh City are taking similar action.[46]

The dispute

Binh Minh Import Export Company (Bitexco), a large Vietnamese construction company, began selling apartments in the Manor residential development in 2007. The apartments set new standards for luxury, attracting competition from wealthy business people and high-ranking state officials. A dispute erupted in 2011, when Bitexco began to charge residents large service fees for using the underground car park. The residents claimed that the car park formed part of the common property that was under their collective ownership and control.

There were two main points of contention. Residents claimed that Bitexco failed to comply with the Law on Residential Housing 2005 to establish a residents' management committee within twelve months of completing construction. If the committee had been established, the residents could have used their majority voting powers to reduce parking fees to a cost-recovery basis. The residents lacked legal recourse because the Law on Residential Housing 2005 does not provide a mechanism to compel recalcitrant investors to establish management committees.

The other ground of contention concerned the legal definition of common property. The Law on Residential Housing 2005 does not define common property. To clarify the issue, Bitexco requested the Ministry of Construction, the state agency that drafted the law, to issue a definitive opinion. Circular No. 37/2009/TT-BXD guiding the method of identifying and managing service condominiums issued by the Ministry in 2009 stated that investors and residents should determine

[46] Residents protests have now spread to the Keangnam, Golden Westlake, and Sky City Tower luxury apartments in Hanoi. See Nguyen Le, "Liên minh chung cư kiến nghị có mức giá trần phí quản lý" ("Condo Alliance Petitioned the Price Ceiling Management Fee"), *Lao Dong Online*, September 19, 2011, available at: http://laodong.com.vn/Tin-Tuc/Lien-minh-chung-cu-kien-nghi-co-muc-gia-tran-phi-quan-ly/58969, accessed May 30, 2013; Nguyen Le, "Cư dân Sky City chỉ phải đóng phí giữ ô tô 1,25 triệu đồng/tháng" ("Sky City Residents Hold the Car Park Fee to only 1.25 million VND per month"), *Lao Dong Online*, April 6, 2011, available at: http://laodong.com.vn/Tin-Tuc/Cu-dan-Sky-City-chi-phai-dong-phi-giu-o-to-125-trieu-dongthang/38785, accessed May 30, 2013.

ownership of common property in the contract of sale.[47] Although this ruling strengthened Bitexco's case, it was not retrospectively binding.[48]

Mapping the relational land market

To understand why the residents could not sue Bitexco for breach of contract, it is necessary to understand how the land market is structured. Property investors in Hanoi, such as Bitexco, prevent the end-users in the retail market – those who intend to reside in the apartments – from buying directly from the project developers. Most investors lack the capital to construct luxury apartments and finance projects by selling apartments off-plan. A practice called *suat ngoai giao* (literally, diplomatic cases) has evolved in which first-tier investors sell apartments to family members, employees, business associates, state officials, and others enjoying a special relationship. Second-tier investors then on-sell the apartments to third- and sometimes fourth-tier investors. It is not unusual for apartments to change ownership many times before eventually being sold to the end-user residents. In the case of the Manor, some apartments had been resold three or four times before they were purchased by the residents.

According to the Civil Code 2005, only the second-tier investors had a legally enforceable contract with the first-tier investor.[49] Since second-tier investors enjoyed a close personal or business relationship with the first-tier investor, they had little inclination to renegotiate contracts on behalf of the end-user residents.

Undeterred by their lack of legal rights against Bitexco, the residents sought redress through relational connections. The use of relational connections to secure land rights has deep historical roots in Hanoi.[50] During the high socialist period (1954–1986), a covert self-regulating

[47] This provision is now governed by Art. 49.2(c), Decree No. 71/2010/ND-CP of the government providing in detail regulations on the Law on Residential Housing, 23 June 2010.

[48] Decree No. 71/2010/ND-CP stated that parking for motorcycles and bicycles was common property, whereas car parking belonged to the developer.

[49] The government has now attempted to regulate abuses of the pre-sale system by limiting this type of transaction to 20 percent of total apartment sales and preventing secondary investors from on-selling until a title is issued. It is too early to determine whether the Decree has been successful. See Decree No. 71/2010/ND-CP. The Law on Consumer Protection 2008, which incorporates oral representations into contracts, does not apply to land transactions.

[50] These comments are based on interviews with Le Trong, land broker, Hanoi, March 2001 and November 2008.

housing market evolved. Initially, most transactions involved the small residential apartments allocated to families in collective housing (*nha chung*), but after market liberalizations gained momentum, most residential housing was sold through informal transactions.[51] Sales contracts created transactional chains that traced ownership back to colonial land titles. Rather than demonstrating legal rights to title – their function under the colonial land system – sales contracts recorded relational chains of title.

This relational environment profoundly influenced the way in which the residents in the Manor conceptualized land transactions. They placed their faith in the personal assurances given by Bitexco staff that residents were entitled to car parking spaces and consequently viewed the decision to charge parking fees as a betrayal of trust. During interviews, residents complained that:

> We accepted the risk of buying million dollar apartments without a "red book" (land title), and expected Bitexco to repay our trust by honoring their promise to provide low cost car parking spaces.

Further exacerbating the dispute, Bitexco insulted the residents by sending a junior company employee to address the residents' grievances. Interviews with the residents suggest that a more conciliatory and personal response by Bitexco might have taken some of the emotional intensity out of the dispute.

Organising resistance to Bitexco

Most residents of the Manor did not know each other before the dispute. What drew them together was the legal fiction that residents of planned communities jointly manage common property. This tenuous connection provided a pretext for the residents to meet and organize. Professor Phap Thu, an eminent retired medical researcher, and Nguyễn Nhung Hạnh, an educational consultant, formed a residents' action group. Approximately 60 percent of the residents supported the protest action – a high response given that some apartments were still owned by investors connected to Bitexco. The residents established an internet mail site to disseminate information and discuss tactics.

[51] See Helen Evertsz, *Popular Housing in Hanoi* (Hanoi: Cultural Publishing House, 2000), pp. 147–151.

After organizing several unsuccessful demonstrations at Bitexco's offices, the residents decided to intensify their campaign. To avoid police intervention, they sought to legitimize their organization in the eyes of government officials by disguising the protest committee to resemble a branch of the state. The protest committee became a *Uỷ ban Thường vụ* (standing committee) – the term used by the state to describe representative agencies. They further integrated themselves into the fabric of government by forming a *To Truong* (resident cluster) – a legally recognized organization at the subward level.[52] To complete the process, Professor Phap Thu, the senior party member in the resident cluster, formed a Party cell.[53] By merging with the state apparatus, the residents could depict the dispute as an internal grievance and avoid being denounced as subversives by the developer.

Once constituted as a government agency, the protest committee organized a series of demonstrations in March 2009. When Bitexco threatened to lock the residents' cars in the car park until outstanding fees were paid, the residents responded by blocking the entrances to the Manor with luxury cars.[54] Before taking this step, the chairs of the resident cluster and Party cell sought permission from the local government and Party committee. The residents were mindful of the punitive laws banning public assembly.

Acting on advice from lawyers, the residents invited support from the daily newspapers. Residents convinced reporters that Bitexco violated *cong ly* (public justice)[55] by failing to establish a management committee and charging parking fees that exceeded the maximum rates set by the Hanoi People's Committee.[56] This media campaign succeeded in forcing Bitexco to the negotiating table. Phi Thai Binh, the vice-chairman of the Hanoi People's Committee, instructed Bitexco to resolve the dispute.

Although most residents were well educated with a sound understanding of the legal framework, private law played a negligible role

[52] See Decision 13 2002 QD BNV, Ministry of Internal Affairs on the Organisation of Resident Clusters.

[53] The Party Statute allows three or more Party members in any organization to form a Party cell.

[54] See VNA, "Investor Asked to Stop Ad Hoc Management of Up-market Complex," *Thanh Nien Online*, November 3, 2009, available at: www.thanhniennews.com/2009/Pages/2009311103019046848.aspx, accessed May 30, 2013.

[55] In urban settings, the term *cong ly* refers to a type of procedural justice, whereas in the Đông Dương village study, the term *cong bang* referred to equality among villagers – a distributive form of justice.

[56] See VNA, "Investor asked to stop ad hoc management of up-market complex."

in this dispute. To breach the deadlock and find a solution, the residents' action group acted like hybrid regulators. They used their political connections to disguise their organization as a government agency – a tactic that enabled them to portray a private property dispute as violation of public order. It also enabled them to enlist state power to force a formidable adversary with strong Party connections to negotiate.

Searching for solutions beyond property rights

The Manor case provides a useful contrast to the other case studies, because the conditions seemed right for property rights to play the decisive role. Not only were the residents highly educated, well travelled, and familiar with laws and legal institutions, but also they were members of a planned community defined by law. But, rather than dominating the regulatory space, the property laws were "place-making" in this case because they were merely one set of regulatory traditions competing with many other regulatory practices. To have made a difference, property law would have to be "place-breaking" and displace the use of relational connections to resolve the dispute. The residents succeeded in persuading Bitexco to reduce the car parking fees, but not to transfer ownership in the car park.

Conclusion

The case studies considered in this chapter narrate an undercurrent of discontent about who has access to land and on what terms. Each of the communities – traditional, spontaneous, and planned – drew on internal epistemic and normative assumptions to frame their responses to land-takings. There was some overlap in these assumptions, and rather than constituting unconnected and self-contained systems of thought, they represent particular positions along a continuum, with traditional regulatory values at one end and rights-based property law at the other end. A defining characteristic of the Đông Dương traditional community was the persistence and reproduction of the sentimental and spiritual connections to place that underpinned village claims to land. For the older generation, land was not a fungible commodity. Their spiritual and moral claims were in fundamental opposition to the state's vision of individual property rights and precise legal boundaries. Although the younger generation in the village were less attached to place and more inclined to view land as a fungible commodity, they were radicalized by the dispute and joined the older generation in rejecting the unequal distribution permitted by the state land regime. Their claim to rightful resistance sought to challenge the moral authority of impersonal and objective rules of law, and the depiction of the countryside as uncivilized and lawless.

The older villagers and state officials resided in different epistemic worlds with few interlinking communicative channels. Villagers rarely saw past the blind spots in their epistemic repertoires to engage with others in meaningful dialog. Mr. Tuan bridged the village and official worlds and brokered a deal that increased compensation. The villagers failed to gain what they wanted most – a sense of community and identity because their highly localized narratives had little resonance beyond the village.

As members of a spontaneous community, residents displaced by the Golden Hills project could not draw on a coherent set of village traditions to support their claim. Initially, they treated their land as a tradable commodity and were willing to leave with the right compensation and resettlement package. As the dispute progressed, emotion transformed their initial pragmatic assessment into the moral belief that the officials had betrayed them.

Nguyễn Bá Thanh, the Da Nang Party chief, used his charismatic power to defuse public anger and allow cost–benefit calculations to determine the outcome once again. He narrated a particular way of seeing the dispute. By portraying the residents as revolutionary heroes, he identified with their struggle against the developer, but also brought them into the Party and state orbit. This regulatory technique encouraged the residents to identify with the state's vision for a developed and modern Da Nang. It also co-opted the residents into a regulatory style that avoided legal, political, and moral accountability for the Party and state. In the process, the Party leader undermined the legitimacy of state discourse about objective procedural rules and official transparency and accountability.

Like the other communities, the residents of the Manor did not use the law to protect their property rights. Instead, they leveraged their political and business connections to mount a public campaign. They first transformed their protest committee into a unit of government and then enlisted the press to publicize their grievances. Officials responded to this narrative, not because they felt obligated to protect the residents' property rights, but rather to prevent legal violations by the investor.

A unifying theme in these studies is the role of law in resolving land disputes. In each case, law added to, without displacing, the pre-existing regulatory approaches to land. Rather than controlling members of the communities directly, the land law coordinated and interacted with other regulatory orders. Party and state officials attempted to apply the law flexibly to seek context-specific outcomes. As Upham argues in Chapter 2, this type of ad hoc resolution provides short-term, contextual solutions without framing broad principles that might build a lasting consensus about land disputes. This creates a regulatory dilemma. To control vast areas of land, states need to operate on a large scale. Simplification, codification, and standardization are prerequisites of effective land management. At the same time, uniform state law seems to be unable to deal with the complexities of plural approaches to land disputes.

It is instructive to ask whether dialogical exchanges between land communities and officials can bring laws into conversation with underlying social practices. In authoritarian Vietnam, the civil space is tightly controlled by the state, and only a limited range of ideas and people is permitted to influence public discourse. For example, as the Manor case study showed, politically connected actors can influence law-makers to regulate in their favor.

Aware of the difficulties farmers face in asserting land claims, a group of Vietnamese public intellectuals is currently exploring new forms of property rights.[57] They argue for private ownership of land to increase government accountability in land-takings and other controversial cases. Their proposal to establish different types of private interests to

[57] This group includes prominent economic advisors, lawyers, historians, and academics advocating radical change to the land law. The group includes Phan Chi Lan, Nguyen Van A, Pham Duy Nghia, Nguyen Lap, Nguyen Khac Vien advocating the (re)recognition of private landownership. See, for example, Nguyen Tien Lap, "Danh Gia Phap Luat So Huu: Nen Mong Cho Nen Kinh Te Thi Truong or Viet Nam" ("The Property Law Foundation of the Market Economy in Vietnam"), Report to Standing Committee of the National Assembly about 5-years of Enforcing Politburo Resolution No. 48," May 24, 2005, pp. 11–12; Hoang Van, "Có nên cho sở hữu tư nhân về đất đai? – Bài 2: Quyền quá lớn dễ dẫn đến lạm dụng" ("Should There be Private Ownership of Land? – Lesson 2: The Right is too Large Leading to Abuse"), *Phap Luat*, March 1, 2011, available at: http://phapluattp.vn/20110228102044 21p0c1013/quyen-qua-lon-de-dan-den-lam-dung.htm, accessed May 30, 2013.

recognize the diverse range of relationships to land offers a useful way give the land communities discussed in this chapter a legal voice. For example, one type of rights suggested would recognize the spiritual and emotional claims to land by traditional communities.[58] What is currently unclear is whether or not this proposal will overcome resolute opposition from the senior Party leaders and investors who steadfastly advocate uniform property rights in Vietnam.

[58] Interviews with Nguyen Tien Lap, senior lawyer, NH Quang and Associates, Hanoi, Vietnam, March and October 2011.

PART IV

Taiwan case studies

12

An overview of Taiwanese land law and dispute resolution

PO-FANG TSAI AND DUAN LIN

Introduction

People in Taiwan rarely look to land law to resolve land disputes, because for centuries such disputes were settled without recourse to formal law. There were no clearly defined land laws in Taiwan before 1949. The Qing Dynasty had no land laws that resembled land titling in Western legal systems, and the Japanese colonial government confined land governance to the colonial system. Clearly defined and generally applicable land laws were not introduced until the Kuomintang (KMT) government after 1949.

Unfortunately, over the past sixty years of KMT land governance, the land laws did not function well. This chapter suggests two reasons for this failure. First, rather than amending the land law to address regulatory problems, the KMT government introduced confusing and contradictory special laws.[1] Second, the land law did not remain relevant to rapid social and economic changes during this period.

To understand how these two factors have influenced land governance, it is necessary to examine how land law functioned in different historical periods. Land law and dispute resolution in Taiwan have been decoupling since the nineteenth century. The state system governing dispute resolution evolved separately from the land law system. The legal systems (prior to 1945) followed the traditional Chinese law system and colonial law, which lasted from the late Qing Dynasty to the Japanese colonial regime, and the legal system of the authoritarian regime of the

[1] In the modern legal doctrines, when judges and lawyers face the conflicts among the different laws or different articles in the same law, the general principles are that special laws or articles precede ordinary ones, laws or articles in the narrow sense precede these in the broad sense, and laws or articles in the whole sense precede ones in the partial sense.

KMT underwent a democratic transformation in the last decade of the twentieth century.

On the one hand, state land law and official dispute resolution did not cover the entire range of social movements, such as conflicts among different ethnicities or the struggles between rich and poor. Although the change from the traditional Chinese law system to the modern Western law system increased the universality of law, it does not cover the major social causes of land disputes, such as economic class and ethnicity. Balancing the universalism of the legal system and particularism in society generated distinct problems for different governments in Taiwan.

On the other hand, the political democratization and economic liberalization of the past two decades has provided new modes of interaction between the state and society. Consequently, in Taiwan today, the legal framework governing land has decreased the discretionary power of the administrative branch and given more power to the judicial branch. Under this new regulatory regime, the gap between legal norms and social practices in land disputes is more likely to be presented as a kind of failure in the system of government. As a result of this transfer of power to the courts, inefficient enforcement has caused the courts to be blamed for failures to resolve disputes, resulting in a vicious circle among the legislative, administrative, and judicial branches.

Before examining land disputes in the current land system, it is useful to consider three historical phases in the evolution of land law and dispute resolution.

Land law and dispute resolution in Taiwan: governing modes in history

The greatest changes in land dispute resolution occurred in Taiwan from the late nineteenth century to the present day. Over this period, regulation changed from the traditional binary mode of official legal norms and non-governmental mediations to adjudication by civil and administrative courts, administrative offices, and non-governmental mediations.[2] In tandem with this change, cooperation among the different branches of government increased the complexity of land dispute

[2] Tay-Sheng Wang, "The Legal Development of Taiwan in the 20th Century: Toward a Liberal and Democratic Country," *Pacific Rim Law & Policy Journal*, 11(3) (2002), 531–559; Tay-Sheng Wang, "The Impact of Modern Western Law on the Chinese in Taiwan," *Australian Journal of Asian Law*, 1(2) (1999), 194–220.

resolution. This transition has not been smooth; rather, changes in the legal system have at various times triggered land disputes. Therefore, we can view these processes in terms of the intersections of three different periods: first, the frontier and colonial regimes of the late Qing Dynasty and Japanese colonial governments, before 1945; second, the period from 1945 to 1990, when the Kuomintang regime governed the country on a wartime footing; and, third, the democratic regime, which began in the last decade of the twentieth century.

Qing Dynasty land governance (1683–1894)

In the shift from the late Qing Dynasty to the Japanese colonial regime, Taiwan experienced a change from the Chinese legal system to the Western legal system. In the nineteenth century, the Qing Dynasty treated Taiwan as one of its many frontiers, such as Tibet, Manchu, and Mongolia, and land governing aimed to "pacify" the local population by dividing land usage among different ethnic groups.[3] According to the historical studies of Mark A. Allee and John R. Shepherd, statecraft in late imperial China focused on separating the land use of Han people as farmers from the aboriginals.[4] Land disputes at that time most commonly arose between landowners and tenant farmers, and also between farmers and aboriginals. The magistrates of the Qing government sent to Taiwan to settle these disputes usually did not involve themselves in the real nature of these disputes, aiming instead to prevent the disputes from

[3] See Fu-san Huang, "The Problems of Settlers on the Farmers in Qing Taiwan and Their Impact on the Aboriginals. Part One," *Shih-Huo: Chinese Social and Economic History*, 11(1) (1981), 19–36 (in Chinese); Fu-san Huang, "The Problems of Settlers on the Farmers in Qing Taiwan and Their Impact on the Aboriginals. Part Two," *Shih-Huo: Chinese Social and Economic History*, 11(2) (1981), 26–46 (in Chinese); Chih-Ming Ka, "Rational State and Historical Contingency: Aborigine Land Rights and Ethnic Politics in Qing Taiwan," *Taiwan Historical Research*, 6(2) (1999), 1–76 (in Chinese); Chih-Ming Ka, "The Classification and Transformation of Aborigine Land Rights in Qing Taiwan," *Taiwanese Journal of Sociology*, 23 (2000), 25–102 (in Chinese); Wen-Liang Li, "Re-thinking Land Reform Policies in Late Qing Taiwan: The Significance and Policy-Making Process of Cutting 40% and Retaining 60% of Large Rents," *Chinese Studies*, 24(1) (2006), 387–416 (in Chinese); Wen-Liang Li, "Aboriginal Land Rent, Subsoil Land Rights and Hakka Society in South Taiwan: A Study on the Rent Arrangements in the 1721 Contract," *Chinese Studies*, 27(4) (2009), 229–260 (in Chinese).

[4] Mark A. Allee, *Law and Local Society in Late Imperial China: Northern Taiwan in the Nineteenth Century* (Stanford University Press, 1994); John R. Shepherd, *Statecraft and Political Economy on the Taiwan Frontier, 1600–1800* (Stanford University Press, 1993).

creating civil unrest.[5] Moreover, Ka Chih-Ming drew on the historical archives to show that the state dealt with land disputes by constructing different social groups with clear status identities.[6] The three-tiered formation of "ethnic politics" proposed by Ka Chih-Ming reflected land governance in the late Qing.[7]

Japanese land governance (1895–1945)

The Japanese colonial regime replaced the Qing system with a Western-style legal system. This change produced major reforms in three aspects of land law: the uniformity of property rights, the centralization of lands, and the separation of administrative and judicial power. First, the colonial government cancelled the link between land usage and group status, standardizing the legal right to own property rights. In the laws concerning landownership and usage, all social groups had equal ownership rights and equal status under the law.[8]

Second, the introduction of the Western legal system coincided with a sharp trend toward centralization of landownership. During the Japanese colonial period, the rapid transferral of land created a new

[5] Wen-Kai Lin, "Local Governance and Land Litigation: A Social Historical Analysis of Land Lawsuits of 'Jin-Shon-Mion Ai' in Taiwan's Zhuqian Region during the Qing," *New History*, 18(4) (2007), 125–187 (in Chinese); Wen-Kai Lin, "Inside and Outside the Local Judicial Space in Qing: An Analysis of Rent Resistance Cases in the Han-Reclamation District of Northern Taiwan," *Taiwan Historical Research*, 14(1) (2007), 1–70 (in Chinese); Wen-Kai Lin, "'Deed Owner, Land Owner?' Land Property Rights and Litigation Culture in Qing Taiwan," *Taiwan Historical Research*, 18(2) (2011), 1–52 (in Chinese).

[6] Chih-Ming Ka, *The Aborigine Landlord: Ethnic Politics and Aborigine Land Rights in Qing Taiwan* (Taipei: Academic Sinica, 2001) (in Chinese).

[7] Chih-Ming Ka, "Formation and Transformation of Aborigine Small-rent Land Tenure: Land Tenancy of Tribesman's Ration Plot in Anli New Territory," *Taiwan Historical Research*, 15(3) (2008), 57–137 (in Chinese); Chih-Ming Ka, "The Invisible Small-rent: Aborigine Small-rent Land Right of Anli Tribe in Land Tax Reforms under Qing and Japanese Colonial Rule," *Taiwan Historical Research*, 15(1) (2008), 31–79 (in Chinese); Chih-Ming Ka, "Abolition of Plain Aborigine Land Rights: Dissolution and Termination of Anli Tribe's Large-rents and Small-rents," *Taiwan Historical Research*, 16(1) (2009), 29–86 (in Chinese).

[8] Wu-Dar Huang, Hideaki Ogawa, and Akira Naito, "Contemporary Taipei City Planning in Japanese Colonial Age (Part I): Beginning and Developing of City Planning," *City and Planning*, 22(1) (1995), 99–122 (in Chinese); Wu-Dar Huang, Hideaki Ogawa, and Akira Naito, "Contemporary Taipei City Planning Japanese Colonial Age (Part II): Enactment and Implementation of Planning Legal System," *City and Planning*, 25(1) (1998), 107–131 (in Chinese); Wu-Dar Huang, Ja-Haur Tsay, and Akira Naito, "Creation of the Contemporary Planning Legislation for Taiwan in Japanese Colonial Age: Scope in the Creation Stage and Implementation Progress in Taipei City Area," *City and Planning*, 24(2) (1997), 99–127 (in Chinese).

landlord class, and this social restructuring shifted land disputes from inter-ethnic to inter-class conflict.[9] Third, the introduction of the idea of the "rule of law" brought about the separation of administrative and judicial power among governing agencies. This separation gave people involved in land disputes two options for settling grievances: lodge petitions with distinct government departments or lodge petitions with local courts. In summary, in the transition from frontier governing to colonial government, it can be said that land law and dispute resolution in Taiwan underwent its first legal modernization, with a major shift away from particularism and toward universalism.

Kuomintang land governance (1945–2000)

The Japanese colonial regime withdrew at the end of the Second World War, when control of Taiwan was transferred to the Kuomintang (KMT, the Nationalist or Citizens' Party). When the Communist Party of China came into power, the KMT retreated to Taiwan. This regime change caused another acute transition in land governance – from colonial to wartime governance. Due to the military's antagonism toward the communist regime in China and the political consolidation within Taiwan, the KMT commenced a series of land law reforms in 1950.[10] The most important reforms were the "thirty-five point five rent reduction," the "land-to-the-tiller," and the "lease of public farm lands."

First, to reduce the economic pressure on the production sector, the KMT government enacted the "thirty-five point five rent reduction" farm rent limitation program. This law favored the tenants and regulated the landlords. Second, the "land-to-the-tiller policy" encouraged tenants to buy the land that they had cultivated for many years by offering government loans and instalment payments. Third, the policy of leasing

[9] Su-Mei Chang and Shu-Jen Yeh, "Taiwan's Land Distribution during the Japanese Period," unpublished National Science Council Project Reports, No. NSC89-2415-H002-010, 2002 (in Chinese).

[10] Shih-Jung Hsu and Hsin-Huang Michael Hsiao, *The Impacts of Class Differentiation and Cultural Construction on Post-War Land Reform in Taiwan* (Taipei: Academia Sinica, 1999); Isaac M. Ofori (ed.), *President Chiang Kai-Shek and Land Reform: Proceedings of an International Seminar held in Taipei, October 1986* (Taipei: China Land Reform Association, 1986); Martin M. C. Yang, *Socio-Economic Results of Land Reform in Taiwan* (Honolulu, HI: East-West Center Press, 1970); Anthony Y. C. Koo, *The Role of Land Reform in Economic Development: A Case Study of Taiwan* (New York: Praeger Press, 1968); Steven N. S. Cheung, *The Theory of Share Tenancy: With Special Application to Asian Agriculture and the First Phase of Taiwan Land Reform* (University of Chicago Press, 1969).

public farmlands economized assets that had lain idle for years and increased the amount of land transactions after the Second World War.

These reforms sparked land disputes concerning the distributive justice of reallocating landownership. The KMT tried to settle these disputes with policy reforms designed to increase equality, rather than by encouraging rights-based litigation. Although scholars have different views about the impact, effectiveness, and efficiency of the three land reforms, they all agree that wartime governance, rather than economic planning, was the most important motive for the reforms.[11]

Eventually, the economic transition in Taiwan forced the KMT to respond to land dispute resolution in a less authoritarian instrumental style. In the 1970s, the KMT government proposed new land laws in a much more inclusive style. The crucial issues in those years concerned the usage and ownership of agricultural and urban land. One set of concerns related to basic food security. The KMT, for example, enacted legislation to regulate the usage and ownership of agricultural land.[12] Only farmers could buy and sell agricultural land, and this land could only be used for agricultural purposes.

At the same time, the KMT government deregulated several aspects of urban land use in order to unleash urbanization in metropolitan areas. The relaxation of restrictions on urban development not only caused an explosion of real estate investment, but it also allowed collusion between the government, local political factions, and construction companies.[13] The disparity between the usage and ownership of agricultural and urban

[11] Chi-Wei Liu and Chih-Ming Ka, "State, Landlords, and Peasantry in Taiwan's Post-war Agrarian Transformation, 1945–1953," *Taiwan Historical Research*, 9(1) (2002), 107–180 (in Chinese); Zhao-Yong Chen, "Land Reform as Regime Consolidation: State, Landlords, and Peasantry in Post-war Taiwan's Land Policy Transformation, 1945–1953," unpublished PhD dissertation, Department of Sociology, National Taiwan University, 2011 (in Chinese); Shih-Jung Hsu and Hsin-Huang Michael Hsiao, "Taiwan's Land Reform Revisited: From the Vantage Point of its Domestic Social Origins," *Taiwan Historical Research*, 8(1) (2001), 89–124 (in Chinese); Shih-Jung Hsu and Hsin-Huang Michael Hsiao, "Landlord and Tenants' Relations in the Post-War Era: Reconsidering the Land to the Tiller Program," *Taiwan Historical Research*, 10(2) (2003), 35–66 (in Chinese).

[12] Su-Jen Huang, "A Reappraisal of Taiwan's Land Reform," *Taiwan: A Radical Quarterly in Social Studies*, 47 (2002), 195–248 (in Chinese); Su-Jen Huang, *The Prison-House of Mind: The Ideology of "Agricultural Land for Agricultural Usage" and the Urban/Rural Development in Taiwan* (Taipei: ChuLiu Publisher, 2002) (in Chinese).

[13] Dung-Sheng Chen, *The City with Money and Power: A Sociological Analysis of the Local Factions, the Consortiums, and the Development of Taipei Metropolitan Area* (Taipei: ChuLiu Publisher, 1995) (in Chinese).

land brought about new land disputes, which the KMT government struggled to control. Looking back at the wartime governance and the authoritarian regime of the KMT government, we find that the land laws and dispute resolution of this period gradually gave in to the social pressures of political democratization and economic liberalization.

Post-democratization land governance (after 2000)

Political democratization and economic liberalization began to flourish during the last twenty years of the twentieth century. As the century drew to a close, the KMT government was forced to consider the complexity of land disputes in its integrative plans. Paradoxically, the transfer of power from the KMT left the Democratic Progressive Party (the DPP, the first meaningful opposition party in Taiwan) with the "Homeland Integrated Development Planning" (HIDP). The DPP faced a dilemma. On the one hand, the HIDP gave local councils powers to decide their own development plan, which they used to promote economic development over environmental protection. On the other hand, the HIDP was supposed to function as an integrating mechanism that balanced economic progress and sustainable development. Although the HIDP created a binary regulatory system with land either falling within or outside this regime, the criteria determining whether the HIDP applied to land came from a political compromise between the central–local relationship rather than a professional judgment of planning.

The HIDP was drafted to maintain social justice in the usage, ownership, and transfer of land. It was based on the principles of the "Planning Permission System" of the United Kingdom and the "Partition Management System" of the United States.[14] However, the HIDP allowed land expropriation by major industries, such as a high-tech original equipment manufacturer (OEM). As a consequence, a growing number of disputes arose over land readjustments and expropriations that benefited the government and industry at the expense of the people.

The HIDP caused another kind of land dispute, one that is handled under the official title of "uncertain land." The term "uncertain land"

[14] Ching-Hui Wu, "Study on Strategy and Application of Land Development Permission (I)," unpublished National Science Council Project Reports, No. 87-2418-H-034-002 (1999) (in Chinese); Ching-Hui Wu, "Study on Strategy and Application of Land Development Permission (III)," unpublished National Science Council Project Reports, No. 89-2415-H034-001 (2001) (in Chinese).

describes land that falls outside the HIDP. The most typical cases are land used by popular religious groups. The temples of folk beliefs or new religions can be classified by the central and local government as "uncertain land." Most of this land belongs to popular religious or family clan groups. The most serious problem with this type of land is the lack of legal protection against expropriation by the government. Land disputes over government acquisition of uncertain lands are thus largely overlooked by the courts, and the owners of this kind of land are often silent victims in the struggle between the economic developmental policies of the government and social pressure for the protection of basic property rights.[15]

In short, political democratization and economic liberalization did not necessarily decrease land disputes. Take the HIDP, for example. There are still obvious problems of land expropriation: the interests of local governments may be limited by central government; the interests of major industries may be prioritized over those of rural farmers; and popular religious or family clan groups may not keep their "uncertain land." Therefore, the planners of land laws and dispute resolution in democratic Taiwan have to face the unintended consequences of the HIDP and improve communication among the different branches of government to develop a consistent version of land justice.

Land law governance during the three historical stages

In order to provide an overview of the historical background of Taiwanese land law and dispute resolution, we must stress that the mode of governance has played an important role in each period. While late imperial China used the frontier-governing mode to pacify the various ethnic minorities, Japan established colonial government to unify different groups by introducing the modern legal system. This transition involved a change from particularism to universalism. The separation of administrative and judicial powers caused rapid centralization of landownership. It also replaced ethnic groups with economic classes as the main social tension animating land disputes.

However, the situation changed again after the KMT took control of Taiwan. Although the modern legal framework of land law and dispute resolution remained similar, the wartime governing mode of the KMT employed first an authoritarian style and then a more consultative style.

[15] These issues are discussed in more depth in Chapter 13 in this book.

Land law and dispute resolution were used by the KMT to maintain political consolidation, even if these policies were often carried out in the name of social justice. It was not until the democratic period of the last two decades of the twentieth century that political and economic liberalization forced the government to abandon its instrumental approach to land law and dispute resolution. Whether the majority party is the KMT or the DPP, the government must balance the efficient administration of land with resolving land conflicts generated by ethnic pluralism and clashes between economic development and customary land use.

The contemporary legal framework and its discontents

Having provided a concise overview of the historical background, we must now turn to the current state of land law and dispute resolution. The existing legal framework is best described by examining a typical land dispute. Before developing a typology of land dispute resolution, we have to mention some additional background information. The term "land law," referring to the laws that regulate landownership, has two different definitions. The narrow definition refers only to the "Land Act," which has five chapters: General Principles, Cadastral Survey, Land Use, Land Tax, and Compulsory Purchase of Land. The wide definition, in contrast, refers not only to the "Land Act," but also to other laws, such as "the National Property Act," "Urban and Regional Planning Act," and "the Act of Advancing Private Participation in Public Construction". In addition, the Civil Code, particularly Part II, Obligations, and Part III, Rights in REM, regulates transactions involving land. In summary, we can view the laws that regulate landownership in a three-tiered framework comprising the Civil Codes, the Land Act, and the other relevant laws, intertwined with general and special codes.

Second, the types of permitted landownership are individual in form, and govern both natural persons and juristic persons.

The laws mentioned above not only allowed horizontal disputes between landholders, but also disputes with the state.[16] In the past two decades, Taiwan has added administrative laws, such as the Administrative Procedure Act and Government Procurement Act. The provisions of

[16] See Li-Fu Chen (ed.), *Land Laws and Regulations in Taiwan*, 14th edn. (Taipei: Sharing Culture Press, 2011) (in Chinese); Li-Fu Chen, *Study on Taiwan Land Law* (Taipei: Sharing Culture Press, 2007) (in Chinese); Li-Fu Chen, "A General Inspection of Land Law in Taiwan," *Taiwan Law Journal*, 16 (2000), 1–13 (in Chinese).

these laws give citizens administrative procedures to challenge state action. However, inconsistent decisions and conflicting judgments by civil and administrative courts have exacerbated social tensions over land.

In some cases, the judgments of civil and administrative courts have conflicted with each other. Moreover, there are sharp contrasts between the capacities of social actors, such as the central or local government, construction and development companies, and social groups and citizens.

First, the legal norms governing land and their discontents are described. Next, three typical cases demonstrating how land laws resolve disputes are selected. The issues in question include the tension between administrative and judicial powers, the disjunction between central and local government policies, and the disparity between land-taking and land-clearing.

Current problems: tension, disjunction, and disparity

The most obvious tension in resolving disputes is caused by the dual track civil and administrative dispute resolution authorities. They follow different reasoning and principles (e.g., autonomy in private law and proportionality in public law) in resolving cases. Litigants exploit the lack of clarity between private and public law by strategically filing appeals on land cases in the different judicial systems. Generally speaking, civil courts investigate the substantive contents and the respective claims of litigants, and administrative courts examine the formal procedures executed by the officials concerned. However, the judges in civil and administrative courts both want to maintain their neutrality in litigation, so in land disputes, their judgments often focus on formal legality, rather than on substantive justice. In addition, judges are reluctant to overrule prior cases. Armed with this knowledge, litigants selectively use civil litigation to resolve administrative issues and administrative litigation to resolve civil claims. These litigation strategies, which are usually adopted by relatively weak litigants such as non-corporate entities, waste legal resources and increase the burden of litigation.

Consider disputes about land in the high-tech industry.[17] These cases of "national economic development versus basic property rights" demonstrate the difficulties inherent in the Land Expropriation Ordinance passed in 2000. There are at least three issues that reveal the legal tension

[17] Ming-Chiang Lin, "Land Use Planning for Sustainable Development," unpublished National Science Council Project Reports, No. 88-2621-Z002-006 (1999) (in Chinese); Ming-Chiang Lin, "A Study on the Legal System of City Development," unpublished National Science Council Project Reports, No. 88-2414-H002-007 (1999) (in Chinese).

between private law and public law. First, the negotiations during land expropriation involve not only formal legalities of both private and public law, but also the autonomy principle of private law, rather than the proportionality principle of public law. When the land is expropriated for an economic development project, the government may not clearly demonstrate that land-taking is for a public purpose and thereby infringe citizens' property rights.

Second, the value of "improvements on land," which according to Article 5 of the Land Act can be divided into constructional improvements and agricultural improvements, are often underestimated during land expropriations. This violates the constitutional principle of property protection.

Third, according to the law governing the standards of compensation for land expropriation, land value should be calculated in accordance with "Rules for Land Value Assessments." However, these rules are scattered among various private and public laws, and consequentially often overlap or are inconsistent. This situation also sharpens the tension between the civil and administrative courts. As a result, legal disputes arising from land expropriation acquire complexity because of the lack of coordination between the civil and administrative courts.

The second key issue is the disjunction of the administrative branch.[18] Because land expropriations may be carried out in different jurisdictions, the central administrative agencies in some circumstances are given sole responsibility for land compensation. However, the general procedures rely on coordination and negotiation between the central and local governments.

The problems caused by the lack of central–local coordination are often shown up in the difficulty of calculating compensation. On the one hand, it is not easy to calculate the public benefits of land expropriation to the local people or the Taiwanese more generally. A land expropriation project for economic development may be good for the people of Taiwan but bad for the local people, or vice versa. The central and local government agencies, which collectively shoulder the costs of land compensation, divide the costs according to case-by-case negotiation. These procedures, which are conducted not with a statutory standard, but under administrative orders, seem to manifest a deficiency in the legality and legitimacy of the system.

On the other hand, due to various budget pressures on the administrative agencies at different levels, any land compensation project may still depend

[18] Li-Fu Chen, "Controversies of Land Expropriation Law," *Journal of Taiwan Land Research*, 11(1) (2008), 1–35 (in Chinese).

on the decisions of both parliament and the local city or county council. In most cases, where land compensation is jointly regulated by administrative agencies, the procedures are time-consuming. Moreover, complicated trivial steps in the procedures, which delay justice in land law and cause additional disputes, also raise the risk of corruption, as stakeholders seek to simplify procedures. Although land law and dispute resolution in Taiwan have traditionally focused on substantive rather than instrumental justice, the procedures and disputes of land readjustment, expropriation, and compensation are commonly criticized for the "devil in the detail," which means that injustice is hidden in the legal framework.

Urban renewal and agricultural land release programs are generally the most procedurally complex styles of administrative cases. These cases lie at the intersections of several sets of laws: the Regional Planning Act, Urban Planning Law, Construction Law, Urban Renewal Regulation, Environmental Impact Assessment Law, and Water and Soil Conservation Law. The most contested point in urban renewal projects is the limitation in Article 25 of the Urban Renewal Regulation that only allows "experienced companies" to participate in projects.

Agricultural land release programs, on the other hand, are caught between two competing viewpoints. One proposes the protection of natural resources, which appeals to government authorities such as the Environmental Impact Assessment Law and Water and Soil Conservation Law. The other promotes land transactions, an objective supported by the Regional Planning Act and Urban Planning Law. These problems cannot be resolved by administrative courts and require reforms to the administrative system.

The third major point is the disparity between land expropriation for public purposes and cadastre clearance where private land has been neglected. The public image of land disputes depends on the motivations of social movements. This is partially shaped by the perceived justice of court cases. Public opinion is also shaped by perceptions about land readjustment, expropriation, and compensation.

For example, under the HIDP, land categorized as "uncertain land" was sold by local governments without the permission of the stakeholders, such as popular religions or family clan groups.[19] The phrase "uncertain land"

[19] Chien-Yuan Lin, "The System of Land Development Control for Highly Uncertain Demand: The Case of Religious Land Use (I)," unpublished National Science Council Project Reports, No. 92-2415-H-002-024 (2004) (in Chinese); Chien-Yuan Lin, "The System of Land Development Control for Highly Uncertain Demand: The Case of Religious Land Use (II)," unpublished National Science Council Project Reports, No. 92-2415-H-002-024 (2005) (in Chinese).

refers to land lacking clear ownership claims and titles. Uncertain land arises from historical processes, such as broken lines of inheritance or the separation of smaller lots from the main land parcel. A typical case involving "uncertain land" can be found in the Cadastral Clean-Up Regulations. This statute was enacted to appropriate and sell uncertain lands to increase revenue. Although this policy did not give rise to as many social struggles as land expropriation, it still harmed the stakeholders of those uncertain lands. For example, most of those uncertain lands belonged to temples operated by popular religions. This type of "ancestral worship property"[20] has no formal title and is controlled by ancestral worship associations.[21] Since such social groups have no legal status, they cannot own land, and "ancestral worship property" is confiscated in cadastral cleanings. To sum up, the injustice caused by the government regulation of "uncertain land" is comparable to the injustice in land expropriation cases.

From the three major issues – tension, disjunction, and disparity – and their respective cases discussed above, we may develop a tentative map of land law and dispute resolution in contemporary Taiwan. The tension between the administrative and judicial branches complicates the litigation strategies in the disputes; the disjunction between the approaches of central and local governments damages the legality of the land laws and the legitimacy of dispute resolution; and the disparity between focused land-taking and neglected land-cleaning robs the silent of justice. Without redress in the legal system, aggrieved land users must mount social protests to reform the relevant laws. Drafts of relevant laws may be proposed not only by governmental agencies, such as the Executive Yuan or the Legislative Yuan, but also by private groups, such as NPOs, NGOs, and professional associations. There is reason to believe that the level of social injustice is sufficiently high that public protest will eventually convince the government to amend the land law.

Conclusion: beyond the image of Taiwanese modernity

Based on our overview of Taiwanese land law and dispute resolution over the last two centuries, a rethinking of orthodox explanations for

[20] These issues are discussed in more depth in Chapter 13.

[21] Jui-Chiao Wu, "A Study on Religious Property Problems in Taiwan: The Case of Temple Illegal Building and Land Issues," unpublished National Science Council Project Reports, No. 96-2415-H-130-004 (2008) (in Chinese); Jui-Chiao Wu, "A Study of Temple Land Use and Illegal Building Issues in Taiwan," *Xuan Zang Fo Xue Yan Jiu*, 16 (2011), 197–221.

land regulation in Taiwan is proposed. Although land regulation in Taiwan has been modernized since the last century, it is still useful to view land disputes as struggles between tradition and modernity.[22] To explain further, we draw two kinds of comparison: one between the Taiwanese and other East Asian societies; and the other between the case studies selected for Chapter 13, which examine ancestor worship.

On the one hand, we have shown that, in the past three decades, legal issues and social criticism have become more internal to the nature of land governance, and land regulation is no longer an instrument for maintaining social order. Externally, however, land law and dispute resolution in Taiwan has followed the principles of the democratic regime and the rule of law. At first glance, it seems that a fully developed legality goes hand-in-hand with economic high growth and gradual political democratization.[23] However, at second glance, this positive image is balanced by two contrasting factors. The first is demonstrated in other East Asian societies, which have different experiences of capitalism and political democracy. The second is demonstrated in the preceding periods, when the frontier, colonial, and wartime governance systems operated in Taiwan. Only in the transition from socialist to post-socialist societies, as occurred in China and Vietnam, and the transition from traditional to colonial to modern governing authorities, such as the Qing to Japanese and the KMT regimes, can we discern that land law and dispute resolution in modern-day Taiwan is not actually modern; in fact, it is still somewhat traditional.

In the following chapter, we use these tentative findings to analyze disputes concerning ancestor worship property in Taiwan. In short, we will attempt to contextualize this case study in the development of Taiwanese land law and dispute resolution, and view it as a struggle between tradition and modernity.

[22] Chi-Jeng Yeh, "Between Globalization and Localization: Toward the Indigenization in Social Research," *Journal of Social Theory*, 4(1) (2001), 41–69 (in Chinese); Chi-Jeng Yeh, *The Struggle Game between Traditions and Moderns* (Taipei: ChuLiu Publisher, 2001) (in Chinese).

[23] Tzong-Shian Yu and Chin-Lih Wang, *The Land Disputes in Taiwan: The Roots of Social Problem* (Taipei: Linking Publishing, 2001) (in Chinese).

13

Customary law and modern society

Land disputes of Jisigongye (祭祀公業, ancestral worship property) in Taiwan

DUAN LIN AND PO-FANG TSAI

> If the mountain won't move, build a road around it. If the road won't turn, change your path.
>
> (Chinese old proverb)

Ancestral worship property in contemporary Taiwan

What we call Jisigongye (祭祀公業, ancestral worship property) is mainly a Han Chinese tradition originating during the Song Dynasty (960–1279).[1] It has a fairly simple nature. Some clan or lineage groups keep pieces of land for ancestral worship. This type of land is treated as inalienable familial property that is inherited by only male descendants. For the family, it is a gathering place to worship their common ancestry. Since the seventeenth century, about 11,994 ancestral worship properties have been established in Han Chinese society in contemporary Taiwan.

In this chapter, we investigate land disputes concerning ancestral worship property. We approach the topic by identifying the epistemic communities that have coalesced around the state and non-state groups that are competing to control ancestral worship property. But first we provide a short introduction to the problems surrounding ancestral worship property and focus on the impact of the Ancestral Worship Property Ordinance 2007.

[1] Yin-chang Chuang, "Some Problems of Clan-Development of Han People in Taiwan: The Patterns of Clan, Temple, and Cultivation," *Bulletin of the Institute of Ethnology Academia Sinica*, 36 (1975), 113–140 (in Chinese); Li-wan Hung, "Historical Studies of Sha-Lu Area: Case Study of Fourteen Ancestor Worship Properties," *Newsletter of Taiwan History Field Research*, 23 (1992), 60–65 (in Chinese); Chen-hua Wen, "A Report of Ancestor Worship Property and Social History in Taiwan: The Example of Dong-shi Area," *Newsletter of Taiwan History Field Research*, 16 (1990), 22–24 (in Chinese).

Then, we discuss our "method and data," before considering the concrete analysis. Next we analyze cases studies and develop a tentative typology of cases. We then examine the strategies of different actors involved in the land disputes and finally present some conclusions.

Legal history of ancestral worship property in Taiwan

Ancestral worship property in Taiwan has undergone several transitions in legal status. Most ancestral worship properties in Taiwan were established under Qing rule (1683–1895).[2] Many Han Chinese families or clans made use of this religious tradition to consolidate their joint responsibility to worship ancestors and raise children, and to face the hard circumstances at that time. Although there was no legal category of landownership in the traditional Chinese legal system,[3] during the colonial period (1895–1945), the Japanese civil law system recognized ancestor worship properties as "customary juridical land." However, when the Chinese Nationalist Government recovered Taiwan in 1945 and started to apply modern Chinese civil law to Taiwan, these lands lost their legal status.[4] Instead, they were treated as "owned-in-common" property (*Gesamthandseigentum* in German civil law). This change in legal status disrupted the function of this old tradition and led to numerous land disputes. According to the case studies, most managers of these properties could only resolve land disputes using non-state customary law.

[2] There are two main types: "lot-allocated" and "contract-charter." Lot-allocated property was created by the ancestors themselves before they died; when they divided their property among their descendants, they set a part aside for use in sacrifices. Such division of property can often be seen in Qing-era land deeds; a part would serve to be used for sacrificing to the ancestors; the remaining property would be divided among the deceased's offspring. Contract-charter property was created by the descendants of a particular ancestor on an individual voluntary basis, with each participant holding a share in the property. Farmland would be bought with the money thus raised, and all income from the land used to sacrifice to the ancestors; only the descendants of those relatives who had originally contributed money would own the assets. See Lin Meirong, "Common Property for Ancestor Worship," *Encyclopedia of Taiwan*, available at: http://taiwanpedia.culture.tw/en/content?ID=1795, accessed May 12, 2011.

[3] As mentioned in Chapter 12 in this book.

[4] Duan Lin, "State Enacted Law and Traditional Custom: A Historical Sociological Analysis of 'Chi-Ssu-Kung-Yeh' (Property-Owning Ancestral Worship Associations) in Taiwan (I)," *Legal History Review*, 1 (2000), 117–151 (in Chinese); Duan Lin, "State Enacted Law and Traditional Custom: A Historical Sociological Analysis of 'Chi-Ssu-Kung-Yeh' (Property-Owning Ancestral Worship Associations) in Taiwan (II)," *Legal History Review*, 2 (2000), 193–216 (in Chinese).

The year 2007 brought a new law – the Ancestral Worship Property Ordinance (祭祀公業條例). Under that law, these properties were again acknowledged as "juridical persons," and Articles 50 and 51 indirectly gave local governments the power to sell unregistered properties. Most managers and descendants of the family clan, as the owners of these properties, refused to follow this law, and they hesitated to register their ancestral worship properties to gain a legal status. In 2011, only sixty of the 11,994 ancestral worship properties had registered their ancestral worship real estate in accordance with the Ordinance. As we shall see, the changes in legal status complicated litigation over ancestral worship properties.

Impact of Ancestral Worship Property Ordinance 2007

In recent years, rapid economic growth in Taiwan has caused land to rise in value. As a result, ancestral worship property appears to have become a problem again from social, legal, and economic perspectives. Unregistered ancestral worship land impeded development by preventing regional governments from implementing new urban planning. Owing to the history of settlement in Taiwan, ancestral worship properties tend to be located in the central regions of the cities and towns. Consequently, the difficulties with their legal status impedes not only transactions involving ancestral worship property, but also the development and renewal of Taiwan's metropolitan areas.

Turning to the legal regime, in the past the government regulated ancestral worship property with two administrative orders, rather than through legislation passed by democratic processes.[5] Stakeholders of the ancestral worship properties and socio-legal scholars have long criticized the lack of legal clarity and legitimacy associated with these administrative orders. Although no legal disputes over ancestral worship properties have risen to the constitutional level, consensus is growing about the

[5] Before the Ancestral Worship Property Ordinance 2007, there were mainly two administrative orders: the Key Points of Land Property Cleaning for Ancestral Worship Property 1982; and the Regulations of Land Property Cleaning for Ancestral Worship Property in Taiwan Province 1998. The former prescribed that the ancestral worship property, whether real estate or movable properties, should be commonly owned by all members of the same ancestral worship property, while the latter prescribed that all the unregistered ancestral worship property should be registered by their managers or descendants in order to tax the real estate or movable properties. For a reflection on these two administrative orders, see *Taiwan Legislative Gazette*, 96, 20(3543), p. 218.

need for legislation on ancestral worship property to replace the Ancestral Worship Property Ordinance 2007.

The taxation of ancestral worship property has generated considerable confusion.[6] On the one hand, the government cannot efficiently tax ancestral worship property because the land often has no clear legal status. On the other hand, it would be unfair to ask managers of ancestral worship property, who are elected from the descendants of family clans, to pay the taxes personally. The government enacted the Ancestral Worship Property Ordinance to rectify these social, legal, and economic problems in one legislative package.

The Ancestral Worship Property Ordinance 2007, however, created new conflicts between central and local governments, on one side, and the managers and the descendants of the ancestral worship property, on the other. The two most controversial issues are: first, whether the Ancestral Worship Property Ordinance relaxed restrictions on the ownership of ancestral worship property (Article 50); and second, the rule allowing the government to sell unregistered ancestral worship property (Article 51).

As far as the advantages of this legislation are concerned, the managers and beneficiaries of ancestral worship property could gain collective legal title on registration. With legal title, the managers and beneficiaries may freely make use of the ancestral worship property according to their internal collective decisions.

In practice, however, collective ownership does not adequately account for the range of practices concerning ancestral worship property. For example, the registration procedures are time-consuming and require a full list of names and the written consent of all the clan descendants. This procedure results in repeated difficulties.

The requirement in Article 51 that land be registered within three years to avoid a government sale has triggered debate over the public interest and private rights. From the point of view of central and local governments, ancestral worship property constitutes a serious barrier to development of public resources, whether it is seen as a method of tax evasion or as impeding urban development. From the point of view of the managers

[6] For example, the same ancestral worship property might be taxed more than once because of its unclear legal status. In practice, government officials often find that there are no taxpayers for ancestral worship property because this land is always "commonly owned." Family clan members might not know each other after the ancestral worship property is established. Even for the property managers and the descendants, there might be uneven tax imposts: some pay all the tax, while others escape this duty.

and beneficiaries, the Ancestral Worship Property Ordinance constitutes an unreasonable and unjust tyranny of the majority. State intervention displaces traditional customs and violates the people's fundamental constitutional rights over property ownership. Despite strident ongoing disputes, by the end of 2011, less than 1 percent of the 11,994 ancestral worship properties had been registered.[7]

The research puzzle: "within a bell jar" or "seeing like a state"?

Concerning the impact of the Ancestral Worship Property Ordinance 2007, two heuristic concepts can be used to describe the relationships between the government, the managers, and the beneficiaries. One is the "bell jar" metaphor, which is used by Hernando de Soto in his *The Mystery of Capitalism* to describe the bounded capitalism mode in Western history. The other is the "seeing like a state" metaphor, which is used by James C. Scott to describe the social engineering of modern Western states.[8] These vivid metaphors provide two distinctive frameworks to re-describe the new mode of interaction between the government and the people – a mode that has been reflected in the legal disputes since the establishment of the Ancestral Worship Property Ordinance 2007.

According to the "bell jar" metaphor, de Soto sees registered property rights as the crucial institutional base of modern capitalism (see Chapter 1). Those within the bell jar enjoy state protection of their registered property rights, while those outside the bell jar must fend for themselves. According to this metaphor, the government has to carry out legal reform in relation to unregistered property, and unify property institutions to break all the "bell jars." In this sense, the key point for de Soto is how to pass efficient legislation, for he believes that to institutionalize property is to transfer an asset into capital.

In contrast, Scott's "seeing like a state" metaphor reflects the contingency hidden in most social reform conducted by modern states (see Chapter 2). To unify and standardize society, policy makers often fail to

[7] Yao, Wen-Chih, "The Current Situation of Ancestral Worship Property: A Short Report," Legislator Yao, Wen-Chih Office, Legislative Yuan ROC, 2011). However, Legislator Wu, Yi-Chen is now in charge of those affairs, such as public hearings or negotiation with managers and descendants.

[8] Hernando de Soto, *The Mystery of Capitalism: Why Capitalism Triumphs in the West and Fails Everywhere Else* (New York: Basic Books, 2000), pp. 61–88, 203–209; James C. Scott, *Seeing Like a State: How Certain Schemes to Improve the Human Condition Have Failed* (New Haven, CT: Yale University Press, 1998), pp. 76–83, 342–357.

deal with the plurality of social practices. Scott reminds us of the risks of legal reform, rather than the possible benefits. In Scott's view, the crucial factor is whether the proposed legal reform seriously considers the diversity of social life. Policy planners should pay more attention to people's practices than to government regulations. The most interesting point that links de Soto to Scott is that their two metaphors form competing arguments with regard to the interaction between state law and customary rule.

Using the "within a bell jar" or "seeing like a state" metaphors, we can see the Ancestral Worship Property Ordinance 2007 as a kind of "legal reform." But has the reform improved conditions for people disputing ancestral worship property? Our research suggests that most managers of ancestral worship property worry that the government will sell their ancestral estate. Thus, our research question can be addressed as follows: does the "legal reform" through the Ancestral Worship Property Ordinance "break the bell jar" or just "see like a state"?

Method and data

In our empirical study of ancestral worship property, we collected research data from three different sources. We will present our case through step-by-step analysis. Since the claims of the disputants do not always match the strategies adopted by the actors, we have different analytical sections for each data set in order to compare and contrast their words and deeds from different angles and multiple sources. Therefore, it is necessary to introduce the multiple sources of the data sets used in our case study.

Our first data set came from the Law and Regulations Retrieving System of the Judicial Yuan of the Republic of China.[9] We searched with the keyword phrase "Ancestral Worship Property Ordinance" for the relevant dispute documents in the written decision database. We found fifty-three cases in administrative courts and 458 cases in civil courts, which range from the district courts to the high courts, and even to the Supreme Court, but not to the Grand Justice Council. This preliminary work revealed that there has not yet been a constitutional interpretation of ancestral worship property. We then classified those

[9] Our data of decisions and judgments came from the website, http://jirs.judicial.gov.tw/index.htm. Those data have not been translated into English, but the relevant laws are available at: http://jirs.judicial.gov.tw/eng.

documents in terms of their dispute contents and selected three representative ancestral worship properties as typical cases. We chose the ancestral worship properties Wang-Wu-Xin, Wu-Da, and Chen-Hwai (hereinafter referred to as the Wang-Wu-Xin property, the Wu-Da property, and the Chen-Hwai property, respectively). We decided to concentrate on the Chen-Hwai property because the Wang-Wu-Xin and Wu-Da cases concerned rent charges and inheritance. The Chen-Hwai cases consisted of fourteen civil cases and one administrative case. We will analyze the respective arguments and draw a tentative typology from the cases involving the Chen-Hwai property.

Our second data set was collected from interviews with the relevant actors in the legal disputes over ancestral worship property. Unlike our previous studies of ancestral worship property,[10] the interviews conducted after the passing of the Ancestral Worship Property Ordinance 2007 reveal the concerns and strategies of both the government actors, such as the civil affairs officers, the municipal land officers, and the judges in the civil or administrative courts, and the non-government actors, such as the managers and the beneficiaries of ancestral worship property.

Combining the interview data with the dispute documents from the courts, we attempt to describe the nature of, and changes in, their strategies regarding state law and customary rule. In particular, we discuss the non-government viewpoints of the property managers and the descendants, as well as government viewpoints shared by the civil affairs officers, the municipal land officers, and the judges in the civil and administrative courts. Understanding these strategies allows us to investigate at close range the interaction of state law and customary rule.

To analyze the data more deeply, we turn to the concepts of "reflexive laws" and "legal hybrids" developed by Gunther Teubner.[11] We will argue that it is necessary to find a way to move beyond the binary conception of the relationship between state law and customary rule. Finally, we use the statements of legislators recorded during legislative debates and field notes from our participant observations in public hearings held by administrative agencies. Although the distinctive positions of non-government and government actors are represented by their different strategies and

[10] Lin, "State Enacted Law and Traditional Custom (I)"; Lin, "State Enacted Law and Traditional Custom (II)."

[11] Gunther Teubner, "Substantive and Reflexive Elements in Modern Law," *Law & Society Review*, 17 (1983), 239–285; Gunther Teubner, "The Parasitic Role of Hybrids," *Journal of Institutional and Theoretical Economics*, 149 (1994), 706–715.

viewpoints, it is possible to create opportunities for them to work together. In our participant observation, the main factor is the emergence of epistemic groups such as the Taiwan Ancestor Worship Property Association (TAWPA) and the Taiwan Ancestor Worship Property Research Association (TAWPRA). We will describe the changes from the official view, based on attaching the Ancestral Worship Property Ordinance to the Cadastral Clean-Up Regulation, to the coordinating view, based on the practical experiences of different actors. We try to argue that neither the binary conception of state law and customary rule, nor the positional conflict[12] between the governments and the people pay sufficient attention to the importance of the epistemic community that is trying to mediate between the opposing two actors. With the emphasis on the professional association as an epistemic community, our case study is able to see the land property disputes in a new way.[13]

Case studies: ancestral worship property Chen-Hwai

We found three leading components in the Chen-Hwai property case, which we will describe in sequence. First, owing to the principle of the autonomy of private law, most officials and judges give priority to internal agreements made since the ancestral worship property was established or transferred with the informed consent of all the beneficiaries. The Chen-Hwai property, for example, had different legal statuses. Since not all written agreements over the last twenty years were signed by all the beneficiaries, some agreements had a different legal status from others. Consequently, the defects in the internal agreements often prevented officials and judges from recognizing the disputants' claims.

Second, most disputants believed that the transfer of registered ancestral worship property guaranteed their claims. The greatest confusion in this type of legal dispute arises from the fact that the disputants often ignore the legal effects of internal agreements on the transfer of ownership. In civil litigation and administrative litigation, it is one thing to have internal agreements about selling or renting the land, but it is another to have the transfer registered. The former is approved by the Municipal or County

[12] As far as this positional conflict is concerned, we are referring to the two viewpoints, government and non-government. In other words, this is an essential conflict between the top-down viewpoint and the bottom-up viewpoint, rather than the different political positions among interest groups and parties.

[13] For a similar analytical approach, see John Gillespie, "Exploring the Limits of Judicial Review in Urban Land Disputes in Vietnam," *Law & Society Review*, 45(2) (2011), 241–275.

Civil Administration, while the latter is approved by the Municipal or County Land Office. Here we find a typical problem: there exist gaps between the private agreements and their legal effect. The government officers suppose that there must be a consensus and register the land creating collective ownership. However, in practice, the private agreements were more complicated than the officers had anticipated.

Third, based on the two components mentioned above, we propose a tentative typology deduced from the legal disputes over the Chen-Hwai property, and attempt to show that such confusion is widespread in legal judgments on land disputes involving ancestral worship property. According to our analysis of the data, the reason why the managers preferred their ancestral worship property to remain unregistered is their distrust and suspicion of the land laws and law-based dispute resolutions.

Internal agreements as trumps?

The original internal agreement of the Chen-Hwai property, made in the early nineteenth century, contained only the name list and norms of membership, but no norms governing transfers among descendants. Three important internal agreements governed the transfer of land rights to some descendants of the Chen-Hwai property. They were the ninth decision of the descendant congress in 1989, the twentieth decision of the descendant congress in 2008, and a mediation settlement statement written in 2010. Facing the impact of the Ancestral Worship Property Ordinance 2007, the disputants appealed to those three internal agreements in their claims in civil and administrative courts. However, the property managers and the descendants received different judgments in their claims. In the following section, we describe two civil cases and one administrative case to discuss the distinctive legal outcomes with an initial typology.

Case I

Descendants A v. *Property Managers M* was dismissed in the civil court.[14] Descendants A claimed their property rights to the lands of the Chen-Hwai property and asked that the lands be transferred to them, based on the ninth decision of the descendant congress in 1989 and the twentieth decision of the descendant congress in 2008. The judges dismissed A's claim in the civil court because a written mediation settlement statement was filed in 2010,

[14] 2010, Chungi-Su-Tze No. 428 Decision, deciding date 10000406, and deciding topic – transfer registration of landownership.

and the descendants had no further rights to raise litigation. In this case, the managers M won and the descendants A lost because the judges gave legal priority to the written mediation settlement statement of 2010, rather than to the two internal agreements of 1989 and 2008. The judgment stated that the legal right *in rem* of real property and transaction security should rest on the written mediation settlement statement, rather than on the private agreements signed internally by the descendant congresses.

Case II

Descendants B v. *Property Managers M* was accepted in the civil court.[15] The descendants B claimed their membership of the Chen-Hwai property, and then asked that the lands be transferred to them, based on the documents that descendants A presented in the previous case. B's claims were not dismissed in the civil court, and the judges ordered the property managers M to transfer the property rights to the descendants B. In this litigation, the managers M lost and the descendants B won because the judges gave legal priority to the membership dispute, rather than to the land dispute. However, the demand in the descendants B's claim also included the transfer of the lands. Although there was a logical and legal order of priority in descendants B's two legal claims – their membership confirmation and the transfer of lands – the judge approved both the claims with the legal emphasis on the ancestral worship property as a membership-based property. The judge dismissed the property managers M's claim that membership created a legal right and postponed subsequent land transfers.

Case III

Descendants C and Property Managers M v. *Civil Affairs Officers and Municipal Land Officers* was dismissed in the administrative court.[16] Descendants C and the property managers M sued for their rights to transfer the land to descendants C when the municipal land officers rejected the application for transfer. The judges dismissed C's and M's claims in the

[15] 2010, Chungi-Su-Tze No. 39 Decision, deciding date 10000530, and deciding topic – confirm the existence of landownership; 2009, Su-Tzu No. 1474 Decision, deciding date 991013, and deciding topic – transfer registration of landownership; 2009, Su-Tze No. 1473 Decision, deciding date 990331, and deciding topic – confirm the existence of membership to the ancestral worship property; 2009, Su-Tze No. 1473 Decision, deciding date 990315, and deciding topic – confirm the existence of membership to the ancestral worship property.

[16] 2010, Su-Tze No. 2529 Decision, deciding date 10000407, and deciding topic – registration of landownership.

administrative court on the ground that descendants C and property managers M were not allowed to take letters of consent from all the descendants, as decided by the 2010 written mediation settlement determination, even though this decision was subsequently upheld by a judge in the civil court. In this case, descendants C and managers M lost, and the municipal land officer won because the judges gave legal priority to the civil and administrative courts, rather than to the internal agreements based on letters of consent from all the descendants and a written mediation statement.

A tentative typology

Having described the three cases, we now attempt to present a tentative typology based on the legal disputes around the Chen-Hwai property.[17] In addition to those three examples of litigation, we have to add another two hypothetical situations, based on our interviews. They suppose that, in similar conditions, the legal outcomes may have an impact on the land dispute over the Chen-Hwai property.[18] In one situation, we suppose that in Case IV, which has conditions similar to those of Case III, descendants D and managers M propose the same claims to transfer the land to descendants D based on their internal agreements in 1989 or 2008, but their claims are rejected by the municipal land officers. They then sue both the civil affairs officers, who are in charge of the membership-confirming process, and the municipal land officers, who are in charge of the land-transferring process. Considering the judgment in Case III, we guess that the claims of descendants D and managers M in Case IV might also be dismissed.

[17] Our tentative typology here is proposed to demonstrate the inconsistency of the legal outcomes in litigation of land disputes over ancestral worship property. However, in our interviews of the managers of the Chen-Hwai property, they still complained that the inconsistency not only happened in the outcome of legal decisions, but also existed in the principles between the civil and administrative courts, in the processing attitudes between the civil affairs officers and municipal land officers, and in the standard of document examination between central and local governmental agencies. Therefore, some managers are inclined to group those inconsistencies of dealing with the juridical and administrative officers with negative factors, such as conspiracy or corruption in government agencies.

[18] Those hypotheticals came from the interviewees and are not based on actual events. Most of the disputants of the Chen-Hwai cases would compare with each other the legal judgments they got, and we draw that thinking, more or less the sources of their discontent, of the legal judgments to construct our typology. In this extended tentative typology, we believe that the actual cases added with the hypothetical ones will enrich our analysis because of the combination of the factual and counter-factual situations.

Table 13.1 *Tentative typology of five cases*

	Case I	Case II	Case III	Case IV	Case V
Claim grounds	Internal agreements	Internal agreements	Letters of consent or written mediation settlement statement	Internal agreements	Ancestral Worship property Ordinance
Judgment	Dismissed	Approved	Dismissed	May be dismissed	Unknown
Legal authority	Civil court	Civil court	Administrative court	Administrative court	Unknown

For the other hypothetical situation, we propose Case V, which has totally different conditions. Unlike Cases I–III, in Case V, descendants D and managers M decide to comply with the Ancestral Worship Property Ordinance 2007, and attempt to register as an "ancestral worship juridical person" or a "business juridical person." However, lacking the proper documents, they fail in the procedure and then sue for compensation for the sale of their lands by the local government. Gathering together all five cases, we propose a tentative typology in terms of their grounds for a claim, final judgment, and legal authority in Table 13.1.

This tentative typology shows the inconsistency in the legal outcomes of the land disputes around the Chen-Hwai property. However, according to our interviews with some Chen-Hwai property managers, underneath their frustration with the legal inconsistencies, they were concerned by the unexpected time and costs incurred during litigation. The managers would rather handle the property through informal or illegal ways, despite the risk that those transactions could be discovered by other descendants and delayed by the government. Moreover, inconsistencies in the litigation, decisions, and outcomes show the disparity of power between the government and the people. Most of the Chen-Hwai managers believed that the judges and officers were not as familiar with the affairs of ancestral worship property as themselves. This lack of understanding of ancestral worship property as traditional land usage damages the reliability of the judicial and administrative agencies.

It is clear from both the legal documents and in-depth interviews that the Chen-Hwai managers obviously distrusted and were suspicious of law-based processes. This distrust explains why the managers might prefer to keep their ancestral worship property unregistered to preserve the consensus between the descendants and the managers. In other words, for the managers, it is easier to negotiate with the other descendants than to deal with the judges and officials.

The strategies of different actors

In addition to the analysis of the cases discussed above and the typology, we investigate further the strategies of four different actors, which are represented with a simple mapping below (Figure 13.1). Before the Ancestral Worship Property Ordinance 2007, there were seldom conflicts between non-government and government actors, but after 2007 conflicts over land rights increased. Both sets of actors chose strategies for dealing with ancestral estates that promoted conflicts, but also revealed implicit contradictions within themselves. Judges and officers in the government hold different positions, and the managers and the descendants have different views. In the following discussion, we list the strategies of distinct actors, present the different conceptions of ancestral worship property in their cognitive frameworks, and explain the changes in these conceptions caused by the impact of the Ancestral Worship Property Ordinance 2007.

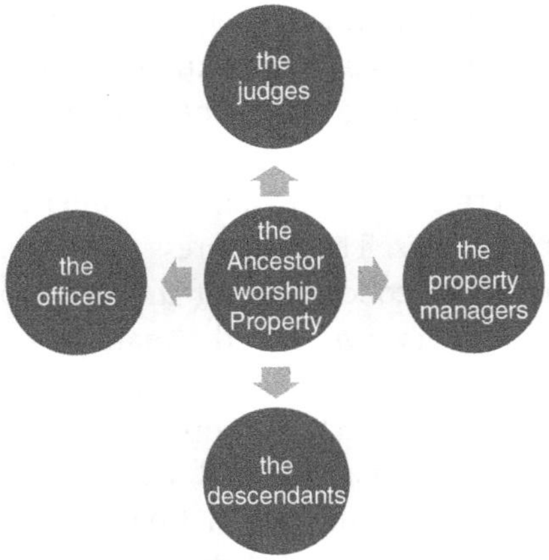

Figure 13.1 Strategies of four actors

The non-governmental viewpoints: property managers and the descendants

Among the non-government actors, the managers were the most active, but they were often sued by other descendants in civil suits. In civil courts, judges tended to make decisions according to the private legal relations between the two parties. In contrast, judges in administrative courts often based decisions on public legal issues rather than on private legal relations. Faced with these different approaches, the managers and the descendants litigated using the following strategies.

In "Strategy I," the non-government actors provided some private legal documents to avoid a review of the transfer of the land by administrative officials. In this way, the non-government actors often tried to appeal to the decision of the descendant congress or written mediation settlements to support the transfer of the property rights. We can find this type of appeal in Case III discussed above.

In "Strategy II," the actor's decision to litigate in civil or administrative courts made an obvious difference to the willingness of the other parties to compromise, the approach taken by the judges, and the burden of proof. Comparing Case II (not dismissed) with Case III (dismissed), we can see that these strategic considerations arose before litigation as kinds of non-legal strategy. Hence, choosing to start a civil or administrative litigation is an important strategic consideration.

There was also "Strategy III," in which the actors appealed to the principle of equality. With Strategy III, the managers and the descendants asked for equal treatment from the administrative officials, and even for the same decision by the civil and administrative courts. We can find evidence of Strategy III in the claims of the managers and the descendants in Case III discussed above. Although the managers and the descendants often cooperate in litigation against the government, the impact of the Ancestral Worship Property Ordinance 2007, especially the deadline on selling the lands by the local government, has irritated the internal conflicts between different descendant factions. The legal pressures have, at the same time, slightly changed the actors' conceptions of ancestral worship property.

As revealed by the interviews with the managers of the Chen-Hwai property, internal disagreements arose about how to deal with the impact of the Ancestral Worship Property Ordinance 2007. Some descendants, insisting that this law had violated their basic property rights, wanted to pursue constitutional litigation. Other descendants were inclined to conform with the Ordinance and register themselves as a collective legal owner, and still other descendants, holding the most passive position, proposed forging a land transaction to bypass the new law. This diversity of positions made it more difficult for the managers to follow a coherent and public agenda in order to handle the reactions of the members of the ancestral worship property and the impact of the Ancestral Worship Property Ordinance 2007.

Moreover, the gradually increasing conflicts between the members fostered different interpretations of the meaning of ancestral worship property. For example, although some descendants retained the traditional understanding, which emphasized the ritual of gathering together and remembering the founding ancestors, other descendants radically chose to honor their ancestors by increasing the value of the ancestral worship property or by participating in social welfare affairs in the name of their ancestors. Thus, in our previous study, we found that most managers had extinguished their ancestral worship property through philanthropy.[19] More and more managers were willing to share some of the benefits from the ancestral worship property with people living in the neighborhood or with socially vulnerable groups having the same family name. Those new management styles are still used to increase the social influence and cultural legitimacy of ancestral worship property in order to counteract the government's forceful regulation.

The government viewpoints: civil affairs officers, municipal land officers, and judges in the civil or administrative courts

Among the government actors, there are two different categories: government officials and judges. The civil affairs officials and the municipal land officials are the government actors with whom the managers and the beneficiaries most often interacted, while the judges in the civil or administrative courts investigate facts and make decisions in the courtroom. Although these two kinds of state actor were connected to land disputes, each of them had their own standpoints concerning the Ancestral Worship Property Ordinance 2007. The civil affairs officials and the municipal land officials would rather accelerate the state management of the ancestral estates. The judges in the civil and administrative courts, however, insisted on judicial neutrality in the land disputes. Drawing on these different viewpoints, these state actors adopted different strategies.

[19] Lin, "State Enacted Law and Traditional Custom (I)"; Lin, "State Enacted Law and Traditional Custom (II)."

As a first strategy, or "Strategy I," the state actors followed formality, neutrality, and accountability in order to avoid becoming overly engaged in the property disputes. This passive and conservative approach might be accepted or re-confirmed by other state actors. For example, a judge in the administrative court might uphold the actions of a municipal land officer again and again. Under this hidden consensus, state actors seemed to decide separately, but in practice acted collectively.

As a second strategy, "Strategy II," the state actors appealed to the substantive reasons behind state policy and law, such as the Ancestral Worship Property Ordinance 2007. In most ancestral estate disputes, the officials referred more frequently than judges to social equality or to the need to clear unregistered lands for urban development. The government actors always justified themselves by claiming to work for the public good.

As a third strategy, or "Strategy III," the state actors maintained their separate decision-making processes, but formally reviewed each other's actions. For instance, in Case III, the municipal land officials allowed the mediation settlement to displace the letters of consent signed by the beneficiaries. Generally speaking, state actors pursued their own professional positions and did not need to consider other approaches. In the eyes of non-state actors, there was some internal coherence or tacit knowledge (or even conspiracy) among the state actors.

The Ancestral Worship Property Ordinance 2007 caused internal conflicts between the state actors. The sharpest conflict arose in the enforcement of registration within the three-year deadline. For the civil affairs and municipal land officials, those on the frontline, it was extremely difficult to push the managers and beneficiaries to prepare the required documents, while the judges in civil or administrative courts needed only to review the legality of those procedures. This resulted in a clear discrepancy between the proactive attitudes of officials and the passive attitudes of judges. This discrepancy led to two different narratives to justify the treatment of ancestral worship property. One emphasized legal formality and valued neutrality from the judges, while the other focused on fairness and efficiency in the political and economic considerations for the people. These two narratives slightly weakened the consistency of the government's policy on ancestral worship property and, at the same time, divided state approaches to traditional land usage. In government agencies, some people began to sympathize with the managers and descendants, and others remained indifferent to their troubles.

Interaction of state law and customary rule

From the cases and the strategies discussed above, we find that the mode of interaction between state law and customary law has obviously changed since the establishment of the Ancestral Worship Property Ordinance 2007. Those changes, which are discussed below, call the metaphors of de Soto and Scott into question.

First, among all the ancestral worship affairs, land disputes have become the most urgent issue discussed by the descendants. Both non-government actors and government actors are concerned with property rights, rather than with consensus or dissent among the beneficiaries and the managers of the ancestral worship property. In this change, we see again the discrepancy caused by the double nature of ancestral worship property: it is both inalienable familial real estate and a gathering place for all the beneficiaries. In our observation, the change in perception from a gathering place to shared real estate profoundly altered the meaning of ancestral worship property.

Second, the majority view shifted. Justice for the whole of society became more important than justice for the ancestral worship property. Some decades ago, the administrative officials and courts considered prioritizing the common norms of ancestral worship properties and customary law derived from familiar traditions. Once the priority changed to land disputes, state actors kept the private customary rights away from public rights relations. This meant that public justice should override private justice.

Third, the gap between the two viewpoints of the state actors and the non-state actors set in place the potential for conflict. The state actors seemed to act in a more coherent way than the non-state actors, while at the same time, disputes between the managers and the beneficiaries fragmented the non-state standpoint. Accordingly, the diversity in the non-government viewpoints was eventually labeled as unofficial, even non-professional or vulgar, and as "arbitrary" opinion. Even before the enforcement of state law, the non-state actors had seemingly been defeated in terms of cultural legitimacy and rational coherence. Based on the findings in our analysis and the three issues discussed above, we evaluate the inappropriateness of the metaphors borrowed from de Soto and Scott. All the complicated claims in legal disputes and the various strategies of different actors force us to realize that there is no simple schema to conceptualize the interaction of state law and customary rule, whether it is a top-down or bottom-up model. Although the burden from traditional land usage, such as ancestral worship, could be viewed as an object of legal reform meriting government enforcement, the "break the bell jar" and "see like a state" metaphors only scratch the surface of the impact of the Ancestral Worship Property Ordinance 2007. The crucial reasons are that various claims, strategies, and narratives are carried out by different actors, and consequently the coalitions and conflicts between them are dependent on, and correlated with, those unstable interpretations.

On the one hand, the "bell jar" metaphor really describes unregistered ancestral worship property as compromised real estate, but the managers and beneficiaries can still make use of that property and detour around the government's policy. Therefore, we may need to develop a better description to capture the land transactions under the Ancestral Worship Property Ordinance 2007. On the other hand, although the "see like a state" metaphor is helpful in explaining the ideal projects of the government, the policy may fail not only because of departmentalism between different branches of the government, but also because of personal empathy toward the managers and beneficiaries.[20]

Communicative hybridization and epistemic communities

Examining the strategies and interpretations used by the different actors to interpret the Ancestral Worship Property Ordinance 2007 has deepened our heuristic and practical understanding of land disputes. We find that new concepts from systems theory can be used to describe the contemporary legal pluralism and the accompanying complexity existing in their justification and communication. As far as conceptual tools are concerned, we are inclined to borrow from Teubner, a leading systems theorist and legal sociologist.[21] Moreover, from our observation of the public hearings, we also find an emerging kind of community, gathering the experiences of the state and non-state actors, which may go beyond binary opposition. Interestingly, there may not be proper resolution of the land disputes at present, but we cannot underestimate the potential for communicative hybridization.

[20] We agree with Scott's critique of "seeing like a state" that the state is not the only regulator and it may ignore the mutualism between state and non-state regulatory systems. However, we believe that it needs to describe our case study with a research framework rather than heuristic metaphors, in order to go beyond this kind of criticism and develop a constructive and productive way.

[21] Teubner, "The Parasitic Role of Hybrids"; Teubner, "Substantive and Reflexive Elements in Modern Law."

Teubner's new concepts: reflexive laws and legal hybrids

On the basis of the findings and discussion above, we have found that neither the "bell jar" nor the "seeing like a state" metaphor can properly describe the interaction between, and the distinct viewpoints of, the state and the people, which are hidden under the legal reform of the Ancestral Worship Property Ordinance 2007. However, two new concepts from Teubner provide a solution to the puzzle. Teubner's "reflexive laws" and the "legal hybrids" were constructed to overcome the dichotomy of "substantive/formal rationality" or "state law/legal pluralism."[22] In the following discussion, we first introduce the two concepts and then use them to explain our participant observation in the public hearings.

According to Teubner, the heuristic concepts of "reflexive laws" and "legal hybrids" are interconnected and can resolve the conceptual dilemma. First, Teubner identifies an emerging kind of legal structure, which he calls "reflexive laws," as a more comprehensive mode of socio-legal co-variation.[23] This new concept, Teubner claims, not only captures the changing map of some legal issues in private laws (family, neighborhood, school), but also prevents scholars from becoming trapped in the "re-materialization of law" theme. In this sense, we can find the interaction of social change and legal structure in a reflexive law, and also a feedback effect of a specific social issue on its reflexive legal norm.

Second, Teubner sees the breakdown of the borderline between hierarchies and markets as a new mode, which he calls "legal hybrids" or "hybrid laws." Although Teubner's writing was not specifically about land disputes, his concept of "legal hybrids" might be helpful for us to re-describe our case study. Given that the network is a third type of private coordination, alongside contract and association, Teubner defines hybrids as not simply mixtures of networks, but as social arrangements in their own right. When we attempt to go beyond the binary of state law and customary rule, there exists a productive way of viewing the land disputants as different actors competing with each other through their legal and non-legal strategies.

22 Gunther Teubner, "Global Bukowina: Legal Pluralism in the World-Society," in Gunther Teubner (ed.), *Global Law Without A State* (London: Dartmouth, 1996); Gunther Teubner, "The Two Faces of Janus: Rethinking Legal Pluralism," *Cardozo Law Review*, 13 (1992), 1443–1462.

23 Gunther Teubner, "Legal Irritants: Good Faith in British Law or How Unifying Law End Up in New Divergences," *Modern Law Review*, 61(1) (1998), 11–32. See also Julia Black, "Regulatory Conversations," *Journal of Law and Society*, 29(1) (2002), 163–196.

Teubner also discussed the extension of constitutional rights into the context of private governance regimes. In our case study, we find that there is a trend of appealing to constitutional rights.[24] With the new concept of legal hybrids, researchers may properly investigate land disputes without referring to the distinction of "public law versus private law." In summary, as the legal structure in contemporary society can be identified as reflexive law, some kinds of land dispute are represented by legal hybrids. With Teubner's new concepts, we are able to re-describe the legislative process of the Ancestral Worship Property Ordinance 2007 and the land disputes over the land property rights of ancestral worship properties.

Emerging epistemic communities

Although Teubner's new concepts are helpful in understanding the legislative process of the Ancestral Worship Property Ordinance 2007, in practice, some actors facilitate hybridization. In our participant observation of the public hearings, we found that mediation is growing in order to develop workable resolutions. Interestingly, some managers and beneficiaries, who were involved in the land disputes for many years, decided to connect with each other and exchange information about litigation. The emerging groups of managers and beneficiaries attracted attention. As far as their social backgrounds are concerned, some of them are professionals, such as land management clerks, land lawyers, or senior or retired land officers. Others may be amateurs, such as freelancers, journalists, or NGO managers. The common characteristic is that they are disheartened and disappointed by the exhausting legal process.

An important group was connected to the TAWPA and the TAWPRA.[25] Representing TAWPA or TAWPRA, they create narratives to shift the balance of land policy from the public interest to private rights. For example, they independently research the diversity of land disputes over ancestral

[24] Gunther Teubner, "In the Blind Spot: The Hybridization of Contract," *Theoretical Inquiries in Law*, 7 (2006), 5–71; Gunther Teubner, "Hybrid Laws: Constitutionalizing Private Governance Networks," in R. Kagan and K. Winston (eds.), *Legality and Community: On the Intellectual Legacy of Philip Selznick* (Berkeley, CA: Berkeley Public Policy Press, 2002).

[25] However, some managers in our interview complained that some people still care about the huge sums of money involved in land disputes over ancestral worship property. Even the TAWPA and TAWPRA cannot displace those members who care more about earning a commission than finding a proper resolution.

worship properties and develop a working typology to persuade the central and local governments and the managers and descendants. In our interviews, we consider their effort to mix the different narratives from distinctive actors as an attempt to create a new epistemic community.

Currently, epistemic communities, consisting of both managers, beneficiaries, and other people (who might have no rights with regard to the ancestral worship properties), have resolved land disputes without following the legal framework. The first proposal for resolving these disputes was presented at public hearings by senior lawyers with extensive experience with ancestral worship property.[26] The senior lawyers wanted to pursue constitutional litigation so that land officials and judges could refer to the highest legal authority when dealing with land disputes. To proceed, this proposal requires an actual case in which ancestral worship property is sold by the local government after the expiration of the three-year period. We could not find any cases where local governments have enforced Article 52 of the Ordinance and sold unregistered land of ancestral worship property. Therefore, people proposing constitutional litigation will have to wait for a concrete case.

The second proposal, advocated by TAWPA and TAWPRA, demands that the land dispute be handled in accordance with the Land Act 2001, in particular, the "Committee on Property Dispute Conciliation" in Article 34(2) of the Land Act 2001.[27] People proposing this approach think that there is an analogy between the conciliation of real estate disputes and the resolution of ancestral worship property. In their opinion, land disputes over ancestral worship properties should be viewed in the same way as disputes over ordinary real estate, so that the results from the Committee on Property Dispute Conciliation can provide a new legal source for resolving disputants under Article 34(2) of the Land Act 2001.

[26] According to the managers' and descendants' complaints about the Ancestral Worship Property Ordinance 2007, the first public hearing was held by the government in November 2011. The participants included the managers and descendants, civil affairs and municipal land officers, and some professional associations, such as TAWPA and TAWPRA. During this meeting, some proposals came out first.

[27] See the Land Act 1930 (amended 2001) in Taiwan, Art. 34(2): "In order to settle property disputes, the Committee on Property Dispute Conciliation shall be set up by the Municipal or County Land Office. The Committee shall employ members with land administration, construction, and legal backgrounds together with local distinguished persons. Rules governing the organization of the Committee on Property Dispute Conciliation, the conditions for the application for conciliation, the procedure, the time limit, conciliation fees and other matters to follow shall be formulated by the Central Land Office."

The third proposal, presented at public hearings by a freelance journalist and some members of TAWPRA, asked the administrative branch to establish an independent committee on ancestral worship property affairs under the Ministry of the Interior. In their opinion, land disputes are best resolved by independent agencies with legal authority. Such a body could also improve knowledge about ancestral worship property for land officials and judges. After two public hearings, these proposals still remain unofficial suggestions and have not attracted much interest from the state. Nevertheless, some professional associations, such as TAWPA and TAWPRA, continue to lobby for change.

Seeing land disputes in a new way

To explain the legal disputes over ancestral worship property with Teubner's "reflexive laws and legal hybrids," we reframe our research puzzle as follows: to what extent can one view the Ancestral Worship Property Ordinance 2007 as a kind of reflexive law?, and to what extent can one conceive of the land disputes after the enactment of the Ancestral Worship Property Ordinance 2007 as legal hybrids? An exploratory answer for these questions is provided below.

Regarding the first question, we find some clues in the legislative process and the public hearings on the Ancestral Worship Property Ordinance 2007. There is a clear departure from formal legal rationality. This departure does not signal a return to substantive rationality, but expresses the features of reflexive law in problematic contexts, legislative concerns, and the reasons for amending the law.

First, it was in the problematic contexts of the cadastre that the government began to consider legislation to govern ancestral worship property. For many years, the government refrained from enacting a law governing ancestral worship property, relying instead on administrative orders. The Ancestral Worship Ordinance 2007 arose from urgent cadastral problems. However, the disputes over unregistered property rights still differed between general cadastre and ancestral worship property.

Second, the description of ancestral worship property in legislation reflects traditional custom, which insists that ancestral worship property should be inherited only by clan descendants. For example, Article 50 of the Ancestral Worship Property Ordinance 2007 prescribes that property rights can be owned by three different kinds of owner: ancestral-worship-juridical-person, cultural foundation based on ancestral worship property, and joint-ownership descendant groups. Article 50 suggests not only that state intervention has allowed for traditional custom, but also that regulation by administrative order had to be replaced with statutory regulation. The enactment of the Ancestral Worship Property Ordinance 2007 was supposed to resolve the problems of legal uncertainty caused by administrative regulation.

Third, among the reasons for amending the law, disputants drew analogies with other kinds of organizational principles, such as the rules governing political parties, corporations, and associations. These proposals were brought forward in a meeting held by the Executive Yuan on unsolved problems following the enactment of the Ancestral Worship Property Ordinance 2007. The proposals included the introduction of constitutional rights into ancestral worship property disputes, the application of general mediation for property rights, and the possibility of forming a commission on ancestral worship property under the Executive Yuan. These suggestions might be integrated into the Ancestral Worship Property Ordinance 2007 through further amendments.

Considering the problematic contexts, legislative concerns, and the reasons for amending the law, the Ancestral Worship Property Ordinance 2007 seems to have some features of reflexive law. Instead of seeing it as de Soto's "legal reform of titling" or as Scott's "legal reform by simplicity," we can characterize the reflexive nature of the Ancestral Worship Property Ordinance 2007 with Teubner's "reflexive law."

Regarding the second question, the extent to which one can conceive of the land disputes after the Ancestral Worship Property Ordinance 2007 as legal hybrids, we find three pertinent issues: legal disputes that confine social solidarity, competing claims, and different types of governance regime.

First, the managers of ancestral worship properties often appealed to their self-governing communities and argued against the government's claim during disputes. In contrast, the judges and officials cared about the security of land dealings, especially for third parties acting in good faith. We identified two definitions of justice circulating in group narratives. One sought justice for private legal affairs and for the ancestral worship community, while the other sought justice for the general citizenry and for the people who might buy the lands involved in legal disputes. Thus, we have observed that the different groups want local justice or universal justice.

Second, disputants justified some competing claims by referring to concepts of justice. For the property managers and the beneficiaries of ancestral worship property, legal disputes over their land property rights involved familiar or common affairs. They argued that the government should not intervene in private juristic disputes. However, from the official viewpoint, ancestral worship properties are of such value that they warrant government monitoring. This transformed private disputes into public disputes.

Third, legal disputes were linked to different governance regimes, and the disputants fought for their rights at different legal levels. On the one hand, the government dealt with disputes in private or public governance regimes. On the other hand, the disputants tried to determine their legitimate rights from private and public, even constitutional, law. The changes in governance regimes have generated new legal norms that interact with the Ancestral Worship Property Ordinance 2007.

What this suggests is that land disputes over ancestral estates are giving rise to legal hybrids. Instead of seeing land disputes as de Soto's "outside the bell jar" or as Scott's "plurality of social practices," we can characterize the interaction between the state and the people as one of Teubner's "legal hybrids."

Conclusion

After decades of isolation, the Ancestral Worship Property Ordinance 2007 brought state and customary regulation of ancestral worship property together. It not only changed the modes of interaction between government and non-government actors and their interpretations of ancestral worship property, but also it led to the emergence of new epistemic communities that opposed the Ordinance. When we reflect on our case studies about ancestral worship property, there are at least three issues to discuss in order to link our findings to the broader context of socialist Asia, such as China and Vietnam, and capitalist Asia, such as Hong Kong.

First, there are no simple and direct correlations between economic growth and legal modernization. We cannot expect a robust legal framework and property dispute resolution to follow after economic liberalization and political democratization, for land disputes are always rooted in human reciprocity and social communities. In recent years, the Taiwanese have witnessed many legal disputes over land expropriations, but disputes over the Ancestral Worship Property Ordinance 2007 receive little attention in the media. Substantive justice in land disputes will not come from economic development. Rather, it needs to be brought about by public communication, and even social struggles between social groups, in both socialist and capitalist Asia.

Second, the difference between socialist and capitalist regimes may be expressed in legal subjecthood for social collectives, such as family groups or clan group, rather than in attitudes toward traditional land usage. Under the socialist regime, the legal concept of collective ownership is well accepted, but the situation is different in the capitalist regime. The ideology of progress appears in the transitions of both socialist and capitalist societies, either from an authoritarian to a democratic regime or from a socialist to a post-socialist regime. From our case study of ancestral worship property, hostility toward traditional land usage arises not only because this practice is considered inefficient, but also from envy of the wealth left by ancestors. Therefore, the contestation and resolution of land disputes must be related to discursive or epistemic factors rather than to institutional backgrounds. Whether a socialist or capitalist regime is the setting of a land dispute, the narratives constructed by different actors have to answer the questions of historical justice with their own reasoning.

Finally, the potential resolution may depend on communities rather than on the individual, especially on the epistemic communities we have discussed above. Where socialist regimes are expected to have more serious governing rules for social groups, our study of the Ancestral Worship Property Ordinance 2007 has shown that the opposing positions of the government and non-government actors always had unproductive effects. One way of breaking the impasse is to develop new epistemic communities that propose novel solutions to resolve disputes. Searching for alternatives and taking alternative actions may not resolve legal disputes immediately, but such actions grant the actors flexibility to communicate with others in pursuit of possible resolutions in the future. The emerging epistemic communities are good examples for those who are also searching for resolutions beyond the limits of the law.

PART V

Hong Kong case studies

14

An overview of Hong Kong land law and dispute resolution

SAY H. GOO

Early days of the colony

Hong Kong consists of three parts: Hong Kong Island; the Kowloon Peninsula south of Boundary Street; and the New Territories.[1] Before Hong Kong formally became a colony, British settlers took possession of unoccupied land on Hong Kong Island, while others purported to buy land from existing Chinese occupiers.

When Hong Kong Island was ceded to the British in January 1841 by the unratified Convention of Chuenpi, it was a barren rock with few inhabitants (about 5,000), mostly in the fishing villages of Aberdeen, Shaukiwan, and Stanley. Under the apparent authority of the Convention, the Royal Navy landed on Hong Kong Island on January 26, 1841, and Captain Charles Eliot began granting land. Whatever land rights the Chinese inhabitants possessed under Qing law were not recognized, and were wiped out by the colonial power and replaced by new leases under British law. There appeared to be little or no resistance from the local population. Charles Eliot decided to auction leasehold interests in suitable land to British settlers with the assurance that, subject to the approval of the British Government, buyers of such leasehold interests could apply later to convert them into freehold estates. On June 12, 1841, the first auction took place where marine, town, suburban, and country lots were sold to the highest bidder for payment of an annual rent. Later, direct leasehold grants were made by private treaty without auctions. While these sales allowed land to be granted to settlers in a reasonably orderly manner, they did not earn the pleasure of the British Government. Immediately after the Treaty of Nanking, signed on August 29, 1842 and ratified on June 26, 1843, which

[1] This part draws heavily on Gordon N. Cruden, *Land Compensation and Valuation Law in Hong Kong*, 3rd edn. (Hong Kong: Butterworths Asia, 2009).

formally ceded the island, the British Government instructed the new governor that no freehold estates were to be granted, and that land was not to be granted for any greater period of time than was necessary to induce tenants to erect substantial buildings. Leases for building land were to be for seventy-five years, other land for twenty-one years, and renewals were to be at the discretion of the governor.[2]

When the Kowloon Peninsula was added to the colony in 1860 by the Convention of Peking, there were very few inhabitants. Those who had land rights under Qing law were either compensated for their rights that were wiped out or granted 999-year leases instead. A Land Commission was set up to determine the compensation payable and to consider applications for crown leases from Chinese owners who were allowed to remain in possession. The compensation claims were settled in 1864, and Chinese owners remaining in possession were granted new leases for 999 years at the same rent as that payable to the Qing Government. Similar to the policy for land grants in Hong Kong Island, new leases to other persons were to be of sufficient length to induce erection of substantial buildings.[3] In 1898, the British Government instructed the governor not to grant 999-year leases, but grant seventy-five-year leases only. This resulted in major protests, and the policy was quickly modified to allow a right of renewal for a further seventy-five years.[4]

The New Territories, except the Walled City just north of Boundary Street between Kowloon and the New Territories, were added to the colony under a ninety-nine-year lease from the Qing Government in 1898 under the Convention of Peking. There were about 700 villages and 102,254 inhabitants in the newly added territories at the time. These inhabitants had been farming there for generations and relied on rural agricultural land for their livelihood.[5] Lands were owned mostly in common tenure.[6] They were held in perpetuity from the Qing emperor subject to payment of land tax and performance of labor services, and

[2] G. B. Endacott, *A History of Hong Kong*, 2nd edn. (Hong Kong: Oxford University Press, 1995), pp. 28, 29, 44, 83; J. W. Norton Kyshe, *The History of the Laws and Courts of Hong Kong* (Hong Kong: Vetch, 1898), vol. I, pp. 7–9, 13, 14, 71, 72, 178, 268, 280, 438, vol. II, pp. 65, 246, 390, 456, 543, 544.

[3] Endacott, *A History of Hong Kong*, pp. 110, 111.

[4] Kyshe, *A History of the Laws and Courts of Hong Kong*, vol. II, pp. 543, 544.

[5] James Hayes, *The Hong Kong Region 1850–1911: Institutions and Leadership in Town and Countryside* (Hong Kong University Press, 2012), p. 33.

[6] *Winfat Enterprises (HK) Co. Ltd.* v. *AG* [1983] HKLR 211, *per* Kempster J. See also D. M. Emrys Evans, “Aliens on British Soil: A Problem of Landholding in Early Hong Kong,” *Hong Kong Law Journal*, 8 (1978), 205.

could be acquired in three ways: by inheritance, by purchase, and by the cultivation of unoccupied or wasteland. They were freely alienable in general, and there appeared to have been no limitations on the use of such land; the character of tenure and the tax payable on such land did not change after the erection of buildings on it.[7]

Recognizing customary land practices

There were rumors after the British took over the New Territories that they would seize all privately owned land, causing many Chinese owners to sell their land to Chinese speculators at far below market value. Resistance to British occupation erupted among villagers in October 1898 and early 1899, but British troops put down the rebellion, arrested resistance leaders, confiscated weapons, and destroyed village gates.[8] The resistance arose due to concerns that the British colonial regime would threaten the power villagers had enjoyed for several centuries. Villagers were concerned about new taxes and land confiscation, as well as disruption to traditional customs and *feng shui* (the harmonious positioning of buildings and objects).[9] The governor toured the New Territories to reassure landowners that their land would not be confiscated and that existing ownership would be fully recognized.

Most resistance subsided when Governor Henry Blake adopted a policy of not interfering in local life and relying on village elders to govern whenever possible.[10] As a result, Chinese custom and customary law were recognized from 1905. For example, the custom of building a small house for sons, and the owning of ancestral land for the purpose of ancestral worship (the Tsos and Tongs) were recognized. This is discussed in Chapter 15.

The governor set up a Land Court for the New Territories to deal with disputed land claims. Surveyors were brought in from India to survey occupied land, and to record the names of the occupiers and the purpose for which their land was being used. This formalization of land proved to be difficult because there were competing claims to landownership, and many long-established informal arrangements concerning land, as well as unregistered interests in the land and land tax irregularities.

[7] *Ibid.*

[8] John Mark Carroll, *A Concise History of Hong Kong* (Lanham, MD: Rowman & Littlefield, 2007), p. 69.

[9] *Ibid.* [10] *Ibid.*, p. 70.

After an inquiry, the Land Court granted new block crown leases to those entitled for ninety-nine years less three days, expiring on June 27, 1997. More than 354,000 lots within block leases were granted, with the remaining large areas of unclaimed New Territories left unalienated.[11]

Over the past forty years, as a result of rapid development in the New Territories, many problems related to the block leases have arisen. Of most relevance to this study is that inaccuracies with the original survey have been exposed. Some initial errors remain uncorrected as there has never been a complete re-survey of the New Territories in relation to boundaries. Compounding the problem, for many years transacting parties handled land transfer without proper legal advice or assistance. Prior to 1982, land transactions in the New Territories were registered at district offices, not at land offices, with the result that they were not brought under the common system of land registration applied to land elsewhere in Hong Kong. In 1982, eight new land offices were opened in the New Territories to take over from district offices.

In February 2005, the Central Registration System was introduced to allow deeds affecting property anywhere in Hong Kong to be registered in the Land Registry's Central office at Queensway Government Offices. But loss of title documents and other public records during the Second World War, compounded by decentralized land offices in the New Territories, remains an issue.[12]

Thus, in the early days of Hong Kong's colonial history, the colonial power resumed land titles, but paid compensation or replaced land-ownership with long-term leases. This had the effect of converting land rights, and hence the resolution of any disputes concerning them, from Qing law to English law.

Fiscalization of land

Land tenure was in constant dispute until at least 1848, with complaints that freehold land would not be granted and that seventy-five-year leases were too short.[13] To meet these criticisms, the governor extended the seventy-five-year leases to leases of 999 years. Another change was to

[11] Peter Wesley-Smith, *Unequal Treaty 1898–1997: China, Great Britain, and Hong Kong's New Territories* (New York: Oxford University Press, 1998), pp. 92–100.

[12] See, for example, *Niceboard Development Ltd.* v. *China Light & Power Co. Ltd.* [1994] HKDCLR 69; [1995] HKDCLR 27.

[13] This part draws heavily on Cruden, *Land Compensation and Valuation Law in Hong Kong*, pp. 6–12.

replace the practice of fixing rents at auction with granting leases at a nominal ground rent subject to the payment of premiums. This practice became an established feature of land tenure and a substantial source of revenue for the Hong Kong Government.

In 1898, the grant of 999-year leases was halted by the Colonial Secretary in London, who instructed the governor henceforth to grant new leases for seventy-five years only or, in some cases, up to a maximum of ninety-nine years. It was thought that 999-year leases were practically equivalent to a freehold tenure, deprived the government of control over land, and diminished future government revenue streams. This policy attracted considerable criticism, but the governor held firm.[14]

When the original term of a large number of these leases began to expire in 1972, the premium payment had increased sharply. To resolve this problem, the Crown Leases Ordinance (Cap. 40) was enacted in 1973 to allow leases to be renewed at a new government rent based on 3 percent of the rateable value.

With the return of sovereignty over Hong Kong to China fast approaching, the uncertainty relating to leases in the New Territories expiring three days before the handover and leases elsewhere extending over June 1997 was resolved by the Joint Declaration between the People's Republic of China (PRC) and Great Britain. This agreement provided that all leases, including rights of renewal extending beyond 1997, were allowed to continue. All leases in the New Territories that expired before June 30, 1997 were extended for a further fifty years until June 30, 2047, and leases in Hong Kong and Kowloon that expired before June 30, 1997 without an option to renew could be renewed by the crown at an annual rent equivalent to 3 percent of the rateable value without additional premium. Since the handover, the practice is for the Hong Kong Special Administrative Region (HKSAR) Government to grant leases for fifty years from the date of the grant.

Changing nature of land disputes

Since the Second World War and the founding of the PRC in 1949, with the influx of immigrants to Hong Kong, and industrialization and urbanization, which greatly transformed the New Territories, the nature of land disputes and their resolution has changed substantially.

[14] Kyshe, *A History of the Laws and Courts of Hong Kong*, vol. II, pp. 543–544.

Resettlement of squatters

First, there was the problem of refugees from the mainland squatting on government land due to a housing shortage.[15] After a large fire in Shek Kit Mei on Christmas Eve 1953 resulted in 58,000 people losing their homes, the government responded by resettling refugees. In the following year, the government accepted the recommendations of the Urban Development Authority to establish a resettlement unit to construct new housing. After 1958, a second wave of immigrants followed a disastrous famine in the mainland. The Hong Kong Government realized that the problem could become not only a land management issue, but also a governance issue. So, in the mid-1960s, the government became determined to deal with the squatter problem as a top priority. It published a White Paper in 1964 and sped up the resettlement process and building public housing. In 1971, when the new governor, Sir Murray MacLehose, arrived, he was concerned about the housing situation in Hong Kong and introduced a Ten-year Housing Programme in 1972 to alleviate the housing shortage. He established the Hong Kong Housing Authority in 1973 to build public housing for the 1.8 million Hong Kong residents who could not afford private housing, and introduced the Home Ownership Scheme to encourage owner-occupation.

Many squatters have been relocated to either public or private housing, and their squatter huts removed. However, there are still settlements dotted around the hillside areas or in the outskirts of townships in the New Territories, Kowloon, and Hong Kong Island, and on the rooftops of urban areas. Government public housing policy since the 1970s has given people on low incomes an expectation that they are entitled to be provided with low-cost housing by the government. With more than 200,000 applicants on the waiting list, the shortage of available land means that this problem is likely to remain a source of grievance for at least the short term.

Small house policy

Second, many indigenous villagers in the New Territories found it difficult to find land to build houses for male offspring. Responding to

[15] Timothy Yuen, "A Brief History of the Changes of the Squatter Control Policy: A Preliminary Account," available at: www.pokfulamvillage.org/bbs3/viewtopic.php?f=6&t=51. See also Bong Yin Fung, *A Century of Hong Kong Real Estate Development* (Hong Kong: Joint Publishing, 2001), ch. 2 (馮邦彥, 香港地產業百年, 三聯書店香港有限公司, 2001版, 第二章).

this problem, the government introduced the small house policy in 1972. However, as land becomes more scarce and demand increases, some commentators have questioned the sustainability of the policy (see Chapter 15 for more details). The villagers, represented by the powerful Heung Yee Kuk, regard the right to land as a customary law that is enshrined in the Basic Law. Tensions have emerged between indigenous villagers and the rest of the population over this issue. With the modernization and Westernization of Hong Kong, and the passing of the Sex Discrimination Ordinance promoting gender equality, the question arises as to the validity of customary law that privileges male offspring. This issue is discussed in Chapter 15.

Illegal structures

Third, as Hong Kong has a small land mass but a large population (over 7 million people), there is a shortage of living space. It is common to find people enclosing their balcony or rooftop to increase their living area. In some urban areas, some property owners or tenants have subdivided their apartments or industrial premises into smaller rooms to let out to low-income people or families who could not afford more than HK$4,000 per month for rental and who are still on the waiting list for public housing. Often these structures are constructed without the Building Department's approval and are therefore technically illegal structures.

Many of these structures do not comply with fire safety regulations and present a serious fire risk. There have been a number of fires in subdivided flats causing death and property damage. In January 2010, a five-story Chinese-style building in Kowloon City collapsed because of unlawful alteration to the internal structure of the building.[16] In the New Territories, even though space is less of an issue, building regulations do not apply to small houses. Villagers have been left to their own devices in constructing these houses. As a result, many are built in excess of the footage and number of stories permitted by the small house grant. As the government took a rather benign approach to enforcing building regulations in the past, many people have come to expect that they could continue to construct illegal structures even after the change in attitude

[16] See "Four killed in Hong Kong Building Collapse," *AFP*, January 29, 2010, available at: www.google.com/hostednews/afp/article/ALeqM5hkV2zgztgphg_TVvRtH2HL2p3HAA.

toward illegal structures (see Chapter 16). The government has vowed to demolish all illegal structures after a number of incidents,[17] and a report from the Director of Audit.[18] This policy has provoked a strong reaction from the villagers in the New Territories. Many have continued to protest, and even threatened to harm the Chief Secretary, and called for the resignation of the chair of the Heung Yee Kuk,[19] Lau Wang Fat, who has encouraged villagers to register their illegal structures.

Reclamation and resumption

As Hong Kong continues to develop, many disputes caused by major infrastructure projects have arisen. There are reclamation projects in Victoria Harbour to create more land for development along the coastline from Central to Wan Chai and on the Kowloon side, which have increasingly narrowed the distance of the harbor from Central to Tsimshashui. Reclamation is not new to Hong Kong. The first major reclamation began in 1852 in Central. However, due to strong opposition by crown lessees who had direct access to the sea, only limited reclamations were completed by 1887.[20] Reclamation work has continued, but public concern over the diminishing size of Victoria Harbour led to the enactment of the Protection of the Harbour Ordinance (Cap. 531) in 1997. The ordinance has been used unsuccessfully by civil society groups to stop the government from completing Phase 3 of the Central and Wan Chai reclamation projects. But the Court of Final Appeal rejected a Town Planning Board's proposal to reclaim land for a Wan Chai North project in 2004.

A major problem associated with urbanization is the compulsory resumption of private land for developments. As there is no freehold land in Hong Kong, the government does not have to compulsorily purchase land, but may simply resume land. The first resumption was as early as 1845. As a result of malaria epidemics, the governor ordered the resumption of the Happy Valley rice fields by prerogative and not contractual or statutory powers. In 1889, the first Crown Lands

[17] Including the collapse of building in Kowloon City, a fire in Garden Street, and ministers, including a former chief executive (CE) and both candidates for the CE election, were found to have illegal structures.

[18] See Report No. 43, 2003, ch. 6, "Buildings Department's Efforts to Tackle the Unauthorized Building Works Problem."

[19] The Kuk is a powerful political organization that represents residents in the New Territories. It has representation in the Legislative Council and at the district council level.

[20] Endacott, *A History of Hong Kong*, pp. 33, 44, 85, 101, 163, 202, 210.

Resumption Ordinance was passed to allow the government to resume and rebuild the Sheung Wan area to improve public health. The large increase in population since the Second World War and subsequent rapid development led to compulsory resumption of large areas of private land for public purposes.

The 1889 Ordinance, which was later replaced by the 1900 Ordinance and subsequent amendments, contained detailed provisions for compensation. Apart from compensation in cash, between 1960 and 1983, the government also granted alternative land in exchange for resumed land. As the government ran out of alternative land to grant, it issued land exchange entitlements (known as Letters A and Letters B), which were assignable, but since 1984 are only redeemable for cash.

Recently, Hong Kong has experienced land-reclamation disputes similar to those discussed in Chapters 6, 8, and 11. One example is the compulsory resumption of land in Choi Yuen village, an agricultural village in the New Territories, which was demolished in 2010 to make way for a new high-speed rail line from Guangzhou to Hong Kong. More than 500 villagers, with support from several Hong Kong students born in the 1980s (otherwise known as the "post-80s generation") and activists, petitioned (with about 14,000 signatures) the government to change the course of the rail line to run through uninhabited neighboring areas.[21] Every week the pressure group organized a guided tour through the village before its demolition. Eventually, the villagers accepted increased compensation from the government and agreed to be relocated to Choi Yuen new village. But they faced the same fate as the villagers in Đông Dương village in Vietnam – losing their old community and cultural traditions.

In an attempt to find more land to meet the housing demand, the government has since 2003 looked into the possibility of developing more new towns in the northeast of the New Territories, and has published a consultation document in this regard. The government wants to use the old approach in resuming all land before it is developed, but this has met with strong resistance from developers, who own large land banks, and private landowners in the area. In a public consultation forum organized by the government, angry protesters shouted and threw objects at the Secretary for Development, calling the plan a plot to provide a back garden for the new rich in Shenzhen at the expense of the local villagers.

[21] See article at: http://en.wikipedia.org/wiki/Guangzhou-Hong_Kong_high-speed_rail_controversy.

Urban redevelopment

As a result of high land prices since 2004, developers have been trying to maximize their landholdings by acquiring old buildings with unused plot ratio space. This has caused the government to change the law to make it easier to force minority owners in old buildings to sell their apartment to developers who have acquired 80 percent of the ownerships in the building under the Land (Compulsory Sale for Redevelopment) Ordinance. This has also generated disputes about how minority owners have been intimidated to sell their apartments. The clever use of plot ratio and gross floor areas by developers has allowed them to increase plot densities and the area available for apartments. This has caused many to question a government policy that brings a huge windfall to developers. But a more ingenious use of unused or residual plot ratio arises in a case involving a housing estate that was developed in the 1970s – the Mei Foo Sun Chuen – which is discussed in the case study in Chapter 16 in this book.

Responses to land disputes

It is clear from the above narrative that many land issues are regulated through law, and that land disputes are resolved through the formal dispute resolution system, principally the courts and other alternative dispute resolution mechanisms. Adverse possession, purchaser summons, landlord and tenant disputes, priority between competing land claims, building management cases, valuation disputes, and other disputes in substantive areas of land law are some examples not discussed in this chapter. The statistics provided below in the Appendix for the period 1999–2012 give some indication of the types and trend of disputes resolved through the courts.

Disputes involving government

The British administration, however, also responded to land disputes in the New Territories politically by allowing Chinese customary practices to continue there and by recognizing these practices in 1905 under sections 11 and 13 of New Territories Land Ordinance (now sections 13 and 15 of the New Territories Ordinance). This was how the British adapted the imported land system into a very different cultural and political context. This practice has continued through to the present day. In other cases, the government has resorted to self-regulation, for example, the sale of uncompleted residential apartments; but things have changed in this area as well, as the government intervened recently by enacting the Residential Properties (First-Hand Sales) Ordinance (Cap. 621).

As we have seen, most land disputes in Hong Kong involve the government, on one side, and private landowners, on the other side, with other interested parties or concerned groups joining the fray. They are often not only a matter of pure legal disputes, but also involve political and social considerations. In most cases, there is clear law on the issue. But the resolution of the disputes is achieved not entirely by strictly enforcing the law through the courts. Take the resettlement program, for example, which created an expectation of entitlement. Other examples are the public housing program, the illegal structures and the small house policies.

But there are cases where the government changed its initially benign stand and sought to resolve disputes by resorting to strict adherence to the law. For example, in the illegal structures cases, the government stance now is that they should be demolished. The only concession the government has made is that owners of exempted village houses (i.e., houses not regulated by the Building Ordinance) in the New Territories can register with the government certain illegal structures that do not pose an imminent danger, and once registered, demolition may be delayed. This approach has not met with complete acceptance. While there were more than 2,000 registrations as of September 2012 since this policy was announced in June 2012, and the chairman of the Heung Yee Kuk has recently encouraged people to register, many villagers have called for his resignation for siding with the government. The former president of the Law Society has also asked people not to register as he argues that this amounts to "admission of guilt." So the registration figure is still very low compared with the estimated number of illegal structures. Many villagers have called for government clemency to allow people to keep their illegal structures if they are safe, and, if the illegal structures give owners extra floor space in excess of the permitted plot ratio, pay an additional premium for the excess area.[22] But the government has refused to give in.

On the other side of the dispute, people affected by government actions have resorted to all possible avenues of redress. For example, in response to the proposed review of the small house policy and the

[22] See "Illegal Structure 'Amnesty' Rebuffed," *RTHK English News*, April 4, 2012, available at: http://rthk.hk/rthk/news/englishnews/20120408/news_20120408_56_831707.htm.

Northeast New Territories Development Plan, villagers have relied on the Heung Yee Kuk to look after their interests, as well as threats of violence, death threats, protests, and demonstrations. Other interest groups have joined in and resorted to protests and demonstrations, marches, petitions to ministers, signature campaigns, media, and sometimes court cases; for example, the judicial review cases by the Society for Harbour Protection. In some cases, the public have also tried to achieve what they want by seeking a change in the law; for example, the enactment of the Protection of Harbour Ordinance; the new guidelines on the sale of uncompleted residential apartments; and the new Residential Properties (First-Hand Sales) Ordinance 2012.

For compulsory resumption of private land by the government, there is a system of compensation similar to the English law; for example, the Acquisition of Land (Assessment of Compensation) Act 1919.[23] An appeal is available against a decision of the Director of Lands on matters relating to resumption to an Appeal Committee, with further appeal to the Secretary for Development. Any disputes between the government and a property owner about the amount of compensation can be referred to the Lands Tribunal, with further appeal in the court system. There can also be judicial review of the government's decision on resumption. However, people affected have resorted to a combination of using the court system and collective or individual actions outside the court system, including demonstrations, participation in political forums, campaigning outside the legislative council building, etc. The government's position in these cases has tended to be to leave matters unresolved through negotiation and the compensation system, while meeting the parties affected and their district councilors to find acceptable solutions, including increasing the amount of compensation. In an interesting development, the Guangdong Land Resources Department sent staff to learn from Hong Kong how to better handle thousands of complaints and compensation claims on land-takings on the mainland.[24]

[23] See Cruden, *Land Compensation and Valuation Law in Hong Kong* and Gordon N. Cruden, *Land Resumption and Compensation in the Urban Area: Guidelines for Owners, Occupiers and Surveyors* (Hong Kong: Lands Department, June 2012), available at: www.landsd.gov.hk/en/images/doc/ulm_resumption.pdf.

[24] See Leu Siew Ying, "Learning from Hong Kong to Resolve Land Disputes," *South China Morning Post*, August 11, 2012, available at: www.scmp.com/article/580771/learning-hk-resolve-land-disputes.

Disputes involving private parties

Where disputes have involved only private parties, such disputes tend to be resolved through the court system. For example, there have been a number of possession actions by developers against squatters for adverse possession. However, in recent years, there has been a tendency for the weaker party in a private dispute to resort to other avenues of redress, such as protests, the media, and court litigation. Consider the actions of a group of residents in Mei Foo Sun Chuen who tried to stop developers from building on retained land that would obstruct the view, airflow, and light to their buildings. Although the residents lost in the Court of First Instance in a judicial review case, the matter is still unresolved.

Since January 1, 2010, under Practice Direction 31,[25] parties are required to explore the possibility of mediation before pursuing litigation in all civil proceedings begun by writ in the Court of First Instance and the District Court, and unreasonable refusal to mediate risks adverse cost orders.[26] There is also mediation available for disputes in compulsory sale cases under the Land (Compulsory Sale for Redevelopment) Ordinance,[27] and building management cases.[28]

Conclusions

The nature of land disputes has changed from the establishment of the colony through to the post-handover period. An effective way in which the colonial government tried to resolve disputes was by recognizing customary rights or practices, for example, the small house policy (see Chapter 15). However, care needs to be taken to prevent recognition of such practices becoming a long-term burden and a drain on limited land resources, and to prevent such practices being discriminatory and

25 See Practice Direction 31, Mediation, available at: http://legalref.judiciary.gov.hk/lrs/common/pd/pdcontent.jsp?pdn=PD31.htm&lang=EN.

26 For details on mediation, see Hong Kong Judiciary website, available at: http://mediation.judiciary.gov.hk/en/index.html.

27 See Directions Issued by the President of the Lands Tribunal Pursuant to Section 10(5)(a) of the Lands Tribunal Ordinance (Cap. 17), Mediation for Compulsory Sale Cases Under the Land (Compulsory Sale for Redevelopment) Ordinance (Cap. 545), available at: http://legalref.judiciary.gov.hk/lrs/common/pd/pdcontent.jsp?pdn=LTPD_CS1_2011.htm&lang=EN.

28 See Directions Issued by the President of the Lands Tribunal Pursuant to Section 10(5)(a) of the Lands Tribunal Ordinance (Cap. 17), Case Management and Mediation for Building Management Cases, available at: http://legalref.judiciary.gov.hk/lrs/common/pd/pdcontent.jsp?pdn=LTPD_BM1.htm&lang=EN.

abused by claimants. A legal framework that allows people who live in vertical communities (e.g., high-rise apartments) to develop their common or customary rules in the form of a Deed of Mutual Covenants has successfully prevented and resolved disputes that arise in high-density housing. Providing squatters who unlawfully occupied government land with affordable public housing has also reduced the potential for land disputes and conflict. Nevertheless, it does raise the expectation of government assistance, which is likely to increase as the property market becomes increasingly less affordable.

The vast majority of other disputes are resolved through the court system, especially in cases where the law is reasonably clear and disputes are more about the application or interpretation of such law. A well-developed system of law and land tribunals based on the English common law has evolved to deal with these disputes. But the legal system cannot resolve every dispute. With the pressure on land resources and the tension between the government and private parties, other methods are used to resolve land disputes. To reduce the high legal cost of dispute resolution through the courts, mediation has become an attractive alternative, or even a prerequisite, in some cases. But, as the next chapters show, the democratization of Hong Kong has opened new extra-legal methods for pressing and resulting land claims.

Appendix

Type of case	1999	2000	2001	2002	2003	2004	2005	2006	2007	2008	2009	2010	2011	2012
(1) Caseload														
(a) District Court														
Distress for rent	12,301	9,024	8,555	10,640	11,059	8,972	7,453	6,194	5,392	5,540	6,320	4,933	2,242	3,857
(b) Lands Tribunal														
Compensation cases	8	59	50	67	64	47	19	28	17	34	17	12	15	14
Building management cases	397	483	574	332	388	413	393	494	329	394	340	407	367	
Tenancy cases	4,509	4,476	5,207	5,295	5,808	5,089	5,144	4,669	4,333	4,611	4,347	4,592	4,457	4,429
Lands compulsory sale application	4	1	3	1	1	3	6	54	14	10	8	21	48	60
Miscellaneous proceedings applications	32	0	30	25	23	20	3	10	5	4	6	10	4	5
(2) Case disposal														
(a) District Court														
Distress for rent	12,147	8,992	8,507	10,646	11,046	8,921	7,419	6,233	5,388	5,497	6,322	51,016	4,513	3,945
(b) Lands Tribunal														
Compensation cases	0	26	46	39	37	33	18	14	27	22	27	20	11	15
Building management cases	134	344	472	244	222	350	252	642	346	389	459	315	333	292
Tenancy cases	2,912	3,665	4,069	4,033	4,474	4,068	3,869	3,733	3,386	3,682	3,497	3,623	3,635	3,461
Lands compulsory sale application	0	1	0	0	0	3	2	5	11	52	9	11	29	33
Miscellaneous proceedings applications	12	0	4	26	14	20	6	5	2	3	6	10	4	

15

The small house policy and Tso and Tong land

Finding the interface between state and customary law in Hong Kong

SAY H. GOO

Introduction

The New Territories have been part of China since at least the Tsing (秦) and Han (漢) Dynasties.[1] Over the centuries, there were migrations from the north, and by the Ming Dynasty the New Territories had developed into a mature agricultural community. However, at the beginning of the Qing Dynasty, the policy of migrating away from the sea, adopted in 1656 to defeat the army led by General Cheng, a loyalist to the Ming Dynasty, forced the population to move inland. As a consequence, the population of the New Territories declined substantially until this policy was finally abolished in 1669, and people were once again allowed to return.

By 1898, the New Territories were once again a flourishing agricultural community. There were schools, towns and villages, and local councils (consisting of the local elites) to manage society. The local councils controlled registration of residency, resolved community disputes, and even collected taxes for the state. There were temples and ancestral places of worship (Tso (族) and Tong (堂)). As David Faure pointed out, villagers not only understood that they were part of a clan and the village, but also their rights as recorded in the imperial records and treaties; and they organized themselves into village associations to defend those rights.[2]

As previously discussed in Chapter 14, when the New Territories were added to the colony of Hong Kong, there were about 700 villages and 102,254 inhabitants who had been farming there for generations, relying

[1] See Ho Yin Lee and Lynne Delehanty DiStefano, *A Tale of Two Villages: The Story of Changing Village Life in the New Territories* (Oxford University Press, 2002).

[2] David Faure, *The Structure of Chinese Rural Society: Lineage and Village in the Eastern New Territories, Hong Kong* (Oxford University Press, 1986), p. 7.

on rural agricultural land for their livelihood.[3] Lands were owned mostly in common tenure under Qing law.[4] They were held in perpetuity from the Qing emperor subject to payment of land tax and performance of labor services. Over the years, the labor services condition fell into disuse, particularly in south China, and was commuted into an additional land tax in lieu of labor collected as a single annual amount. Land could be acquired in three ways: by inheritance, by purchase, and by the cultivation of unoccupied or waste land. It was freely alienable, and there appeared to have been no limitations on usage. Furthermore, the character of land tenure and the tax levied did not change after the construction of buildings.[5]

When the British took over the New Territories in 1898, the villagers did not understand why their property rights and entitlement should change. But, according to the colonial government's perspective, the crown now controlled all land tenure rights. To overcome resistance to the British occupation by villagers in October 1898 and early 1899, the governor reassured landowners that their land would not be confiscated and that existing ownership would be fully recognized. It adopted a policy of not interfering radically in local life and relying on village elders whenever possible.[6] As a result, Chinese custom and customary law were recognized from 1905, including the custom of building small houses for sons, and ownership of ancestral land for the purpose of ancestral worship (the Tsos and Tongs). However, their common tenure was replaced by block crown leases. Moreover, after the British takeover, it was no longer possible to acquire landownership by cultivating what now became unalienated land. So villagers could only build on land they already owned or had bought from the government. After the Second World War, many indigenous villagers found it difficult to find land to build for their male children, and many of them lived in poor conditions.

As explained later, this led the government to introduce the small house policy in 1972. However, as there is increasingly less land in the

[3] James Hayes, *The Hong Kong Region 1850–1911: Institutions and Leadership in Town and Countryside* (Hong Kong University Press, 2012), p. 33.

[4] *Winfat Enterprises (HK) Co. Ltd.* v. *AG* [1983] HKLR 211, *per* Kempster J, adopting the affidavit of Mr. Anthony Dicks, a barrister and professor at the School of Oriental and African Studies. No reference to the historical source of this was made in the affidavit. See also D. M. Emrys Evans, "Aliens on British Soil: A Problem of Landholding in Early Hong Kong," *Hong Kong Law Journal*, 8 (1978), 205.

[5] *Winfat Enterprises (HK) Co. Ltd.* v. *AG* [1983] HKLR 211, *per* Kempster J.

[6] Hayes, *The Hong Kong Region 1850–1911*, p. 70.

New Territories and more demand on housing, some people, including government officials, have questioned the sustainability of the policy. The villagers, represented by the powerful Heung Yee Kuk, regard the policy as their customary birthright enshrined in the Basic Law. This has caused a new tension between the indigenous villagers and the rest of the population in this regard. With the modernization and Westernization of Hong Kong, and the passing of the Sex Discrimination Ordinance promoting gender equality, there is also a tension between the sexes among villagers about the male villagers' right to small houses, a right that their female counterparts do not enjoy.

The Heung Yee Kuk

The Heung Yee Kuk was formed at a meeting of more than 100 Chinese village elites in Tai Po in 1924 with the aim of negotiating collectively with the colonial government over land issues in the New Territories. The Kuk started out as the New Territories Agricultural, Industrial and Business Research Association, and was renamed the Heung Yee Kuk in 1926. Later, it was recognized and controlled as a statutory body by the Heung Yee Kuk Ordinance in 1959. The Ordinance provides for the establishment of the Kuk, its chairman and deputy chairmen, full council and executive committee of the full council, and their election, and the rules for conduct of elections, powers, and functions of the Kuk, and rules for the exercise of powers and functions. Elections are held every four years. The elected representatives of the 700 villages are ex officio members of the Council.

Role of the Heung Yee Kuk in defending land rights in the New Territories

Land disputes have been a major issue in the history of the New Territories since the British took over in 1899.[7] As residents and land-owners in the New Territories have always been unhappy with the colonial government's land policy, the Kuk has always been in negotiation with the government over land disputes. These disputes include levying of premiums for building on agricultural land, modification of

[7] This part is drawn from《新界鄉議局史》作者薛鳳旋、鄺智文, 出版: 三聯書店, 2011年 (English translation, Sit Fung Shuen *et al.*, *The History of the New Territories's Heung Yee Kuk* (Hong Kong: Joint Publishing (HK), 2011)), p. 190.

land use, compensation upon resumption by the government, land exchanges, and village houses. After many years of negotiation, the government introduced measures such as the small house policy, Letters A and Letters B, and amendments to the New Territories (Crown Lease Resumption) Ordinance.

However, it has been suggested that the government's intention of using the lowest price to get the maximum land from landowners remained unchanged. Thus, on the basis of the Crown Lease Resumption Ordinance 1902 and the system of block crown lease introduced in 1906, the government used various methods to resume village land and reduce the compensation amount payable to the landowners. On the other hand, the Kuk used the provision[8] in the Convention for the Extension of Hong Kong 1898 and the proclamations of the governor directed to the inhabitants of the New Territories that their landed interests would be preserved to fight for the rights and entitlement or compensation that they regarded as reasonable. In addition to engagement with the government, the Kuk also took legal and political steps in their fight; for example, they engaged local counsels to draft a "Joint Opinion" and went to London to present it to the Foreign Secretary and Commonwealth Deputy Commissioner, Robert Perry, and the then opposition Conservative Party leader, Margaret Thatcher, in 1977. They also raised issues with members of parliament in the United Kingdom through their members who were residing there.

Small house policy as an example of recognition of customary rights by administrative measure

The custom and the small house policy

Recognition of customary rights by the state law system is nothing new in land law and has proved to be the most effective way to resolve land disputes. In fact, much of the case law and many statutes in land law are but a restatement of customs that had been practiced in the communities for a long time before their formal recognition in law, and the custom provides a basis for the recognition of such rights. Thus, for example, easement by prescription (common law and the Prescription Act) is based on long-term use, and easement of fencing agricultural land in

[8] That "there will be no expropriation or expulsion of the inhabitants of the district included within the extension [the New Territories], and that if land is required for public offices, fortifications, or the like official purposes, it shall be bought at a fair price."

England was recognized because it was a local custom. However, with the transformation of society from small rural communities to urbanization, some customary rights have come into conflict with other competing claims to limited land resources, sometimes with irreconcilable demands and consequences. The small house policy in the New Territories is one such example – one type of customary governance that existed before 1898 when the New Territories were leased to Britain. Prior to 1898, there was a custom among villages that sons of local inhabitants could build themselves a village house on their land in accordance with the orderly layout of the village.[9] "They had the right to convert agricultural land into building land without prior permission of the Manchurian Government of the Qing Dynasty."[10] When the British took over the New Territories, the perpetual rights of the villagers were replaced by block crown leases in 1906, and, from 1923, building village houses on agricultural land required permission from the government and the payment of a premium.[11] This caused great concern to villagers who already owned land. They argued that such conditions were inconsistent with the assurance made in the 1902 New Territories Regulation Ordinance that guaranteed that such villagers did not have to pay additional premiums.

Thereafter, the villagers organized themselves (which led to the establishment of the Heung Yee Kuk in 1926) and petitioned the New Territories Land Officer. However, initially, the government was only willing to amend the rules as follows:

- villagers who built houses for self-use needed to pay only the additional crown rent, but not the premium;
- villagers who built and rented houses to others had to pay the additional crown rent plus half of the premium;
- non-villagers had to pay additional rent and the premium whether or not they had built the house for self-use or for lease.

The villagers were still unhappy about this compromise and sent their representatives to meet with the Secretary for Chinese Affairs, Edwin

[9] Denis Bray, *Hong Kong Metamorphosis* (Hong Kong University Press, 2001), p. 163.

[10] Lisa Hopkinson and Man-lei Lao, *Rethinking the Small House Policy* (Hong Kong: Civic Exchange, 2003), p. 31. See also *Winfat Enterprises (HK) Co. Ltd.* v. *AG* [1983] HKLR 211.

[11] Under the Private Land and the Housing Premium Rules set by the New Territories District Office, so it was not gazetted. Before this, they only had to pay additional crown rent, not premium, and only villagers who built on land they bought from the government were required to pay additional crown rent and premiums.

R. Hallifax, and Legislative Council members, Sir Shou-son Chow and Sir Robert Kotewall. Later, in November 1923, the villagers petitioned the governor, Sir Reginald Edward Stubbs, as the Secretary for Chinese Affairs and the Land Officer who had not replied to their earlier petitions. The villagers pointed out that the rules had in effect treated villagers' lands and alienated land in the same way. This was tantamount to resuming villagers' lands and was inconsistent with the promise in the 1898 Convention. They argued that the second method meant that half of their income was taken by the government, and the third method also caused loss to them because non-villagers had to buy land from the villagers and the additional premium they had to pay to the government would be reflected in the price that they would be willing to pay.

In April 1925, 671 village representatives petitioned the Colonial Secretary, Leo Amery, with an opinion written by a barrister arguing that the 1922 Crown Lands Resumption Ordinance was inconsistent with the 1898 Convention. As a result, the government delayed the enforcement of the new rules. In 1925, the villagers again petitioned the new governor, Sir Cecil Clementi, who eventually promised that no premium was required for building on agricultural land in the New Territories.

Before 1950, these "village-type houses" were exempt from the requirements of the Building Ordinance. So, although their common tenure had been replaced by leasehold tenure, the villagers could continue to build village houses on their agricultural land without paying the extra premium, except for the brief period between 1923 and 1926. Nonetheless, from 1950, village houses were subject to the Building Ordinance; villagers had to submit plans drawn up by an architect, buildings were not to exceed 700 ft^2 and 25 ft in height, and had once again to pay the premium. In 1955, the District Office announced that the premium was 20 to 30 cents per square foot. Additionally, villagers had to exchange their agricultural land for building land in the ratio of 3:1.

In November 1955, the Heung Yee Kuk chairman expressed the villagers' dissatisfaction about the new policy to Chief Secretary Edmund Teesdale and the Director of the New Territories Administration, Kenneth Barnett. In 1956, the Kuk issued a statement on the matter and petitioned the governor, Sir Alexander Grantham, restating that the District Office's policy was contrary to the 1898 Convention and the 1900 Governor's proclamation, and that the Land Officer was arbitrary and manipulative. On May 18, 1956, the Kuk held a village representatives meeting asking the government to withdraw the policy, otherwise they would ask all villagers to go to Hong Kong Island to petition the governor. However, later, the acting chairman of the Kuk canceled the plan, which led to a split in the Kuk. The Kuk's stand on the land issue also led to the governor's determination to further control the Kuk.

In a report to the governor, Kenneth Barnett pointed out that the first principle in the land policy toward the New Territories was the need for control, and in dealing with the Kuk's petition, one should not refer to the Convention or other irrelevant matters. This was to become the government's position in the years to come. However, Barnett did feel that, for those agricultural lands granted in block crown leases, it should not be necessary to pay the premium.

In 1959, the Kuk became a consultative body under the Heung Yee Kuk Ordinance. From then until 1971, the Kuk's land policy committee continued to negotiate with the government, and succeeded in finally dispensing with the requirement for architectural plans and in extending the permitted build area to 1,000 ft^2 and a two-story house, but there was still little progress on the premium. There were inconsistent practices regarding village houses in various districts, so the villagers often found matters confusing.

The main problem for the villagers was that, if they did not already own land, they had to buy it from the government at a public auction. It was no longer possible for them to acquire land by the cultivation of unoccupied or waste land, as these lands had now become crown land. As land was sold by auction, non-villagers could buy them and build village houses in a village, which was unacceptable to the villagers. To overcome this problem, in many villages, auctions were held at dawn, and permits for temporary structures were granted by the District Officers, which did not grant title to the land. These wooden structures with tin roofs have been lived in for decades and were not really temporary.[12]

Finally, in 1971, the Kuk established a special committee to fight for the rights of the villagers, and called a meeting in June to express their dissatisfaction with the government's village house policy. Almost 1,000 village representatives attended the meeting in the district of Sai Kung alone. The government was surprised by the unity of the villagers, and their action was described by the new New Territories Commissioner, Denis Bray, who was still on a 12-month probation, as a "village uprising." The number of villagers attending revealed the Kuk's ability to organize and mobilize the villagers.

[12] Bray, *Hong Kong Metamorphosis*, p. 163.

The Kuk had four requests:

- remove the restrictions on village houses;
- fair compensation on resumption;
- protect villagers' land rights; and
- allow private parties to be involved in the development of land in the government's development plan.

These requests were claimed to be the villagers' rights as promised under the Convention and the proclamation. In his report to Bray, the District Officer of Tai Po pointed out that, as the villagers were united and the Kuk understood that the Convention was the trump card in their negotiation with the government, the government had to make concessions and could not ignore the Kuk's requests any longer. Bray eventually responded to the Kuk's plan to mobilize 10,000 people to march on the Governor's House and boycott meetings of the Home Affairs Department by changing government policy.

Bray introduced the small house policy, which allows male descendants of original indigenous villagers who do not own land or who have held crown licenses for ten years to apply to the government, once in their lifetime, for land on a private treaty grant (PTG) at a concessionary premium of two-thirds of the full market value for the purpose of building themselves a small house. The right given by the policy has come to be known as the Ding Right.[13] The policy was formulated and implemented in just six weeks without any legislation. It was approved by the Governor-in-Council in November 1972, and, in the same month, the Legislative Council passed the Building Ordinance (New Territories) 1972 to exempt small houses in the New Territories from the Building Ordinance with effect from December of that year. The policy was intended as a temporary solution to the social problem at the time, and both the villagers and the government agreed that the right could be abolished if it was abused.[14]

In the early years of the policy's implementation, there were teething problems with regard to details concerning the structure permitted to be built, who was qualified to apply and the application procedures, and inconsistency in the implementation of the policy by different district offices, about all of which the Kuk continued to negotiate with the government. In 1974, the Kuk pointed out in its correspondence to Governor MacLehose that there were many unreasonable minor

[13] A Ding is a male descendant. [14] Bray, *Hong Kong Metamorphosis*, p. 166.

technicalities preventing villagers from applying, including raising the premium arbitrarily, using the user restriction as recorded in the block crown lease as grounds for refusing an application, and abolishing the right of those who had held licenses for ten years to apply. Over the years, there were many negotiations between the Kuk and the government concerning various aspects of the small house policy – including the permitted square footage and height limit – with the government making concessions on some aspects but not others.

Problems with the small house policy

While the small house policy has undoubtedly improved the living conditions of indigenous people in the New Territories, with the ten-year housing development plan introduced in 1973 and the subsequent urbanization of the New Territories to meet the housing demands of the population, the land available for PTG for small houses is shrinking rapidly. Yet the number of descendants of indigenous villagers is an infinitely growing class. The government is currently finding it difficult to find suitable land for qualified villagers. Some 250,000 people are estimated to have the right, and many are on the waiting list for land to build small houses. At the same time, there is an estimate of more than 200,000 people waiting for public housing. It has been suggested that the policy is not sustainable.[15]

Added to this, as small houses are exempt from the Building Ordinance, there are many problems relating to sewage and illegal structures. Also, as only male descendants are entitled to apply under the policy, this raises questions about discrimination against female descendants, which is contrary to the Bill of Rights Ordinance and the Sex Discrimination Ordinance. Yet, if female descendants are also entitled to apply, this will exacerbate the demand on available land. Furthermore, the vast majority of the population who are not descendants of villagers consider the policy to be discriminatory and unfair.[16] This feeling is exacerbated by the fact that many villagers are still able to apply for land even though they no longer live in the village, and many

[15] See Jake van der Kamp, "Dubious Rights and Plenty of Wrongs Behind Small-house Policy," *South China Morning Post*, September 23, 2004, available at: www.scmp.com/article/471424/dubious-rights-and-plenty-wrongs-behind-small-house-policy.

[16] Peter Kammerer, "Small House Policy Can't Go Unchallenged for Much Longer," *South China Morning Post*, February 19, 2013, available at: www.scmp.com/comment/insight-opinion/article/1153234/small-house-policy-cant-go-unchallenged-much-longer.

collaborate with developers who have agricultural land to apply for building licenses or sell small houses almost as soon as the certificates of compliance are issued.[17]

Abuses and failure of safeguards

Abuses of the system occurred not long after the introduction of the small house policy. In 1978, the government even planned to abolish the policy.[18] But, after negotiation with the Kuk, a compromise was reached in August 1978. To prevent abuses of the system, restrictions on alienation were introduced; for example, within five years of obtaining Certificates of Compliance (CCs) in the case of building licenses and land exchanges, and perpetually in the case of PTGs.[19] Villagers have to pay the government premium for removing the restrictions. The premium payable is the difference between the full market value of the site as at the date of the application for consent for removal and any premium previously paid.

It might be assumed that there would be no incentive for villagers to abuse the system or cash in their "Ding Right." However, there are several reasons why the restrictions have failed to prevent abuses. First, for years, the Lands Department has applied a discounting factor (from 70 percent in the first year to 93 percent in the fifth year) to the premium payable under the above formula in assessing the premium actually payable.[20] According to Land Department Records,[21] the villagers (or their collaborating developers) have only to pay as little as HK$0.6 million for a site that is worth HK$2 million in the market, thereby cashing in HK$1.4 million if the small house is sold in the first year, and pay HK$0.1 million if the small house is sold in the fifth year.

Second, if the small house is sold five years after the CC is obtained, no premium is payable, which means an even bigger windfall. Third, while there is no discounting factor for a PTG, so in principle villagers (or their

[17] See Audit Commission Report, Hong Kong, No. 39, 2002, ch. 8 "Small house grants in the New Territories." In the 2002 report, the Audit Commission found fifty-three cases of indigenous villagers applying for permission to sell their small houses within an average of three days after the issue of the Certificate of Compliance (CC). Nearly all the flats of the fifty-three small houses were sold in about five months after the removal of the restriction on alienation.

[18] Audit Commission Report, Hong Kong, No. 10, 1987.

[19] For PTGs under the Village Expansion Scheme, there is also a moratorium on the removal of restriction within the first three years of obtaining the CCs.

[20] Audit Commission Report, 2002, p. 21. [21] *Ibid.*

collaborating developers) do not gain from any difference between the full market value and concessionary grant, this still presents a money-making opportunity in the profit margin in selling small houses. A villager who does not live in the village can apply for a PTG to build and then sell the small house to make a profit to which a non-villager would not be entitled. For those developers hungry for land but who do not have a Ding Right, collaborating with villagers is one way of getting land without having to compete for it in a public auction with wealthy developers. The Chief Secretary's Committee certainly regarded the ability to develop small houses by indigenous villagers in a way not open to other people as a valuable privilege, especially in a rising property market.[22]

Government reports have shown that villagers have used various devices and documents to avoid the "waiting time" and the "premium" restrictions.[23] For example, a Letter of Confirmation by the indigenous villager to say that they intend to transfer the land to the collaborator at a certain time in the future and a power of attorney to authorize the collaborator to manage the land in the meantime have been used.[24] At various times, the Lands Department has put in place different measures to counteract these devices; for example, since July 1997, villagers have been required to sign a declaration prior to the grant of the building license, land exchange, or PTG that they have not made arrangements for their rights to be sold to other individuals or developers, or that they have not made an agreement with anyone to hold the land in trust or to transfer it at a later time.[25] Since October 2001, villagers have had to make an additional declaration that they have never entered into any arrangements or agreements with any person or persons to transfer, alienate, dispose, or otherwise deal with their rights in and over the lot, including, but not limited to, the right to develop the lot pursuant to any grant or approval to be issued by the government.[26]

While these measures have made it harder to abuse the system, old declaration forms that do not contain the additional declaration are still being used in some districts in the New Territories, before this was

[22] See Chief Secretary's Committee Paper No. 16/94, December 12, 1994, referred to in Audit Commission Report, 2002, para. 2.6.

[23] See Audit Commission Report, 2002, ch. 8. [24] *Ibid.*

[25] See *Lau Kwai Kiu* v. *Bian Xintian (Personal Representative) & Another* [2012] 4 HKC 313, CA, paras. 7–13.

[26] See Audit Commission Report, 2002, para. 2.19.

discovered by the Audit Commission in July 2002,[27] and there are still villagers willing to risk being prosecuted for false declarations in a rising market due to inherent weaknesses in enforcement actions.[28]

Finding solutions to the problems

Because of the problems and abuses mentioned above, there were calls for the small house policy to be reconsidered as long ago as 1997. In a report, the Civic Exchange identifies three options in regard to the small house policy:

- abolish it;
- create a tall house policy; or
- create a centralized village.[29]

The Audit Commission has also made recommendations for the system surrounding the policy to be improved to prevent abuses.[30]

The villagers, represented by the Heung Yee Kuk, on the other hand, have argued that they always had the right to convert agricultural land to building land without the permission of the Qing Government or the payment of a premium before the British took over the New Territories, and the aim of the policy was partly to restore the right that was taken away in 1905 by the block crown lease.[31] Further, they have argued that this lawful, traditional right or interest is protected by Article 40 of the Basic Law.[32] Moreover, the small house policy may have created a legal right or legitimate expectation,[33] but the government and critics of the policy have disagreed.[34]

It appears that much depends on what was the custom pre-1898. There appears to be no written or definitive statement in the early Government

[27] *Ibid.*, para. 2.20. It is not clear whether any declarations have been made using the old forms in this brief period.

[28] See Audit Commission Report, 2002, para. 2.25(a)(ii).

[29] Hopkinson and Lao, *Rethinking the Small House Policy.*

[30] See Audit Commission Report, 2002.

[31] W. F. Lau, Paper No. CB(2)1634/96-97(01), 1996, Meeting of Bills Committee to discuss the Equal Opportunities (Family Responsibility, Sexuality and Age) Bill, Equal Opportunity (Race) Bill and Sex and Disability Discrimination (Miscellaneous Provisions) Bill 1996, April 1, 1997, referred to in Hopkinson and Lao, *Rethinking the Small House Policy*, p. 31, fn. 143.

[32] *Hansard* (1997), Minutes of the Bills Committee on the Equal Opportunities (Family Responsibility, Sexuality and Age) Bill, Equal Opportunity (Race) Bill, and Sex and Disability Discrimination (Miscellaneous Provisions) Bill 1996, April 1, 1997, cited in Hopkinson and Lao, *Rethinking the Small House Policy*, p. 32, fn. 148.

[33] C. Robinson, personal communication, May 2003, cited in Hopkinson and Lao, *Rethinking the Small House Policy*, fns. 157–158.

[34] Hopkinson and Lao, *Rethinking the Small House Policy*, pp. 30–31.

Gazette or by the Chinese authorities of what constitutes a traditional right and interest of an indigenous villager.[35] While certain pre-1898 customs, such as traditional burial customs, communal property, and rights of inheritance, were explicitly recognized in the New Territories Regulations Ordinance 1910, there is no such recognition of the Ding Right.[36] From Bray's account, and the expert evidence of Anthony Dick accepted by the court in *Winfat Enterprises (HK) Co. Ltd* v. *AG*,[37] it seems clear that villagers who owned agricultural land could build a small house on it without permission or payment of an extra premium or land tax. However, what is not clear is whether a villager who did not own any land could apply for one at a concessionary premium or land tax from the Qing Government. Dick says there were three ways to obtain land of common tenure: by inheritance, by purchase, or by cultivation of unoccupied land or wasteland subject to payment of land tax.[38] It seems that there is no concessionary tax. But, in the case of purchase, Dick does not tell us whether the Qing Government could refuse to sell land to villagers, although in theory it must have had the power to refuse, being sovereign. It may be that this was never an issue in practice as the Qing Government probably never refused, or, in any case, the villagers probably obtained their land through the cultivation of unoccupied land, which ceased to be possible after the British takeover. If the Qing Government could refuse to sell, then the PTG under the small house policy has gone beyond what was permitted in the original traditional right. And the PTG at a concessionary premium also appears to exceed the villagers' entitlements under their traditional rights.

Future of the small house policy

As the numerous newspaper articles on the subject suggest, the future of the small house policy remains a hotly debated economic, cultural, and political issue. It is proving to be difficult to replace customary governance with legal governance. It is an example of a traditional land community (bound by long-standing village traditions) that, over time, has converted into a spontaneous community brought together by a shared objective, but no longer viewing the land through a

[35] Hopkinson and Lao, *Rethinking the Small House Policy*, p. 30. [36] *Ibid.*

[37] *Winfat Enterprises (HK) Co. Ltd.* v. *AG* [1983] HKLR 211, *per* Kempster J, adopting the affidavit of Mr. Anthony Dick, a barrister and professor at the School of Oriental and African Studies, University of London.

[38] *Ibid.*

"traditional" framework. In fact, villagers are now trying to force the state to adhere to this long-standing land policy.

Disputes relating to the small house policy can be divided into three groups between different parties:

- the legitimacy of the small house policy and its future (involving indigenous villagers, on the one hand, and non-indigenous people and the government, on the other hand);
- the decision of the Director of Lands to refuse to grant PTG (involving indigenous applicants and the government);
- disputes between indigenous villagers and collaborators in relation to the ownership of a small house.

Many have resorted to the courts to resolve their disputes. Since 1996, there have been no less than fourteen reported cases and forty-two unreported cases. In resolving these disputes, the courts have applied principles of common law and equity that are familiar to them, and have recognized rights according to their principles, even though such recognition has the effect of upholding the collusion between indigenous villagers and outsiders that allows outsiders to enjoy the Ding Right in violation of the spirit of the small house policy.

Thus, in *Lau Kwai Kiu* v. *Bian Xintian (Personal Representative) & Another*,[39] for example, the Court of Appeal held that a claimant who paid HK$100,000 to an indigenous villager to apply for a PTG, HK$24,590 to pay the premium for the PTG and the construction costs of the small house, and who moved in with her family to reside there when the house was completed, was entitled to a beneficial interest in the house pursuant to a common intention constructive and/or resulting trust. The court was undeterred by the argument that illegality was involved in the acquisition of the beneficial interest as the claimant did not need to establish a cause of action by reference to the illegal transaction.[40]

Tso and Tong as an example of the government's recognition of customary governance by ordinance

Like the Ding Right, Tso and Tong are another example of a spontaneous community brought together by shared values and tradition, but, in the

[39] *Lau Kwai Kiu* v. *Bian Xintian (Personal Representative) & Another* [2012] 4 HKC 313, CA.
[40] Applying *Tinsley* v. *Milligan* [1994] 1 AC 340, HL.

case of Tso and Tong, the state has co-opted the customary governance into the state system by expressly recognizing it in legislation.[41] The arrangement created by the legislation has worked reasonably well, and disputes are still resolved by the customary mechanisms that have been brought within the legal framework with the court system ultimately acting as a final adjudicator, but following the customary practices that have been brought within the legal system in its adjudication.

Tso and Tong are traditional Chinese institutions of landholdings recognized by section 13 of the New Territories Ordinance (originally section 11 of the New Territories Land Ordinance 1905). They are basically land held by male descendants of a named common ancestor for the purpose of worship of the common ancestor and the upkeep of their grave. In Western terms, in a Tso or Tong, ancestral land is often described as being held under a Chinese customary *trust* for the purpose of worship. However, as one author has pointed out, it is not a true trust.[42]

In the case of Tong, the common ancestor is often the settlor. The intention of this custom is that the parcel of land is to be perpetuated and not disposed of, and male descendants who are for the time being alive are the beneficiaries. Thus, traditionally, under Chinese customary law, Tso and Tong land is generally not alienable, unless the sale is beneficial to the Tso or Tong and all members agree to it.[43] It used to be necessary for all the members to execute the assignment, but this requirement was simplified by section 15 of the New Territories Ordinance (originally section 13 of the New Territories Land Ordinance 1905) by the appointment of a manager to represent the Tso or Tong. The manager is responsible for the day-to-day management of the Tso or Tong land and has the power to dispose of or deal with the land subject to the consent of the Secretary for Home Affairs, who will consent to a sale only if there is no objection from any member and the sale is for a good purpose.[44] The English law of partition and the rule against perpetuities does not apply to Tso or Tong,[45] although if Tso or Tong land is co-owned it would be possible to partition under the Partition Ordinance.[46]

[41] For a detailed account, see Stephen Selby, "Everything You Wanted to Know About Chinese Customary Law (But Were Afraid to Ask)," *Hong Kong Law Journal*, 45 (1991), 45.

[42] Malcolm Merry, "Are Tsos Really Trusts?," *Hong Kong Law Journal*, 42 (2012), 669.

[43] *Kan Fat-tat* v. *Kan Yin-tat* [1987] HKLR 516 at 534.

[44] *Tang Kai Chung* v. *Tang Chail Shang* [1970] HKLR 276. [45] *Ibid.*

[46] *Brisilver Investment Ltd.* v. *Wong Fat Tso & Another* [1999] 3 HKC 567.

There are nearly 4,000 Tsos and more than 2,000 Tongs, which collectively control some 6,000 acres of land.[47] Some of them existed before 1898. There have been relatively few reported cases relating to Tso and Tong land, most of which have been dealt with by the court in accordance with the Chinese customary law relating to Tso and Tong. However, as there are no written rules concerning the control and governance of Tso and Tong, nor are there any memorandum or articles of association or written by-laws, and managers (who are often the elderly in the family) are appointed for life, there is potential for abuse by managers, although there are no reported cases where managers have been found liable for breach of trust.

Disputes

An area of dispute concerns the compensation to be paid to Tso or Tong when such land is compulsorily resumed by the government under the Government Law Resumption Ordinance. No consent has to be obtained from any member of the Tso or Tong for accepting government compensation. There will, however, be negotiation with the government on the amount of compensation or letters of exchange. The Heung Yee Kuk often plays a part in these negotiations.[48] But the issue concerns whether Chinese customary law continues to apply to such compensation, as opposed to land. It was held in two decisions of a Deputy High Court judge – *Kan Fat-tat* v. *Kan Yin-tat*,[49] and more recently *Tang Che Tai* v. *Tang On Kwai*[50] – that, under section 13 of the New Territories Ordinance, Chinese customary law only applies to land but not compensation, so the compensation money is governed by Hong Kong law, but the rule against perpetuities should be disapplied to compensation as it would be unjust and oppressive to apply it as Tsos would be destroyed by such application.[51] On appeal, in the *Tang Che Tai* case, Cheung JA said that, while he appreciated the approach taken by the court below to

[47] Roger Nissim, *Land Administration and Practice in Hong Kong* (Hong Kong University Press, 2008), p. 111.

[48] Belinda Wong Sheung-Yu, "Chinese Customary Law: An Examination of Tsos and Family Tongs," *Hong Kong Law Journal*, 20 (1990), 13 at 26.

[49] *Kan Fat-tat* v. *Kan Yin-tat* [1987] HKLR 516.

[50] *Tang Che Tai* v. *Tang On Kwai* [2007] 5 HKC 277.

[51] It has been suggested that the definition of "land" in s. 13 of the New Territories Ordinance should be amended to include compensation: see Wong, "Chinese Customary Law: An Examination of Tsos and Family Tongs," p. 26.

finding a practical solution, this was a very cumbersome way of dealing with the matter.[52] Without citing any authority and dealing with the limitation placed upon the meaning of the word "land" in section 13 of the New Territories Ordinance, Cheung JA said that the hallmark of Tso and Tong land is inalienability, and that the British Government had recognized this ancient landholding system when it leased the New Territories, so that the most appropriate way to give full effect to this recognition is to apply Chinese law and custom to the compensation.[53] Lam J took the same view, but, while recognizing that section 13 does not include compensation, said that Chinese customary law continues to apply to compensation under Articles 8 and 18 of the Basic Law, which provide that common law and customary law prior to 1997 continue to apply. Since common law is subject to modification to suit the local circumstances under the Supreme Court Ordinance 1844 and the Application of English Law Ordinance 1966, this means that common law is not applicable if its application would cause injustice and oppression, and in such circumstances the court can apply Chinese customary law.[54] It follows, therefore, that since the rule against perpetuities should not be applied to compensation as it would destroy Tso and Tong, Chinese customary law would continue to apply to Tso and Tong after the ancestral land has been changed to other forms of assets.

However, there is still an unresolved issue as to the mode of distribution of Tso and Tong monies if there is to be a distribution. There can be a distribution only if there is unanimous agreement for distribution and its mode of distribution. There is no customary law on the mode of distribution;[55] it all depends on agreement between the members. Government compensation for ancestral land resumed would not be paid out until there is an agreement on distribution.[56] Different agreements have been reached by different Tsos and Tongs.[57] Managers play an important role in influencing the members in reaching an agreement, and there have been allegations or complaints that managers may be

[52] *Tang Che Tai* v. *Tang On Kwai* [2008] 3 HKC 521, *per* Cheung JA at para. 59.

[53] *Ibid.* [54] *Re Tse Lai Chiu* [1946–72] HKC 160; [1969] HKLR 159.

[55] *Kan Fat-tat* v. *Kan Yin-tat* [1987] HKLR 516, *per* Deputy Judge Robert Tang QC at 543.

[56] City and New Territories Administration, "New Territories Ordinance: Customary Succession, Trusteeship and Tso and Tong Managers," unpublished report, December 3, 1986, p. 10.

[57] Heung Yee Kuk's letter to the Land Commission, dated July 28, 1987, cited in Wong, "Chinese Customary Law: An Examination of Tsos and Family Tongs," p. 29.

bribed by fang (房) heads into favoring one fang over another.[58] Some managers may even refuse to sign relevant documents unless the members agree to the mode of distribution favorable to the fang to which the manager belongs. It has been suggested that there should be legislation to solve the distribution problem.[59] As land resources in Hong Kong are shrinking, there will be greater pressure on the Tso and Tong, which control 6,000 acres of land, to sell, and the issue relating to distribution is likely to remain important in the future.

[58] *Ibid.* [59] *Ibid.*

16

Flexibly applying the law to regulate illegal buildings in Hong Kong

ALICE LEE

Introduction

In this chapter, the interaction and convergence between formal state-sanctioned rules and informal community regulation is illustrated through two case studies. The first case study concerns property encroachment in the form of illegal structures, while the second case study concerns justifiable restraints to the lawful exploitation of property rights exemplified in a private housing dispute being resolved through public/private dialogues. Incidentally, these cases have brought about fundamental changes in the dispute resolution framework and political landscape in Hong Kong.

The two case studies discussed in this chapter both concern property rights: the former is about property encroachment, while the latter is about exploitation. They illustrate the emergence of self-regulation, through tacit agreement or social norms, and its interaction with state-sanctioned rules. In one case, people shun the law, while in another, people pursue justice by taking the law into their own hands without resorting to state-sanctioned remedies. These are relatively new phenomena in Hong Kong, particularly in relation to property-related legal matters. The first case study – "Illegal structures, distrusted officials" – shows how public disobedience trumps state-sanctioned enforcement, while the second – "Private dispute, public forum" – illustrates how public campaigning preempts private development. Both cases appeared, at least at the outset, to be instances of a spontaneous community (see Chapter 1 in this book) trying to take over resolution of property disputes from the formal law enforcement regime. As it turns out, these ad hoc attempts have triggered an irreversible, seemingly permanent, change in the attitude of Hong Kong residents toward the ruling elite and the rich.

By way of background, the property market has been one of the pillars of the Hong Kong economy and prosperity since the arrival of the

British, who brought with them not only modern governance, but also a capitalist ethos (see Chapter 14 in this book). The Swire Group, for instance, established overseas branches in Shanghai and Hong Kong in the late nineteenth century, and Swire Properties has been a leading player in the Hong Kong property market, developing and managing large-scale commercial and residential properties, since it was founded in 1972. A local example is the all-sweeping conglomerate, or "property kingdom," owned by tycoon Ka-shing Li, the founder of the listed property group Cheung Kong Holdings Limited. Li has been hailed as the richest man of Asian descent in the world and an Asian icon of success, earning him the nickname "Superman Li."

The predominance of property developers in the local economy had never been a concern to the general public, provided the public were also able to reap some benefits from Hong Kong's property market, which has been one of the most volatile in the world.[1] It was only when property prices rocketed to a level that was beyond the reach of the public, most notably in the 2000s, that resentment began to grow over the allegedly high-handed and sometimes not-so-honest marketing strategies and business models of the developers. The term "developer hegemony"[2] was coined to ridicule the omnipotence of those developers who had branched out into retail, telecommunications, and other businesses, leaving little room for small businesses or sole proprietorships to survive. At the same time, the local administration was blamed for not taking effective measures to curb soaring property prices or to bridge the gap between the rich and the poor. The anti-government sentiment soon escalated into allegations of "collusion between the government and

[1] See, for instance, Ray Forrest and James Lee, "Cohort Effects, Differential Accumulation and Hong Kong's Volatile Housing Market," *Urban Studies*, 41(11) (2004), 2181–2196. In *Kwan Siu Man Joshua* v. *Yaacov Ozer* [1999] 1 HKLRD 216 at 226, Litton PJ of the Hong Kong Court of Final Appeal also referred to the "highly volatile" property market of Hong Kong in discussing the significance of the date of completion in a contract for the sale and purchase of land.

[2] The term originated from a book titled *Land and the Ruling Class in Hong Kong* (Hong Kong: Enrich Professional Publishing, 2005) by Alice Poon, a former personal assistant to one of the property tycoons in Hong Kong. The book was written in English when it was first published, and was translated and published in Chinese in 2010 with the title 地產霸權. The Chinese title became so popular that it was translated by bloggers and columnists as "developer hegemony." See, for instance, Sunita Sue Lend, "Hong Kongers Fight Developer Hegemony," *The Edge Singapore*, April 26, 2011, available at: www.theedgesingapore.com/blog-heads/sunita-sue-leng/28439-sunita-sue-leng-hong-kongers-fight-developer-hegemony.html.

individual property developers or consortia" (see Chapter 14),[3] and resulted in distrust and doubts over the integrity of senior government officials, including those running for the chief executive office. In September 2011, when a local businessman, Henry Tang, who was believed to be Beijing's favorite to be Hong Kong's next chief executive, announced his candidacy for the highest post in local administration, his personal life and family properties suddenly came to the attention of the press[4] to such an extent that one might wonder whether invasion of privacy should be made actionable in Hong Kong.[5] The widespread media coverage about the presence of illegal structures on his luxurious property not only resulted in unexpected twists and turns in the local administration's succession plan,[6] but also triggered a territory-wide campaign against illegal structures.

Case study 1: illegal structures, distrusted officials

A history of tolerating non-conformity

In Hong Kong, illegal structures are ubiquitous. Ordinary citizens, as well as the Buildings Department (the government authority responsible for granting approval for building works[7]), had ignored them until

[3] A reply by the Acting Secretary for Transport and Housing, Mr Yau Shing-mu, to a question raised by Legislative Councilor the Hon Emily Lau in the Legislative Council on May 19, 2010, available at: www.info.gov.hk/gia/general/201005/19/P201005190228.htm.

[4] For the first time in Hong Kong there was media intrusion into the private life of a public figure. Media-hired cranes were crowded outside Tang's luxurious villa in order to film over the high walls what was believed to be an illegal basement – illegal in the sense that it was built without the necessary approval of the authority. The incident soon got the attention of the press as well as bloggers and satirists, who began to refer to it as "Basement-gate," a play on the word "Watergate."

[5] Invasion of privacy is not actionable as such in Hong Kong despite the positive recommendations of the Law Reform Commission in its report "Civil Liability for Invasion of Privacy," December 9, 2004. See Rebecca Ong, "Is There a Case for Tort of Invasion of Privacy in Hong Kong?" *International Journal of Liability and Scientific Enquiry*, (2009), 69.

[6] The incident turned out to be a heavy blow to Tang's integrity, bringing to an end what was believed to be Beijing's "succession plan" for Hong Kong's top government position.

[7] Under the Buildings Ordinance (chapter 123 of the Laws of Hong Kong), s. 2(1), "building works" that require approval include any kind of building construction, site formation works, ground investigation in the scheduled areas (including railway protection areas and sewage tunnel protection areas as well as designated districts such as the Mid-Levels on Hong Kong Island and the Northwestern part of the New Territories), foundation works, repairs, demolition, alteration, addition, and every kind of building operation, including drainage works. Simplified procedures and exemptions are available for certain small-scale works in private buildings under the Minor Works Control System as implemented by the Building (Minor Works) Regulation (chapter 123N of the Laws of Hong Kong).

recently when some government officials were found to be harboring illegal structures in their homes.[8] The lack of attention and the low rate of enforcement were probably consistent with the Chinese tradition of "minding one's own business" and "living in harmony with neighbors." First, illegal structures constitute a kind of property encroachment in which a party is exploiting their property beyond the legitimate limits as conferred by the original grant, encroaching the interest of the land (ultimately the original grantor, the government), which would otherwise be of value if included in the original grant. The most common example is the extension of habitable areas or the addition of recreation facilities to the property beyond the original plan.

The Chinese proverbs mentioned above are not only cultural artifacts, but also point to underlying tacit agreements and social norms.[9] "Tacit agreements" and "social norms" are:

> the labels attached to behavioral patterns that emerge and persist in the absence of organized, conscious direction by individuals. According to some commentators, these behavioral patterns result from the interactions of individuals acting in their rational self-interest.[10]

On this reading, the tacit agreements concerning illegal structures balance household control over property against toleration of property encroachment by neighbors. This type of reciprocal understanding flourishes when the encroachment is at the expense of "public/government" land. In these circumstances, it is the wider public who bear the social costs of any disturbed view, compromised public safety standards, and reduced government land sale revenues that might arise from illegal structures. Drawing on the discussion about land communities in Chapter 1, the owners of illegal structures have evolved into a community in which they tacitly tolerate each other and ignore each other's illegal construction. They form a united front when challenged by other communities or by the government. This constitutes a form of collective property encroachment in the sense that members of the community derive more value from their property than the

8 Augustine Tam, "Hong Kong Rocked by Illegal Structures," *Asia Times Online*, August 18, 2011, available at: www.atimes.com/atimes/China/MH18Ad01.html.

9 The literature on the relation between social norms and law is vast. See, for instance, the entry "Social Norms and the Law," in Peter Newman (ed.), *The New Palgrave Dictionary of Economics and the Law* (London: Macmillan, 1998). For a more sophisticated treatment of social norm or non-legal cooperation, see Eric Posner, *Law and Social Norms* (Cambridge, MA: Harvard University Press, 2000), ch. 2. In the context of the present chapter, "tacit agreement" is used interchangeably with "social norm."

10 See Posner, *Law and Social Norms*, p. 8.

tenure rights originally granted by the state. Owing to the illicit nature of the encroachment, the agreement is tacit and unwritten, but can be vividly inferred from the parties' conduct. When one family erects structures such as rooftop shacks or extended balconies to increase their living space, their neighbors are likely to acquiesce and do nothing, or some might follow suit quietly, hoping for reciprocal indulgence within a peaceful neighborhood. Such a phenomenon was common in the 1970s in Hong Kong, especially in densely populated districts, such as Yau Tsim Mong, Sham Shui Po, and Kowloon City, where many families could not afford an apartment big enough to house the entire family. There, residents were generally reluctant to report their neighbors' additions or alterations to their flats to the Buildings Department. They were unlikely to know whether neighbors had sought or obtained approval for such building works unless they had made the necessary enquiries or investigation. Until recently, unsolicited investigations were rare, but following the previously discussed media focus on "unauthorized building works," reportings have become more common.[11]

The low reporting rate was probably also due to the obscurity of the statutory scheme of approval. The Buildings Ordinance provides that no person shall commence or carry out any building works without having first obtained the written consent of the Director of Buildings, that is, the Buildings Department.[12] The statutory definition of "building works," referring as it does to building construction, site formation, ground investigation, and drainage works,[13] might easily give the impression that only large-scale building works such as those undertaken by developers would require approval. In fact, any addition or alteration to any private property, such as supporting frames for air-conditioning towers, canopies, or rooftop structures,[14] require approval. To explain the coverage of the approval scheme, which is not immediately discernible from the statutory definition, the Buildings Department included hypothetical illustrations in the "Frequently Asked Questions" on its website as follows:

> Q: If I wish to erect storage cabinets on the roof of my property, do I need approval and consent from the Buildings Department?
>
> A: Prior approval and consent from the Buildings Department are required for erecting prefabricated structures including mobile houses

[11] "Unauthorized Building Works" (or "UBW") is the official term for any additions or alterations to buildings without the prior approval of the Buildings Department or not following the simplified procedures under the Minor Works Control System.

[12] Buildings Ordinance, s. 14. [13] Buildings Ordinance, s. 2(1).

[14] Examples given by the Buildings Department, available at www.bd.gov.hk.

and man-size storage cabinets on the main roof, podium roof or open yard of a building. It is because large storage cabinets occupying space will likely contravene the floor area limitation and other building regulations. However, storage cabinets at such locations are generally not subject to immediate enforcement action when:

- the cabinet does not exceed a height of 1.5 metres nor the parapet wall,
- the cabinet does not affect the structure of the building,
- the fire escape route is not obstructed, and
- the drainage system is not affected.

It is doubtful how far such illustrations helped. The proviso that structures of a certain size and nature would not be subject to immediate enforcement action was confusing. Due to the overwhelming number of unauthorized building works, or "UBW" as they are referred to in the Buildings Department's enforcement policy, only UBWs causing overloading of the building were actionable items subject to priority enforcement action. There is explicit provision in the Buildings Ordinance that, with the exception of minor works commenced under the simplified requirements,[15] any building works that have been carried out in contravention of the Ordinance may be ordered to be demolished.[16] Nevertheless, such orders would be issued only if the UBW in question was classified as "priority," according to the so-called "enforcement policy," which is not part of the legislation, but only informal announcements made by the Buildings Department from time to time. On its website, the department would announce that, "in accordance with the established procedures," a removal order would be issued to the owner concerned, requiring them to rectify the irregularities within sixty days. The questions arose what exactly those "established procedures" were and what would happen if they were not complied with? Only the department would know.

As expected, "wait-and-see" or just idling therefore became a sensible strategy commonly adopted by property owners, who simply had no means or no incentive of finding out whether and when enforcement action would be taken by the authority. What might be surprising was that even the Buildings Department itself did not seem to have any realistic estimate of the time and effort the battle against UBWs would take. There was no systematic monitoring or reporting of the number of UBWs until the late 1990s when the department revealed that there were about 800,000 UBWs

[15] The requirements refer to those stipulated in the Building (Minor Works) Regulation (chapter 123N of the Laws of Hong Kong).

[16] Buildings Ordinance, s. 24.

hanging on buildings in old residential districts. It was estimated that, without public cooperation, it would take the government 133 years to remove all UBWs – assuming no new ones were constructed.[17] To set the ball rolling, in September 1999, the department started large-scale clearance operations known as "blitz" against all UBWs projecting from the external walls of identified buildings,[18] and followed up in 2001 with a ten-year demolition program, which was bundled with an enforcement policy that accorded priority to clearing UBWs constituting an obvious or imminent danger to life or property, newly erected UBWs, and UBWs constituting a serious health hazard or a serious environmental nuisance. In the absence of objective transparent guidelines, it was doubtful if the department's own categorization of UBWs into "immediate" (i.e., those that must be removed immediately) and "non-immediate" (i.e., those that could wait) would help in promoting public awareness of building safety or soliciting public cooperation in combating UBWs.

Changing official attitudes toward non-conforming buildings

As it turned out, it did not take the Buildings Department a century to tighten up its enforcement policy against UBWs. The process was accelerated, rather unexpectedly, by a series of triggering events; the first one being a tragic accident in January 2010: the collapse of a five-story fifty-five-year-old residential building at Ma Tau Wai Road, a densely populated area of the Kowloon Peninsula, leaving four dead. As revealed by subsequent investigations, the building was disproportionately burdened with numerous unauthorized internal partitions (or "subdivided units") in such a way that its main supporting columns became vulnerable to disturbance or damage by external forces. Before the tragedy happened, such kind of unauthorized subdivision of a residential flat into smaller self-contained units, which were to be rented out to separate households, was commonly condoned as an acceptable means of maximizing low-cost accommodations. No one would complain – in accordance with the Chinese philosophy of staying away from others' business – as long as it was done within the four walls. It was not until the tragic loss of life that

[17] "Illegal Structures: Time Bombs Overhead," *Varsity* (magazine of the School of Journalism and Communication, Chinese University of Hong Kong), December 1999.

[18] "Background Brief on Unauthorized Building Works" for a Special meeting of the Legislative Council Panel on Development, June 20, 2011, LC Paper No. CB(1)2487/10-11(03), para. 4.

the danger posed by unauthorized structural alterations became a focal point for public discussion. The discussion was centered on the safety hazard, but, understandably, soon grew to be a platform for criticizing the inadequacy of the government's housing policy. However, it did not touch on the righteousness of the many illegal structures prevailing in the territory. It appeared that the illegality of the illegal structures would not attract criticism per se unless, and until, they caused safety concerns – no moral hazard without safety hazard! It was at that juncture that the social costs of public safety incurred by illegal structures and borne by the public exceeded the tolerable latitude (what that exact latitude was supposed to be is always an unknown before it is transgressed) that the tacit agreement was assaulted or even broken up. Apparently, the tragic incident was the tipping point that triggered the ensuing social and media concern over the matter. The accumulation of awakened public and media concern, it is observed, even disturbed the ethos of "no moral hazard without safety hazard," and bundled the tolerance of illegal structures with the morality of integrity, a moral hazard per se, thanks to the timely local political upheaval in 2012.

The Buildings Department first responded with a territory-wide inspection of more than 4,000 buildings aged fifty years or above to ascertain their safety, which was completed within a month after the accident and followed by a detailed report,[19] while Donald Tsang, the then Chief Executive of the Hong Kong Government, announced in his 2010/2011 Policy Address a new multi-pronged approach to enhance building safety. Four directions were identified: legislation, enforcement, support and assistance to owners, and publicity and public education.[20] In April 2011, the Ombudsman in his annual report blamed the government for its ineffectual clearance of unauthorized structures or rooftop additions in the New Territories.[21] These measures were widely expected and consistent with the trouble-shooting mentality of the government. What was unexpected was the powerful and effective attack from the press. In the months following the accident, there was constant media coverage of illegal structures found on the properties of legislative councilors and senior government officials, including even the

[19] Buildings Department, "Buildings Department Report on Building Collapse in Ma Tau Wai Road and Inspection Results of Buildings aged 50 or Above with Photos/videos," press release, April 26, 2010, available at: www.info.gov.hk/gia/general/201004/26/P201004260229.htm.

[20] "Background Brief on Unauthorized Building Works," for a Special meeting, June 20, 2011, para. 8.

[21] Tam, "Hong Kong Rocked by Illegal Structures."

candidates for Hong Kong's top government position. C.Y. Leung, who eventually became the new chief executive in July 2012, was one of the targets of attack. It was after he won the election in March 2012 that illegal structures were found in his house, and this became the climax, or anti-climax, of the episode.[22]

The scandals created an unprecedented opportunity for print and electronic media to join hands to reveal the prevalence and severity of illegal structures in Hong Kong.[23] The ad hoc media alliance against illegal structures turned out to be more effective in exposing matters than the lobbying by political parties. A mandatory building inspection scheme was introduced by virtue of the Buildings (Amendment) Ordinance 2011, while the Buildings Department's enforcement policy was amended to extend the scope of "actionable UBW" beyond the "high-priority items under the ten-year programme."[24] Even the Secretary for Development of the Hong Kong Government admitted that:

> In view of the completion of [the] ten-year UBW demolition programme in March this year [2011], and the fact that the [Legislative Council] Members and the public are still paying close attention to building safety, in particular the requests expressed by the councillors from districts to the Administration over the years for further clearing those UBWs not constituting imminent danger, the Development Bureau and the Buildings Department have conducted a comprehensive review on the strategy to enhance building safety.[25]

With the ten-year program coming to an end, the Buildings Department took the step of revising its UBW enforcement policy. Under the new policy promulgated in April 2011, the department has refocused its priorities and broadened the scope for enforcement action against UBWs to cover the following:[26]

22 Had it happened before the election, the incident could have affected his winning in the same way as "Basement-gate" did to the other candidate Henry Tang. See fn. 4 above.

23 Alvin Wong, "Media Unite to Spotlight the Wrongs of the Rich and Famous: CE not Excluded," *The Journalist*, August 2011, available at: http://hkthejournalist.blogspot.com.au/2011/08/e06.html.

24 "Background Brief on Unauthorized Building Works," for a Special meeting, June 20, 2011, paras. 9, 13.

25 A reply by the Secretary for Development, Mrs. Carrie Lam, to a question raised by Legislative Councilor the Hon. Tse Wai Chun in the Legislative Council on June 8, 2011, press release, available at: www.info.gov.hk/gia/general/201106/08/P201106080210.htm.

26 "Unauthorized Building Works," available at: www.bd.gov.hk. See also "The Buildings Department's Internal Guidelines on Prioritization of 'Actionable' Unauthorized Building Works: A Summary," also available at the Buildings Department website.

(a) items constituting obvious hazard or imminent danger to life or property;
(b) new items (excluding statutorily exempted building works under the Buildings Ordinance) irrespective of the date of completion of the building where such items have been carried out;
(c) items on the exterior of buildings, including those on rooftops and podiums, in yards and lanes and projecting from external walls (excluding projecting structures covered by the Household Minor Works Validation Scheme and the proposed Signboard Control System and other minor amenity features);
(d) items in the interior of buildings, constituting obvious hazard or imminent danger to life or property (e.g., building works associated with subdivided units with obstruction to means of escape, serious water seepage causing deterioration of structural members or over-loading problem);
(e) items in or on buildings, constituting a serious health or environmental nuisance (e.g., misconnection of drainage systems);
(f) major standalone items;
(g) a specific type of UBW, or items identified in buildings or groups of buildings, targeted for large-scale operations; and
(h) unauthorized alterations to or works in green and amenity features of a building (e.g., balconies, sky gardens and podium gardens) for which exemption from calculation of gross floor area has been granted by the Buildings Department.

What would have taken the government a century to achieve was accomplished by an ad hoc alliance in less than two years. The anti-UBW campaign waged by the Hong Kong media was the first of its kind. While the media was playing its role of public supervision, there were political parties and politicians who viewed the building safety scandals as a golden chance to drag down their rivals.

The politicization of illegal buildings

Integrity, not just safety, has also been put in issue. Chief Executive C. Y. Leung, who managed to win the March 2012 election before illegal structures were discovered on his property, has been facing investigation and interrogation by the press, legislators, and political parties since he assumed office. Ironically, it was Leung who, during the 2012 election debates, questioned the integrity of his rival Henry Tang when an unauthorized basement was found on Tang's luxurious villa. That election turned out to be a shameless mud-slinging exercise with much string-pulling behind the scenes by different players, including the Central Government in Beijing. According to the Basic Law, Hong Kong's mini-constitution, the Chief Executive is the head of the administration nominated and elected by a college of 1,200 members, who are supposed to represent different sectors of the population, while members of the public are ironically denied the right to elect the Chief Executive. This is more a selection than an election proper. During the last election campaign, Leung, regarded as an underdog at the initial stage of the election, stepped up his attack on Tang's illegal structures, which turned into a bombshell targeting Tang's honesty and integrity instead. As argued above, having illegal structures at one's home is an illicit property encroachment, an exemplification of human greed. Any effort to conceal it is a further act of dishonesty, a denial of greed, and an evasion of responsibility. Leung painted his rival with such heinous color, incidentally exposing the insidious nature of the tacit agreement or social norm of tolerating each other's illegal structures. Leung not only reported Tang's misdeeds, but also used them for his own cause. He succeeded and was elected to office. However, no sooner had the dust from the election settled than it transpired that Leung did not come with clean hands either. A chartered surveyor by profession, Leung should have known that the "additional structures" on his own property, whether or not constructed by him, required the approval of the Buildings Department. After months of inquisition, Leung chose to appear at the December 2012 session of the Legislative Council in an attempt to "dampen controversy over his illegal structures."[27] It ended up doing more harm than good to his efforts to salvage credibility.[28] When asked whether he had cheated in order to get the position of Chief Executive, Leung said: "I did not say I had no illegal structure." Notwithstanding the government effort to gauge public sentiment afterwards, the Pan-Democrats accused Leung of lying his way up the ladder to the city's top post, while the Democratic Party immediately pressed on with a motion of no confidence against Leung.[29]

[27] Joyce Ng and Dennis Chong, "CY Leung Denials Cause More Damage, Say Analysts," *South China Morning Post*, December 11, 2012, available at: www.scmp.com/news/hong-kong/article/1102482/cy-leung-denials-cause-more-damage-say-analysts.

[28] *Ibid.*

[29] Eddie Luk, "Dust Yet to Settle," *The Standard*, December 11, 2012. There was allegedly evidence that, prior to declaring his Chief Executive bid, C. Y. Leung had in fact told the press that he had no illegal structures at his homes.

As at July 2013, the heat erupting from the scandal remains in the air, although not escalating, even though Leung has not answered all questions about his alleged illegal structure. His integrity is not in question.[30] But his evasive and equivocal stance on the matter contrasts with the heightened public awareness about the issue, diluting, if not defying, the effort to curb illegal structures and to expose the community's tacit toleration and illegal building. It is possible that his actions send a signal to the community that the government is not serious in opposing illegal construction. When the chief of the administration could not stand up and give an account of his own illegal structure story, he is unlikely to press others to comply, fearing a return of the media spotlight on his own affairs.

Currently, the tacit community approach to illegal structures is spreading; from high officials to ordinary members of the public, now everyone feels more comfortable in "not being governed."[31] This is no anarchy, but a rule by contractualism, in which a tacit toleration of illegal structures is spreading throughout society.[32] One can see the odd standoff between this tacit understanding and the state-sanctioned regulatory framework. It is interesting to speculate whether or not this standoff reflects the underlying strength of non-state approaches to property. Alternatively, the current situation may be attributed to the failure of the state regime to adequately enforce the law. In the language of H. L. A. Hart, the great jurist, people need an "internal point of view," or to have internalized the law, in order to develop the habit of obedience to the law.[33] If that is the case, in spite of the heightened territory-wide awareness of the matter, what was brought about by the illegal structure scandals simply reinforces people's belief in the legitimacy of expanding their property without seeking state approval.

[30] The cover of *Time* magazine dated July 9, 2012, published right after Leung's victory in the Chief Executive election, says it clearly, "Can Hong Kong Trust This Man?"

[31] The phrase is borrowed from James C. Scott, *The Art of Not Being Governed: An Anarchist History of Upland Southeast Asia* (New Haven, CT: Yale University Press, 2009), a work on the land and people in Zomia, which has not been fully incorporated into the effective rule of nation-state.

[32] This is the very essence of contractualism as expounded by Harvard philosopher Thomas Scanlon in his many works, most prominently, *What We Owe to Each Other* (Cambridge, MA: Harvard University Press, 1999).

[33] See H. L. A. Hart, *The Concept of Law*, 3rd edn. (Oxford University Press, 2012), pp. 89–91. It is interesting to note that there are parties seriously lobbying for the legalization of illegal structures, arguably bringing the legislation more in line with the social context.

Case study 2: private dispute, public forum

Mei Foo Sun Chuen, the oldest private housing estate in Hong Kong, is situated at a former oil depot of Mobil Oil Limited (whose Chinese trading name was "Mei Foo") in Lai Chi Kok, Kowloon, which was converted into a residential development in stages from the late 1960s to 1978 (the estate is divided into eight zones for management, Stages I–VIII). The name "Mei Foo Sun Chuen," which literally translates as "Mobil new estate," reveals its origin and link with Mobil Oil.

The estate's ties with Mobil have faded since the change of the oil company's name to ExxonMobil in 1999. In the same year, the oil company further severed its links with the housing estate by removing its liquefied petroleum gas (LPG) storage site from a small plot of land ("the land"[34]) by the side of Stage VIII of Mei Foo Sun Chuen. The land, which had an area of 1,291 m^2, was left vacant for a decade until it was sold in 2009 to Billion Star Development Limited, a local developer that had successfully applied to the Building Authority for permission to erect a twenty-story residential building on it.[35] What the developer purported to do was a legitimate property exploitation in every sense, but it was a "nightmare come true" for Stage VIII residents, who had always been concerned about the adverse effects of any redevelopment of the land, which, like a wind corridor, had ensured fresh air and an unblocked view of the adjoining park.[36] Not only guaranteeing a better and healthier living environment, the land, as a buffer between Stage VIII and the adjacent Stage III, also enhanced the marketability and resale value of the blocks it abutted. The residents were worried that such environmental and market benefits would be dispossessed by the projected legitimate development. People do not like unwelcome development in their backyard. As the saying goes, "Not in my backyard!"

Understandably, the proposed twenty-story project met with strong opposition from the residents of the adjoining blocks. One of those residents even applied for, but was denied, leave to seek judicial review of the Building Authority's decision to approve Billion Star's building

[34] In legal terms, the land is described as "The Remaining Portion of New Kowloon Marine Lot No. 25 and Section B of New Kowloon Marine Lot No. 25."

[35] Judicial review of the Building Authority's decision was sought but ruled out in the case *Re Ho Mei Ling*, HCAL No. 51 of 2011 (August 29, 2011), an unreported decision of Lam J.

[36] The park, which was constructed on reclaimed land as a "buffer outer space" between Mei Foo Sun Chuen and a highway, was a project winning architectural "greening effect" awards in 1996.

plans.[37] What needs explanation is that opposition to the scheme was shared by other residents of Stage VIII and even the rest of the estate, leading to the formation of a Concern Group against the Construction of Screen Buildings in Mei Foo Sun Chuen ("Concern Group"). Both the Concern Group as well as the Incorporated Owners of Stage VIII have taken action to object, including writing to the Building Authority, meeting with Legislative councilors, lobbying through the relevant District Council, and applying to the Town Planning Board for change of use of the land, but all in vain.[38] Although not yielding the desired outcome, these resident-led activities have attracted much attention and support. It is where civil society met the media while the media reinforced the cohesion of the civil society.[39]

From March to April 2011, when construction work was due to commence on the land, members of the Concern Group and their supporters formed patrol teams, launched blocking action, and "staged a dramatic lie-down protest" against construction of the proposed twenty-story building.[40] Unable to commence any construction work, Billion Star, the current owner of the land, issued a writ of summons on April 20, 2011[41] against defendants who were either active members of the Concern Group or their supporters, such as former and current Legislative councilors. By the writ, Billion Star applied for an interlocutory injunction to prevent the defendants from trespassing on the land and from interfering with Billion Star's exercise of its right of way over

[37] *Re Ho Mei Ling*, HCAL No. 51 of 2011 (August 29, 2011). Ho Mei Ling was the owner of a unit in Stage VIII. Her main contention was that the Building Authority erred in calculating the permissible redevelopment potential for Billion Star's land in terms of plot ratio and site coverage. As Lam J found it, the calculation principles proposed by Ho differed from those established in previous cases and her application was dismissed.

[38] *Re Ho Mei Ling*, HCAL No. 51 of 2011 (August 29, 2011), para. 14.

[39] "Civil society," although an elusive concept, aptly describes the residents' voluntary bonding together to raise objections to the relevant development. For the flourishing of civil society in the Hong Kong context, see Elaine Chan, "Civil Society," in Lam Wai-man, Percy Luen-Tim Lui, and Wilson Wong (eds.), *Contemporary Hong Kong Government and Politics*, expanded 2nd edn. (Hong Kong University Press, 2012).

[40] Diana Lee, "Sleepless in Mei Foo," *The Standard*, April 4, 2011, available at: www.thestandard.com.hk/archive_news_detail.asp?pp_cat=30&art_id=109827&sid=31902147&con_type=3&archive_d_str=20110404.

[41] The application for an interlocutory injunction was refused by Deputy Judge Au-Yeung in *Billion Star Development Ltd.* v. *Wong Tak Chuen & Others*, HCA No. 708 of 2011 (April 29, 2011). The plaintiff's application for leave to appeal from the Deputy Judge's decision was dismissed by the Court of Appeal in *Billion Star Development Ltd.* v. *Wong Tak Chuen & Others*, HCMP No. 1042 of 2011 (July 15, 2011).

private roads for accessing the land to carry out the intended construction work.[42] The application was refused by Deputy Judge Au-Yeung, who, after balancing the plaintiff's financial loss and the defendants' need to file evidence in opposition to the application, concluded that no interlocutory injunction should be granted pending the substantive hearing, which was henceforth adjourned to December 19–20, 2011.[43]

As the Chinese saying "Sweep the snow from your own doorstep, and don't worry about the frost on your neighbor's roof" suggests, there is a strong social norm for people to mind their own business. However, the scope of what constitutes one's "own business" is fluid. In the Mei Foo case, whose interest was at stake? At first glance, it seemed to be the collective interest of the residents of the adjacent blocks, the value of which depended on whether the land in question could be preserved as a wind corridor as they wished. In fact, those living in other parts of Mei Foo Sun Chuen also felt that it was their business – that their "home" had been invaded. As the first private housing estate in Hong Kong, and the largest in the world at the time it was built, Mei Foo Sun Chuen has grown into a community with its own identity. It is in a way a planned community with its own Deeds of Mutual Covenants and House Rules governing the use of the property and regulating the behavior of residents. In an earlier court decision where the validity of a clause in the House Rules was put in issue,[44] it was confirmed that the House Rules, which were made and revised from time to time by the manager of the estate in exercise of the power conferred by the Deeds of Mutual Covenants, could not contradict the Mutual Covenants.[45]

Since the Billion Star land dispute was brought to light, residents of other parts of Mei Foo Sun Chuen have been worried that another non-residential plot ("the plot") inside the estate might also be turned into a multi-story building against their wishes. On the plot sits the Mei Foo community hall "Foo Yau Tong," meaning "Mei Foo Blessing Hall," which has been a

[42] *Billion Star Development Ltd.* v. *Wong Tak Chuen & Others*, HCMP No. 1042 of 2011 (July 15, 2011), para. 4.

[43] The matter took a dramatic turn when it came to the substantive hearing. The first to sixth defendants consented to final judgment for an injunction in the terms as sought by the plaintiff, while the case against the remaining defendants turned on whether the plaintiff had acquired a right of way over the land in question. It was held that the plaintiff was entitled to an injunction to restrain the unlawful interference with its right of way: *Billion Star Development Ltd.* v. *Wong Tak Chuen & Others* [2012] 2 HKLRD 85.

[44] *Tsang Chi Ming* v. *Broadway-Nassau Investments Ltd. & Another* [2009] 1 HKLRD 96. The clause in question prohibited the keeping of pets on the premises.

[45] *Ibid.*, para. 53.

popular venue for sports and cultural activities, as well as meetings and gatherings of the Mei Foo residents, since it was built forty years ago. A one-story structure with a traditional Chinese rooftop, the hall is not only an architectural and aesthetic asset, but it also brings more space and fresh air to the surrounding blocks, as the former LPG site does. Most importantly, it also signifies the bonding and sense of belonging among Mei Foo residents. Situated in Stage II, "Foo Yau Tong" has been a focal point of the estate, both geographically and sentimentally. Fearing that this monumental structure might be subject to residential development, some Mei Foo residents and their supporters applied to the Town Planning Board for the plot to be re-zoned as "Government, Institution or Community" to reflect its current use as a community center. Turning down the request, the Town Planning Board concluded that the "Government, Institution or Community" zoning should be for the provision of facilities serving the needs of the local residents and/or a wider district, region, or the territory, and for the provision of land for uses directly related to, or in support of, the work of the government, organizations providing social services to meet community needs, and other institutional establishments. This description was not applicable to "Foo Yau Tong," which is privately owned and mainly open to the local organizations of Mei Foo Sun Chuen.[46] Instead, the Board found it appropriate to re-zone the plot as "Other Specified Use – Private Community Centre" to reflect its existing use as a private community center,[47] thereby putting the Mei Foo residents' minds at ease, at least for the time being.

Both the Stage VIII Concern Group and the ad hoc group advocating for the re-zoning of "Foo Yau Tong" could be viewed as spontaneous communities, an instance of civil society, within the larger, planned community of Mei Foo Sun Chuen, which has been in existence for more than forty years. The power and effectiveness of such spontaneous communities could be seen on November 9, 2011 when an attempt by Billion Star's contractor to resume construction work at the former LPG site was brought to a halt by Mei Foo residents who were protesting by standing or sitting in the middle of the road that provided access to the site. The residents reportedly "refused to move as the truck drove towards them without slowing down before stopping suddenly."[48]

[46] Minutes of the 451st Meeting of the Metro Planning Committee of the Town Planning Board held on October 7, 2011, para. 6(l).

[47] *Ibid.*, para. 26.

[48] Joyce Ng, "Political Turn at Mei Foo as Protesters Halt Truck," *South China Morning Post*, November 10, 2011, available at: www.scmp.com/article/984384/political-turn-mei-foo-protesters-halt-truck.

The ensuing ninety-minute stalemate turned out to be effective in preventing Billion Star from bringing through the back door an injunction that had been rejected earlier by the court.

Comparing this case and the "illegal structure" case study discussed above, one is struck by the similarities. Here, the developer's project is sanctioned by law, just as is the policy of curbing illegal structures. Resistance to the development and building controls both arise from land communities that reinforce tacit assumptions among their respective members about the appropriate way to regulate land. More importantly, both cases could not be settled through legal norms or processes. The land communities displaced (in the first case) and challenged (in the second case) state land regulation. It is not surprising that the state and developers were perceived as joint actors, because they drew on state power to override the common interest of the land communities.[49]

A paradigm shift in land dispute resolution with long-term impact on the political landscape

A special administrative region of the People's Republic of China since July 1, 1997, Hong Kong has maintained its common law system and a high degree of autonomy as enshrined in its constitutional document – the Basic Law (see Chapter 14).[50] With a stable political and regulatory environment, a highly respected judicial and law enforcement system, and comparatively low corruption levels, Hong Kong has been a safe destination for investment,[51] as well as a community more interested in accumulating wealth than anything else.[52] Hong Kong people used to have faith and trust in the colonial administration, the judiciary, and the

[49] The two cases studied here echo the civil resistance campaign against land-grabbing in Taiwan in 2010. Called a community land justice movement, it was established to oppose land dispossession and displacement under the legal regime. For details, see www.taiwanruralfront.org and also Chapter 12 in this book.

[50] Article 5 of the Hong Kong Basic Law: "The socialist system and policies shall not be practiced in the Hong Kong Special Administrative Region, and the previous capitalist system and way of life shall remain unchanged for 50 years."

[51] Hong Kong was ranked first in the IMD *World Competitiveness Yearbook* in 2011 and 2012, available at: www.imd.org/research/publications/wcy/World-Competitiveness-Yearbook-Results/#.

[52] Hong Kong may be, as some have described, "one of the most materialist societies as its inhabitants put accumulating wealth ahead of anything else": Yojana Sharma, "Work Not 1997 Stresses Hong Kong People," IPS News Agency, November 18, 1994, available at: www.ipsnews.net/1994/11/hong-kong-work-not-1997-stresses-hong-kong-people-1-an-inter-press-service-feature. Some still hold the view that "Hong Kong focused its

law enforcement agencies. Even if there were political rallies, protests, or demonstrations once or twice a year, such events were usually orderly, non-violent, and non-confrontational.

It is only in recent years that protesters have begun to take proactive action such as lying on the road, blocking the traffic, or bringing a paper coffin to government buildings. The success of the ninety-minute stalemate at Mei Foo Sun Chuen further proved that mass civil disobedience could be an effective mode of communication when social groups lacked other effective forums for expressing their views. Once labeled apolitical or politically apathetic, Hong Kong people have become more willing to engage in, and even shape, the political discourse in public and to fight for that to which they aspire through spontaneous communities such as those considered above.

In the first case study, social groups, in alliance with some media outlets, used illegal structures as a rallying point against the Chief Executive alliance that is likely to continue until the end of his term. For the first time, the press and the Pan-Democratic legislators have joined hands in a political campaign against the highest government official in Hong Kong. After a no-confidence motion was voted down earlier at the Legislative Council,[53] C. Y. Leung, the much-attacked Chief Executive, had to face yet another more serious challenge: an unprecedented impeachment motion. It was only after a heated eight-hour debate that the motion was voted down.[54] However, ironically, the political outcry that seemingly drowned the more problematic legal issues surrounding illegal structures had shifted attention away from the latter. A comprehensive revamp of the law and enforcement policy against illegal structures, which could have commenced immediately after the recent scandals, has been put on hold.

energy on accumulating wealth as a means of security and status, and everything else, like environment, healthcare and religion, became secondary": Celene Loo, "Does this City Need God?" *Giving Bread*, December 8, 2010, available at: www.givingbread.org/?p=93&lang=zh.

53 Luk, "Dust Yet to Settle."

54 Joshua But, "Pan-Democrats will Table Motion to Impeach CY Leung," *South China Morning Post*, December 12, 2012, available at: www.scmp.com/news/hong-kong/article/1109312/pan-democrats-will-table-motion-impeach-cy-leung; "Lawmakers Move to Impeach CY Leung," *South China Morning Post*, January 9, 2013; Te-Ping Chen, "Hong Kong Leader Survives Bid Against Him," *Wall Street Journal*, January 9, 2013. In the *Wall Street Journal* article, the "symbolic impeachment bid" was referred to as "the latest twist in an escalating struggle between pro-democracy activists and the Beijing-backed chief executive."

In the second case study, the parties ended up going to court, with the plaintiff developer being granted an injunction to restrain unlawful interference with its right of way over the land in question.[55] One of the defendants appealed on the ground that, *inter alia*, he was entitled to exercise his constitutional right of freedom of speech and assembly.[56] The appeal, which was based on the social injustice caused by the harm to the local community, was dismissed by the Court of Appeal. The Court agreed with the trial judge that "the right of assembly and the right of freedom of expression are not absolute and cannot override the constitutionally entrenched rights to protection of property."[57]

Public demonstrations and processions have suddenly become a common and regular occurrence, almost every weekend, in the areas surrounding government headquarters. At the same time, Legislative councilors have started to express their disagreement with, or disapproval of, the government by "filibuster," the use of obstructionist tactics, especially prolonged speech-making, to delay or prevent the deliberation or passing of proposed legislation.[58] The most recent and large-scale incident of civil resistance is a movement entitled "Occupy Central," meaning occupying the central business district of Hong Kong, which was initiated by an associate professor at a local law school in March 2013, calling for universal suffrage for election of the position of chief executive in 2017.[59] The list would only be extended with the emergence of fresh issues and the feeble responses afforded by the existing legal and political regimes. Hopefully, the change in the public's attitude to social injustice may facilitate the resolution of emerging issues by unconventional means. The evolution of the political landscape is gradual but irreversible. The two cases above are only parts thereof.

[55] *Billion Star Development Ltd.* v. *Wong Tak Chuen & Others* [2012] 2 HKLRD 85.

[56] *Billion Star Development Ltd.* v. *Wong Tak Chuen & Others*, CACV No. 49 of 2012 (March 8, 2013).

[57] *Ibid.*, para. 55, citing *HKSAR* v. *Au Kwok Kuen* [2010] 3 HKLRD 371.

[58] "Filibuster" has hit the headlines in Hong Kong: see Eddie Luk, "Legco Chiefs Clash on Filibuster," *The Standard*, May 21, 2012; Wendy Wong, "Marathon Legco Filibuster Fails," *RTHK English News*, June 1, 2012; "Legco in Marathon Sitting over Filibuster Attempt," *South China Morning Post*, August 15, 2012; "Legco President Jasper Tsang Vows not to Surrender on Filibusters," *South China Morning Post*, October 10, 2012; "'Long Hair' in Appeal to Challenge Legco Filibuster Decision," *South China Morning Post*, January 11, 2013.

[59] "Occupy Central" has caught so much attention that there is a Wikipedia page describing it as "a proposed non-violent occupation protest for universal suffrage that would take place in Central, Hong Kong in July 2014." See http://en.wikipedia.org/wiki/Occupy_Central_(2014).

INDEX